STUDIES IN IMPERIALISM

general editor John M. MacKenzie

When the 'Studies in Imperialism' series was founded
more than twenty-five years ago, emphasis was laid upon
the conviction that 'imperialism as a cultural phenomenon had as significant an effect on the dominant as on
the subordinate societies'. With more than ninety books
published, this remains the prime concern of the series.
Cross-disciplinary work has indeed appeared covering the
full spectrum of cultural phenomena, as well as examining
aspects of gender and sex, frontiers and law, science and
the environment, language and literature, migration and
patriotic societies, and much else. Moreover, the series has
always wished to present comparative work on European
and American imperialism, and particularly welcomes the
submission of books in these areas. The fascination with
imperialism, in all its aspects, shows no sign of abating,
and this series will continue to lead the way in encouraging
the widest possible range of studies in the field. 'Studies
in Imperialism' is fully organic in its development, always
seeking to be at the cutting edge, responding to the latest
interests of scholars and the needs of this ever-expanding
area of scholarship.

*Empire, migration and identity
in the British World*

MANCHESTER
1824

Manchester University Press

Empire, migration and identity in the British World

Edited by Kent Fedorowich and Andrew S. Thompson

MANCHESTER
UNIVERSITY PRESS

Published by Manchester University Press
Altrincham Street, Manchester M1 7JA, UK
www.manchesteruniversitypress.co.uk

British Library Cataloguing-in-Publication Data is available

Library of Congress Cataloging-in-Publication Data is available

ISBN 978 1 5261 0670 4 *paperback*

First published by Manchester University Press 2013

This edition first published 2017

The publisher has no responsibility for the persistence or accuracy of URLs for any external or third-party internet websites referred to in this book, and does not guarantee that any content on such websites is, or will remain, accurate or appropriate.

Printed by Lightning Source

For our fathers
Ed Fedorowich (1930–2007) and
John Thompson (1936–2009)

CONTENTS

CONTENTS

LIST OF TABLES

NOTES ON CONTRIBUTORS

Rachel Bright is a Lecturer in Modern History at Keele University, specialising in modern British imperial and African history. She has a particular interest in migration and information networks in the British Empire, especially concerning race, violence, labour, law, popular politics and identity. She obtained her doctorate at King's College London in 2009 which examined the impact of Chinese indentured labour in South Africa and its impact on the formation of the Union between 1902 and 1910. A post-doctoral fellowship at the University of East Anglia followed soon after completion of the thesis, as did teaching at the London School of Economics and Goldsmith's College, London, before her move to Keele.

Hilary M. Carey is Professor of History at the University of Newcastle, New South Wales, and Life Fellow of Clare College, University of Cambridge. Her most recent works are an edited collection, *Empires of Religion* (2008), and the highly acclaimed *God's Empire: Religion and Colonialism in the British World, c.1801–1908* (2011).

Lisa Chilton is an Associate Professor in the History Department at the University of Prince Edward Island. She is the author of *Agents of Empire: British Female Migration to Canada and Australia, 1860s–1930* (2007). Her current research project explores immigrant reception programmes and policies in Canada from the 1770s to 1930.

Stephen Constantine is a graduate of Oxford University, and has been at Lancaster University since 1971. His research has mainly concerned modern British and British Empire history, and often the relationship between the two, and hence his interest in empire migration. Related publications are (ed.), *Emigrants and Empire: British Settlement in the Dominions between the Wars* (1990); 'Migrants and Settlers', in Judith Brown and Wm Roger Louis (eds), *Oxford History of the British Empire: The Twentieth Century* (1999); *Community and Identity: the Making of Modern Gibraltar* (2009); and *Migration and Empire*, co-authored with Marjory Harper (2010); plus several journal articles on child migration to the empire. He is a Fellow of the Royal Historical Society.

Jo Duffy is a graduate of the University of Oxford where she was awarded her DPhil in 2001. A revised version of her thesis was published in the Routledge African Studies series in 2006 entitled, *The Politics of Ethnic Nationalism: Afrikaner Unity, the National Party, and the Radical Right in Stellenbosch, 1934–1948.* She now works in the Research and International Directorate within the Economic and Social Research Council (ESRC) headquartered in Swindon, Wiltshire.

Kent Fedorowich is Reader in British Imperial and Commonwealth History at the University of the West of England, Bristol. He is author of *Unfit for Heroes: Reconstruction and Soldier Settlement between the Wars* (1995) and co-editor, with Martin Thomas, of *International Diplomacy and Colonial Retreat* (2001), and, with Carl Bridge, *The British World: Diaspora, Culture and Identity* (2003). A leading authority on the history of prisoners-of-war and civilian internees, he has co-edited with Bob Moore, *Prisoners of War and their Captors in World War II* (1996), and, co-authored with Bob Moore, *The British Empire and its Italian Prisoners of War, 1940–1947* (2002).

A. James Hammerton taught history at La Trobe University in Melbourne, Australia, from 1969 until his retirement at the end of 2004. His teaching fields and research interests ranged across modern British and Australian history, the history of migration, the history of women, of marriage and of masculinity. His latest co-authored book, with Alistair Thomson, *'Ten Pound Poms': Australia's Invisible Migrants*, was published in 2005. He is currently working on the oral history of British emigration and the 'British Diaspora' since the 1960s, a project funded by the Australian Research Council.

Aled Jones is the Sir John Williams Professor of Welsh history at the University of Aberystwyth. His current research focuses on Welsh Protestant missions in India 1840–1966, and he was elected Fellow of the Royal Asiatic Society in 2004 for his work on the history of the Welsh in Bengal. He has served as Head of the Department of History and Welsh History (1994–2002), Dean of the Faculty of Arts (2004–5) and is currently the University's Pro-Vice Chancellor with responsibility for Research, Language Policy and International Development. He is joint editor of the *Welsh History Review* and served as Literary Director (Modern) of the Royal Historical Society (2000–4).

Michele Langfield is Associate Head of School (Research) in the School of History, Heritage and Society, Faculty of Arts and Education, Deakin University, Melbourne, Australia. Her research interests include migration, ethnicity, identity and cultural heritage in which she has published widely in these areas. Her books include *Welsh Patagonians:*

The Australian Connection, with Peta Roberts (2005); *More People Imperative: Immigration to Australia, 1901–39* (1999); and *Espresso Bar to EMC: A Thirty-year History of the Ecumenical Migration Centre* (1996). Much of her work utilises oral histories and video-testimonies, particularly in the field of Jewish and Holocaust studies, and she is joint editor of *Testifying to the Holocaust*, with Pam Maclean and Dvir Abramovich (2008). A further edited collection (with William Logan and Mairead Nic Craith) entitled *Cultural Diversity, Heritage and Human Rights: Intersections in Theory and Practice* was published by Routledge in 2009.

Kathrin Levitan is an Assistant Professor of History at the College of William and Mary, where she teaches courses on modern British history, modern European history, and the history of British and European empires. Her book, *A Cultural History of the British Census: Envisioning the Multitude in the Nineteenth Century* was published by Palgrave/Macmillan in 2011. Levitan also has published articles in the *Women's History Review* and the *Gaskell Society Journal*.

Eleanor Passmore completed an MA by research (with Distinction) at the University of Leeds in 2006, comparing British and French welfare policy for post-colonial migrants after the Second World War. She has since worked as a social policy researcher in a number of UK think tanks, and led the Work Foundation's programme on public service reform before joining the Cabinet Office in 2008. She is currently a Senior Policy Advisor in the Cabinet Office, where she works on a range of domestic policy issues.

Eric Richards is a prize winning author and Professor of History at Flinders University in Adelaide. A leading specialist in the history of Australia, British and international migration, his most recent published work includes *Britannia's Children: Emigration from England, Scotland, Wales and Ireland since 1600* (2004); *Destination Australia: Migration to Australia since 1901* (2008); and, *The Highland Clearances: People, Landlords and Rural Turmoil* (2008).

Andrew S. Thompson is Professor of Modern History at the University of Exeter, and a Council member of the Arts and Humanities Research Council. His research has focused on the effects of empire on British private and public life during the nineteenth and twentieth centuries, including *Imperial Britain* (2000) and *The Empire Strikes Back?* (2005). Most recently, he has published a companion volume to the Oxford History of the British Empire series entitled *Britain's Experience of*

Empire in the Twentieth Century (2012). He has also written on public memories and the legacies of empire. A project on Asian Britishness, undertaken with the Institute of Public Policy Research and Tameside Metropolitan Borough Council, led to an invitation to address the Prime Minister's Strategy Unit on the subject in 2005. His co-authored monograph, with Professor Gary Magee of Monash University, entitled, *Empire and Globalisation. Networks of People, Goods and Capital in the British World, 1850–1914*, published by Cambridge University Press in 2010, offers a fresh perspective on the historical roots of modern globalisation and its relationship to imperial expansion.

GENERAL EDITOR'S INTRODUCTION

The historiography of imperialism is staggeringly rich and, just as importantly, it continues to show signs of repeatedly reinventing itself. One of the most productive phases in this process has been the work surrounding the concept of the 'British World' (and its variant, the British World System), which stimulated a whole succession of conferences and publications, mainly in the twenty-first century. This book, focusing on questions of migration, makes a notable contribution to this on-going debate. The conference at which these papers were first delivered, held in Bristol in 2007, was a strikingly lively affair, and some of that vibrancy comes through here. For a start, the extensive introduction by the two editors forms an exceptionally valuable survey of the idea of the 'British World' and the manner in which it can be applied to many forms of migration, embracing territories of settlement, so-called 'dependent' colonies, areas often known as 'informal empire', as well as the ways in which such global movement became far more transnational and indeed less 'British' in modern times. All of this not only pulls together the themes of the papers with great skill, but implicitly indicates fresh directions for research. It should indeed constitute a starting point for all students wishing to acquaint themselves with this field.

Meanwhile, the papers themselves strike out in a variety of new directions. They cover such fields as migration in relation to nineteenth-century demographic theory, various aspects of religious and missionary dispersal, producing tensions between forms of nationalism and Christian universality, the presence or absence of imperial sentiment in the minds of migrants, as well as non-white migration in the form of the extensive movement of Asian people in the second half of the nineteenth century and the early years of the twentieth. The invariably forced migration of children has been much written about and has stimulated forms of apology in recent years. Here we have a significant case study which casts fresh light on these often disturbing processes. We also hear of the plight of single female emigrants and the conditions they endured in Canada in the 1920s, as exposed by a public-spirited member of the Imperial Order Daughters of the Empire. Yet another case study relates to a cache of correspondence, illustrating the means whereby migrants maintained connections with 'home', transmitting news of the circumstances in which they found themselves and their attempts to familiarise the unfamiliar. In addition, we have several papers on the decolonisation era, less well covered in past studies of migration. In African territories where Europeans had settled, independence created new dilemmas, notably whether to 'stay on' or not. There is much to be written about this and the chapter on Zambia should stimulate other studies. In recent decades, we have new forms of cosmopolitan migration and 'sojourning' as well as continuing questions of integration and multiculturalism in countries like Britain and France which have experienced major migrations from their former empires. These two significant fields are covered in the last two chapters.

Thirty years ago, the distinguished historian of science and of the environment, Roy MacLeod, substituted the notion of the 'moving metropolis' for simplistic dispersal theories in respect to the spread of western scientific notions. The 'moving metropolis' idea fits the British World well, in at least two respects. The conferences themselves took place not just in Britain, but also in Australia, New Zealand, Canada and South Africa (as it happens almost mirroring the moving conferences of the British Association for the Advancement of Science in the early twentieth century). But beyond that it is apparent that the British World concept embraces many forms of territorial, demographic, and cultural pluralism, as well as ideas about networks within a web of intra-colonial connections, and transnationalism moving from imperial to global contexts. Moreover, the British World idea showed itself capable of providing a framework for those connections among economic and social, religious and intellectual, environmental and cultural histories that became part of the historians' quest from the 1980s onwards.

The question arises where do we go from here? There will of course continue to be a place for national histories, but the emerging studies (some in this series) that compare the experience of different territories mainly within the British Empire need to be encouraged and extended. But my answers to the question of future directions go beyond this and are entirely personal: I think we need more work that moves across the borders of different empires, perhaps even in chronological as well as geographical terms. In other words, we need to think in much more comparative terms about empires in general and parallel forms of modern imperialism in particular. We also need to recognise that white people can be divided up into different ethnicities as much as indigenous peoples in Asia, Africa and elsewhere. It is for this reason that I have been promoting the concept of a 'four nations' approach to the history of the British Empire, in pursuit of what may be termed Irish, Scottish, English and Welsh Worlds. Each of these ethnicities had distinctive social, cultural, religious and intellectual forms to offer to empire and the world. As always, the 'Studies in Imperialism' series will set out to be in the forefront of both the comparative and the four nations approaches, while responding, of course, to the many other suggestions that may emerge.

John M. MacKenzie

ACKNOWLEDGEMENTS

Versions of several of these essays were first presented at the British World Conference held in Bristol in July 2007. That conference, which saw 140 delegates from fourteen different countries, was jointly hosted by the (then) British Empire and Commonwealth Museum, the University of Bristol and the University of the West of England, Bristol. The conference would not have been the success it was without the hard work of many people who laboured tirelessly behind the scenes. There are simply too many to acknowledge individually, but two people deserve special mention. Dr Rob Skinner at the University of Bristol, where the conference was hosted, was the link person in the Department of Historical Studies who provided invaluable liaison work between the department and the conference organising committee. Dr Jayne Gifford, then a doctoral candidate at UWE (Bristol), proved indispensable in providing vital support and a cheeky sense of humour at critical stages during final preparations.

Generous financial support was also bestowed in 2007 by a number of agencies which provided timely funds in the form of conference subventions, monies which were used to allow over forty post-graduates and early career researchers to participate. The editors would therefore like to express their gratitude to the Economic History Society, the Royal Historical Society, and the British Academy for their support. Departmental funds were also tapped as were monies from the Vice-Chancellors of each of the host institutions. Writing space and quiet reflection were also provided by residency and visiting fellowships which allowed Dr Fedorowich to revise the manuscript in 2010–11. He would like to acknowledge the generosity of the Stout Research Centre for New Zealand Studies at the Victoria University (Wellington), and the Humanities Research Centre at the Australian National University (Canberra). An Australian Bicentennial Fellowship awarded through the Menzies Centre for Australian Studies, King's College, London, was extremely beneficial in tapping into crucial Australian-based material.

The editors would also like to extend a heartfelt appreciation to the support and friendship of a number of people who have been instrumental while this project was unfolding: Professor Robert Bickers (Bristol), Professor Carl Bridge (King's College, London), Dr John Darwin (Oxford), Professor Saul Dubow (Sussex), and Professor John M. MacKenzie (Lancaster). Drafts of the introduction were also aired at a number of research seminars during the final preparations on the manuscript. The editors would like to acknowledge the convenors and participants at the Humanities Research Centre (ANU), the Department of History and Art History at the University of Otago (Dunedin), the Stout Research Centre for New Zealand Studies at the Victoria University (Wellington), and the Department of History at the Rijk Universtait, Groningen, in the Netherlands. In particular, the editors would like to thank Dr Debjani Ganguly and Professor Paul Pickering (ANU); Dr Vanessa Ward, and Professors Angela McCarthy, Tony Ballantyne, Tom Brooking, and John Stenhouse (Otago); Professors James Belich, Richard Hill and Lydia Wevers (Stout Research Centre, Wellington); and Professor Raingard Esser (Groningen). Earlier drafts of the introduction were also kindly read by Professors Dane Kennedy (George Washington University), Paul Pickering (ANU), Philippa Mein Smith (Canterbury, Christchurch), and Angela Woollacott (ANU). Their comments and constructive criticisms were both helpful and much appreciated. Finally, the editors would like to thank Palgrave/Macmillan for granting us permission to publish substantially reworked elements from chapter 6, ideas of which first appeared in Kathrin Levitan's *A Cultural History of the British Census* (2011).

Colleagues at Exeter, Leeds and UWE (Bristol) have also been very supportive of our efforts and to them we would like to express our gratitude. Equally important, the editors would like to thank the contributors. So, too, are we appreciative of Emma Brennan and her production staff at Manchester University Press. Finally, it is to our respective wives who have borne the brunt of the editorial process and dealt with numerous phone calls, editorial meetings over dinner and extended periods away from home. Our thanks and love to Gudrun Fedorowich and Sarah Lenton who with their quiet support were always there for us. This book, however, is dedicated to our fathers; men from blue collar/working class backgrounds who were steadfast in their belief that a good education was invaluable. This book honours that commitment and their memory.

Kent Fedorowich and Andrew S. Thompson
April 2012

INTRODUCTION

Mapping the contours of the British World: empire, migration and identity

Kent Fedorowich and Andrew S. Thompson

For half a century or more, theories of imperialism have juggled with an array of factors – economic, political, military, strategic and, more recently, ideological and cultural – in their efforts to explain the causes and consequences of European overseas expansion. Emigration has figured less explicitly in such scholarship than one might have imagined. It is not that its importance is denied, more that emigration remains what one scholar has recently termed a 'hidden phenomenon'[1] whose relationship to empire was considerably complicated by the fact that diasporas, of whatever ethnicity or nationality, rarely mapped neatly on to the formal boundaries of colonial rule. This is beginning to change, however. The migratory process, and the resulting encounters and conflicts between settlers, indentured migrants and indigenous peoples, are increasingly regarded as fundamental to the world made by modern empires. In particular, the recent literature on the relationship between globalisation and empire underscores the importance of emigration to racial thinking and the 'imperial imaginary'; the profound impact of migration cycles upon the development of settler societies and economies; and the economic, social and cultural ways in which movements of population – Asian as well as European – shaped relations between colony and mother country.[2]

What emerges from this new scholarship is the necessity for a better conceptualisation of the reciprocal effects of empire and emigration. In framing this relationship we need both to grasp how the political economy and racial taxonomies of colonialism generated particular types of long-distance population movement, but, equally, how empire, in turn, was to a large extent defined by the very same demographic forces that it had helped to set in train. This is especially true of the British Empire as it strove to organise global mobility in the nineteenth and twentieth centuries. Indeed, it can be argued that the whole *raison d'être* of Britain's empire lay in the constant shifting of people between different parts of the world in ways that were likely to destabilise old identities and forge new ones.[3] From the mid-nineteenth century onwards the British were portrayed as a colonising people whose institutions, culture, and outlook had been shaped above all by their migrant experience.[4] They saw the 'wider world in general, and empire in particular, as vast regions over which to roam'.[5] But, crucially, as well as finding vocal supporters and exponents at home, Britishness also had to be refashioned overseas in societies that, far from being deferential to Britain, were rather selective and critical of metropolitan society, and often confident that they could improve on what existed 'at home'.[6]

Since 1998, historians primarily from the former settler dominions, the United States and the United Kingdom have participated in a series of conferences established to explore the making and remaking of Britishness across a 'British World'. This abstraction, which was open to a variety of interpretations both within Britain and its overseas empire, extends well beyond the physical confines of those regions on the map painted red. Although still relevant, it has less to do with the military, political and constitutional legacies of Anglo-dominion relations; topics which have been examined by historians for decades. Rather, the British World is an idea based on the three broad themes of diaspora, culture and identity. It examines those elements which bound people together as part of what two Commonwealth-born historians, long resident in Britain, have referred to as 'an imaginary or imagined empire, an empire of the mind which projected a common set of ideas, opinions and principles'.[7] This, however, was not a world created simply by sentiment, a common heritage and shared institutional values. It was a world whose peoples were connected by a series of interlocking networks, webs and information flows, which ranged from family and community affiliations, to commercial, scientific and professional bodies, to educational, philanthropic, religious and labour groups – associational and organisational ties which, if anything, strengthened over time.[8]

The concepts elaborated at the first British World conference, held in London in 1998, have proved central to the development of Commonwealth–Imperial historiography in the intervening years. One of the goals of this first conference, which has remained a core undertaking at subsequent events, was to escape from the static confines and parochial constraints of 'national' historiographies in order to provide a more integrated and comparative approach to the British World. Thus the British World concept is not – nor has it ever been – a simple 'repackaging' of British imperial history.[9] Rather, it is a reshaping and reorientation of the subject, which offers new and multiple avenues of research within a wider analytical framework.[10] Within this plea to broaden the investigative agenda, is the recognition that the British World concept draws on a number of complex, multifaceted and interlinked ideas generated within other disciplines and cross-fertilised by other scholarly traditions. Indeed, far from being binary in outlook or linear in approach, the very essence of the British World idea is its plurality. Through its exploration of the ways in which people, ideas and institutions circulated between Britain and its settler colonies, British World scholarship has thus engaged with the contemporary debates generated by 'globalisation', as well as new thinking surrounding 'transnationalism' as an analytical tool.[11] As several historians have recently argued, the 'seeds of transnationalism [were] imperial, rather than post-colonial'. Empires were among the most 'critical sites where transnational social and cultural movements took place', and might even be described as the 'principal global conveyer-belt' for the transmission of such activities.[12] Similarly, A. G. Hopkins' analysis of global imperialisms has sought to explain how transnational impulses and ideas were intrinsic to the operations of empire and therefore had far-reaching historical consequences. As Hopkins notes, what were empires if not 'transnational organisations ... created to mobilise the resources of the world? Their existence and their unity were made possible by supranational connections. Their longevity was determined by their ability to extend the reach and maintain the stability of these connections.'[13]

If scholarship on the British World has been instrumental in putting the former colonies of settlement – or 'neo-Britains'[14] – on the radar of imperial historiography, a key focal point has been an analysis of imperial migration, its shifting patterns and processes, its socio-economic bases, and the transfer of ideas, identities and investment capital along the various networks established by British migrants throughout the empire, both formal and informal. Furthermore, taking a cue from the British-born, New Zealand-raised historian J. G. A. Pocock,[15] British World scholarship has also moved beyond these familiar axioms to provide more sophisticated notions of 'Britishness' as contested forms of identity.[16] As Stephen Constantine reminds us, practitioners of the British World are 'emphasising the Britishness of Greater Britain, even in the self-governing Dominions', where for so long the annals of earlier dominion historians 'had opted to emphasise the historical roots of distinctive nation states'.[17] In a similar vein, Stuart Ward has taken up the transnational baton by demonstrating how the tensions between metropolitan and colonial conceptions of Britishness arising from the 'interplay between familiar ideas and institutions from home and the unfamiliar exigencies of colonial experience' were played out in a variety of arenas. Of particular note here is the language of race nationalism, which, as Ward and others show, could be inflected with different meanings across and within the (settler) colonies, albeit in ways that were compatible – for settlers at least – with the idea of an overarching ethnic and cultural unity.[18]

However, Britishness is not simply about 'whiteness' or its global reach. There were, as several scholars are at pains to remind us, 'subaltern' forms of Britishness which developed among indigenous peoples – a multiplicity of responses that originated at the local and regional levels.[19] This rich topic requires a more systematic investigation,[20] but it is essential to highlight the racial plurality of the British World even if the scholarship to date has been uneven and/or perceived as overtly and overly 'white' in its focus.[21] There is also the need, as Paul Pickering has posited, to examine the impact over time of the ever growing 'native-born' population in the colonies of settlement on ideas of 'home', 'nation' and 'empire'. More importantly for him – and this is another opportunity for British World scholars – there is the question of how far local and regional identities were equal to, or perhaps more significant than, the transnational dimension of the British World. In other words, where is the place for the idea of 'the local', or to use his phraseology the 'trans-local', in the fashioning of settler and British identities?[22]

What is emerging under the banner of the British World, therefore, is a more subtle yet far-reaching investigation of what at one level seem to be competing forms of empire and nation-building. Fundamental to the conceptualisation of the British World is the rejection of the naive and unsophisticated contrast between a metropolitan nucleus and colonial periphery. If 'traditional' imperial history has largely focused on binary conceptions of metropole and periphery, the 'new' imperial history has consciously developed alternative networked conceptions of empire. David Lambert and Alan Lester have been prominent among those scholars who have highlighted the limitations of the geographies of the 'traditional' genre. They seek to show how a narrow focus of categories of 'metropole' and 'periphery' upon impulses emanating from the centre has been at the expense, and to the exclusion of, other types of interaction, such as the 'extensive networks connecting multiple colonial and metropolitan, as well as extra-imperial, sites'. The result has been a failure to 'retrieve a sense of the imperial whole from the viewpoint of this metropolitan "core"'.[23] Yet, and Lambert and Lester argue, far from being on the periphery, however, metropolitan hubs like Winnipeg, Wellington, Sydney, Cape Town, Bombay, Calcutta and even Hong Kong were themselves powerful agents that extended and blended British culture and society, aspects of which were then reconfigured and retransmitted back to the United Kingdom or to other parts of the empire.[24]

This volume explores several of the ongoing tensions between the national and imperial, the global and transnational. Its chief aim is to introduce the reader to new and emerging research in the broad field of 'imperial migration' and, in so doing, to show how this 'new' migration scholarship is helping to develop and deepen our understanding of the British World. The volume is appropriately published in the 'Studies in Imperialism' series, which, for over twenty-five years, has assiduously promoted the comparative and cross-disciplinary approach to the study of empire and its impact on British society. In fact, migration has arguably been among the leading themes of a series rapidly approaching its centenary publication.[25]

Using the British World concept as the lens through which to investigate this 'new' migration scholarship, a number of analytical benchmarks can be set down – benchmarks that connect the history of empire to world and transnational histories, as well as to histories of globalisation. Above all, British World scholarship is bringing into sharper relief the dynamics of settler-identity formation by presenting settler identities across the different colonies 'as part of a singular, integrated historical experience',[26] by developing new geographies of empire (especially the networked conceptions referred to above), and by recognising the extent to which white settler histories and histories of indigenous peoples were entwined. The latter is of particular significance, for whereas in the past migration scholarship was prone to fragmentation – with artificial boundaries erected between free-European and Asian and African indentured migratory streams – more recently there has been welcome recognition of the need to explore the interplay of these mass movements of peoples. Indeed, the very political economy of colonialism, it is argued, was based around racial divisions of labour and the emergence and development of racially exclusive principles of migration control. Hence, in the words of one leading migration historian, the imperative must now be to view these mass movements of people as a 'spectrum of overlapping migrations', where integration and inclusion, not segregation or exclusion, are the watchwords.[27]

'Britons of Greater Britain' and the making of the British World

Central, then, to the creation of this British World was the emergence of a group of settler societies or 'Britons of Greater Britain',[28] which shared a set of common, yet distinctive, social and economic characteristics.

These hitherto lightly populated regions occupied a privileged position in the first global economy wrought by British free traders. With an abundance of fertile land, but lacking in capital and labour, these societies easily attracted and firmly held the interest of British emigrants and investors. Such integration into the international economy was to prove an essential prerequisite of their development as 'better Britains'.[29] By enticing large numbers of immigrants and large volumes of capital to their shores, by constructing modern infrastructure, and by exporting a narrow range of staples, they were able to achieve rapid rates of economic growth and offer their settler populations levels of per capita income that, for the time, were impressively high. Even more remarkable, as Donald Denoon argued long ago, these settler societies *chose* dependent development and flourished as a result.[30]

The emphasis of recent British World scholarship on migration is no accident therefore. Integral to a proper analysis of 'global Britishness', is a better understanding of the role played by the mass movement of people. Globalisation, it has been said, is 'mediated by migration',[31] while evolving definitions of transnationalism are similarly underpinned by migration, whether permanent or transitory.[32] Waves of emigration not only helped to integrate large portions of the world materially, intellectually, culturally and politically, but engendered new, more transnational, ways of thinking.[33] In particular, the great transatlantic migrations, as well as those across Africa, Asia and the Pacific, are understood to have been pivotal to the first wave of modern globalisation between the 1850s and 1914.[34]

While migration may be 'as old as humanity itself', it was during these years that the world witnessed an unprecedented exodus of fifty or so million Europeans, causing significant shifts in the distribution of the world's population.[35] As prolific migrants, the British peoples were a significant part of this process. According to one of the pioneers of migration history, Charlotte Erickson, with the possible exceptions of Jewish and Chinese communities, the British were unrivalled for the 'degree of dispersal' around the globe: 'The British had an extraordinary range of choice as to destination and rarely experienced discrimination or exclusion anywhere.'[36] Between 1815 and 1930 some 13.5 million British people settled across Australia, New Zealand, South Africa, Canada and the United States.[37] The consequences of this outflow of population were profound. On the one hand emigration was a force for global economic growth, integrating labour, commodity and capital markets to an extent never previously seen. Yet on the other this industry of white settlement – for that is what it was – led to the widespread dispossession and delocalisation of indigenous peoples, the effects of which were felt powerfully at the time and still resonate today. Such migration made transnationalism – by which we mean living in and identifying with more than one country or place at once – a normal way of life for many British people in the second half of the nineteenth and first half of the twentieth century.[38] In the eyes of many, those who had migrated to Britain's settler colonies, or whose forefathers had migrated there, remained 'British', or at least partly so. Being British, moreover, had material implications. Not only did it shape tastes and consumer preferences: it impacted on the very nature and orientation of economic activity and behaviour.

The greater prominence of Britain's settler colonies in imperial historiography, tied in with a growing interest in the origins and evolution of British identity, has thus been an important feature not only of British World scholarship, but of the branching out of imperial historians into transnational, global and world history and, indeed, of the heightened emphasis on cultural discourses and practices in understanding how colonialism was articulated, experienced and understood. It also goes a long way to explain why migration history and imperial history have moved closer and closer together since the turn of the twenty-first century. Their symbiotic relationship is well illustrated by several of the key developments and innovations in the latest scholarship on imperial and international migrations, such as the greater attention paid to the circulation of information and ideas around the empire, to the formation of diasporas – religious, ethnic and political, and to what one scholar refers to as global or transnational 'biopolitics'. In each of these spheres migration scholarship has helped to expand the boundaries of the so-called 'new' imperial history demonstrating that, with a little patience and imagination, fertile ground exists for dialogue between these two branches of scholarship. For example, the study of information flows by migration scholars has fed directly into the new imperial history's growing interest in 'spaces and places'. External stimuli emanating from outside Britain are rightly being given greater analytical prominence, in an effort to highlight how the colonies interacted not only directly with the metropole but increasingly with each other. The themes of 'collaboration' and 'resistance' – inherited from an older imperial historiography – are also being revisited and reworked by a new generation of migration historians eager to explore the diasporic intersections of religion and ethnicity in a multi-level analysis between the metropole, missionary/settler agencies and indigenous communities. Meanwhile, new perspectives on the importance of racial ideology and imaginings, in particular the theoretical codes and philosophical canons that lay behind imperial governance and expansion, are being opened up by scholarship on 'global biopolitics' and 'racial demographies'.[39] Given the centrality of migration scholarship to the key historiographical shifts associated with the 'new' imperial history, it is worth pausing to examine these developments in greater detail.

Scholars have been drawn to the subject of how information moved around the empire,[40] and how the mass media was used to disseminate colonial ideas and news. The introduction of the imperial penny post in 1898 standardised postal rates and facilitated the sending of letters and parcels overseas. When combined with new communication technologies (such as telegraphs and trans-oceanic cables) and revolutionary advances in ship design and propulsion (introduced from the 1870s), it is clear that information, goods and people travelled much faster around the empire by the turn of the nineteenth and twentieth century, albeit with significant differences between the colonies.[41] Interestingly, the revolution in communications and transportation which allowed writers such as Charles Dilke, Anthony Trollope and J. A. Froude to move around the settler empire so effortlessly between the 1860s and 1880s, coincided with an increased public appetite in Great Britain for news of the colonies, which these authors eagerly satiated. Put another way, this genre of travel writing and the ideas conveyed were excellent examples of the 'geopolitics of travel'.[42]

Studies of the imperial press demonstrate just how crucial print media was to integrating constituent parts of the empire, as well as its importance in providing information to British settlers about possible migration opportunities.[43] They also reveal the role the authorities could play in the management, if not manipulation, of these information flows and networks in the interests of imperial control.[44] Indeed, a key function of newspapers was to propagandise and promote, as research into the nineteenth-century British transoceanic steamship press in India and Australia, in which information about market and settlement opportunities were extensively reported and advertised, has powerfully conveyed.[45] Similarly, with respect to the broadcast media, it has been shown how, during the Second World War, dominion and colonial propaganda was transmitted back to the British home front to better inform 'domestic' listeners about the imperial war effort, the wartime sacrifices of their 'colonial' cousins, and the many post-war opportunities that awaited Britons overseas after the war.[46] The accumulation, dissemination and manipulation of the news (and other sources of information) throughout the British World were therefore inextricably tied to the migratory process.

The study of religious diasporas, of which Hilary Carey and Aled Jones are leading advocates,[47] has likewise been a growth area for migration scholars.[48] The spread and maintenance of Christianity in the colonies was propelled by the expansion, numerically and spatially, of settler communities along and deeper into the frontiers.

For most of the nineteenth century, the settler dominions relied on home seminaries and colleges to provide ministers and a religious infrastructure within their emerging societies. Carey, for instance, has demonstrated the dependence of Australia on the recruitment of clerics in the United Kingdom well into the twentieth century. Meanwhile, Jones illustrates that Welsh missionary activity in north-east India was not simply about taking Christianity to the Indian peasantry. As time moved on, Welsh missionaries had to redevelop their attitudes and methods when negotiating with their Indian charges, so that, by the twentieth century, work in the field was being used to transform missionary work within Wales itself. Taking these respective cues, Heather McNamara has cleverly combined the themes of the press and religious diaspora by explaining, through the *New Zealand Tablet*, how the Irish Catholic community in New Zealand kept in touch with, and networked into, the wider Irish diaspora.[49] Nonetheless, British World historians have yet to provide a comprehensive investigation similar to Robert Swierenga's examination of Dutch immigration and settlement in the United States, which focuses on the role of faith and family in the migratory process.[50]

Another fresh avenue of research, intersecting migration and imperial histories, is the emerging field of global or transnational 'biopolitics'.[51] By combining health and hygiene with the familiar debates about population control and eugenics, we can examine how nations and empires sought to enhance, maintain and protect their racial purity, national strength and global reach. A key component of this exclusionist mantra was the increased use of medical restrictions – the 'medicalisation' of the migratory process – which the host settler societies increasingly invoked to the consternation of the multitudes seeking a new life overseas.

Canada provides an interesting illustration. From 1890, medical inspection was used regularly by Canadian immigration officials as a measure of social control and nation-building. Public health issues were easily and conveniently employed by Canadian eugenicists, many of whom were leading medical professionals. The influential C. K. Clarke, head of the Toronto Psychiatric Clinic, was a leading exponent of medical inspections to exclude immigrants on racial grounds.[52] Indeed, prior to 1920, Canada's doctors were at the forefront of this growing discomfort over immigration, and championed stricter selection criteria based on ethnicity and race where the 'widening of medical grounds for exclusion became their weapon'.[53] Medical inspection combined with deportation, therefore, became an increasingly powerful bludgeon in the Canadian government's arsenal to exclude not just the unhealthy and mentally unfit, but also the politically mutinous.[54] These draconian measures were not confined to non-European migrants. Increasingly, after 1920, many assisted migrants from the British Isles fell victim to the growing corpus of legislation because they had become public charges and hence an unwelcome burden on the senior dominion's fledgling welfare system.[55]

Paralleling this interest in global or transnational 'biopolitics' is an emerging literature on 'racial demographies'. At its heart are the construction, collation and manipulation of census data. In this volume, Kathrin Levitan explores how, in the mid-nineteenth century, US census material reinforced the bonds between Britain and America – the construction of an Anglo-World. Her investigations lend weight to William E. Van Vugt's observation that between 1820 and 1860 the United States and the United Kingdom were the two 'most interconnected countries in the world in terms of culture and economic growth'.[56] If the inclusion of the United States was a key element in the formation of an Anglo-British World, Rachel Bright's chapter also shows how the exclusion of non-white peoples was integral to the process. Within a British colonial context keeping a detailed inventory was not just about monitoring the condition of, and improvement in, the human condition of its citizenry; it was equally crucial to the maintenance of imperial hegemony. According to one historical geographer, the 'collection and manipulation of statistics became an essential part of the operation of the state as it assumed a greater role in the direction of population'.[57] Therefore, from the 1830s onwards, several white setter societies used census data to either construct a racially exclusive, anti-Asian stance – as in the case of 1890s British Columbia; or, as in the instance of colonial Australia to justify the extension, at the expense of an already beleaguered Aboriginal population, of a white settler society on an ever-expanding frontier.[58]

Mapping global networks

Much can be learnt, therefore, about the British World by conceiving it as a species of global networking – networks that enable us to analyse, with greater precision, long-distance connections over extended periods of time. Such networks connected private, unofficial and provincial interests in Britain with their overseas contacts and communities. It was through them that ideas and information were exchanged, trust was negotiated, goods were traded, and people travelled. Two key facets of the 'new' migration history seek to show both the integrative power and exclusionary tendencies of these networks: namely, the different forms and expressions of family and kinship networks, and the scale and significance of migrant remittance flows.

Transnational family or kinship networks – explored by Stephen Constantine, Jo Duffy and James Hammerton – have attracted the attention of a growing number of scholars eager to chart an individual's migrant experience through oral testimony or the letters they wrote to and received from family and friends over time. Using emigrant letters as a source can be rewarding;[59] but the methodological pitfalls and 'blatant biases' contained within them are many.[60] For instance, how does one interpret the silences? Why and to what extent are letters self-censored? Understandably, when emigrant letters are printed in contemporary newspapers, journals, travelogues and almanacs, there is a natural aversion by historians to dismiss them as unabashed propaganda.

Others, however, have suggested that this mistrust may sometimes be misplaced. Bill Jones, for example, highlights how these letters provide information about personal networks, and, in particular, how some emigrant communities, like the Welsh, used these letters to negotiate a cultural space between and within an adopted but foreign public sphere.[61] Indeed, for historians such as Maldwyn Jones, the 'private letter was beyond question the most trusted source of information about emigration and may well have been for that reason the most effective stimuli'.[62] The letter became the fulcrum of transnational family and kinship networks facilitating the augmentation, melding and dispersal of information flows. The growing plethora of published material from the 1820s onwards, the increasing speed and efficiency with which these materials were despatched and disseminated, coupled with rising literacy rates, fuelled this revolution in knowledge exchange and inspired many individuals with means and education to up sticks for new challenges overseas. It also allowed migrants to keep abreast of settlement and investment opportunities as more families, increasingly facilitated by assisted migration schemes, began to pool their resources to exploit lucrative commercial ventures both at home and abroad.[63]

Prepaid passages were another key factor within transnational family networks which oiled the wheels of migration overseas. Oliver MacDonagh has suggested that the majority of nineteenth-century Irish migration was financed this way. According to the estimates of one leading Liverpool shipping agent in 1834, of the 3,000 bookings undertaken by his firm, approximately 45 per cent were prepaid or paid by remittance. Increasing amounts of money travelled back across the chain helping families to join their friends and relatives in North America (and later Australasia). In 1848, £400,000 was remitted in Liverpool to help Irish migrants make their overseas journey; 40 per cent of this figure took the form of prepaid passages. During the next season, in 1849, British emigration officials reported that 75 per cent of the Irish emigrants had received their fares from North America in one form or another.[64] Funds transferred this way were prodigious. In 1855 the Colonial Land and Emigration Commissioners recorded in their annual report that nearly £1.75 million had been remitted home from North America, although it was acknowledged that the actual sum was significantly greater.[65] Indeed, it is staggering to think that during the nineteenth century approximately 10 per cent of all European migrants journeyed overseas using a government subsidy, while another 25 per cent had their voyage underwritten by friends and family.[66]

In seeking to show how migrants were key players in Britain's exploitation of global resources, scholars have also recently opened up a much-neglected dimension of their experience, namely the one-off and regular payments they made to support their families and communities 'back home'. Studies of contemporary remittance activity highlight the positive role such monetary transfers have played in alleviating poverty in recipient countries. Yet they also criticise remitters, like the Chinese in Australia, for not 'making a life' in their adopted country, and for sending their earnings 'home'.[67] By comparison, remittances have received much less attention from historians – until recently, it was not even clear what type of source material could be used to reconstruct them.[68]

The extensive remittance culture of the long nineteenth century, unleashed by successive rounds of migration, put into play streams of capital that not only supplied vital financial support to British families literally stretched across the globe. Data discovered in the British Post Office offer unparalleled insights into the scale of these remittance flows, and the range of purposes to which they were put. It was in the later nineteenth century that the volume of remittances rose rapidly, a product of the growing wealth and numbers of emigrants and the ease with which they could transfer funds internationally via the money and postal order systems operated by the British and colonial post offices.[69] From their inception in the early 1870s, these systems proved very popular, allowing for small amounts of cash to be sent regularly through the mail.

What, then, persuaded ordinary men and women to put their trust in postal and remittance services? The Victorian Post Office was one of very few government services to reach into all parts of the country and touch all classes.[70] Its ethos was one of efficiency and reliability. And discipline from the centre was not only exercised on the provinces in Britain – colonial post offices were likewise subject to the strictures of the British Postmaster-General, with staff sent out from Britain to run them.[71] Anthony Trollope, for example, had an acute appreciation of the value attached to the overseas mail by colonists, and of the excitement occasioned by its arrival. During his frequent trips abroad, he made a point of examining the post office whenever he arrived in a new city.[72] As Trollope observed, post office buildings in the colonies were often the grandest public edifices in town – a sign of how symbolic forms of authority could reinforce the confidence placed by colonists in money and postal orders.

From the 1870s to 1914, over £200 million was remitted to and from the United Kingdom – a very considerable sum of private capital. One significant source of remittances came from the Cornish mining diaspora.[73] From the 1880s the Cornish provided a highly mobile work-force: on the Witwatersrand in South Africa, for example, they formed a quarter of the white mine workforce, some 10,000 miners in all.[74] Many of these miners travelled alone, and the families they left behind anxiously awaited the arrival of a regular remittance.[75] When the South African mail arrived, people would flock into the towns from the surrounding villages to collect their money, and business in local shops boomed.[76] Conversely, when the 'home pay' did not arrive, the county's Board of Guardians were left to pick up the pieces – albeit helped by the charitable work of several Cornish associations on the Rand. The constant flow of remittances from South Africa provided a lifeline for the Cornish economy until at least the First World War.

What these two case studies exhibit is how, separated from their family by great distances, many migrants clearly felt responsible for the wives, children and dependent relatives they left behind. Nor was the tenacity of 'old' world social ties confined to the British imperial world. Transatlantic remittance flows show how a sizeable proportion of British migrants in the United States displayed an ongoing psychological commitment to their 'homeland'. Moreover, it was not just British migrants who were sending money home. Between 1873 and 1923, scores of Canadian oil drillers who had developed their unique trade while exploiting oil deposits in Enniskillen Township in south-western Ontario, were lured abroad by higher wages when the deposits in Petrolia and Oil Springs had played out. Their specialist skills and technical expertise were highly sought after by companies eager to exploit newly discovered oil reserves in the Dutch East Indies, Persia, Galicia, Russia, India, the West Indies and the United States. Like their Cornish brethren, they became part of an imperial 'overclass' by virtue of their 'whiteness', 'Britishness', and technical know-how. Moreover, their remittances were crucially important to the continued well-being of their families and to local manufacturers and businesses who profited by the regular supply of money being sent home.[77] Whether migrants left for the settler colonies, America or indeed sojourned to other empires, their departure was not so much a case of 'cut and run', as of run, remit and later (perhaps) return.[78]

Europeans were not the only migrants, of course.[79] The Indian and Chinese contract labourers who moved around the empire in search of employment had their own motives for emigrating.[80] Like their European counterparts, they too strove to save money to send to their family during indenture, or to take back home with them after it ended.[81] Much less has been written about this, however, raising the possibility of further and fruitful comparative study of non-European migratory behaviour across the different diasporas that were partly the product of empire. What we do know is that in those regions where European and non-European migratory streams *did* mix the power of imperial networks to discriminate against indigenous peoples, and to exclude them from 'the privileges of responsibility and skill', was striking.[82]

British migrants, by contrast, enjoyed privileged access to these networks and were adept at exploiting them for their own gain.[83] Take the controversy, re-examined by Rachel Bright below, over Chinese indentured labour in early twentieth century South Africa. Skilled workers from Britain (and Australia), who had migrated to the Transvaal, invoked a doctrine of 'white labourism' or 'racial socialism' to challenge the presence of 'ethnic outsiders' in the workplace who threatened to undercut their wages. Understood in this way, remittances might almost be likened to a form of imperial-wide social insurance – part of a bigger push to shore up a separate racial status, including job security, better pay and welfare, for (white) *British* subjects.

Such a privileged position for white migrants did not necessarily mean that they had it all their own way all the time. Labour historians in Australia, Canada, New Zealand and the British Isles, while lamenting the need for more comparative study,[84] have over the years demonstrated that despite the positive contributions made by British migrants to the social and economic development of their new societies, the transplantation of their ideas and working practices did not necessarily make them easy to accommodate. British coalminers and iron and steel workers who migrated to the Antipodes are a case in point. On the positive side, retail cooperatives or 'Rochdales' were transplanted to Australia relatively easily in the mid-nineteenth century, despite some subtle local adaptations and variations.[85] Working practices in the coalfields of New South Wales and along the west coast of New Zealand mimicked those of Fyfe, Northumberland and Co. Durham. Indeed, British coalminers were eagerly sought after for their technical proficiency. Much less welcome were their trade union practices which led to confrontation with colonial capitalists; but as Robin Gollan noted almost fifty years ago the origin of unionism in Australian mines 'scarcely need[ed] explanation'.[86] The establishment of 'labour aristocracies' by the miners was not welcomed by unskilled (colonial) labour or the mine owners. This eventually led to confrontation and industrial action.[87] The recruitment of British labour in the Antipodean coal and iron and steel industries was therefore a double-edged sword, but it was essential if standards were to be maintained and the skill base updated and replenished.[88]

Exclusion versus inclusion

By its very nature, migration is transformative.[89] It changes the way in which individuals – and the families they left behind – imagine their social and political spaces, thereby making their migration a defining aspect of their identity. By encouraging people to see themselves as part of a global chain of kith and kin, who shared common standards, forms of communication and expectations, the mass migration of people from the British Isles during the 'long' nineteenth century turned national (and indeed regional) identities into transnational ones.[90]

When one looks more closely at the migrant networks that established themselves across this British World, what one sees is a multitude of recurring personal interactions which, over the second half of the nineteenth century, brought ever wider groups of peoples together.[91] Almost by stealth, the workings of a multitude of transnational networks bypassed national boundaries and unwittingly took large and historically important steps toward the emergence of a truly global market.[92] While Britain was often the hub of these networks through which people, capital and goods moved, Australia, Canada, New Zealand and South Africa were rapidly-evolving and maturing societies and economies in their own right, remarkably open to the world beyond their shores, and each thus contributing distinctively to, as well as feeding off, the transnational networks under consideration. And this was not confined to the worlds of finance, commerce and industry. Fraternal associations, like the Freemasons or the Orange Order were equally adept at spreading their secret webs through and along a multi-centred British World.[93]

Yet, care is needed here. One should not assume that this process of network-sponsored growth was all rosy or uni-directional.[94] Networks, after all, are specifically created to be exclusive and to promote the interest of insiders, if need be, at the expense of others. When opportunities falter, the natural instinct of networks is to turn inwards. Moreover, the common cultural identity underlying these networks now acted to facilitate this transition. In other words, the social, cultural and economic possibilities of the British World were also racially circumscribed and hence exclusive to peoples or regions not deemed white and 'British'.[95]

The 'White Australia' policy is one example where exclusion along racial lines became a powerful and emotive domestic political issue until the mid-1970s when it was officially abandoned.[96] Canada and New Zealand operated similar policies until the 1960s which, like Australia, were driven, in part, by the perception of white workers and their unions that the large-scale introduction of cheaper foreign labour was a pernicious and ever-present threat that demanded unremitting vigilance. As a result, the need to continually guard the gates from the 'subversive' masses of non-white labour fed into the battery of exclusionist legislation which intensified during times of economic downturn. Similarly, these issues continuously spilt over into imperial affairs and marred relations with their Asian neighbours well into the twentieth century.[97]

As well as understanding how a developing sense of global Britishness aided economic and social integration in the half century before the First World War, we also need to be aware therefore of the historical diversity of globalising forces – to quote John Darwin: 'The past patterns of trade and conquest, diaspora and migration, that have pushed and pulled distant regions together and shaped their cultures and politics have been exceptionally complex.'[98] With this in mind, the clarion call is for migration historians to cast aside the narrow and exclusive confines of ethnocentric analyses and embark on bolder comparative studies that situate the experiences of specific migrant groups, as Lindsay Proudfoot has demanded, within the 'wider histories they shared with others'.[99] Globalisation, transnationalism and the British World model are examples of these new conceptual forces at work that are indeed providing a more integrated approach to migration studies. This includes the integration of European, Asian and African migrations as well as free and coerced; an approach long advocated by David Eltis and recently reiterated by two early modern scholars.[100] Indeed, as we have seen above with work on transnational networks and remittances, significant advances have been made in the field of British migration studies since the mid-1990s; in particular the growing awareness that migrants and their kinship and community networks were key conduits in the transmission of political ideas, investment capital, cultural transfer and identity (re)formation.[101]

Empire and emigration: the ongoing debates

So what does this volume tell us about the relationship between empire and emigration? One fundamental question, posed by Eric Richards, is that we have yet to fully grasp the dynamics of the British diaspora: what made people migrate? It is an appeal for more in-depth research into what he calls the 'social psychology of emigration'. Furthermore, Richards argues that one of the neglected but rewarding aspects of the migration story is how this mass departure of tens of millions of people over two centuries affected Britain itself. For, in population terms, despite unparalleled emigration and renewed imperial impetus, most of the inhabitants of the British World remained on the 'Home Islands'. Richards's chapter focuses on the Reverend Thomas Malthus, arguably the most important Victorian thinker on emigration, and his ideas about how population movements presaged forces within sectors of a pre-industrial economy. Emigration was seen by Malthus as only a temporary expedient that would never provide enduring relief to the social afflictions facing Great Britain. To illustrate the limitations of Malthus's work, ideas which have largely been dismissed by scholars today, Richards examines the rural responses in three localities within the United Kingdom: the Isle of Man, the West Highlands of Scotland, and Swaledale in the North Yorkshire Pennines. This reveals wide-ranging responses to the pressures (including resistance) of these agrarian communities to emigrate; areas still locked into a pre-industrial sector of the economy that was being forced to engage with monumental economic forces from outside.[102]

The formation of national and imperial identities along racial lines in the mid-nineteenth century is the theme of Kathrin Levitan's incisive analysis of the mid-nineteenth century British censuses. Initiated in 1801, the British census (which was administered every ten years) played a central role in helping people envisage their nation in novel ways. The census was first and foremost an exercise in gathering information, but by 1851 British people at home and overseas began to picture their nation and empire in terms of racial proportions. Migration allowed the British 'race' to 'expand', which was key to the hierarchical constructs now being established between the white 'Anglo-Saxon' or 'British' races (which included the United States) and the 'less white' Irish and non-white, indigenous colonial 'other'. The census quickly developed into an instrument of parliamentary and extra-parliamentary power; especially in the settler colonies where colonial governors and administrators used and manipulated census data to guarantee white control and subjugation over indigenous peoples. By 1860, especially in the colonial environment, race had been brought to the forefront of the enumeration process. Racial purity became a chief concern of census taking hereafter as it easily slipped into the eugenics discourse that accelerated after 1850. And it was not just in the United Kingdom where large-scale Irish migration was causing concern about 'national' and racial degradation; but also in the overseas empire where physical and moral traits were becoming key indicators in early eugenic philosophy that was increasingly used to justify white British settler control of the ever-expanding colonial frontier. Racial potency, as Levitan argues convincingly, was ever more characterised by migration and the development of global racial demographics that put the United States and Great Britain at the apex.

Oonagh Walsh, in her study of the Irish abroad, has argued that, with the welcome easing of the theoretical frameworks in regard to migration, scholars have been able to be more imaginative when including 'career' migrants such as missionaries, the professional classes, soldiers, and policemen into the migrant pool.[103] The need for a wider appreciation of groups or categories who may not have thought of themselves as immigrants, therefore, demands a more in-depth investigation. This would include itinerant workers of all kinds – transported felons, musicians, thespians, domestic servants, merchant seamen, indentured labourers, customs officials and railway engineers – transnationalism or globalisation from below.[104] Hilary Carey's chapter surveys one of the more neglected of these careers, the clergy. Although Catholic Australia's dependence on Irish émigré clergy is well known, what is less familiar is that all the major denominations were intensely reliant on British-born clerics until well into the twentieth century. Using as her focus one of the most vital, but little understood British colonial institutions – that of the emigrant churches – she argues that the clergy played a pivotal role in the importation and diffusion of a sense of British identity (and morality) to Australian churchgoers. By exploring one of the more complex cultural connections between Britain and the settler colonies in Australia, Carey sets out a new and exciting agenda for migration historians to develop. Building on the work of Howard Malchow,[105] she provides additional insights into how the church played an important role in the emigration process itself. Providing spiritual solace to emigrants was only one small, but important role performed by the clergy. By the mid-nineteenth century, they not only took an active role on Boards of Guardians, Poor Law committees and emigration societies – writing letters of recommendation for would-be migrants[106] – but they themselves became part of the migratory process to meet the pastoral demands of burgeoning colonial flocks throughout the southern British World.

Aled Jones's chapter on the resistance and accommodation of Welsh Presbyterianism in Eastern Bengal investigates the varieties of engagement with Indian Christians and non-Christians between 1860 and 1940 that uncover strategies of both an individual and shared nature for addressing cultural and religious diversity. The town of Sylhet and its surroundings had long featured in the mind's eye of Welsh Nonconformism, nourished as it was by decades of press comment, lectures, sermons, exhibitions, novels, stage plays and later films. Sylhet itself was created by flows of internal migrants, largely Hindu workers from the North-West Provinces and Bihar, who were transported in large numbers after 1850 to clear land for the burgeoning Assamese tea industry. It was here that many Christian evangelicals, both Protestant and Catholic, migrated and traversed with these workers. In other words, Sylhet provides an excellent example of the intersection of internal regional migrant labour flows mixing with a vector of international missionary migration. This chapter points to the dynamics of inter-faith dialogues between Christians, Hindus and Muslims and the cultural transfers which occurred at all levels of Welsh missionary activity both in the field and at home. It also highlights the counter-strategies implemented by Hindu and Muslim communities in confining, avoiding and fending off Christian influence. This forced the Welsh missions and the home churches to adapt to these complex sets of circumstances which in the end demonstrated that, whatever the doctrinal and cultural accommodations made by the Welsh to Sylheti society, they were only ever to occupy a marginal site within it.

In a timely re-examination of the Asian 'menace', Rachel Bright argues that Asian migration and the perceived threat it posed to the settler colonies was *the* issue which could unite these seemingly incongruent elements of the British World. She argues that not only did the Asian 'other' captivate settler imaginations in the late nineteenth and early twentieth centuries; it was fundamental in shaping the British World and moulding the national identities of those white settler colonies. The racial discourse – 'whiteness' contrasted with 'yellowness' – dominated the political arenas in Australia, South Africa, British Columbia and California prior to 1914. It was an issue that transcended the British World and unified the English-speaking or Anglo-World.

Race, however, was not the only factor at play here. The contest between Europeans and Chinese was also fought between white labour and capitalists – the latter charged with subverting the labour market by introducing cheaper Chinese labour to lower wages and prevent the spread of trade unionism. Interestingly, most of the Chinese (and Indian) migration was out of the control of Europeans. When gold was discovered mid-century in California, British Columbia and Australia, Chinese labourers or 'free' migrants were recruited, organised and financed by Chinese capital working independent of European controlled networks. Indeed, the gold fields were initially reliant on Chinese mining skills and expertise. Soon after, white settlers became fearful of being 'swamped' by a flood tide of Asian migrants that threatened their livelihoods. Apprehensive about the growth of this foreign, non-white element in their midst – described as an invasion by stealth – the settlers used the fear of disease to implement segregation and, later, a raft of exclusionary policies (including the introduction of passports) designed to curb the influx of Chinese, Japanese and Indian immigrants.[107]

The use of censuses also provoked growing anti-Asian feeling. What emerges from this chapter is the extent to which colonial and US administrations would go to restrict Asian migration. The sharing of information became common practice and demonstrates the interconnectedness of the dominions (and the United States) when refining exclusionary legislation; legislation which was underpinned by the over-riding conviction within these 'better Britains' that Asians would not fit into the new democratic societies under construction in the settler colonies. Moreover, the stereotype of the Asian intruder inspired the formation of a robust white identity that was shaped by transnational labour interests and ideologies under the umbrella of white labourism, which by 1907 had succeeded in all but stopping Asian migration to the United States and the settler dominions.

Child migration has become a very sensitive and politically charged issue. In November 2009, the former Australian Prime Minister Kevin Rudd addressed several hundred of the 7,000 surviving former child migrants at Parliament House in Canberra where he made a moving apology to the Forgotten Australians and those children sent to Australian shores without their consent.[108] Prime Minister Gordon Brown in February 2010 announced with 'regret' the British government's role 'in the shameful deportation of thousands of children to former colonies'. Many were not impressed with Brown's statement calling it an 'empty apology'. One year on, both Brown and his successor as prime minister, David Cameron praised the work of Margaret Humphreys and the Child Migrants Trust, founded in 1986; Cameron, in particular, showing his 'delight' at the government-funded £6 million Family Restoration Fund that has already reunited many former child migrants with their relatives.[109] The work of the Child Migrants Trust, whose motto is 'Reuniting Families, Reclaiming Identity and Restoring Dignity', has become a powerful pressure group, which continues to provide support for those 'robbed' of their childhood. The Canadian government has never issued an apology instead declaring 2010 the 'Year of the British Home Child'.[110]

In a measured but insightful chapter, Michele Langfield examines one of the lesser studied child migration agencies, the Middlemore Children's Emigration Homes, which operated out of Birmingham. Much smaller than Barnardo's and the Salvation Army,[111] it placed over 8,000 children in foster homes throughout Canada and Australia between 1872 and 1972. She first supports the entreaties made by other scholars, such as Geoffrey Sherington, Chris Jeffrey and Stephen Constantine, that historians must provide a balanced understanding of the circumstances surrounding these child migration organisations. Echoing Constantine, she warns against 'constructions of history that are ignorant of the contemporary context and cautious against imposing twenty-first century values on beliefs and practices of earlier times'. This is quite challenging when media interest has been intense and demands for compensation, however valid, can easily skew the historical narrative.[112] Surprisingly, what Langfield demonstrates is that John T. Middlemore was perhaps further ahead of his time when it came to attitudes to juvenile migration and child care. What her chapter also highlights is the need for a more sophisticated approach in the study of child migration, education, social reform and the construction of an imperial citizenship.[113]

In her chapter Lisa Chilton asks: what sorts of privileges did British migrants, especially women, expect or seek overseas prior to the Second World War? Why did Canadians go out of their way to support these expectations? And why did Canadian immigration and railway officials agree to enact policies and enable structures that made these privileges possible? Using the broader discussion revolving around concepts of Britishness, white settler hegemony, and British superiority in pre-1939 Canada, she examines the cultural cross-currents and, at times, contradictions in the construction of an Anglo-Canadian or 'Britannic' national identity. Undeniably, Britishness was its bedrock. As migrants, therefore, Britons were given an elevated cultural status in the senior dominion. They were seen as less problematic and easier to acculturate to the Canadian way of life because for many Canadians being British *and* Canadian were one and the same. In other words, as Alan Sears has argued, the crux of the problem in 'forging a "national people" [hinged on] defining some people as more naturally Canadian (or capable of becoming Canadian) than others'.[114] Hence, they received preferential treatment while in transit, as individuals and as a group. This was particularly important for British women whose needs were assumed by their hosts to be different from foreign women. Segregated along ethnic lines during medical inspections, British women were granted separate amenities and better living quarters while en route than their less fortunate European sisters.

A closer examination of the documentation that has survived in the Canadian official correspondence of the 1920s demonstrates that 'ethnicity was classed'. Britons were a caste above most immigrants from other European countries and Canadians worked hard to promote and facilitate this social distance between newcomers from the United

Kingdom and those primarily from southern, east-central and south-eastern parts of continental Europe. Britons were deemed the 'right' type of immigrant because they possessed the moral fortitude, social beliefs, and cultural virtues that Anglo-Canadians valued. Despite the growing number of complaints about the quality and character of British migrants in the 1920s – evidenced by the increasing numbers of British deports – Britons were given the status of colonists, while most continental Europeans were simply foreigners.

If British migrants expected to be given preferential treatment and privileged status in the British World prior to the Second World War, what happened when they became just another influx of immigrants arriving alongside recent arrivals from other European or extra-European sources into societies made up of native-born Australians, Canadians and New Zealanders? Stephen Constantine, in a thought-provoking chapter highlighting the ambiguities and complexities of the ever-changing demographics of settler societies, examines how being just one of many immigrant streams impacted on the self-perception of British migrants in their new environments. Eavesdropping on the private voice of one early twentieth-century English migrant woman – and using an incomplete set of family correspondence written between 1926 and 1967 – he charts one migrant's transnational story. Recognising the epistolary shortcomings of this particular cache of letters, he nevertheless situates his analysis within the methodological parameters of the 'new' migration history.[115] For example, how do you navigate a set of incomplete correspondence largely written by one person who makes constant reference to other letters either lost or long destroyed? How do you interpret the silences, the irregularities and the gaps in the dates of the surviving letters? Most significantly, what do these letters say about identity formation and can we as historians recover them and make sense of them? Did this woman consider herself an empire settler, and hence a citizen of the British World? Or did she become assimilated to the Australian way of life, and invent or take up an Australian identity? Moreover, what tensions exist between the public and private domains contained within this correspondence?

These questions also form the basis of the chapters by Jo Duffy and A. James Hammerton. Duffy's chapter on white settlers' decisions to stay on after independence was granted to Northern Rhodesia in October 1964 is instructive for two reasons. Deploying a series of oral testimonies gleaned in 2005 and 2006, it first fills an important gap in our understanding of Africa's colonial legacy and reveals that the 'settler' community was far from being a monolithic group possessing one single dynamic or perspective. Second, and more importantly from the viewpoint of the British World, it provides hitherto neglected but fertile ground from which to survey their diverse experiences in one part of post-independence Africa. Crucially, her interviews reveal the multiplicity of experiences and overlapping identities that were engendered over forty years; in particular, settler conceptions of 'home' and whether they (and their offspring) considered themselves 'British' or 'African'.

Again using oral testimony, A. James Hammerton, in a stimulating chapter investigates post-1945 British migration where an increasing number of these migrants willingly assumed the title 'world citizen', adopting a cosmopolitan identity while possessing no fond connection with their birthplace or country of abode. They had become serial migrants adapting to a nomadic lifestyle in a highly globalised, transnational setting. Whereas between 1945 and the early 1970s many British migrants would have been consoled that they were actually moving to another part of Britain, by the 1980s as British migration to Australia slumped, many of those who arrived 'Down Under' considered themselves refugees from Thatcherism. Hammerton, building on earlier and pioneering work,[116] reflects on the changing ways these emigrants have come to depict and contemplate their lives at the turn of the twenty-first century.

And he makes some striking observations. Since the mid-1970s there has been a steady increase in permanent British settlement in non-British countries like Spain and France.[117] As the British World shrivels, British migrants of all walks of life are eager to look beyond the once familiar destinations where common cultural, sporting and linguistic awareness were the determining factors in making a new life overseas in the British Commonwealth. Mobility, however, is a critical factor running through Hammerton's analysis, where new employment and lifestyle opportunities are matched with an abiding determination to leave a country that is perceived by some as being over-run by asylum seekers and economic migrants from Eastern Europe, Africa and Central Asia – an issue in which successive British governments have continually failed to address.

Despite this outflow to the non-British World, Hammerton's analysis provides crucial glimpses at what he calls the 'creeping global outlook' that continues to influence those migrants to settle in the former settler dominions. For instance, Australia remains the most popular 'old' Commonwealth destination and ranks first in the top ten migrant destinations. Weather is a key factor for many families wanting to move to Australia. Educational opportunities are another. The ease of travel and knowledge obtained down the chain from friends and family is another prime factor in one's decision to move to Australia; a country which is hungry for skilled labour such as nurses, doctors, teachers, engineers, machinists and industrial apprentices. A useful illustration of these and other determining factors is the BBC's 'Wanted Down Under' programme – in its fifth season, at the time of writing – where UK families are given an opportunity to experience Australia or New Zealand for a week to see if they are ready for what is a life-changing decision.[118] Recent statistics demonstrate that of the 26,000 British citizens who migrate to Australia annually, 10,000 or almost 40 per cent return to the UK within a year. Some of these returnees – known as 'Ping Pong Poms' – then re-migrate to Australia a second or even third time highlighting not just their mobility and creation of multiple identities, but also their adaptability to a cosmopolitan, transnational lifestyle.

Finally, the last chapter in this volume by Eleanor Passmore and Andrew S. Thompson introduces a long-neglected, comparative analysis of post-1945 migration from the decolonising British and French empires. After the Second World War the concept of an imperial citizenship, based on a self-confident, white 'Britannic' identity, was undermined by the dominions' need to define their own separate citizenship. The various citizenship acts that were rolled out between 1946 and 1949 finally severed the 'indivisibility of subjecthood', which for so long had underpinned the British World. Canadians, for example, were still British subjects but only by dint of their being Canadian citizens first. London's response was the British Nationality Act of 1948, which was not, as some have argued, a deliberate attempt to 'racialise' future British immigration policy. This was to come later with the introduction in 1962 of the Commonwealth Immigrants Act. Rather, the 1948 Act was meant to maintain the essence of the pre-1946 arrangements, including the right of all British subjects to enter Britain. In other words, at least for the 1950s, it kept the door open for subsequent waves of non-white migration into Britain.[119]

Beginning with an overview of immigration trends to Britain from the 'new' Commonwealth between 1945 and 1962, Passmore and Thompson then compare and contrast British and French approaches to integration. At the core of their analysis are the tensions which existed between internal political pressures and the administration of Commonwealth relations with the newly emerging states in South Asia, Africa and the West Indies. At one level, the challenges facing Britain were greater than those of France because of the ethnic diversity of the new migrants seeking a new life in Britain. France however, even though the majority of new migrants were largely from North Africa, especially Algeria, had an equally problematic set of obstacles to negotiate as many Algerians were fleeing a nasty colonial conflict that was creating intense division within French society. How then were these new citizens to be assimilated into British and French civil society? How effectively did these respective governments cater for the welfare of these new arrivals as decolonisation gathered pace? How far did they tackle racial discrimination, and what were the differences between French Republican and British multicultural models of integration as each nation sought, eventually, to restrict the flow of these new immigrants? What this chapter gives us is not only a deeper understanding of the complex forces at work as two of the largest decolonising powers had to grapple with the legacy of empire; it also provides insights into how contemporary British immigration policy with its array of border controls, integration policies and anti-discrimination legislation is influenced today by the vestiges of decolonisation. In other words, multiculturalism was defined, in part, by the British government's responses to the interplay between immigrant welfare, the new Commonwealth and the related debates about 'Britishness'.

The above chapters explore the key points on the compass that are critical in mapping in greater detail what is meant by the British World. If this is an ongoing process, the signposts as plotted by our contributors signify that migration cannot be confined to simplistic notions that people moved merely because they were 'pushed', 'pulled', 'enticed' or 'coerced'. By setting free and un-free, European and non-European migration flows into a single investigative framework the British World concept can counteract the tendency toward fragmentation and segmentation that has haunted a number of disciplines, including imperial and migration history, for too long. Migration was imperial, transnational and global; it relied on a variety of networks and webs that facilitated the sharing of local knowledge and the exchange of ideas that flowed and rebounded on a regional, national and international scale. These networks, and migrants' contributions to them, shaped subsequent waves of emigration which were foundational to the earlier history of what today we call transnationalism or globalisation. These chapters, which encompass a variety of perspectives on imperial migrations, profile emerging research and demonstrate how this new migration scholarship is enhancing and enriching our understanding of the interplay of empire and emigration in the making of the modern world.

Notes

1 J. M. MacKenzie, 'Passion or Indifference: Popular Imperialism in Britain, Continuities and Discontinuities over Two Centuries', in J. M. MacKenzie (ed.), *European Empires and the People: Popular Responses to Imperialism in France, Britain, the Netherlands, Belgium, Germany and Italy* (Manchester, 2011), p. 63.
2 Much of this scholarship has been brought together by J. Belich, *Replenishing*

the Earth: The Settler Revolution and the Rise of the Anglo-World, 1783–1939 (Oxford, 2009); J. Darwin, The Empire Project. The Rise and Fall of the British World-System 1830–1970 (Cambridge, 2009); A. G. Hopkins (ed.), Globalization in World History (London, 2002); G. B. Magee and A. S. Thompson, Empire and Globalisation: Networks of People, Goods and Capital in the British World, c.1850–1914 (Cambridge, 2010); A. M. McKeown, Melancholy Order: Asian Migration and the Globalization of Borders (New York, 2008); and D. Bell, The Idea of Greater Britain: Empire and the Future of World Order, 1860–1900 (Princeton and Oxford, 2007).

3 J. Darwin, 'Empire and Ethnicity', Nations and Nationalism, 16:3 (2010), p. 391.
4 Ibid., p. 393.
5 MacKenzie, 'Passion or Indifference', in MacKenzie (ed.), European Empires and the People, p. 62.
6 Darwin, 'Empire and Ethnicity', p. 396.
7 C. Bridge and K. Fedorowich (eds), The British World: Diaspora, Culture and Identity (London, 2003), p. 6.
8 For the interconnectedness of Empire see, A. Lester, Imperial Networks: Creating Identities in Nineteenth Century South Africa and Britain (London, 2001); Z. Laidlaw, Colonial Connections, 1815–45: Patronage, the Information Revolution and Colonial Government (Manchester, 2005); U. Hillemann, Asian Empire and British Knowledge: China and the Networks of British Imperial Expansion (Basingstoke, 2009). For scholarship on migration networks and information flows see P. Hudson, 'English Emigration to New Zealand, 1839–1850: Information Diffusion and Marketing a New World', Economic History Review, 54:4 (2001), pp. 680–98; M. Harper, Emigration from Scotland between the Wars: Opportunity or Exile? (Manchester, 1998); D. Baines, 'European Emigration, 1815–1930: Looking at the Emigration Decision Again', Economic History Review, 47:3 (1994), pp. 525–44; T. Ballantyne, Orientalism and Race: Aryanism in the British Empire (Basingstoke, 2002), pp. 1–17, and 'Empire, Knowledge and Culture: From Proto-Globalization to Modern Globalization', in Hopkins (ed.), Globalization in World History, pp. 115–40; Magee and Thompson, Empire and Globalisation; M. Harper and S. Constantine, Migration and Empire, Companion Series, Oxford History of the British Empire (Oxford, 2010). For labour markets, labour hierarchies and trade unions, see J. Hyslop, 'The Imperial Working Class Makes Itself "White": White Labourism in Britain, Australia and South Africa before the First World War', Journal of Historical Sociology, 12:4 (1999), pp. 398–421; and N. Kirk, Comrades and Cousins: Globalization, Workers, and Labour Movements in Britain, the USA and Australia from the 1880s to 1914 (London, 2003), and most recently his Labour and the Politics of Empire: Britain and Australia 1900 to the Present (Manchester, 2011), pp. 3–30. See also the two special issues in Labour History Review, 74:3 (2009) and 75:1 (2010), guest edited by N. Kirk, D. M. MacRaild, and M. Nolan. For Irish and American dynamics, see E. O'Connor, 'William Walker, Irish Labour and "Chinese slavery" in South Africa, 1904–6', Irish Historical Studies, 37:145 (2010), pp. 48–60; and J. Higginson, 'Privileging the Machines: American Engineers, Indentured Chinese and White Workers in South Africa's Deep-Level Gold Mines, 1902–1907', International Review of Social History, 52:1 (2007), pp. 1–34. Professional and philanthropic organisations are further discussed in A. S. Thompson, The Empire Strikes Back (London, 2005), but two recent additions to this scholarship on professional networks are C. Poullaos and S. Sian (eds), Accountancy and Empire: The British Legacy of Professional Organisation (New York, 2010), and B. M. Bennett, 'The Consolidation and Reconfiguration of "British" Networks of Science, 1800–1970', in B. M. Bennett and J. M. Hodge (eds), Science and Empire: Knowledge and Networks of Science across the British Empire, 1800–1970 (London, 2011), pp. 30–43.
9 N. Kirk, D. M. MacRaild and M. Nolan, 'Introduction: Transnational Ideas, Activities, and Organizations in Labour History 1860s to 1920s', Labour History Review, 74:3 (2009), p. 223.

10 For a useful outline of the British World concept and its positioning within the so-called 'new' imperial history see G. A. Barton, 'What is the British World?', *British Scholar*, 2:2 (2010), pp. 177–80; and P. A. Pickering, 'An Afterthought: Why we should tell Stories of the British World', *Humanities Research*, 13:1 (2006), pp. 85–90, where he makes an interesting plea to use biography as a lens through which to examine the British World.

11 A good entry point to a growing body of literature on transnationalism is N. Glick Schiller, L. Basch, and C. Blanc Szanton, 'Transnationalism: A New Analytic Framework for Understanding Migration', *Annals of the New York Academy of Sciences*, 645 (1992), pp. 1–24, and their expanded analysis in *Unbound Nations: Transnational Projects Postcolonial Predicaments and Deterritorialized Nation-States* (Amsterdam, 1995), especially chapters 1 and 7. See also: A. Portes, L. E. Guarnizo and P. Landolt, 'The Study of Transnationalism: Pitfalls and Promise of an Emergent Research Field', *Ethnic and Racial Studies*, 22:2 (1999), pp. 217–37; S. Vertovec, 'Conceiving and Researching Transnationalism', *Ethnic and Racial Studies*, 22:2 (1999), pp. 447–62; P. Kivisto, 'Theorising Transnational Immigration: a Critical Review of Current Efforts', *Ethnic and Racial Studies*, 24:4 (2001), pp. 549–77; P. Levitt, J. DeWind and S. Vertovec, 'International Perspectives on Transnational Migration: an Introduction', *International Migration Review*, 37:3 (2003), pp. 565–75; P. Clavin, 'Defining Transnationalism', *Contemporary European History*, 14:4 (2005), pp. 421–39.

12 K. Grant, P. Levine and F. Trentmann (eds), *Beyond Sovereignty: Britain, Empire and Transnationalism, c.1880–1950* (Basingstoke, 2007), pp. 2 and 6. This idea is picked up by Antoinette Burton in a thought-provoking essay, 'Getting Outside the Global: Re-positioning British Imperialism in World History', in C. Hall and K. McClelland (eds), *Race, Nation and Empire: Making Histories, 1750 to the Present* (Manchester, 2010), pp. 199–216. For New Zealand migration historians, however, the nation remains an important reference point: see, for example, a special issue of the *New Zealand Journal of History*, guest edited by L. Fraser, 'Migration Histories and Writing the Nation', 43:2 (2009).

13 A. G. Hopkins, 'Back to the Future: From National History to Imperial History', *Past & Present*, 164 (1999), pp. 198–243 [quotation on p. 205].

14 This phrase was first coined by the New Zealand historian, J. Belich, in his paper entitled 'Neo-Britains', delivered at the first British World conference at the Institute of Commonwealth Studies, London, June 1998. This theme has been developed further in his two-volume history of New Zealand, *Making Peoples: A History of the New Zealanders. From Polynesian Settlement to the End of the Nineteenth Century* (Auckland, 1996), and *Paradise Reforged: A History of the New Zealanders from the 1880s to the Year 2000* (Auckland, 2001). He has subsequently expanded his thesis to encompass a host of settler societies, including the United States, in his highly acclaimed *Replenishing the Earth*.

15 J. G. A. Pocock, *The Discovery of Islands* (Cambridge, 2005), brings together almost thirty years of work aimed at widening the parameters of British history, and including the white settlement colonies as integral elements to the development of Britain as a global entity. E. Richards makes a similar point when he argues that Australian sources were valuable when writing British history: 'Voices of British and Irish Migrants in Nineteenth-Century Australia', in C. Pooley and I. Whyte (eds), *Migrants, Emigrants, and Immigrants: A Social History of Migration* (London, 1991), p. 22.

16 The Bridge and Fedorowich collection was largely based on a selection of papers presented at the British World Conference in Cape Town in January 2002, but contained papers by S. Constantine and P. Buckner first presented at the inaugural conference held in London in 1998. Two volumes edited by P. Buckner and R. D. Francis, *Rediscovering the British World* (Calgary, 2005) and *Canada and the British World: Culture, Migration, and Identity* (Vancouver, 2006), were published from the Calgary conference (2003). No volume of essays was published following the Auckland conference (2005), but K. Darian-Smith, P. Grimshaw and

EMPIRE, MIGRATION AND IDENTITY

S. Macintyre edited a selection from the Melbourne gathering entitled, *Britishness Abroad: Transnational Movements and Imperial Cultures* (Melbourne, 2007).

17 S. Constantine, 'British Emigration to the Empire-Commonwealth since 1880: From Overseas Settlement to Diaspora?', in Bridge and Fedorowich (eds), *The British World*, p. 16. More recently, historians of colonial Canada have been wrestling with these new conceptual frameworks in a transatlantic context by making a plea for a broader British history that includes the overseas settlement colonies. See N. Christie, 'Introduction', in Nancy Christie (ed.), *Transatlantic Subjects. Ideas, Institutions, and Social Experience in Post-Revolutionary British North America* (Montreal and Kingston, 2008), pp. 3–44. P. Buckner made a similar plea to the Canadian historical community when he was president of the Canadian Historical Association. See his 'Whatever Happened to the British Empire?', *Journal of the Canadian Historical Association*, new series, 4 (1993), pp. 3–32. An expanded version of this presidential address, 'Making British North America British, 1815–1860', appeared in C. C. Eldridge (ed.), *Kith and Kin: Canada, Britain and the United States from the Revolution to the Cold War* (Cardiff, 1997), pp. 11–44. For a useful examination of British identity in Winnipeg and how the British World concept is beginning to influence a younger generation of Canadian scholars see, K. Korneski, 'Britishness, Canadianness, Class, and Race: Winnipeg and the British World, 1880s–1910s', *Journal of Canadian Studies*, 41:2 (2007), pp. 161–84. For New Zealand, see R. McClean, '"How we Prepare them in India": British Diasporic Imaginings and Migration to New Zealand', *New Zealand Journal of History*, 37:2 (2003), pp. 131–52.

18 S. Ward, 'Imperial Identities Abroad', in S. Stockwell (ed.), *The British Empire: Themes and Perspectives* (Oxford, 2008), pp. 219 and 226–34. For further references, see Ward's footnotes and M. Lake and H. Reynolds, *Drawing the Global Colour Line: White Men's Countries and the International Challenge of Racial Equality* (Cambridge, 2008). A useful benchmark in the contestation of 'national' versus 'imperial' identities was pioneered by D. Cole, 'The Problems of "Nationalism" and "Imperialism" in British Settlement Colonies', *Journal of British Studies*, 10:2 (1971), pp. 160–82. For the cultural construction of settler identities through the natural world see J. M. MacKenzie, *Museums and Empire: Natural History, Human Cultures and Colonial Identities* (Manchester, 2009).

19 See, especially, B. Nasson, 'Why they fought: Black Cape Colonists and Imperial Wars, 1899–1918', *International Journal of African Historical Studies*, 37:1 (2004), pp. 55–70; A. Spry Rush, 'Imperial Identity in Colonial Minds: Harold Moody and the League of Coloured Peoples, 1931–1950', *Twentieth Century British History*, 13:4 (2002), pp. 356–83; H. Sapire, 'African Loyalism and its Discontents: The Royal Tour of South Africa, 1947', *Historical Journal*, 54:1 (2011), pp. 215–40; V. Bickford-Smith, 'African Nationalist or British Loyalist? The Complicated Case of Tiyo Soga', *History Workshop Journal*, 71 (2011), pp. 74–97.

20 For two exploratory essays, see A. Thompson, 'The Languages of Loyalism in Southern Africa, c.1879–1939', *English Historical Review*, 118:477 (2003), pp. 617–50; D. Lowry, 'The Crown, Empire Loyalism and the Assimilation of Non-White Subjects in the British World: An Argument against "Ethnic Determinism"', in Bridge and Fedorowich (eds), *The British World*, pp. 96–120, where Jews, French Canadians and the Irish are also examined alongside non-white communities throughout the Empire.

21 These threads and the tensions between British World scholarship and postcolonialism have recently been explored by K. Pickles, 'The Obvious and the Awkward: Postcolonialism and the British World', *New Zealand Journal of History*, 45:1 (2011), pp. 85–101.

22 The editors wish to thank Professors Dane Kennedy and Paul Pickering for their incisive thoughts contained within this paragraph on intriguing questions of subaltern forms of Britishness and 'trans-local' identities respectively.

23 D. Lambert and A. Lester (eds), *Colonial Lives Across the British Empire: Imperial Careering in the Long Nineteenth Century* (Cambridge, 2006), pp. 3–10. Also see

[28]

A. Lester, 'Imperial Circuits and Networks: Geographies of the British Empire', *History Compass*, 4:1 (2006), pp. 124–41.

24 For these regional variants, see A. Perry, *On the Edge of Empire: Gender, Race and the Making of British Columbia 1849–1871* (Toronto, 2001); P. Mein Smith, P. Hempenstall and S. Goldfinch, *Remaking the Tasman World* (Christchurch, 2008); T. R. Metcalf, *Imperial Connections: India in the Indian Ocean Arena, 1860–1920* (Berkeley, CA, 2007); C. Markovits, *The Global World of Indian Merchants, 1750–1947: Traders of Sind from Bukhara to Panama* (Cambridge, 2000). For an incisive analysis of the South African dimension see S. Dubow, 'How British was the British World? The Case of South Africa', *Journal of Imperial and Commonwealth History*, 37:1 (2009), pp. 1–27. The idea of 'empire' as a multi-centred entity was highlighted by Carl Bridge and Kent Fedorowich, 'Mapping the British World', in Bridge and Fedorowich (eds), *The British World*, pp. 1–15. One leading historian has argued that historically, globalisation was a multi-centred phenomenon, and that, 'even today, it can be understood fully only by recognising that it is not simply the result of a dominant center [*sic*] activating lesser peripheries, but is jointly produced by all parties to the process'. See A. G. Hopkins, 'Introduction', in A. G. Hopkins (ed.), *Global History: Interactions Between the Universal and the Local* (Basingstoke, 2006), p. 5. An interesting assessment of the interactions between Western and Japanese corporations and how they tapped into Chinese social networks and information flows is examined by S. Cochran, *Encountering Chinese Networks: Western, Japanese, and Chinese Corporations in China, 1880–1937* (Berkeley, CA, 2000).

25 A key volume, anchoring migration studies in the series, is S. Constantine's (ed.), *Emigrants and Empire: British Settlement in the Empire between the Wars* (Manchester, 1990). Many of the authors who explored other aspects of the migration story in the series are cited throughout this work. Professor MacKenzie's own work has been instrumental in shaping ideas which resonate throughout this volume. Of particular importance are: *Propaganda and Empire: the Manipulation of British Public Opinion, 1880–1960* (Manchester, 1988); and, written with N. R. Dalziel, *The Scots in South Africa: Ethnicity, Identity, Gender and Race, 1772–1914* (Manchester, 2007). His edited volume, *Imperialism and Popular Culture* (Manchester, 1989) remains a keystone as well.

26 Ward, 'Imperial Identities', in Stockwell (ed.), *The British Empire*, p. 219.

27 A. McKeown, 'Global Migration, 1846–1940', *Journal of World History*, 15:2 (2004), pp. 155–89 [quotation on p. 160]. Also incisive is D. Hoerder, 'Negotiating Nations: Exclusions, Networks, Inclusions. An Introduction', *Histoire sociale/ Social History*, 33:66 (2000), pp. 221–9.

28 *Toronto Globe*, 25 September 1901, cited in P. Buckner, 'Casting Daylight upon Magic: Deconstructing the Royal Tour of 1901 to Canada', in Bridge and Fedorowich (eds), *The British World*, p. 183.

29 This concept, first enunciated by Belich, saw the development of his 'neo-Britains' to 'better Britains'. See Bridge and Fedorowich (eds), *The British World*, p. 2.

30 The pioneer of the comparative study of dominion economies is D. Denoon: see 'Understanding Settler Societies', *Historical Studies*, 18:73 (1979), pp. 511–27; and *Settler Capitalism: the Dynamics of Dependent Development in the Southern Hemisphere* (Oxford, 1983). For a transatlantic perspective, see D. Hoerder, 'International Labor Markets and Community Building by Migrant Workers in the Atlantic Economies', in R. Vecoli and S. M. Sinke (eds), *A Century of European Migrations, 1830–1930* (Urbana, IL, 1991), pp. 78–107. See also, Magee and Thompson, *Empire and Globalisation*, pp. 40–1.

31 M. Kearney, 'The Local and the Global: the Anthropology of Globalization and Transnationalism', *Annual Review of Anthropology*, 24 (1995), p. 549.

32 Kirk, MacRaild, and Nolan, 'Transnational Ideas', p. 225.

33 For an insight into the range of migration's global consequences, see, for example, A. Bashford, *Imperial Hygiene: A Critical History of Colonialism, Nationalism and Public Health* (Basingstoke, 2004); A. Bashford, *Medicine at the Border:*

Disease, Globalisation and Security, 1850 to the Present (Basingstoke, 2006) on the fascinating relationship between migration, globalisation and public health.

34 For three thought-provoking essays on the interconnectedness of migration and world/global history see, McKeown, 'Global Migration', pp. 155–89; U. Bosma, 'Beyond the Atlantic: Connecting Migration and World History in the Age of Imperialism, 1840–1940', *International Review of Social History*, 52:1 (2007), pp. 116–23; and T. Pietsch, 'A British Sea: Making Sense of Global Space in the late Nineteenth Century', *Journal of Global History*, 5:3 (2010), pp. 423–46. Also see E. Christopher, C. Pybus and M. Rediker (eds), *Many Middle Passages: Forced Migration and the Making of the Modern World* (Berkeley, CA, 2009), where contributors try and break away from the Euro- and terra-centric foci of migration to explore the so-called 'middle passage', or ocean voyage(s), for the dispossessed such as African slaves, convicts, trafficked Asian women and children, and coerced Chinese and Melanesian labour migrants. The analysis of the 'middle passage' for white migrants is also an emerging area of interest: see A. Hassam, *Sailing to Australia: Shipboard Diaries by Nineteenth-Century British Emigrants* (Manchester, 1994); R. Haines, *Doctors at Sea: Emigrant Voyages to Colonial Australia* (Basingstoke, 2005); B. Bell, 'Bound for Australia: Shipboard Reading in the Nineteenth Century', *Journal of Australian Studies*, 68 (2001), pp. 5–18; and K. Foxhall, 'From Convicts to Colonists: The Health of Prisoners and the Voyage to Australia, 1823–53', *Journal of Imperial and Commonwealth History*, 39:1 (2011), pp. 1–19. Originally published in 1937, a still useful study on the shipboard experiences of British migrants travelling to Canada can be found in E. C. Guillet's, *The Great Migration. The Atlantic Crossing by Sailing-Ship Since 1770*, 2nd edn (Toronto, 1963). For a South African perspective see the special feature, 'The Story of the Voyage', guest edited by M. Titlestad and P. Gupta, *South African Historical Journal*, 61:4 (2009). New Zealand is also touched upon by D. Hastings, *Over the Mountains of the Sea: Life on the Migrant Ships 1870–1885* (Auckland, 2006).

35 For a survey of the different phases of modern migration, see D. S. Massey *et al.* (eds), *Worlds in Motion. Understanding International Migration at the End of the Millennium* (Oxford, 1998), pp. 1–7 [quotation on p. 1].

36 C. Erickson, *Leaving England. Essays on British Emigration in the Nineteenth Century* (Ithaca, 1994), p. 10. For the contribution made to America's industrial and agricultural development by British migrants see R. T. Berthoff, *British Immigrants in Industrial America, 1790–1950* (Cambridge, MA, 1953); W. E. Van Vugt, *Britain to America: Mid-Nineteenth-Century Immigrants to the United States* (Chicago, 1999).

37 At least 52 million migrants left Europe for overseas destinations between 1815 and 1930, with Britain supplying approximately a quarter of the total: see D. Baines, *Emigration from Europe, 1861–1900* (Cambridge, 1991), pp. 9–11. For an imperial overview of flows, trends and policies see K. Fedorowich, 'The British Empire on the Move, 1760 to 1914', in Stockwell (ed.), *The British Empire*, pp. 63–100.

38 R. Bickers rightly makes great play of this in his excellent introduction, 'Britains and Britons over the Seas', in R. Bickers (ed.), *Settlers and Expatriates*, Companion Series, *Oxford History of the British Empire* (Oxford, 2010), pp. 1–17.

39 S. Howe (ed.), *The New Imperial Reader* (London, 2009) outlines the theoretical frameworks used by proponents of the 'new' imperial history.

40 D. S. A. Bell, 'Dissolving Distance: Technology, Space, and Empire in British Political Thought, 1770–1900', *Journal of Modern History*, 77:3 (2005), pp. 523–62.

41 R. M. Pike, 'National Interest and Imperial Yearnings: Empire Communication and Canada's Role in Establishing the Imperial Penny Post', *Journal of Imperial and Commonwealth History*, 26:1 (1998), pp. 22–48; and D. R. Headrick, *The Tentacles of Progress: Technology Transfer in the Age of Imperialism, 1850–1940* (Oxford, 1988), especially chapters 2 and 4 on imperial shipping and telecommunications networks. For an examination of technology transfer in a colonial setting, see J. Todd, *Colonial Technology: Science and the Transfer of Innovation to Australia* (Cambridge, 2009). For technological diffusion brought about by British migrants

to the United States, see D. Jeremy, *Transatlantic Industrial Revolution: The Diffusion of Textile Technologies between Britain and America, 1790s-1830s* (Oxford, 1981), and G. Tweedale, *Sheffield Steel and America: A Century of Commercial and technological Interdependence, 1830–1930* (New York, 1987).

42 The term was coined by D. Nally, '"Eternity's commissioner": Thomas Carlyle, the Great Irish Famine and the Geopolitics of Travel', *Journal of Historical Geography*, 32:2 (2006), pp. 313–35.

43 S. J. Potter, *News and the British World: The Emergence of an Imperial Press System* (Oxford, 2003); S. J. Potter, 'Communication and Integration: The British and Dominions Press and the British World, c.1876–1914', in Bridge and Fedorowich (eds), *The British World*, pp. 190–206. Also see D. Read, *The Power of News: The History of Reuters, 1849–1989* (Oxford, 1992).

44 C. Kaul, *Reporting the Raj: The British Press and India, c.1880–1922* (Manchester, 2003), and her edited collection, *Media and the British Empire* (Basingstoke, 2006).

45 P. Puntis, 'The British Transoceanic Steamship Press in Nineteenth-century India and Australia: an Overview', *Journal of Australian Studies*, 91 (2007), pp. 69–79.

46 S. Nicholas, '"Brushing Up Your Empire": Dominion and Colonial Propaganda on the BBC's Home Services, 1939–45', in Bridge and Fedorowich (eds), *The British World*, pp. 207–30.

47 H. Carey, *God's Empire: Religion and Colonialism in the British World, c.1801–1908* (Cambridge, 2011); and her edited collection, *Empires of Religion* (Basingstoke, 2008).

48 J. Ridden, 'Britishness as an Imperial and Diasporic Identity', in P. Gray (ed.), *Victoria's Ireland? Irishness and Britishness, 1837–1901* (Dublin, 2004), pp. 88–105; A. Jones and Bill Jones, 'The Welsh World and the British Empire, c.1851–1939: An Exploration', in Bridge and Fedorowich (eds), *The British World*, pp. 57–81; J. Stuart, 'Beyond Sovereignty?: Protestant Missions, Empire and Transnationalism, 1890–1950', in Grant, Levine and Trentmann (eds), *Beyond Sovereignty*, pp. 103–25; I. Talbot and S. Thandi (eds), *People on the Move: Punjabi Colonial, and Post-Colonial Migration* (Oxford, 2004); T. Ballantyne, *Between Colonialism and Diaspora: Sikh Cultural Formations in an Imperial World* (Durham, NC, 2006).

49 H. McNamara, 'The *New Zealand Tablet* and the Irish Catholic Press Worldwide, 1898–1923', *New Zealand Journal of History*, 37:2 (2003), pp. 153–70.

50 R. P. Swierenga, *Faith and Family: Dutch Immigration and Settlement in the United States, 1820–1920* (New York, 2000). D. Schurer made the same observations about kinship and family over twenty years ago, but acknowledged that historians of overseas migration – unlike those dealing with internal migration within the UK – had long recognised the influence of family in the migration process. See his, 'The Role of the Family in the Process of Migration', in Pooley and Whyte (eds), *Migrants, Emigrants, and Immigrants*, pp. 106–42.

51 A. Bashford, 'Nation, Empire, Globe: The Spaces of Population Debate in the Interwar Years', *Comparative Studies in Society and History*, 49:1 (2007), pp. 170–201.

52 A. Sears, 'Immigration Controls as Social Policy: The Case of Canadian Medical Inspection 1900–1920', *Studies in Political Economy*, 33 (1990), pp. 91–112; I. Dowbiggin, '"Keeping this Country Sane": C. K. Clarke, Immigration Restriction, and Canadian Psychiatry, 1890–1925', *Canadian Historical Review*, 76:4 (1995), pp. 598–627; D. Hoerder, *Creating Societies: Immigrant Lives in Canada* (Montreal and Kingston, 1999), especially pp. 237–77. For the Australian dimension on the medicalisation of immigration policy, see W. Anderson, *The Cultivation of Whiteness: Science, Health, and Racial Destiny in Australia* (New York, 2003). A new dimension on this theme is A. McCarthy and C. Coleborne (eds), *Migration, Ethnicity, and Mental Health: International Perspectives, 1840–2010* (London, 2011).

53 Z. Godler, 'Doctors and the new immigrants', *Canadian Ethnic Studies*, 9:1 (1977), p. 6.

54 H. E. Drystek, '"The Simplest and Cheapest Mode of Dealing With Them":

Deportation from Canada before World War II', *Histoire sociale/Social History*, 15:30 (1992), pp. 407–41; F. A. Miller, 'Making Citizens, Banishing Immigrants: The Discipline of Deportation Investigations, 1908–1913', *Left History*, 7:1 (2000), pp. 62–88; B. Roberts, 'Doctors and the Deports: The Role of the Medical Profession in Canadian Deportation, 1900–1920', *Canadian Ethnic Studies*, 18:3 (1986), pp. 17–36; B. Roberts, '"Shovelling Out the Mutinous": Political Deportation from Canada Before 1936', *Labour/Le Travail*, no. 18 (1986), pp. 77–110; and her book-length study, *Whence They Came: Deportation from Canada 1900–1935* (Ottawa, 1988).

55 J. Cavell, 'The Imperial Race and the Immigration Sieve: The Canadian Debate on Assisted British Migration and Empire Settlement, 1900–1930', *Journal of Imperial and Commonwealth History*, 34:3 (2006), pp. 345–67; K. Fedorowich, 'Restocking the British World: Empire Migration and Anglo-Canadian Relations, 1919–1930' (unpublished paper).

56 Van Vugt, *Britain to America*, p. 3. Also see P. A. Kramer, 'Empires, Exceptions, and Anglo-Saxons: Race and Rule between the British and United States Empires, 1880–1910', *Journal of American History*, 88:4 (2002), pp. 1315–53.

57 A. J. Christopher, 'The quest for a census of the British Empire c.1840–1940', *Journal of Historical Geography*, 34:2 (2008), p. 269. Also see Jean-Pierre Beaud and Jean-Guy Prévost for the failure to construct an empire-wide statistical gathering agency: 'Statistics as the science of government: the stillborn British Empire Statistical Bureau, 1918–1920', *Journal of Imperial and Commonwealth History*, 33:2 (2005), pp. 369–91.

58 P. A. Dunae, 'Making the 1891 Census in British Columbia', *Histoire sociale/Social History*, 31:62 (1998), pp. 223–41; R. Watts, 'Making Numbers Count on the Racial Frontier: An Historical Sociology of the Birth of the Census, Victoria (Australia), 1835–1840', *Histoire sociale/Social History*, 35:70 (2002), pp. 423–46; R. Watts, 'Making the Numbers Count: The Birth of the Census and Racial Government in Victoria, 1835–1840', *Australian Historical Studies*, 34:121 (2003), pp. 26–47; A. J. Christopher, 'Race and the Census in the Commonwealth', *Population, Space and Place*, 11:2 (2005), pp. 103–18; Jean-Pierre Beaud and Jean-Guy Prévost, 'Immigration, Eugenics and Statistics: Measuring Racial Origins in Canada (1921–1941)', *Canadian Ethnic Studies*, 28:2 (1996), pp. 1–24. For the simple problems of enumeration and data collection in these early days, see B. Curtis, 'On the Local Construction of Statistical Knowledge: Making up the 1861 Census of the Canadas', *Journal of Historical Sociology*, 7:4 (1994), pp. 416–34.

59 P. Hudson and D. Mills, 'English Emigration, Kinship and the Recruitment Process: Migration from Melbourn in Cambridgeshire to Melbourne in Victoria in the Mid-Nineteenth Century', *Rural History*, 10:1 (1999), pp. 55–74; R. Arnold, 'English Rural Unionism and Taranaki Immigration, 1871–76', *New Zealand Journal of History*, 6:1 (1972), pp. 20–41; A. McCarthy, '"Bands of Fellowship": The Role of Personal Relationships and Social Networks Among Irish Migrants in New Zealand, 1861–1911', *Immigrants & Minorities*, 23:2–3 (2005), pp. 339–58; W. Cameron, S. Haines and M. McDougall Maude, *English Immigrant Voices: Labourers' Letters from Upper Canada in the 1830s* (Montreal and Kingston, 2000); A. McCarthy, *Personal Narratives of Irish and Scottish migrants, 1921–1965: 'For Spirit and Adventure'* (Manchester, 2007); D. A. Gerber, *Authors of Their Lives: The Personal Correspondence of British Immigrants to North America in the Nineteenth Century* (New York, 2006).

60 B. Elliot, D. A. Gerber, and S. M. Sinke (eds), *Letters across Borders: The Epistolary Practices of International Migrants* (Basingstoke, 2006). For over thirty years Erickson has pioneered the use of emigrant letters as a source in tracing the 'invisible' English migrant in nineteenth-century America. This corpus of work has been re-encapsulated in *Leaving England*. [quotation on p. 16]. Another key work is D. Fitzpatrick's, '"Oceans of Consolation": Letters and Irish Immigration to Australia', in D. Fitzpatrick (ed.), *Visible Immigrants: Neglected Sources for the History of Australian Immigration* (Canberra, 1989), pp. 47–86 – expanded

in his *Oceans of Consolation: Personal Accounts of Irish Migration to Australia* (Ithaca, 1994). Also see A. McCarthy's, '"A Good Idea of Colonial Life": Personal Letters and Irish Migration to New Zealand', *New Zealand Journal of History*, 35:1 (2001), pp. 1–21; and T. Bueltmann, '"Where the Measureless Ocean between us will Roar": Scottish Emigration to New Zealand, Personal Correspondence and Epistolary Practice, *c.*1850–1920', *Immigrants & Minorities*, 26:3 (2008), pp. 242–65.

61 W. R. Jones, '"Going into Print": Published Immigrant Letters, Webs of Personal Relations, and the Emergence of the Welsh Public Sphere', in Elliot, Gerber and Sinke (eds), *Letters across Borders*, pp. 175–99. For the Irish story in New Zealand, see L. Fraser, '"The Ties that Bind": Irish Catholic Testamentary Evidence from Christchurch, 1876–1915', *New Zealand Journal of History*, 29:1 (1995), pp. 67–82. For a brief but illuminating analysis of personal narratives, see D. M. MacRaild's review article, 'Personal Narratives of Emigration and Adjustment', *Irish Historical Studies*, 36:141 (2008), pp. 91–4.

62 M. Jones, 'The Background to Emigration from Great Britain in the Nineteenth Century', *Perspectives in American History*, 7 (1973), p. 16.

63 R. Dalziel, 'Emigration and Kinship: Migrants to New Plymouth 1840–1843', *New Zealand Journal of History*, 25:2 (1991), pp. 112–28; E. Johnson, 'The Role of the Family and Community in the Decision to Emigrate: Evidence from a Case Study of Scottish Emigration to Queensland 1885–1888', *Family & Community History*, 9:1 (2006), pp. 5–25; M. Rodwell, 'Assisted Immigration and the Family Economy at Ollera Station, Guyra, 1840–*c.*1860', *Journal of Australian Colonial History*, 9 (2009), pp. 45–72; R. Duncan, 'Case Studies in Emigration: Cornwall, Gloucestershire and New South Wales, 1877–1886', *Economic History Review*, second series, 16:1 (1963), pp. 272–89. Personal and family networks were not the monopoly of the well read or well off. For the illiterate, local elites acted as intermediaries and helped facilitate the labouring poor through their own personal and professional networks; and word of mouth could be equally effective. See here G. Howells, '"For I was Tired of England Sir": English Pauper Emigrant Strategies, 1834–1860', *Social History*, 11:2 (1998), pp. 181–94; G. Howells, 'Emigration and the New Poor Law: the Norfolk Emigration Fever of 1836', *Rural History*, 11:2 (2000), pp. 145–64.

64 O. MacDonagh, *A Pattern of Government Growth 1800–60* (London, 1961), pp. 27–9.

65 P. A. M. Taylor, 'Emigration', in D. V. Glass and P. A. M. Taylor, *Population and Emigration* (Dublin, 1976), p. 70.

66 D. Baines, *Emigration from Europe, 1815–1930* (London, 1991), pp. 50–2; C. Newbury, 'Labour Migration in the Imperial Phase: An Essay in Interpretations', *Journal of Imperial and Commonwealth History*, 3:2 (1975), pp. 240–2.

67 See, for example, *BME Remittance Survey. Research Report* (27 July 2006), prepared for the Department of International Development by ICM. A similar complaint was lodged by Canadian immigration officials and trades unionists, especially in British Columbia, about Chinese and Japanese migrants at the turn of the twentieth century. Without understanding the cultural factors at work, it was claimed by the 'British' community that the Asian propensity to remit damaged the economy because Asian migrants spent next to nothing in the country. See D. Hoerder, '"Of Habits Subversive" or "Capable and Compassionate": Perceptions of Transpacific Migrants, 1850s–1940s', *Canadian Ethnic Studies*, 38:1 (2006), p. 12.

68 Social scientists have led the way on modern day remittance analysis. A survey of the *International Migration Review* reveals that, since 1985, remittance behaviour among Asian, Greek, Caribbean, Mexican, Salvadoran, Filipino and Moroccan labour migrants has received growing attention. The Asian case is significant for early investigations revealed that, in 1981, 2.5 million Asians remitted $7.9 billion to their home countries. See C. W. Stahl and F. Arnold, 'Overseas Workers' Remittances in Asian Development', *International Migration Review*, 20:4 (1986), pp. 889–925.

69 For a fuller account of migrant remittances in the English-speaking world, see G. B. Magee and A. S. Thompson, 'Lines of Credit, Debts of Obligation: Migrant Remittances to Britain, c.1875–1913', *Economic History Review*, 59:3 (2006), pp. 539–77; and 'The Global and the Local: Explaining Migrant Remittance Flows in the English-speaking World, 1880–1914', *Journal of Economic History*, 66:1 (2006), pp. 177–202. Also see Gerber, *Authors*, pp. 140–61.

70 R. Mullen, *A. Trollope: A Victorian in his World* (London, 1990), p. 244.

71 A. Trollope, *An Autobiography* (Oxford, 1950), p. 128.

72 N. J. Hall, *Trollope. A Biography* (Oxford, 1991), pp. 235, 368 and 426; A. Trollope, *Australia*, ed. P. D. Edwards and R. B. Joyce (St Lucia, Qld, 1967), pp. 87–8, 305–6, 377, 596–7 and 640.

73 There is a particularly rich historiography on the Cornish diaspora, much of which has been published under the aegis of the Institute of Cornish Studies at the University of Exeter. See, especially, here P. Payton, *The Cornish Overseas* (Fowey, 1999). That said, the social and economic impacts of remittance transfers can also be explored for other regions in the UK. See, for example, M. Harper's pioneering studies of Scottish emigration, summarised in her *Adventurers and Exiles: The Great Scottish Exodus* (London, 2003), which, inter alia, highlights the function of remittances in chain migration; the close relationship between remittances and migrant correspondence; the different patterns of remittance behaviour between farmers and artisans; and the hardship caused by a breakdown in the transmission of earnings to dependants at home: see pp. 93, 111, 188, 279, and 306. Meanwhile C. Erickson's, *Emigration from Europe, 1815–1914. Select Documents* (London, 1976), pp. 139 and 231–2 and E. Richards's, *Britannia's Children: Emigration from England, Scotland, Wales and Ireland since 1600* (London, 2004), pp. 144 and 166–8, lay emphasis on the importance of remittances in providing the pre-paid tickets which brought the friends and relatives of migrant labourers and artisans to the United States.

74 R. Dawe, *Cornish Pioneers in South Africa: 'Gold and Diamonds, Copper and Blood'* (St Austell, 1998), pp. xv and 123. For Cornish in North America, see J. Rowe, *The Hard-Rock Men: Cornish Immigrants and the North American Mining Frontier* (Liverpool, 1974).

75 S. Schwartz and R. Parker, *Tin Mines and Miners of Lanner. The Heart of Cornish Tin* (Tiverton, 2001), pp. 157–8.

76 Payton, *Cornish Overseas*, p. 245.

77 C. Burr, 'Some Adventures of the Boys: Enniskillen Townships "Foreign Drillers", Imperialism, and Colonial Discourse, 1873–1923', *Labour/Le Travail*, no. 51 (2003), pp. 47–80.

78 The nature of British emigration to the United States did, however, result in distinctive patterns of remittance behaviour. Lower transport costs to America facilitated short-term, seasonal labour migration, so that a significant number of skilled workers who migrated across the Atlantic had no fixed intention of staying. Such migrants – or 'birds of passage' – were rarely accompanied by their dependants, and tended to accumulate relatively high rates of saving out of their earned income. Their aim was to build up a nest egg in America with a view to setting up in business or acquiring land on their return, or providing for their retirement. English bricklayers in New York, Welsh colliers in Pennsylvania, Aberdeen granite masons in New England, and Sheffield steel workers in Pittsburgh all fit this pattern. They either remitted money in anticipation of their return, or returned home with their savings. See here: J. E. Bodnar, *The Transplanted: A History of Immigrants in Urban America* (Bloomington, IN, 1985), pp. 60–1; W. D. Jones, *Wales in America: Scranton and the Welsh, 1860–1920* (Cardiff, 1992), passim; M. Harper, 'Transient Tradesmen: Aberdeen Emigrants and the Development of the American Granite Industry', *Northern Scotland*, 9 (1989), pp. 53–74; A. Murdoch, *British Emigration, 1603–1914* (Basingstoke, 2004), pp. 111 and 118.

79 K. Saunders (ed.), *Indentured Labour in the British Empire 1834–1920* (London, 1984); M. Carter, *Servants, Sirdars & Settlers: Indians in Mauritius* (Delhi, 1995);

W. L. Lai, *Indentured Labor, Caribbean Sugar: Chinese and Indian Migrants to the British West Indies, 1838–1918* (Baltimore, 1993); McKeown, *Melancholy Order*; P. Jones, 'The View from the Edge: Chinese Australians and China, 1890–1949', in C. Ferrall, P. Millar and K. Smith (eds), *East by South: China in the Australasian Imagination* (Wellington, 2005), pp. 46–69; K. N. Tiwari, 'The Indian Community in New Zealand: A Historical Survey', in K. Tiwari (ed.), *Indians in New Zealand. Studies of a Sub-culture* (Wellington, 1980), pp. 1–84; T. Ballantyne, 'India in New Zealand: The Fault Lines of Colonial Culture', and J. Leckie, 'A Long Diaspora: Indian Settlement', in S. Bandyopadhayay (ed.), *India in New Zealand: Local Identities, Global Relations* (Dunedin, 2010), pp. 21–44 and 45–63 respectively; H. Johnson and B. Moloughney (eds), *Asia in the Making of New Zealand* (Auckland, 2006); S. Bhana and J. B. Brain, *Setting Down Roots: Indian Migrants in South Africa, 1860–1914* (Johannesburg, 1990); A. Desai, *Inside Indian Indenture: A South African Story, 1860–1914* (Cape Town, 2010).

80 H. Tinker, *A New System of Slavery: the Export of Indian Labour Overseas 1830–1920* (Oxford, 1974), argues that indenture was simply another form of slavery. By contrast, while recognising that many contemporaries saw Asian and African indenture as a 'disguised continuation' of slavery, David Northrup emphasises that both European and non-European systems of indenture were voluntary and of a limited duration. See D. Northrup, *Indentured Labour in the Age of Imperialism, 1834–1922* (Cambridge, 1995), pp. 1–15.

81 Northrup, *Indentured Labour*, pp. 135–7, and 'Migration from Africa, Asia and the South Pacific', in A. Porter (ed.), *The Oxford History of the British Empire*, 4 *The Nineteenth Century* (Oxford, 1998), pp. 88–100; O. W. Parnaby, *Britain and the Labour Trade in the South West Pacific* (Durham, NC, 1964); S. Marks and P. Richardson (eds.), *International Labour Migration: Historical Perspectives* (London, 1984); H. L. Wesseling, *The European Colonial Empires, 1815–1914* (Harlow, 2004), pp. 18–19; J. Ng, 'The Sojourner Experience: The Cantonese Goldseekers in New Zealand, 1865–1901', in M. Ip (ed.), *Unfolding History, Evolving Identity: The Chinese in New Zealand* (Wellington, 2003), pp. 5–6.

82 A. Offer, *The First World War: An Agrarian Interpretation* (Oxford, 1989), p. 168; D. Avery, *'Dangerous Foreigners': European Immigrant Workers and Labour Radicalism in Canada, 1896–1932* (Toronto, 1979). D. Goutor's, *Guarding the Gates: The Canadian Labour Movement and Immigration, 1872–1934* (Vancouver, 2007) is a welcome examination of the Canadian labour movement's aggressive actions to protect jobs for Anglo-Canadians. Nonetheless, even more arresting – and this is an important area for future study – was the ability of non-European communities to broker and mediate their own 'belonging' and identity with their settler hosts. Some useful theoretical markers are provided by E. Bonacich in two pioneering essays: 'A Theory of Ethnic Antagonism: The Split Labor Market', *American Sociological Review*, 37:5 (1972), pp. 547–59; and 'A Theory of Middleman Minorities', *ibid.*, 38:5 (1973), pp. 583–94. Also see L. R. Mar, *Brokering Belonging: Chinese in Canada's Exclusion Era, 1885–1945* (Toronto, 2010); A. Kobayashi and P. Jackson, 'Japanese Canadians and the Racialization of Labour in the British Columbia Sawmill Industry', *BC Studies*, 103 (1994), pp. 33–58; and a special issue of the *Journal of Australian Colonial History*, 6 (2004), entitled 'Active Voices, Hidden Histories: The Chinese in Colonial Australia', especially A. Rasmussen, 'Networks and Negotiations: Bendigo's Chinese and the Easter Fair', pp. 79–92; and 'Dragon Tails: New Perspectives in Chinese Australian History', a special issue of *Australian Historical Studies*, 42:1 (2011) for new areas of nuanced research of the Chinese in Australia and their brokering with white settlers. The New Zealand experience for Chinese migrants and how they negotiated their own identities within this settler society is equally engaging and complex. See T. Ballantyne and B. Moloughney, 'Asia in Marihuku: Towards a Transnational History of Colonial Culture', in T. Ballantyne and B. Moloughney (eds), *Disputed Histories: Imagining New Zealand's Pasts* (Dunedin, 2006), pp. 63–92; H. Johnson, 'Performing Identity, Past and Present: Chinese Cultural Performance, New Year

Celebrations, and the Heritage Industry', in Ferrall, Millar and Smith (eds), *East by South*, pp. 217–42; and M. Ip, 'Chinese New Zealanders: Old Settlers and New Immigrants', in S. W. Grief (ed.), *Immigration and National Identity: One People – Two Peoples – Many Peoples* (Palmerston North, 1995), pp. 161–99; M. Ip, 'Redefining Chinese Female Migration: From Exclusion to Transnationalism', in L. Fraser and K. Pickles (eds), *Shifting Centres: Women and Migration in New Zealand History* (Dunedin, 2002), pp. 149–65. For Chinese migrant information flows or 'feedback' to China see W. T. Yuen, *The Origins of China's Awareness of New Zealand 1674–1911* (Auckland, 2005), pp. 41–67.

83   M. Boyd, 'Family and Personal Networks in International Migration: Recent Developments and New Agendas', *International Migration Review*, 23:3 (1989), pp. 638–70.

84   G. S. Kealey and G. Patmore (eds), *Canadian and Australian Labour History: Toward a Comparative History* (Griffith, NSW, 1990); G. S. Kealey and G. Patmore, 'Comparative Labour History: Canada and Australia', *Labour/le Travail*, no. 38 (1996), pp. 1–15; S. Berger and G. Patmore, 'Comparative Labour History in Britain and Australia', *Labour History*, no. 88 (2005), pp. 9–24.

85   E. Eklund, 'Retail Cooperatives as a Transnational Phenomenon: Exploring the composition of Australian colonial society and culture', *Journal of Australian Colonial History*, 9 (2007), pp. 127–54.

86   R. Gollan, *The Coalminers of New South Wales: A History of the Union, 1860–1960* (Melbourne, 1963), pp. 17–18.

87   See L. Richardson, 'British Colliers and Colonial Capitalists: the Origins of Coalmining Unionism in New Zealand'; E. McEwen, 'Coalminers in Newcastle, New South Wales: a Labour Aristocracy?'; and A. Reeves, '"Damned Scotsman": British Migrants in the Australian Coal Industry, 1919–1949', in E. Fry (ed.), *Common Cause: Essays in Australian and New Zealand Labour History* (Sydney, 1986), pp. 59–76, 77–92 and 93–106, respectively. This volume of essays is seen by many Antipodean labour historians as the catalyst which initiated more in-depth comparative Trans-Tasman labour studies. See the special issue 'Trans-Tasman Labour History', guest edited by R. Markey and K. Taylor, *Labour History*, no. 95 (2008), in particular the essay by R. Frances and M. Nolan, 'Gender and the Trans-Tasman World of Labour: Transnational and Comparative Histories', pp. 25–42 where Eric Fry is praised for his pioneering work. Also see G. Patmore, 'Iron and Steel Unionism in Canada and Australia, 1900–1914: The Impact of the State, Ethnicity, Management, and Locality', *Labour/Le Travail*, no. 58 (2006), pp. 71–105; and J. D. Belshaw, 'The British Collier in British Columbia: Another Archetype Reconsidered', *Labour/Le Travail*, no. 34 (1994), pp. 11–36. For the South African dimension of British immigrant influence on trade union politics, see J. Hyslop, *The Notorious Syndicalist J. T. Bain: A Scottish Radical in Colonial South Africa* (Johannesburg, 2004); J. Hyslop, 'The World Voyage of James Kier Hardie: Indian Nationalism, Zulu insurgency and the British Labour diaspora, 1907–1908', *Journal of Global History*, 1:3 (2006), pp. 321–41.

88   L. Layman, 'To Keep Up the Australian Standard: Regulatory Contract Labour Migration, 1901–1950', *Labour History*, no. 70 (1996), pp. 25–52. British trade unions also sponsored emigration and the emigration of their members overseas. For the activities of British agricultural unions in the 1870s and early 1880s, see P. Horn, 'Agricultural Trade Unionism and Emigration, 1872–1881', *Historical Journal*, 15:1 (1972), pp. 87–101; and D. Goutor, '"Stand by the Union, Mr. Arch": The Toronto Labour Establishment and the Emigration Mission of Britain's National Agricultural Labourers Union', *Labour/Le Travail*, no. 55 (2005), pp. 9–35. Also see the pioneering work of C. Erickson, 'The Encouragement of Emigration by British Trade Unions, 1850–1900', *Population Studies*, 3:3 (1949), pp. 248–73; R. V. Clements, 'Trade Unions and Emigration, 1840–80', *Population Studies*, 9:2 (1955), pp. 167–80; H. L. Malchow, 'Trade Unions and Emigration: A National Lobby for State Aid', *Journal of British Studies*, 15:2 (1976), pp. 92–116. Two influential artisan unions also facilitated the migration process in the later nineteenth

MAPPING THE CONTOURS OF THE BRITISH WORLD

and early twentieth centuries – the Amalgamated Society of Engineers (ASE) and the Amalgamated Society of Carpenters and Joiners (ASC&J). See H. Southall, 'British Artisan Unions in the New World', *Journal of Historical Geography*, 15:2 (1989), pp. 163–82; and, more generally, K. Buckley, 'Emigration and the Engineers, 1851–87', *Labour History*, no. 15 (1968), pp. 31–9; R. A. Buchanan, 'The Diaspora of British Engineers', *Technology and Culture*, 27:3 (1986), pp. 501–24.

89 For the neglect of migrant diasporas in globalising processes, see J. N. Pieterse, *Globalization and Culture. Global Mélange* (Oxford, 2003), pp. 4 and 32.

90 See, for example, S. J. Potter, 'Webs, Networks, and Systems: Globalization and Mass Media in the Nineteenth- and Twentieth-Century British Empire', *Journal of British Studies*, 46:3 (2007), pp. 621–2. For an interesting examination of ethnic and individual identities, transformed by migration, see A. McCarthy (ed.), *A Global Clan: Scottish Migrant Networks and Identities since the Eighteenth Century* (London, 2006); T. Bueltmann, A. Hinson and G. Morton (eds), *Ties of Bluid, Kin and Countrie: Scottish Associational Culture in the Diaspora* (Guelph, 2009). A double issue of *Immigrants & Minorities*, guest edited by E. Delaney and D. M. MacRaild entitled, 'Irish Migration, Networks and Ethnic Identities Since 1750: An Introduction', also appeared in 2005; as did a 'Symposium: Perspectives on the Irish Diaspora', *Irish Economic and Social History*, no. 33 (2006), pp. 35–58 where contributions by E. Delaney, K. Kenny and D. M. MacRaild appeared. The Scots and Irish dominate the literature on ethnic networking and identity formation in the migratory process. The most recent examples are: A. McCarthy, *Scottishness and Irishness in New Zealand since 1840* (Manchester, 2011); T. Bueltmann, *Scottish Ethnicity and the Making of New Zealand Society, 1850–1930* (Edinburgh, 2011); and T. M. Devine, *To the Ends of the Earth: Scotland's Global Diaspora, 1700–2010* (London, 2011). The English diaspora remains understudied, but a welcome benchmark is T. Bueltmann, D. T. Gleeson and D. M. MacRaild (eds), *Locating the English Diaspora, 1500–2010* (Liverpool, 2012). For a pioneering work on English societies overseas in the migratory/identity process see, J. Watson, 'English Associationalism in the British Empire: Yorkshire Societies in New Zealand before the First World War', *Britain and the World*, 4:1 (2011), pp. 84–108; and T. Bueltmann and D. M. MacRaild, 'Globalizing St George: English associations in the Anglo-world to the 1930s', *Journal of Global History*, 7:1 (2012), 79–105.

91 For the argument that much of contemporary globalisation is regional rather than truly 'global' in nature, see A. Rugman, *The End of Globalization: Why Global Strategy is a Myth & How to Profit from the Realities of Regional Markets* (New York, 2001), pp. 1–12; U. Beck, *What is Globalization?* (Malden, MA, 2000), pp. 119–20.

92 For a historical perspective on the transnational networks forged by migrants, see S. Vertovec, 'Transnationalism and Identity', *Journal of Ethnic and Migration Studies*, 27:4 (2001), pp. 576–7.

93 J. Harland-Jacobs, *Builders of Empire: Freemasonry and British Imperialism, 1717–1927* (Durham, NC, 2007); D. Fitzpatrick, 'Exporting Brotherhood: Orangeism in South Australia', *Immigrants & Minorities*, 23:2–3 (2005), pp. 277–310; P. Coleman, 'Who wants to be a Grand Master? Grand Masters of the Orange Lodge of the Middle Island New Zealand', in B. and K. Patterson (eds), *Ireland and the Irish Antipodes: One World or Worlds Apart?* (Spit Junction, NSW, 2010), pp. 96–107; D. A. Wilson (ed.), *The Orange Order in Canada* (Dublin, 2007).

94 See Magee and Thompson, *Empire and Globalisation*, esp. p. 238.

95 R. A. Huttenback, *Racism and Empire: White Settlers and Colored Immigrants in the British Self-Governing Colonies 1830–1914* (Ithaca, 1984); C. A. Price, *The Great White Walls Are Built: Restrictive Immigration to North America and Australasia 1836–1888* (Canberra, 1974); S. Brawley, *The White Peril: Foreign Relations and Asian Immigration to Australasia and North America,1919–1978* (Sydney, 1995); J. Martens, 'A Transnational History of Immigration Restriction: Natal and New South Wales, 1896–97', *Journal of Imperial and Commonwealth History*, 34:3

(2006), pp. 323–44; J. Martens, 'Richard Seddon and Popular Opposition in New Zealand to the Introduction of Chinese Labour in the Transvaal', *New Zealand Journal of History*, 42:2 (2008), pp. 176–95; B. Moloughney and J. Stenhouse, '"Drug-besotten, Sin-begotten Fiends of Filth": New Zealanders and the Oriental Other, 1850–1920', *New Zealand Journal of History*, 33:1 (1999), pp. 43–86; Lake and Reynolds, *Drawing the Global Colour Line*. The transfer of English traditions of liberty overseas were also powerfully exclusionary as settler societies repressed indigenous peoples and asserted their control over property rights, the rule of law and government. See J. P. Greene (ed.), *Exclusionary Empire: English Liberty Overseas, 1600–1900* (Cambridge, 2010).

96   M. Willard, *History of the White Australia Policy to 1920* (Melbourne, 1923); L. Jayasuriya, D. Walker and J. Gothard (eds), *Legacies of White Australia: Race, Culture, and Nation* (Crawley, WA, 2003); J. Carey and C. McLisky (eds), *Creating White Australia* (Sydney, 2009). A word of caution: the term 'White Australia' has more recently become synonymous with settler-Aboriginal relations, whereas the earlier work dealt with Oriental and Melanesian immigration in the later nineteenth and early twentieth centuries.

97   H. H. Sugimoto, *Japanese Immigration, the Vancouver Riots, and Canadian Diplomacy* (New York, 1978); H. Johnston, *The Voyage of the Komagata Maru: The Sikh Challenge to Canada's Colour Bar* (Oxford, 1979); N. Buchignani, D. M. Indra and R. Srivastava, *Continuous Journey: A Social History of South Asians in Canada* (Toronto, 1985); W. P. Ward, *White Canada Forever: Popular Attitudes and Public Policy Toward Orientals in British Columbia* (Montreal and Kingston, 1978), and P. Roy, *A White Man's Province: British Columbia's Politicians and Chinese and Japanese Immigrants, 1858–1914* (Vancouver, 1989); P. Roy, *The Oriental Question: Consolidating a White Man's Province 1914–1941* (Vancouver, 2003); K. Niergarth, '"This Continent must Belong to the White Races": William Lyon Mackenzie King, Canadian Diplomacy and Immigration Law, 1908', *International History Review*, 32:4 (2010), pp. 599–617. Also see P. S. O'Connor, 'Keeping New Zealand White, 1908–1920', *New Zealand Journal of History*, 2:1 (1968), pp. 41–65; S. Brawley, 'No "White Policy" in New Zealand: Fact and Fiction in New Zealand's Asian Immigration Record, 1946–1978', *New Zealand Journal of History*, 27:1 (1993), pp. 16–36.

98   J. Darwin, *After Tamerlane: The Global History of Empire* (London, 2007), p. 505.

99   L. Proudfoot, 'Landscape, Place and Memory: Towards a Geography of Irish Identities in Colonial Australia', in O. Walsh (ed.), *Ireland Abroad: Politics and Professions in the Nineteenth Century* (Dublin, 2002), p. 172.

100 D. Eltis, 'Free and Coerced Transatlantic Migrations: Some Comparisons', *American Historical Review*, 88:2 (1983), pp. 251–80; J. Horn and P. D. Morgan, 'Settlers and Slaves: European Migrations to Early Modern British America', in E. Mancke and C. Shammas (eds), *The Creation of the British Atlantic World* (Baltimore, 2006), pp. 19–44.

101 See B. Patterson (ed.), *Ulster–New Zealand Migration and Cultural Transfers* (Dublin, 2006); McCarthy (ed.), *Global Clan*; A. R. McCormack, 'Networks among British Immigrants and Accommodation to Canadian Society – Winnipeg, 1900–1914', *Histoire sociale/Social History*, 17:34 (1984), pp. 357–74. See S. J. Hornsby, 'Patterns of Scottish Emigration to Canada, 1750–1870', *Journal of Historical Geography*, 18:4 (1992), pp. 397–416, where he argues that Highland emigration was concentrated in a few major avenues because of its community nature, as compared to the diffuse nature of Lowland emigration which was more individualistic.

102 For studies which explore the internal migration patterns of British migrants, and which connect internal migration with stimuli linked to overseas migration, see C. W. J. Withers and A. J. Watson, 'Stepwise Migration and Highland Migration to Glasgow, 1852–1898', *Journal of Historical Geography*, 17:1 (1991), pp. 35–55; S. Nicholas and P. R. Shergold, 'Internal Migration in England, 1818–1839', *Journal of Historical Geography*, 13:2 (1995), pp. 155–68; S. King, 'Migrants on the Margin?

Mobility, Integration and Occupations in the West Riding, 1650–1820', *Journal of Historical Geography*, 23:3 (1997), pp. 284–303.

103 'Introduction', in Walsh (ed.), *Ireland Abroad*, pp. 9–10. The term career migrant is used by C. Tilly, 'Transplanted Networks', in V. Yans-McLaughlin (ed.), *Immigration Reconsidered: History, Sociology, and Politics* (Oxford, 1990), pp. 79–95. For the contribution of migrants to colonial police forces, see K. Fedorowich, 'The Problems of Disbandment: the Royal Irish Constabulary and imperial migration, 1919–1929', *Irish Historical Studies*, 30:1 (1996), pp. 88–110; E. Malcolm, '"What would People say if I became a Policeman?": the Irish Policeman Abroad', in Walsh (ed.), *Ireland Abroad*, pp. 95–107; G. Sinclair, *Colonial Policing and the Imperial Endgame 1945–80: 'At the End of the Line'* (Manchester, 2007). Soldiering overseas, which took a drastic toll on these men, is now seen as an important aspect of migrant activity. See U. Bosma, 'European Colonial Soldiers in the Nineteenth Century: their Role in White Global Migration and Patterns of Colonial Settlement', *Journal of Global History*, 4:2 (2009), pp. 317–66; P. Burroughs, 'The Human Cost of Imperial Defence in the Early Victorian Age', *Victorian Studies*, 24:1 (1980), pp. 7–32.

104 For pioneering work on convict transportation, see S. Nicholas and P. R. Shergold, 'Transportation as Global Migration', and 'Convicts as Immigrants', in S. Nicholas (ed.), *Convict Workers: Reinterpreting Australia's Past* (Cambridge, 1988), pp. 28–39 and 43–61 respectively. Also see D. Oxley, *Convict Maids: the Forced Migration of Women to Australia* (Cambridge, 1996); A. Woollacott, *Gender and Empire* (Basingstoke, 2006), pp. 14–37; K. Reid, *Gender, Crime and Empire: Convicts, Settlers and the State in Early Colonial Australia* (Manchester, 2007).

105 H. L. Malchow, 'The Church and Emigration in Late Victorian England', *Journal of Church and State History*, 24:1 (1982), pp. 119–38. In the Canadian context, the church played a key role in maintaining long-term stability of immigrant rural communities, which has not been explored by historians for the Anglo-Celtic communities, but has been explored in depth for the non-Anglo-Saxons such as Mennonites, Doukhobors, Jews, Mormons and Ukrainians. See J. C. Lehr and Y. Katz, 'Crown, Corporation and Church: the Role of Institutions in the Stability of Pioneer Settlements in the Canadian West, 1870–1914', *Journal of Historical Geography*, 21:4 (1995), pp. 413–29.

106 C. S. Hallas, 'Migration in Nineteenth-Century Wensleydale and Swaledale', *Northern History*, 27 (1991), pp. 153 and 156; G. Howells, '"On Account of the Disreputable Characters": Parish Assisted Emigration from Rural England, 1834–1860', *History*, 88:4 (2003), p. 592.

107 R. V. Mongia, 'Race, Nationality, Mobility: A History of the Passport', *Public Culture*, 11:3 (1999), pp. 527–56, examines the Canadian insistence that Indians possessed passports when migrating to Canada between 1906 and 1915. Our thanks to Tony Ballantyne, University of Otago, for pointing us in the direction of this valuable reference. Also see J. Doulman and D. Lee, *Every Assistance & Protection: A History of the Australian Passport* (Sydney, 2008); S. Mazumdar, 'Empire and Migration', *The Palgrave Dictionary of Transnational History*, ed. A. Iriye and Pierre-Yves Saunier (Basingstoke, 2009), pp. 319–25; and R. Mayer, 'Paper Citizens and Biometrical Identification: Immigration, Nationality and Belonging in Chinese America during the Exclusion Era', in V. Künnemann and R. Mayer (eds), *Trans-Pacific Interactions: The United States and China, 1880–1950* (Basingstoke, 2009), pp. 85–104.

108 www.nla.gov.au/pressrel/ForgottenAustraliansandformerChildMigrantshavetheir say_mediarelease.html (accessed 20 April 2011).

109 www.childmigrantstrust.com/news/uk-apology-to-former-child-migrants (accessed 20 April 2011).

110 www.cic.gc.ca/english/multiculturalism/homechild/index.asp (accessed 20 April 2011). For a late extension of child migration to Southern Rhodesia just prior to the Second World War through the Fairbridge Memorial Settlers Association, see E. Boucher, 'The Limits of Potential: Race, Welfare, and the Interwar Extension of

Child Migration to Southern Rhodesia', *Journal of British Studies*, 48:2 (2009), pp. 914–34.

111   The references in her footnotes are superb and do not need to be replicated here. Suffice it to say that the two voluntary organisations mentioned, combined with the Fairbridge scheme to Australia and Southern Rhodesia, have received the lion's share of scholarly attention. Also see M. Rutherdale, '"Canada Is No Dumping Ground": Salvation Army Immigrants, Public Discourse and the Lived Experiences of Women and Children Newcomers, 1900–1930', *Histoire sociale/Social History*, 39:79 (2007), pp. 75–115; and J. Eekelaar, '"The Chief Glory": The Export of Children from the United Kingdom', *Journal of Law and Society*, 21:4 (1994), pp. 487–504, which examines the lack of legal control in the emigration of pauper children from the United Kingdom in the nineteenth and twentieth centuries.

112   www.nla.gov.au/oh/fafcm/ (accessed 20 April 2010). Until recently, Dr J. Sassoon was the project manager leading a three-year oral history project entitled 'Forgotten Australians and Former Child Migrants' based out of the National Library of Australia to record the lives of many child migrants who were 'deported' to Australia. This is a term used by the former migrants themselves and indicates just how many, but not all, felt about their ordeals. The editors would like to express their thanks to Dr Sassoon for valuable insights given to Dr Fedorowich into her ongoing work while he was a visiting fellow at the Humanities Research Centre at the Australian National University (April–June 2011).

113   Patrick Dunae has pioneered the investigation of relationships between upper-class public schools and emigration: *Gentlemen Emigrants. From the British Public Schools to the Canadian Frontier* (Manchester, 1983); Patrick Dunae. 'Education, Emigration and Empire: the Colonial College, 1887–1905', in J. A. Mangan (ed.), *'Benefits Bestowed'? Education and British Imperialism* (Manchester, 1988), pp. 194–210. Equally important was the development of a state school curriculum where geography held a central place in promoting emigration to the colonies. See here A. M. C. Maddrell, 'Empire, Emigration and School Geography: Changing Discourses of Imperial Citizenship, 1880–1925', *Journal of Historical Geography*, 22:4 (1996), pp. 373–87; D. Gorman, *Imperial Citizenship: Empire and the Question of Belonging* (Manchester, 2007). School curriculum was also a site where colonial regimes through education and racial stereotypes could reinforce the hegemony of the white settler communities. See J. A. Mangan (ed.), *The Imperial Curriculum: Racial Images and Education in the British Colonial Experience* (London, 1993).

114   Sears, 'Immigration Controls', p. 103.

115   Gerber, *Authors*; Elliot, Gerber and Sinke (eds), *Letters Across Borders*.

116   A. J. Hammerton and A. Thomson, *Ten Pound Poms: Australia's Invisible Migrants* (Manchester, 2005); A. J. Hammerton, 'Life Stories, Family Relations and the "Lens of Migration": Postwar British Emigration and the New Mobility', in D. Deacon, P. Russell and A. Woollacott (eds), *Transnational Ties: Australian Lives in the World* (Canberra, 2008), pp. 135–47.

117   British retirees are a different animal but for an examination of how they negotiate their Britishness in the Mediterranean see R. King, T. Warnes and A. Williams, *Sunset Lives: British Retirement Migration in the Mediterranean* (Oxford, 2000); K. O'Reilly, *The British on the Costa Del Sol: Transnational Identities and Local Communities* (London, 2000). Over the years the Institute for Public Policy Research has conducted a number of studies on British migration and re-migration. See D. Sriskandarajah and C. Drew, *Brits Abroad: Mapping the Scale and Nature of British Emigration* (London, 2006); T. Finch, M. Latorre, N. Pollard and J. Rutter, *Shall We Stay Or Shall We Go? Re-migration Trends among Britain's Immigrants* (London, 2009).

118   www.gettingdownunder.com/2010/01/09/wanted-down-under-series-4–back-on-the-bbc/ (accessed 20 April 2011).

119   For this debate, see R. Hansen, *Citizenship and Immigration in Post-war Britain: The Institutional Origins of a Multicultural Nation* (Oxford, 2000), who refutes the notion by the two authors listed below that the 1948 Act was the beginning

of the racialisation of British immigration policy. K. Paul, *Whitewashing Britain: Race and Citizenship in the Post-War Era* (Ithaca, 1997); I. R. G. Spencer, *British Immigration Policy since 1939: The Making of Multicultural Britain* (London, 1997).

CHAPTER 1

Malthus and the uses of British emigration
Eric Richards

The dynamics of emigration

The British World, in its most basic origins, started with people moving along country lanes from cottages in the towns and villages of rural Britain. This movement extended across several centuries and ultimately stretched across the globe. It reached its flood tide in the middle decades of the nineteenth century, when it became increasingly an urban phenomenon.[1] How exactly it was activated remains largely a mystery.

In his seminal work on the Atlantic world at the end of the eighteenth century, Bernard Bailyn speculated about the grand, almost tectonic forces that impelled vast movements of people within the three connecting continents and across the ocean itself. In a series of scintillating metaphors Bailyn imagined the Atlantic basin being convulsed into intercontinental flows of human beings over a territory that stretched from Luanda to Shetland, and from the Danube to the Mississippi.[2] These dynamic mechanisms are still obscure and have not yet been absorbed into the general literature.

A similar imaginative challenge is required of the even larger idea of the 'British World'. In this case the British spread themselves territorially over a global scale. The fact is that we have relatively few clues about the underlying dynamics of that great diasporic process, that is, the articulation of the grand movements of emigrants from the British Isles who eventually numbered tens of millions, greater even than the black slave trade in the Atlantic.

What ultimately animated these out-seeking people? It was evidently a complicated and long-term shifting process that had more than a single connecting cause. It was obviously more than a simple extrusion of population from the land. But the disengagement of people from rural society was a common prior requirement in the arousal of mobility in Britain as elsewhere. We also have a rather poor grasp on the ways in which the exodus of perhaps thirty million British migrants affected Britain itself. Moreover, despite unprecedented emigration and renewed imperialism, in population terms most of the 'British World' remained within the British Isles.

Upon these large spheres Thomas Robert Malthus (1766–1834) continues to cast his ghostly influence. Malthus was an equivocal advocate of emigration. He was, nevertheless, immensely influential among those who urged emigration as a solution to the problems of poverty, destitution and over-population across the British Isles in the nineteenth century. Their idea was to populate the British World while simultaneously relieving the British Isles of its excess population. In the outcome Malthus's predictions about emigration were not well-borne out and their applicability in the new industrial world is now generally discounted.

Yet there were certainly regions in each of the home countries which were caught in severely negative conditions and where labour supply outran the long-term possibilities of employment. The efficacy of migration as a means of relief, in terms of Malthusian doctrine, is the central issue in this essay. Malthus offered a surprisingly wide range of propositions on the question and these are re-examined in terms of the timing, dynamics, diversity and psychology of emigration from the British Isles in the nineteenth century. Malthus and his reputation provide a convenient peg for two connected issues which had a fundamental bearing upon the making of the British World. One is the manner in which Malthusian doctrine related to emigration; the other is the overhanging problem of rural evacuation in the nineteenth-century economy.

Malthusian predictions

Malthus's most famous propositions on emigration related to the short run and were concerned with the utility or otherwise of emigration as a means of relieving the pressure of population on subsistence. His prescriptions were connected with his broad principle that population tended always to expand to the limits of subsistence unless other influences actively intervened. The evolution of his thinking on emigration occurred in a critical context – namely the volatile conditions in Britain during the Napoleonic Wars and especially in the years after Waterloo when constricted demand for labour caused serious mass unemployment in most sectors of the economy. In these circumstances, in 1817, Malthus was prepared to allow that 'emigration is most useful as a temporary relief', and could be used to reduce the adjustment required until population would 'conform itself to the state of the demand for labour'. Nine years later he repeated his earlier proposition, that: 'A certain degree of emigration is known to be favourable to the population of the mother country.'[3]

The essential point was that emigration could exert a benefit only in a strictly temporary fashion; it could not provide any permanent relief to society's woes. Emigration alone was entirely inadequate to affect the level of population; it could not reduce the population permanently and consequently would never lead to depopulation. As he expressed it: 'There are no fears so totally ill-grounded as the fears of depopulation from emigration.'[4] It was, however, marginally useful 'as a partial and temporary expedient'. And emigration, incidentally, would help to spread the benefits of civilisation and 'the more general cultivation of the earth'.[5]

In 1827, in his famous explication before the Emigration Committee of Parliament, he argued that the ineffectiveness of emigration as a permanent remedy was a consequence of the much repeated 'vacuum effect'[6] – that the space released by the removal of emigrants was inevitably replenished by a subsequent regrowth of population, facilitated by the return to subdivision of the land holding and early marriages and followed by a further round of 'prolificness'. As Malthus put it: 'There is always a natural tendency towards the filling up of a vacuum', which would render the effect of emigration 'nugatory'.[7] And again 'there is always a very strong tendency to fill up the vacuum; and you might even encourage a greater proportion of births by an emigration, unless it were accompanied by some measures of the kind before referred to.'[8] Malthus was alluding especially to Ireland and the Scottish Highlands but also the feared inundation of England by destitute Irish. He was prepared to allow that the refilling of the vacuum could be diminished if people were prevented from reoccupying the land from which the emigrants had departed. This would be accomplished by the prohibition of sub-division and the literal destruction of houses and cottages previously occupied by the departed emigrants. As he put it: 'I think it is possible that the vacuum might not be filled up, because those miserable hovels that had been deserted might be pulled down and not be replaced.'[9] This would 'be something like an effectual remedy' because it would deter early marriages, which were the root of the evil.[10]

This was the Malthusian doctrine of emigration in its limited role as a palliative.[11] In the British experience of emigration in the nineteenth century it is now utterly clear that the record was highly varied, but that many parts of the country did indeed register permanent reduction in population levels and that the vacuum effect was eventually shown to be inoperative in practice. This was true of very large rural tracts of the country; it was also eventually true of the two sites to which

Malthus particularly pointed. The population of the Highlands began to fall absolutely after 1851; and, most sensationally, the population of Ireland fell like a stone after the Great Famine and did not begin to recover for another hundred and fifty years. Emigration was part of the cause; emigration indeed diminished population and the vacuum simply did not work in the manner Malthus predicted.

Even more fundamentally for Malthusian predictions, the population of the British Isles as a whole rose cumulatively for 200 years, from the early part of the nineteenth century, and this period was clearly associated with rising living standards. The wrongness of Malthus seems to be complete. Indeed, when in mid-2005, the 125th anniversary issue of *Science* magazine rank-ordered the really 'Big research questions' of the day, it identified number twenty-five as: 'Will Malthus continue to be wrong?'[12]

Nevertheless, the influence of Malthus caused his contemporaries and their immediate successors to dismiss emigration as a relieving mechanism on the demographic pressures of the day. According to Mark Blaug this was 'a generation drunk on Malthusian wine'.[13] Thus Herman Merivale, in this *Lectures on Colonisation* in 1839–41, cited the well-known case of the Isle of Skye from which 8,000 of a total population of 11,000 emigrated in the late eighteenth century. Yet within a generation Skye had recouped its original numbers, which then proceeded to grow much further. This seemed to be a perfect example of the Malthusian vacuum effect. It encouraged generalised scepticism about the possible benefits of large-scale emigration, even from Ireland. In the outcome Merivale lived to witness the impact of the Great Famine and, in the post-famine edition of his lectures in 1861, he conceded that emigration had hugely reduced the Irish population; and emigration certainly helped to sustain its gradual betterment over the following century.[14] In the case of the Isle of Skye, its population history followed a similar path, rising until 1851 and then beginning at last its long, continuous decline.[15]

It can be argued that there is a let-out clause for Malthus particularly if we consider his doctrine in its longer-run mode. One school of thought claims that there was less rigidity and less pessimism in Malthusian doctrine than is conventionally thought. Malthus was not saying that humanity was doomed forever to retreat to bedrock subsistence and misery.[16] He was just as emphatic that the supplies of subsistence could be increased. J. J. Spengler for instance, says that Malthus was a Smithian and believed that urban and industrial development would ultimately increase 'the expandability of employment', which would lead to a better balance of population with subsistence. How much flexibility this permitted in the Malthusian framework is not entirely clear. But it is worth consulting a lineal descendant of Malthus, the economist J. M. Keynes, who had interesting things to say about the course of growth in the nineteenth-century world. Keynes regarded the great expansion of trade, settlement and migration as the engine of development in the long Victorian era. But when the territorial expansion of the European people seemed to reach its geographical limits by 1914, Keynes was pessimistic. He sensed the end of the extended Malthusian limits. This was one of his recurrent themes in the 1920s and 1930s, causing him to be greatly dispirited about, in essence, the future supply of food. This, of course, had been a vital element in the great age of emigration, much of it in the form of the extension of the British World.[17]

Thus there is some doubt, which is not unusual, about the implications of Malthus's prescriptions with regard to the emigration variable. But there is no doubt about the story of economic growth and ultimately the rising living standards during the Victorian Age – which is a recognition of the success of the supply side that he had emphasised. Indeed, emigration was certainly a vital component in the widening scale of British production around the world.

The social psychology of emigration

Malthus was a keen observer of the course of emigration from the British Isles at the end of the eighteenth century. Apart from his principal theoretical propositions on the subject he was also fascinated by the social psychology of migration, although these elements in his thinking have been somewhat neglected. He was clear-minded about the essential differential that was required to induce emigration. Thus in the 1798 exposition, he remarked that 'a great emigration necessarily implies unhappiness of some kind or other in the country that is deserted', some serious uneasiness to justify the loss of 'families, connections . . . and native land' to take up a new life 'in untried foreign climes'. But he also acknowledged the 'hope of some great advantage' in the new place.[18] He emphasised the risk factor in any kind of emigration, noting that 'the emigrant, impatient of the distresses which he feels in his own country, is by no means secure of finding relief in another'.[19]

Here his emphasis is on the reluctance to emigrate, the inertia of rural people – of 'how much misery and hardship men will undergo in their own country, before they can determine to desert it' – and how even the most tempting settlements were rejected 'by people who appeared to be starving'.[20] Malthus probably had in mind the Irish and the Highland peasantries. It was a theme to which observers of even the English rural population in the mid-nineteenth century frequently reverted.[21]

Malthus was however adamant about the self-defeating consequences of emigration and drew on cases from the West Highlands of Scotland, most notably the island of Jura. On Jura the population regenerated despite successive rounds of emigration. The island was 'absolutely overflowing with inhabitants in spite of constant and numerous emigrations': recurrent waves of emigration produced no lasting benefit to the landlord looking for a reduction in population, nor to the people who remained. The migrants evidently responded to better opportunities in America especially, but their places were soon filled up by renewed population growth. Thus emigration 'will appear but a weak palliative', never more than 'a partial and temporary expedient'.[22]

In this light it is surprising that Malthus spoke so warmly of the Earl of Selkirk's recent writings on emigration since Selkirk emerged as the apostle of the idea that emigration was the great solution to the Highland problems of poverty and over-population. Nevertheless, Malthus declared that 'it would surely be unjust to oblige people to leave their country and kindred against their inclinations'. Indeed, Malthus set his face against the active encouragement of emigration. People should be left to themselves even when not emigrating consigned them to lives of 'celibacy or extreme poverty in their own country'.[23]

Emigrants in Malthus's exposition were not necessarily either predictable or rational. And here he put his finger on the problem of analysing migrant behaviour, migrant psychology. He celebrated the courage of emigrants labouring under great difficulties in new places, which they overcame by 'those powerful passions, the thirst of gain, the spirit of adventure, and religious enthusiasm' – which, in their combinations, enabled them to overcome every obstacle. He noted also that emigrants often wreaked devastating effects on indigenous peoples: it made 'humanity shudder', he said.[24]

At the same time, he noted cases where the 'excessive tendency to emigrate' had encouraged extreme procreation in the home parish. He referred to 'whole tribes, who enjoyed the comforts of life in a reasonable degree' had left 'from mere humour, and a fantastical idea of becoming their own masters and freeholders'.[25] This 'humour' and these 'fantastical ideas', common among emigrants then and since, continue to challenge our understanding of the mechanisms and psychology of emigration.

Malthus: the pre-industrial political economist

Obscurities surrounding the precise implications of Malthus's doctrines have bred unsatisfactory controversies and polemics.[26] Moreover Malthus, understandably, had little grasp of the actual course of British population trends. His earliest writings pre-dated the first censuses and he laboured under the severe delusion that the population of Britain in 1798 was only 7 million whereas it was soon to be revealed that it was actually much closer to 11 million, an underestimate of 44 per cent.[27]

Nor was it surprising that Malthus misunderstood the actual capacity of the economy to expand its supply of foodstuffs and its demand for labour. As E. A. Wrigley points out, these were revolutionary economic times: at the very moment that Malthus was writing gross national product was rising unprecedentedly to an average growth rate of between 2 and 5 per cent per annum. This was a quantum leap over the typical pre-industrial rates of between 0.5 per cent and 1 per cent per annum.[28] It was, of course, a revolution beyond the limits of Malthus's mind and was unaccounted for in his predictions. Malthus derived his thinking and premises from a world which was being overturned as he wrote. The Malthusian world was a pre-industrial world in which population growth seemed always most likely to outstrip and swamp any achievable economic growth. Now, for the first time in human existence, 'rising numbers no longer posed a threat to living standards'. The Industrial Revolution changed the underlying relationship between population and society.[29]

Malthus therefore was a political economist of the pre-industrial world, and drawing on past experience; he could hardly be blamed for his 'failure to forecast the future'.[30] This also inevitably undermined most of his predictions about the consequences of emigration. For most of the time in most of Britain after 1820, the 'vacuum effect' did not apply; people emigrated in large numbers without much consequence for the growth of population and living standards. In reality, Britain was not repeatedly dragged back to older levels of subsistence; and living standards increased cumulatively beyond the level of population growth.[31] The Malthusian spectre lacked substance, at least on the British mainland.

Types of migration and the disengagement with the land

Malthus's usefulness in explaining the phenomenon of British emigration in the nineteenth century is limited. This was, after all, a massive inter-continental transfer of people which reached a crescendo in the middle decade of the century. Furthermore, it possessed many roots and mechanisms. There were numerous categories of migration out of Britain, often associated with different dynamics, moving with different velocities and under widely different pressures. Malthus's exposition is particularly helpful in explaining migration from the pre-industrial sectors of the economy – many of which persisted into the late nineteenth century. Malthus's outline of the social psychology of the migration was applicable especially in these cases. But other types of emigration were emerging in the new industrial age and a more elaborate typology of migrant behaviour is necessary if we are to make better sense of the otherwise chaotic outflows from the British Isles in the great age of migration.

The central overarching question was the adjustment of the primarily rural population to the facts of revolutionary demographic growth which occurred simultaneously with unprecedented advances in agricultural productivity. The movement of people out of agriculture is sometimes described as an 'evacuation',[32] entailing the removal (sometimes by actual emigration) of large numbers of people from the land. Agriculture was divested of a large part of the rural population. It was a vast readjustment of population in relation to the land following in the wake of large-scale demographic development. This was, of course, a crucial feature of the modern age, first in the British case, then across the industrialising world, often associated with considerable dislocation and turmoil. C. F. G. Masterman in 1909 described it as 'the largest secular change of a thousand years: from the life of the fields to the life of the city. Nine out of ten families have migrated within three generations.'[33] Against Malthus's predictions, migration and emigration diminished the populations of many peripheral parts of Britain.

These mechanisms operated quite differently in different parts of the British Isles. The transition appears to have been greater and easier in locations near towns and much more difficult in remoter zones of the British Isles. Internal migration was always an easier option than emigration. The role of emigration was variable and in some places subject to sudden bursts of enthusiasm and activity: the vocabulary of emigration is full of 'fevers', outrushes, obsessions, and floods, as though barely rational. Most migration was more often a seepage, a scarcely perceptible exiting of small numbers over many years. But, over the long run, they accumulated into massive aggregate migrations – and indeed drained the countryside. This was achieved mainly by internal migration, but it also fed emigration. Three variants of the rural emigration process spring to mind: the Isle of Man, the Western Highlands of Scotland and Swaledale in North Yorkshire.

These cases are chosen to exemplify the broad range of precipitants which accompanied the evacuation of rural people in nineteenth century Britain. All three exhibited both relative and absolute declines in their population bases, but in different local conditions and on different timetables and on different scales. In the first case, set in an island society in which shifting price differentials eased out people from several strata of the rural community, the process was eventually expressed in transatlantic migration. In the West Highlands rapid population growth occurred on a narrowing economic base, which created concentrations of local poverty and subsequent out-migration in many directions. In North Yorkshire complicated intersecting forces restrained the outflow for many decades before the rural population began to decline. These provide three well-documented cases along a wide spectrum of contrasting circumstances, which, in turn, capture some of the divergent circumstances shaping rural adjustments in the nineteenth century, with Malthus always looming in the background.

Islands sometimes provide simplified conditions in which to examine the operation of migratory flows, especially where they are unaffected by direct industrialisation – for example the Isle of Man in the 1820s and 1830s. A particularly rapid and concentrated outflow of Manx people to Ohio at that time developed into a strong connection which lasted for more than a century.[34] In the island context in the post-Waterloo years there was a general tightening of rural conditions and a very rapid rise of population; there were some poor harvests, rising rents and intensifying competition for the land, and falling prices; and there were parallel problems in the fishing industry – yet none of these adverse conditions assumed catastrophic proportions.

A sequence of departures from certain localities on the island was established among rural people, fishermen and, later, construction workers and miners.[35] It was commonplace economic migration involving a straightforward calculation of the widening differential between income and prospects in Ohio compared with those available in the Isle of Man. It was a perfectly rational reciprocation between two particular components of the Atlantic system, a relocation of population, technology and capital. The mechanism which started the flow required some initial risk-taking by the first contact migrants. This was followed by the usual paraphernalia of correspondence, advertising, persuasion and family-based chains of movement and connection. Manx people responded in substantial numbers and their movements were registered in their letters back and forth.

In the original migration, in the years after 1825, some 200 Manx farmers and families found their way towards the Western Reserve and their descendants made Cleveland and the Cuyahoga the capital of the Manx in the United States, setting up churches and benevolent societies that maintained a degree of cohesion. There was a pronounced degree of clustering and solidarity. The original groups enthusiastically encouraged fellow-Manx people to join them. Many were Methodists, some spoke the Manx language. The economic argument was put bluntly by William Kelly when he wrote back home from Ohio: 'A man can earn three times as much here in America per day and provisions are thrice as cheap, as in the Isle of Man . . . It makes no odds whether a man be rich or poor.' And he gave precise detailed information about how to transplant to 'this land of liberty and luxuries'. Land itself was cheap, yields were high, acres boundless: 'the son of the poor man had the same chance as the son of the rich'. The main problem of the prospective migrants was their disengagement from their ties (including leases and debts) in the Isle of Man.

The striking aspect of the Manx migration was the composition of the departing people. Many of the relatively prosperous people left for America: there was local astonishment 'that people as well off as they are would think of going to a far off and unknown land of America, which was very nearly outside the world'. There was report of 'almost a panic . . . by a middle class going to America' – activated by letters sent back from Ohio. 'It makes no difference, where that a man is rich or poor, if he can get there.' The critical problem was the actual cost and dislocation of emigration: 'we often lament that so many of our countrymen have not the means of emigrating here . . . The poorest man can purchase land here', reported another migrant.[36]

This was perfectly rational migration without extreme pressure; the main impediment was the cost of the passage and the disengagement with 'home', both economic and emotional. It exchanged a land-scarce context for a land-rich place. It meant that emigration favoured the better off, the young and the unattached – though family migration seemed to be the main model. Its principal effect was to reduce rural pressure in the Isle of Man – not particularly dramatically, and secondary to internal movements – and fed the needs of expansion on the Ohio frontier. It was a story often retold across the Anglosphere: a modest and selective evacuation, an agricultural adjustment by way of emigration, which helped to reduce the absolute numbers dependent on Manx agriculture without impeding rising productivity on the home farms.[37] There was no refilling of the Manx vacuum. Malthus's prescriptions had little purchase in these conditions.

In the West Highlands of Scotland in the middle decades of the nineteenth century the problem of poverty and rural congestion was much more acute. Emigration was urged by the landlords, social reformers, some charities and by a succession of government commissions, even by parish ministers. These people had the most to gain by emigration or migration. But they also had the least capacity to pay the passages

[51]

and they were remote from the main ports of migration. On the other hand, they were part of a long tradition of Atlantic migration stretching back to the early eighteenth century. Michael Flinn argued that out-migration from the north-west Highlands in the late eighteenth century 'helped to stave off what must certainly have otherwise been a gathering Malthusian crisis'.[38] But the outflow was fitful and not reliable nor large enough to prevent the growth of a vulnerable population, heavily dependent on the potato crop (most notably in Skye, Lewis, Harris, Mull, Eigg, Tiree, Coll and the north-western coastal lands) by the mid-nineteenth century. Here the sequence of migration reflected local realities, but it also manifested a significant resistance to use escape routes out of the region. The documentation of the times is replete with evidence of reluctance to migrate, which was widely regarded as bloody-minded and self-defeating.[39]

The problem in the West Highlands was the great build-up of population from 1770 to 1860, and later in some parts. Even where emigration was substantial the population in many of the most remote places was replenished very quickly and seemed to drag the communities back to the original congestions and vulnerability of the past.[40] This, of course, was the precise Malthusian prediction and Malthus himself drew examples from the Highlands before 1801. But the cycle continued well into the nineteenth century. The regenerative powers of the Highland population were put to an early test in the Napoleonic Wars when vast numbers of young men were enlisted in the regiments and served abroad for very long periods. The population, nevertheless, grew at unprecedented rates and then redoubled at the end of the wars.[41]

Some of the psychology of resistance, of clinging on despite severe deprivation in the famine years, was exposed in emigrant letters of the time. A small clutch of correspondence between family members in Gairloch in the West Highlands and outback New South Wales revealed some of the prevailing mentalities towards emigration. Gairloch was part of the western littoral of northern Scotland, much damaged by the potato famine and its aftermath. In one letter, in the spring of 1852, Murdo McDonald in Gairloch told his son in New South Wales that local conditions were still no better: 'the poorer class are in a state of starvation, the potato failure still continues'. Another family member had 'made up his mind to go to Australia, and both his mother and myself agree to it now, seeing as there is no prospect for a young man in the country'. McDonald also told his other son not to return home but to make a success of his own emigration in New South Wales. An uncle had died just before he had decided to emigrate, 'for fear he might be a burden on his friends in this country'. He had said in 1851: 'There is nothing now in Gairloch but Starvation and Poverty.' But emigration was slight despite generous assistance available to prospective emigrants prepared to go to Australia. Even when the fishing and the potato crop improved in 1853, conditions were still straitened – as one family member put it: 'I do believe that some people would do better in Australia if they would muster the courage to go.'[42]

There was evidently increasing domestic negotiation about emigration in these communities. which sometimes ended in substantial communal outflows. More typical were small seepages, usually to distant towns, perhaps as a prelude to emigration; other communities seemed to turn inwards and battled poverty in time-honoured fashion, against the odds. A compromise was seasonal migration, which was well documented: income from the south propped up remote communities for many decades; overseas remittances operated in much the same way, though they were not so easily detected.

The Highland model was an extreme version of the general retentiveness of several such peripheral zones that persisted for many decades. They were characterised by an initial rapid accumulation of population and then a prolonged decline which was never prompt nor large enough to satisfy the landlords and the critics. The reluctance to emigrate impeded the convergence of living standards between regions which, very slowly, eventually brought the Highlands a rising per capita living standard – the main propellant of which was most probably the actual decline of population.

These were long surviving pre-industrial communities which did not shift their patterns of subsistence for many decades. Emigration from the West Highlands was often followed by population regeneration and further population growth and undiminished rural congestion. It took many decades to break out of this late pre-industrial mould. The survival of many West Highland communities was a remarkable achievement within that mould and fitted closely the doctrines enunciated by Malthus himself. His ideas indeed applied much more to the pre-industrial world than to the new industrial future.

The third example, Swaledale, probably constituted the most common model of population redistribution over the long run. The demographic and economic career of the upland Swaledale region in the North Yorkshire Pennines can be followed longitudinally and shows several sequences within the long-term decline of rural population.[43]

The first people to emigrate from Swaledale were farmers and tradesmen with capital. They were departing for America in the late 1820s and 1830s, their relocation facilitated by the sale of their farms. In 1833 many of the poor yeomen and small farmers were beginning to take off for Canada, and 'if they could afford it, to Australia'. Christine Hallas notes that 'the poorest families, due to lack of capital, generally could not leave unless assisted by the local vestry'. By the 1840s emigration was gathering pace, many taking advantage of free passages to Australia and to the Cape of Good Hope. Emigration operated as a safety valve and there is a suggestion that the 'pull' force was crucial for the people at the top of the ladder; meanwhile the 'push' factor was more decisive for those at the bottom of the rural ladder. But, as Hallas says, 'many chose to accept a lower standard of living rather than leave the area', and this was clearly a vital choice. Out-migration from Swaledale was not replenished in the Malthusian model, but there was a clear enough tendency for some of the pre-industrial forms of local occupation to persist even against the pressures of economic maximisation and rationality. Emigration was the safety valve; out-migration in effect permitted a continuance of the old 'pre-industrial economic and social structures virtually intact'.[44]

The process of emigration was accompanied by the relative decline of agricultural employment in the region. Eventually – and notably in the Swaledale district – the population fell by a quarter in the 1880s and by two-thirds over the longer period of 1821–1911; though it was still greater than the earlier aggregate population of the district in 1801. Out-migration seems to have permitted the continuing coexistence of older forms of economic and social life in parallel with the new agriculture. Many of the local farmers coped, but only 'because most of the population growth was syphoned off during these years . . . A large part of the natural increase was surplus to local employment requirements.'[45]

Comparable adjustments were experienced across rural Britain – there was a phenomenal increase in rural productivity; eventually employment in agriculture began to fall but the population of rural areas declined more slowly, and later.[46] In many parts of agricultural Britain rural people were choosing to remain on the land despite the fact that their living standards were under the greatest pressure.[47]

Conclusion

These contrasting examples suggest a wide range of rural responses to population imperatives in the nineteenth century. The diagnoses of Malthus were essentially applicable to those regions that remained closest to the pre-industrial world. In the Isle of Man the rationalisation of agriculture was achieved by a continuous and definitive evacuation which included emigration; in the West Highlands emigration was sporadic and counteracted by continued regrowth of the local population which rested on the old pre-industrial base and was accompanied by extreme congestion and deprivation; in Swaledale both processes operated in tandem with considerable retention of the old system, cheek by jowl with the new. Malthus did not cover all cases but his emphasis on the social psychology of migration remains relevant though difficult to systematise.

E. A. Wrigley pointed out that there was very little expansion of the agricultural labour force in England in the early nineteenth century, yet the massive growth of the home population 'remained very largely home fed'. He estimates that output per man increased by 42 per cent in the period 1811–52, which was part of the 'very handsome long-term rise in output per man' for the entire period 1600–1850. 'Each man at work on the land in the 1850s was capable of meeting the food needs of significantly more people engaged in other work than his predecessor in the 1800s had been able to do.' This was the one great industry 'in which output per head rose markedly but in which employment grew very little in absolute terms, and fell sharply as a fraction of the workforce'. Paradoxically, even though employment in agriculture grew very little the total population of rural England continued to grow vigorously during most of the first half of the century. Only after 1850 did stagnation set in and then often accompanied by persistent structural unemployment in the countryside. Consequently, there remained many people on the land who were not actually contributing directly to the great productivity increases. There were, for example, tailors, butchers, blacksmiths, carpenters, and bricklayers – that is, trades which were not subject to much specialisation and served only local markets.[48] Thus the contrast between advanced areas of English agriculture and, say, the remote Highlands was less than definitive – there were retentive tendencies in both spheres.

The surge in rural output occurred when the population was generally rising at an unprecedented rate. The problem, therefore, was to adjust population to the needs of the rural economy by way of a diversion, a redeployment of the labour force out of the rural areas. Mostly this was achieved spontaneously with people responding to better incentives beyond the rural sector. The social consequences, given the scale of the structural upheaval, were relatively well contained. But there were parts of the system which did not experience this smooth transition, where labour remained literally unmoved.[49] It was here that the emigration stratagem was advocated almost as the last resort of a frustrated adjustment to the realities of the shift in the economy. The three cases outlined in this chapter are variants on this theme.

Migration was often heavily patterned and followed a relatively clear sequence, repeated in many rural districts of the British Isles in the nineteenth century. The timing and chronologies varied, but the end result was usually a progressive decline of the rural population after many decades of adjustment and, in many cases, persistent intractable poverty. Almost always it reflected the pressure of population numbers on the availability of land, but usually was exacerbated by changing land uses which simultaneously reduced the demand for labour in those rural sectors. This was part of the replicated pattern in rural zones.

The problem of rural evacuation was strikingly differentiated across the British Isles and the purchase of Malthus's ideas varied with the variety of conditions. There were different degrees of suggestibility, or propensity, to migrate. In some parts of rural Britain the reluctance to emigrate was notoriously frustrating to landlords and some of the social commentators and reformers of the mid-nineteenth century. Thus, in England, the Cornish possessed the highest rates of out-migration; rural outposts seem to have clung on most tenaciously, even in deteriorating conditions, in some of the worst-off regions. But of greatest contrast were the Irish who, of course, before and after the Famine, seemed to be fleeing destitution at very high rates. Malthus's analytical insights applied most specifically to pre-industrial zones, and even they eventually escaped the trap that he had identified for an earlier era.

Notes

1　On the emergent urban bias in emigration in the mid-nineteenth century, see P. Dewey, 'Farm Labour', in E. J. T. Collins (ed.) *Agrarian History of England and Wales, 7:1, 1850–1914* (Cambridge, 2000), p. 849, citing D. E. Baines, *Migration in a Mature Economy: Emigration and Internal Migration in England and Wales, 1861–1900* (Cambridge, 1986), p. 279.

2　B. Bailyn, *The Peopling of British North America: An Introduction* (London, 1987); B. Bailyn, *Voyagers to the West: A Passage in the Peopling of America on the Eve of the Revolution* (New York, 1986).

3　T. R. Malthus, *An Essay on the Principle of Population: the sixth edition (1826)*, ed. E. A. Wrigley and D. Souden, vol. 2 (London, 1986), p. 307. Malthus made the same assertion in 1798; T. R. Malthus, *An Essay on the Principle of Population: the first edition (1798)*, ed. Wrigley and Souden, vol. 1 (London, 1986), p. 41.

4　T. R. Malthus, *An Essay on the Principle of Population*, 2nd edn (1803), ed. P. James, Variorum edition (Cambridge, 1989), 1, p. 346.

5　*Ibid*. Malthus's mildly approving attitude to the encouragement of emigration was expressed in a letter to Wilmot Horton in February 1830 though it was hardly a ringing endorsement. See J. M. Pullen and T. Hughes Parry (eds), *T. R. Malthus: The Unpublished Papers in the Collection of Kanto Gakuen University*, 2 vols (Cambridge, 1997 and 2004), 1, pp. 103–4.

6　Malthus's 1803 edition declared that emigration was, at most, a 'weak palliative' to the problem of overpopulation [*Principle*, ed. James, 1, p. 340]. He remarked that 'no plans of emigration . . . can prevent the continued action of a great check to population in some form or other' [*Ibid.*, 2, p. 87]. Emigration could never be an adequate remedy: 'emigration is perfectly inadequate' for the purposes of making room for an unrestricted increase of population [*Ibid.*, 1, p. 346]. In the 1817 edition he was a little more positive for a temporary solution: 'Emigration if it could be freely used, has been shown to be a resource which could not be of long duration. It cannot therefore under any circumstances, be considered as an adequate remedy' [*Ibid.*,

2, p. 237]. Huzel, citing this text, points out that many contemporaries, including Martineau and Marcet, ignored Malthus. J. P. Huzel, *The Popularization of Malthus in Early Nineteenth-Century England* (Aldershot, 2006), pp. 83–4.

7   House of Commons Parliamentary Papers (HCPP), no. 550, *Third Report from the Select Committee on Emigration from the United Kingdom, 1827* (1827), pp. 311–27, Q.3198, Q.3231, Q.3222, and Q.3395. The doctrines of Malthus in relation to contemporary opinion regarding emigration are discussed in A. Gambles, *Protection and Politics. Conservative Economic Discourse, 1815–1852* (Woodbridge, Suffolk, 1999), pp. 167–9 and 181–2.

8   HCPP, no. 550, *Third Report . . . on Emigration*, Q.3380.

9   *Ibid.*, Q.3231. See also A. Digby, 'Malthus and the Reform of the English Poor Law', in M. Turner (ed.), *Malthus and His Time* (Basingstoke, 1986), pp. 18–19.

10 HCPP, no. 550, *Third Report . . . on Emigration*, Q.3251. Malthus was straightforward in his advocacy of clearances in Ireland and the Scottish Highlands and encouraged emigration in conditions in which the regeneration of the population was fully controlled – including the destruction of houses to prevent their reoccupation. There is good evidence that Malthus's ideas actually guided landlord policy in both places, including the pre-emptive destruction of cottages to prevent re-occupation. See E. Richards, *Patrick Sellar and the Highland Clearances* (Edinburgh, 1999), *passim*.

11 The strength of his scepticism about emigration is displayed most fully in G. H. Ghosh, 'Malthus on Emigration and Colonization: Letters to Wilmot-Horton', *Economica*, 30:117 (1963), pp. 45–62.

12 Quoted in R. H. Steckel, 'Big Social Science History', *Social Science History*, 31:1 (2007), p. 4.

13 M. Blaug, 'The Myth of the Old Poor Law and the Making of the New', in M. W. Flinn and T. C. Smout (eds), *Essays in Social History* (Oxford, 1974), pp. 125 and 143.

14 See B. Thomas, *Migration and Economic Growth: A Study of Great Britain and the Atlantic Economy* (Cambridge, 1954), p. 5.

15 The vacuum theory was still in the minds of commentators at the time of the Irish Famine in 1850. Anon. author [attrib. H. Hill Burton] in the *Edinburgh Review* argued that emigration did not permanently reduce population even from Ireland and the Scottish Highlands and that employment and industrial training were required as well as emigration. People indeed needed to be trained for emigration to give them hope and progress as well as a better welcome when they arrived in the destination countries. Anon., 'Emigration and Industrial Training', *Edinburgh Review*, 92 (October 1850), pp. 491–3.

16 For the long term Malthus was optimistic, in effect advocating balanced growth and small families. With regard to his principle of population, he said future prospects were not necessarily 'entirely disheartening, and by no means preclude the gradual and progressive improvement in human society . . .' Quoted by D. Winch, *Malthus* (Oxford, 1987), p. 103.

17 See E. Richards, *Britannia's Children: Emigration from England, Scotland, Wales and Ireland since 1600* (London, 2004), 238 ff.

18 Malthus, *Principle* (1798), p. 13.

19 Malthus, *Principle* (1803), ed. James, 1, p. 46.

20 Malthus, *Principle* (1798), p. 75.

21 The advocates of emigration were frustrated by the failure of rural people to solve the problem of congestion and poverty by migrating out of their own predicaments. They were not behaving in their own best interests, especially when the colonies beckoned so vigorously and offered to pay their fares and provided employment and even land. Part of the trouble was that the colonies would only take the young and the able, those who could be quickly inducted into the labour force. They did not want the old, the sick and the lame and the mass of dependants who were part and parcel of typical poverty. None of this made Highlanders unusual – it was generally difficult to persuade rural folk to emigrate.

22 Malthus, *Principle* (1803), ed. James, 1, pp. 284, 340 and 346.

23   See the note on Selkirk in Malthus, *Principle* (1803), ed. James, 2, pp. 332–3; see also *ibid.*, p. 220; and *Principle*, 1, p. 344.

24   *Ibid.*, 1, p. 340.

25   Malthus, *Principle* (1803), 1, p. 285.

26   See E. A. Wrigley, 'Men on the land in the countryside: employment in agriculture in early nineteenth century England', in L. Bonfield, R. M. Smith and K. Wrightson (eds), *The World We Have Gained* (Oxford, 1986), pp. 295–337.

27   This of course was the source of much late eighteenth-century demographic controversy which took another three decades to disperse. Had Malthus been properly aware of the true population size he might well have been even more alarmist about the immediate future. See E. A. Wrigley, 'Malthus Reassessed', *Journal of Historical Geography*, 8:2 (1982), p. 192, footnote 2.

28   Wrigley, 'Malthus Reassessed', pp. 189–90. See also W. Petersen's review of D. A. Coleman and R. Schofield, *The State of Population Theory* (Oxford, 1986) in the *European Journal of Population*, 2 (1986), pp. 407–10.

29   On the remarkable growth of productivity in British agriculture, see C. O'Grada, 'Farming High and Low, 1850–1914', *Agricultural History Review*, 49:2 (2001), pp. 210–18, esp. 211.

30   Wrigley, 'Malthus Reassessed', p. 190.

31   The modern case is clear, as E. A Wrigley has shown. Wrigley examines Malthus's *postulata* against 'the test of modern historical knowledge of the behaviour of economic and demographic variables in England in the centuries immediately before he wrote'. E. A. Wrigley, 'Elegance and Experience: Malthus at the Bar of History', in D. Coleman and R. Schofield (eds), *The State of Population Theory* (Oxford, 1986), pp. 46–64, especially 46, 51–2 and 63.

32   The term is employed by Thomas, *Migration and Economic Growth*, p. 118.

33   C. F. G. Masterman, *The Condition of England* (London, 1909), p. 76, quoted by D. Lodge, *Consciousness and the Novel* (Cambridge, MA, 2002), p. 149.

34   This was later celebrated in F. Kermode's memoir *Not Entitled* (New York, 1995), pp. 261–2. See also S. Thernstrom (ed.), *Harvard Encyclopaedia of American Ethnic Groups* (Cambridge, MA, 1980), pp. 695–7.

35   The decline of the Manx mines was a clear expulsive force and miners found new employment at Laxey and Foxdale in Ohio (on the Cornish migratory pattern).

36   Letters from the *Manx Advertiser* in the 1820s reproduced by *The Historical Society Quarterly*, 4:4 (Lake County, OH, 1962); *Annals of the Early Settlers' Association of Cuyahoga County*, 1:4 (Cleveland, 1893); *History of the Manx People who Came to America*, compiled by M. Steed (Lake County Genealogical Society, OH, 1950).

37   Most parishes (16 out of 21) reached their maximum populations in 1851 or before. The total population of the island, however, rose continuously to the end of the century, most of the increase relocated in the urban centres of Douglas and Ramsey. See A. W. Moore, *History of the Isle of Man*, 2 vols (Douglas, 1992 reprint [1900]).

38   M. W. Flinn, 'Malthus, Emigration and Potatoes in the Scottish North-west, 1770–1870', in L. M. Cullen and T. C. Smout, *Comparative Aspects of Scottish and Irish Economic and Social History, 1600–1900* (Edinburgh, 1977), p. 50.

39   See Richards, *Britannia's Children*, pp. 189 footnote, and 288. W. A. Armstrong, *Farmworkers*, says that rural emigration was not great enough in practice to produce improvements in living standards in the mid nineteenth century: 'Many farmworkers were notoriously averse to long-distance migration.' Emigration was often opposed by rural interests in the late nineteenth century. There was a widespread belief that emigration left behind the feeble minded, pp. 78–9, 107–8, 115–17 and 247.

40   Barra was a particularly good example where, between 1755 and 1821, the population doubled and continued to grow vigorously despite repeated large-scale emigrations and recurrent destitution. The landlords' policies may have contributed to the increase but, even when the landlord attitudes were reversed the surge in numbers continued. See K. Branigan *et al.*, *From Clan to Clearance. History and Archaeology on the Isle of Barra c.850–1850 AD* (Oxford, 2005), 140 ff.

41   See J. Mackay, *The Reay Fencibles* (Glasgow, 1890), and A. Mackillop's, *More*

Fruitful than the Soil: Army, Empire, and the Scottish Highlands, 1715–1815 (East Linton, 2000).

42 National Archives of Scotland, Edinburgh, Letters of Hector McDonald, Goulburn, New South Wales, from his brother Duncan, Gairloch, Ross and Cromarty, GD 1/1190/1, Murdo McDonald to Hector McDonald, 5 May 1852; Donald McDonald to Hector, 24 October 1853. For a general Malthusian interpretation of the Highland situation in the north-west Highlands, see Flinn, 'Malthus, Emigration and Potatoes'.

43 C. S. Hallas, 'Migration in Nineteenth-Century Wensleydale and Swaledale', *Northern History*, 27 (1991), pp. 141–57; C. S. Hallas, *Rural Responses to Industrialization: The North Yorkshire Pennines, 1790–1914* (Bern, 1999); C. S. Hallas, 'Poverty and Pragmatism in the Northern Uplands of England: the North Yorkshire Pennines, c.1770–1900', *Social History*, 25:1 (2000), pp. 67–84.

44 Hallas, *Rural Responses*, pp. 286–7, 293–4 and 311.

45 *Ibid.*, pp. 310 and 268.

46 See Dewey, 'Farm Labour', pp. 851–2 and 856.

47 Hallas, *Rural Responses*, p. 294.

48 E. A. Wrigley, 'Men on the Land in the Countryside: Employment in Agriculture in Early Nineteenth Century England', in Bonfield *et al.* (eds), *World We Have Gained*, pp. 295–337.

49 Richard Jefferies stands as an exemplar of the advocacy of labour migration as a vital solution for rural poverty. See E. L. Jones, 'The Land that Richard Jefferies Inherited', *Rural History*, 16:1 (2005), pp. 83–93.

CHAPTER 2

'Sprung from ourselves': British interpretations of mid-nineteenth-century racial demographics

Kathrin Levitan

In an article on the British and colonial censuses of 1861, a writer for *The Times* explained: 'As a race we assign a high place to the command to increase and multiply and replenish the earth. We consider it our vocation to people the wilderness'.[1] The recent population growth in Britain and in certain British colonies had provoked great pride, and the census seemed to quite naturally inspire such ruminations on the relation between population, race, and empire. The quotation is ambiguous, however, not only because the 'race' and the 'we' are unspecified, but because the site of population growth remains unclear. Is it in Britain that the race is multiplying, or in the 'wilderness?' How are nation and empire connected to one another, and what role do race and migration play in connecting them? Race became a widespread aspect of discourse about empire and population in the middle decades of the nineteenth century, and the census allowed people to view their empire and the world as ones in which different races competed for demographic dominance. By examining British interpretations of colonial statistics we can gain insight into the tensions within British national and imperial identity, particularly as they related to racial proportions in both metropole and colonies.

The British census, which has been conducted every ten years, beginning in 1801, played a major role in allowing people to visualise their nation in new ways. As a technology capable of describing the nation as a whole, the census allowed people to view that nation as an aggregate and at the same time to understand its population in terms of increasingly differentiated groups. By placing population at the centre of discourse about the nation, the census encouraged people to visualise groups as proportions of the whole, and the harmony of the social body as understood by many nineteenth-century observers depended primarily on the maintenance of healthy proportions of people. Discussions about the census often revolved around supposedly problematic groups such as Irish immigrants, unemployed workers, and single women, who, partly owing to their numbers, were all thought to threaten the security of the nation.

The precise borders of the nation, however, were fluid and shifting, and as global communication and migration increased during the nineteenth century, new ways of understanding those borders emerged. Britain's large, diverse, and scattered empire was also counted by census-takers, and the data, which was widely circulated and analysed in the press, helped British people to visualise their empire, like their nation, as a vast and shifting aggregate in which different kinds of people moved and interacted with one another. The census thus served as a technology that brought the empire together and helped people make sense of a world in which large-scale migration was the norm.[2] The notion that a healthy society was one made up of healthy proportions of people living together in harmony extended from Britain to the empire as a whole.

As the British public's preoccupation with class hostility began to abate after 1850, and the fear of overpopulation gradually gave way to anxiety about racial survival, the empire and its racial proportions became ever more important. Strength on the world stage, census analysts believed, would depend not only on a large and productive population at home, but on racially 'healthy' colonies. The question of how large a role race played in British people's understandings of their empire has received renewed attention since the publication of David Cannadine's *Ornamentalism: How the British Saw Their Empire*.[3] Cannadine argues that in most colonial contexts, the empire was both ruled and imagined as if it were an extension of Britain's individualised social hierarchy, and that status was as important as race in making sense of that hierarchy. Examining the census categories that British rulers created for the colonies provides a lens into this debate, because it indicates precisely what types of distinctions administrators considered important.[4] A summary of these distinctions suggests that understandings of colonial hierarchies varied greatly, and that class, race, religion, and other categories of analysis were all considered important in certain places. While Cannadine is right to insist on close examination of local hierarchies rather than broad generalisations about race, the latter did play an important role in nineteenth-century understandings of imperial populations. The details of hierarchy were different everywhere, but one way for British people to imagine their empire as a whole was in terms of racial proportions of people.[5] Migration, which allowed the British or the English 'race' to 'expand,' was central to this conception.

Until 1861, when the process was partially standardised, the population of Britain's colonies was counted sporadically. Colonial censuses were usually conducted on the initiative of the colonial governor or another local administrator, and the questions asked were dependent on local concerns.[6] For most of the first half of the nineteenth century, the censuses taken in the colonies tended to be locally oriented and thus less totalising than the metropolitan British census. But by mid-century, the empire as a whole, which was in some ways understood as a macrocosm of the nation, was coming to be seen as an aggregate that could be studied as one, and calls for a more consistent and standardised census were heard.[7] William Farr, the architect of the metropolitan mid-Victorian censuses, explained that 'it is desirable on many grounds that the population of the Queen's dominions should be enumerated simultaneously'.[8] Census Commissioner James Hammack agreed that 'by uniformity of plan, not only at home but in our colonial possessions, we might obtain results capable of being summed up for the entire British empire'.[9] According to this view, the colonies could be absorbed into the increasingly centralised metropolitan government, making the empire understandable as a single unit. In 1861 a census was taken in almost all of the colonies simultaneously, and the colonial censuses thus began to reflect not only the local dilemmas that the British faced in governing their empire, but more abstract concerns about worldwide racial demographics. This chapter demonstrates the ways in which anxieties about migration and racial proportions in the metropole were intricately connected to notions about the expansion of the race to other parts of the world. It then returns to the metropole to discuss the connection between the census and early eugenic thinking. As ideas about race circulated throughout the empire, it became clear that racial strength could be defined both through migration and other types of 'improvement'.

'Peopling the world' and the English race

In 1853, the *Manchester Guardian* wrote that Britain's enormous population increase since 1801 'indicat[ed] the transition from a kingdom to an empire'.[10] British census analysts often expressed pride in the fact that the colonies were growing and that British people were settling all over the world. At first, emigration to the colonies was considered helpful as a means of ridding Britain of its surplus population, but as Malthusian fears gradually gave way to language surrounding the reproduction of the race that was very similar to language later used by eugenicists, emigration also came to demonstrate Britain's material power and worldwide influence. The size of the empire, in terms of population as well as land and resources, was increasingly understood to mean strength in a competitive world. Even more important to observers was the fact that members of the British (or in many cases the English or the Anglo-Saxon) 'race' were being 'exported' all over the world.[11] As race became increasingly important in discussions of national strength throughout Europe, and social scientists theorised about the development and possible extinction of different races, many British people accepted the notion that their empire would be strong only if certain racial proportions existed.[12]

Census analysts were not always consistent about what kinds of demographics made the empire strong. As statistical data from the colonies began arriving in Britain more regularly during the 1830s, the most immediate response was usually simple satisfaction in the empire's size. In 1841 *The Times* wrote proudly:

> it will be found that the subjects of the British Crown are more numerous than that of any other civilised monarchy or republic on the face of the globe ... we may safely say, that Her Majesty Queen Victoria is the sovereign of a hundred millions of subjects – a larger portion of the human race than has ever obeyed any one European sovereign since the downfall of the Roman Empire.[13]

Size alone, however, was not enough to ensure the health of the empire. One way for British people to visualise their empire was as a large body, with a metropolis and extremities that all had to be in good health. This was simply the domestic social body writ large, extending over the entire world, and like British society itself the empire was thought to need appropriate proportions of people.

During the early nineteenth century, proportions were thought to be especially important in the 'settler' colonies, which could not succeed unless the settlers themselves gained a demographic advantage. It was in this context that European and non-European, or 'white' and 'black' or 'coloured' gained potency as categories for understanding the empire. In 1809 a *Quarterly Review* author described 'settlements ... [that] resemble garrisons rather than colonies; their white inhabitants forming scarcely a tenth of their total population'.[14] Seen as particularly problematic were the West Indian colonies, which had been founded by large numbers of European settlers, but as a result of the slave trade had acquired a substantial non-European majority. In Barbados, the journalist wrote, security, property, and British rule were all threatened by the disproportion, because plantation owners were sometimes forced to delegate authority to their slaves, and 'a great numerical disparity between these two classes is the worst evil that can befall the community. It has an obvious tendency to produce insurrection on one side, and harshness on the other'.[15]

[63]

But 'healthy' proportions were also needed to ensure the reproduction of the British race. In the Australian territories for example, early nineteenth-century censuses counted the numbers of convicts as compared to the numbers of 'respectable' characters. By the 1850s, Australia had a large and diverse population and a new reputation as a thriving destination for emigrants, whereby questions of racial demographics had overcome questions of criminal proportions. The various immigrants mingled with one another and with Aboriginals, who were themselves considered to be on the verge of extinction. While in some colonial contexts census-takers made detailed distinctions between people from different European countries, in the Australian colonies Europeans were described as making up a single race in terms of their likelihood to breed with one another. In a discussion of the ratio of the sexes, the many Chinese male immigrants were simply discounted; the assumption was that they would not marry white women.[16]

But in a world where many people were travelling long distances, the racial proportions were constantly shifting. If the empire was a macrocosm of the nation, and both needed healthy distributions of people, then migration was central to both national and imperial stability. By the Victorian era migration was a fact of modern life, and the 1851 census report noted that 'the Irish have entered the British population in large numbers, and great numbers of all the British races have annually left the United Kingdom; settled and multiplied into millions in the United States, in the colonies of North America, of Australia, and of South Africa'.[17] In 1861, William Farr wrote that 'the people of these islands are more moveable than other nations', and the British citizens who were living abroad at the time of the census were found 'in the strangest places'.[18]

Migration was considered necessary because it distributed labour where it was needed. Discussions of surplus, primarily during the 1820s and 1830s, often relied on the assumption that unemployment could be remedied by simply relocating people to where there was work. This was true on an empire-wide level as well as within Britain, and the importation of East Indians to the Caribbean, for example, indicates that the British government was well aware of the potential for increased productivity that such redistribution of labour could bring. But at the same time, migration caused anxiety to people who, perhaps remembering a more sedentary and local society, believed that people 'belonged' in certain places.[19] The question about birthplace, first added to the metropolitan census in 1841, reflected this anxiety, and can be understood in part as an attempt to pin down an overly mobile population. Hundreds of thousands might live in Manchester and Liverpool, but where, the census asked, were they *really* from?

Discussions of both the metropolitan and the colonial censuses constantly reflected this anxiety. Migratory or seasonal workers, for example, were considered a problem for the census-takers, because they were believed to skew the results.[20] In 1861 the *Manchester Guardian* noted that people who were leaving for the countryside at the time of the census were 'lost to the town in the numbering of the population'.[21] People often protested against these 'distortions' because they were worried about the numerical strength of various groups. But such discussions betray the assumption that constantly moving was not entirely natural, and that one of the goals of the census was to determine where people actually belonged.[22] Large towns, with people constantly coming and going, were especially confusing to those who found sedentary populations easier to understand. London, wrote Farr, 'contains natives of every county of England and Wales, of every part of the United Kingdom, and of all the principal countries of the world'. The *Manchester Guardian* chimed in that 'only 645,000 men and women would be left in London, if the 750,000 recruits marched back to their homes'.[23] Although such a statement served as an expression of pride in London's greatness, the very fact that the writer was considering the possibility of people going back 'home' is significant. While London might not have been what it was without its immigrants, those immigrants were also thought to have more genuine homes elsewhere.

The anxiety became even more acute when the migrants were of different 'races'. British understandings of race were complex and shifting, and it is evident that the word could be used in many ways. But while Victorians' use of the word was famously fluid, their understanding of an individual's race tended to be rigid: one's race certainly did not change simply by moving from one place to another. And if race was permanent then the census could be, according to some, misleading. From the very beginning of the British census, the government was interested not only in the numbers of people living on British soil, but in their origins. 'The mere population of the natives was not the only thing to be considered', one MP pointed out in 1800: 'It was well known that, for some years past, there had been a great number of foreigners in the country, who consumed their proportion of its annual produce.'[24] Fifty years later, the notion that the census ought to distinguish between natives and foreigners remained common: before the 1851 census one MP said that 'as a very great number of foreigners would probably be in London at that time, care must be taken not to include them in the census'.[25]

Within Britain, concern about migration centred primarily on poor Irish labourers, who were often thought to threaten the social and political stability of British cities. Children born in England of Irish parents, however, were registered as English in the census, because the census only asked about birthplace, not ancestry. Analysts often described this as misleading, and suggested that there was no way to determine the 'real' number of Irish people in Britain. Furthermore, the supposed Irish propensity to wander – to arrive in one city but then travel to where there was work – made them seem temporary or impermanent, and at times they were spoken of as a naturally 'migratory' people.[26] It was found that the Lancashire town of Warrington, for example, 'has also decreased in its native population, and ... the apparent increase is caused by the immense numbers of Irish who are continually passing through the borough'.[27] The other 'races' of Britain (Welsh, Scottish, Anglo-Saxon), were equally unidentifiable with the current census machinery. As Farr wrote in 1851, 'no attempt has been made to ascertain the number of the people of different races that can still be distinguished by their speech or by their characters'.[28]

Ireland's ambiguous position on the outskirts of the nation continued to place it at the centre of debates about national strength throughout the nineteenth century, and the question of racial difference remained a shifting one. Observers like James Kay, Friedrich Engels, and Thomas Carlyle believed that the Irish were racially different from and inferior to the English, but they also expressed anxiety about the possibility of these two races becoming amalgamated; the English workers, polluted by the contagion of Irish immigration, would become as bad as the Irish, and individuals would no longer be recognisable as either Irish or English. As Thomas Carlyle pointed out, 'having a white skin and European features, [the Irish] cannot be prevented from circulating among us at discretion'.[29] Census categories were one strategy used to keep the Irish separate from the English, but these categories did not quite succeed in alleviating anxiety.

Yet even though migration was problematic, it was at the same time considered necessary, because one needed to be able to transport surplus populations to where there was work.[30] Farr wrote that 'a free circulation of the people is now necessary in Great Britain, to meet the varying requirements of the Public Industry'.[31] In addition to redistributing labour where it was needed, migration could be used to manipulate racial proportions in such a way as to create healthier colonies. Finally, if race was permanent, then migration could indicate the expansion of the race and could therefore bring great pride. When the 1851 census indicated that there were more British people abroad than there were foreigners in Britain, commentators expressed satisfaction in this further proof of the size of the British population.[32] If British people remained British wherever they went, then Britain was constantly growing and expanding. This rigid understanding of race and nationality is made especially clear by British discussions of the United States.

Since the United States took its census only one year before the British did, comparisons between the two were obvious. As the *Illustrated London News* wrote in 1851, '[we can] compare their material and moral progress with our own, and ... take warning, should we on any great point find them wiser or more fortunate than ourselves'.[33] The United States held a unique place in the British imagination: no longer a colony, yet not quite foreign, this new country had 'sprung from ourselves', and the two nations were viewed as inextricably linked by language, culture, race, and economic ties.[34] British people were especially impressed by the evidence that the US census provided of astounding growth in the population and economy; growth that outstripped even that of Britain itself. The ways in which British people understood their relationship with Americans were complex and multifaceted. But it is clear that British people tended to view not only white settlers in their own colonies but also white Americans as extensions of themselves. The United States had been founded by British settlers – had been settled in the same way that the British were now continuing to settle Canada, Australia, New Zealand and Southern Africa. Thus, British discussions of their empire during the Victorian period often blurred the distinction between their own colonies and the English-speaking world more generally. The British press spoke of 'emigration which has spread our race and language over half the world', and while independent for many years, the United States was included in this conception.[35]

While economic and demographic competition was strong between Britain and the United States, British people were also proud of US growth. If Britain was to be surpassed as the nation with the fastest growing population and economy, it was best that the country surpassing it was the one most closely tied to Britain. 'The survivors and descendants of the races' made the British population even larger, even if those descendants were by now in the United States, and a large American population was therefore a source of satisfaction.[36] As the *Westminster Review* remarked:

> in surveying the progress of our state and nation, we cannot throw aside our brethren's interests and honours, as a bad government threw off their allegiance and duty; and when we have to tell of advance and improvement at home, we have hearty pleasure in showing the far more striking progress of those who are placed in a newer position, and under fresher influences, than ourselves.[37]

If British emigrants were still British, whether they settled in the colonies or the United States, then the vast numbers of people leaving the British Isles during the period from 1820 through 1860 could be considered not a loss, but a success of 'colonisation'. The 1851 census report asserted that emigration 'cannot exhaust the vast resources of these islands, but will rather extend, as they have done hitherto, the commerce, manufactures, and numbers of the nation from which they sprang, and from which they can never be divided in interest, language, or affection', and 'armies of peaceful emigrants from the United Kingdom every year crossed the Atlantic in increasing numbers to swell the States' Census'.[38] The 1861 report explained that 'to determine the increase of the English race the emigrants must be taken into account'.[39] And in 1853, a *Manchester Guardian* report on the census expanded on the same theme:

> Contemporaneously with the increase of the population at home, emigration has preceded since 1750 to such an extent, as to people large states in America, and to give permanent possessors and cultivators to the land of large colonies in all the temperate regions of the world, where, by a common language, commercial relations, and the multiplied reciprocities of industry, the people of the new nations maintain an indissoluble union with the parent country.[40]

When British writers emphasised their connection with the United States they rhetorically enhanced the strength of their empire. In 1851 a journalist for *The Times* wrote, 'with North America and many other portions of the earth's surface occupied by our own flesh and blood, speaking our language and inheriting our laws, if not our allegiance, we must ever occupy an honourable and useful position'.[41] And the image of Britain as the mother country was taken seriously and was frequently repeated. The article explained that 'the results of the British and of the American census ... bring this relation of the parent State and her numerous progeny into unusual prominence ... We can never forget that it is an Anglo-Saxon population which is thus expanding itself, and that the laws and language of the new Empire have descended from our own.'[42]

While British commentators were sometimes vague when praising American population growth, they clearly viewed only white Americans as descendants of the British. In a discussion of the US census of 1850, *The Times* explained that if the black population was subtracted from the total:

> this would leave the American citizens of British or other European extraction about 20,000,000. It thus appears that there are about 52,000,000 persons of British extraction, or of some other European race amalgamated with them, occupying the best geographical positions in the world, possessing the largest maritime trade and the most profitable

manufactures, enjoying the freest institutions, commanding the vastest extents of fertile territory and the finest climates, and receiving the services of many millions of useful auxiliaries, of various races and hues, living either in comfortable slavery, or willing subjection, or dignified alliance.[43]

Such hyperbole regarding the empire is familiar to historians of Victorian Britain. But this particular interpretation of the numbers augmented the British Empire by many millions, bringing satisfaction to imperialists and indicating that certain kinds of racial categories were at least in this context trumping political or geographical categories. Yet while the British constantly pointed out that race was one of the things that they shared with the United States, this emphasis belied the radically different racial situations in the two countries. The United States, although initially settled by British people and sharing language as well as other perceived cultural characteristics with the mother country, had its political independence and in some people's minds, its own political and social disgrace in the form of slavery. Thus, statistics of race were another aspect of the US census that was of great interest to British people. The British recognised that rates of regional population growth and racial proportions in the United States would have profound implications as tensions over slavery grew.[44]

Both the British government and the wider public participated in discussions of American racial statistics.[45] Some people in Britain were opposed to slavery not only because of its moral questionability but because they believed that a large proportion of black people were a threat to order. Black people, wrote an author for the *Quarterly Review* in 1845, are 'elements of discrepancy in the composition of a state. The coloured race pervades the whole Union, and being more equally spread, the virus may be considered as diluted by diffusion.'[46] The only cause for relief seemed to be that whites were increasing faster than blacks were (because of immigration). Current ideas about racial survival and extinction suggested that if blacks were not as demographically significant as whites they would not survive as a major element in the population. We can see how the British concern with social harmony and their anxiety about maintaining correct proportions influenced their understandings of the demographic situation in the United States. It is also clear that as tensions grew and the American Civil War began, much of the British public saw itself as deeply implicated in events across the Atlantic. As the *Leicester Guardian* wrote in September of 1861, 'every tide of events [in the United States] have been anxiously watched, and that not on account of the great commercial interests involved but a feeling that those taking part in the contest are bone of our bone and flesh of our flesh'.[47]

The emphasis on shared race blurred the lines between mother country and colonies, nation-state and empire. The US racial situation was, at least on the surface, more comparable to the situation in the British Empire as a whole than it was to Britain itself. Yet here too, things were different, because the abolition of slavery in the British colonies had occurred in 1833. And if Britons were always ready to express pride and complacency in their empire, they also had anxieties about it, particularly in regard to the economic plight of their West Indian colonies. The decrease in productivity there since abolition helped to gradually change British ideas about race, as a liberal concept of the equality of all races largely gave way after 1850 to an idea of the inherent inferiority of non-whites.[48] Economic competition with the United States was therefore inevitably tied up with the issue of slavery. While many British people saw their own nation as the morally superior one, the question of black productivity was thought to be very much unresolved. Furthermore, by the 1850s cries for political representation were being heard both at home and in the colonies, and numbers again played an obvious role. The large black majority in Jamaica and other West Indian colonies seemed, to many British people, to forecast political and economic chaos. After the Jamaica rebellion of 1865 the shift in attitudes towards race seemed to be complete, and British colonial policy shifted in tandem.[49] The centrality of representation and power in the US census, therefore, spoke to British concerns about their political system at home and in the colonies. The United States, with its peculiar circumstances arising from slavery as well as its historical and economic ties to Britain, could serve as a mirror – albeit a distorted one – for anxieties about race and labour within Britain's post-abolition empire.

What was clear to British imperialists was that the empire provided great opportunities for racial expansion in addition to military, political, and commercial expansion. The 1851 census, wrote the *Illustrated London News*, would reveal statistics of emigration, colonisation, and manufactures 'which carry our name, and fame, and usefulness to the remotest regions of the globe'.[50] And in these remote regions, 'there is so much waste and unoccupied land yet, that it is rather to be described as an untenanted wilderness than overcrowded with human beings'.[51] Thus, by the time that a large population had come to be considered positive, the immense population increases at home and abroad were thought to complement one another and together to contribute to Britain's greatness. This was an image of an empire (and a former empire, in the case of the United States), that was united by free trade capitalism as well as a shared culture and race. In 1854 Farr remarked proudly that 'the United Kingdom is now covered by *twenty-eight millions of people*; and has thrown out towards the west a long line of colonies, and independent states, that speak her language, that preserve the purity of the English family, that have lost none of the courage or industry of their race'.[52] It was a goal 'that the British race, growing better and greater, may increase in numbers at home, and continue to send out every year thousands of new families to the colonies'.[53] Population growth at home and abroad was one and the same. The domestic discourse of proportions was thus reproduced both on the level of individual colonies, and also on the level of the empire and even the world as a whole.

The discussion of racial proportions happened in the context of broader debates about the nature of empire. If, as many Britons argued, the colonies should be self-sufficient, then settlers would need to be able to defend themselves and cultivate the land. After the Indian rebellion of 1857 it became evident that the existing policy of ruling millions of potentially hostile subjects with only tens of thousands of British men was no longer safe for the government. So, just as the renewed international tension of the early 1850s brought a large domestic population back into favour, problems of governance in the colonies helped transform emigration and settlement from a mode of disposing of surplus to a signpost of national strength. Yet despite the general shift towards the embrace of a large population, the British did not completely give up their faith in emigration either as a means of redistributing surplus labour or of disposing of those who were considered incurably unproductive. In 1861 *The Times* wrote that 'vast cities have risen up in the Antipodes, peopled by men and women who would otherwise have pressed on the common resources of home'.[54] And, as is evident in discussions surrounding the census, some elements of the English race were thought to be of higher quality than others.

The strength of races and the improvement of the English race

This chapter has argued that many British observers took their expanding empire to mean not only military strength, but racial strength, and by the 1850s discussions of the relative strength of different races were common in the British press. While the easiest way to maintain the strength of the race, however defined, was through targeted migration and manipulation of racial proportions, statisticians were also very interested in the possibilities that selective breeding held. Census questions about health and disabilities as well as numbers more generally addressed both the quality and quantity of different races, and census-takers, who combined knowledge of population with a concern about the strength of the nation, often found the shift to eugenic thinking an easy one.

From the very beginning of the nineteenth century, foreign census results were reported in the press and the assumption was that censuses demonstrated the relative strength of different nations. The first British census was taken, in large part, to determine such strength, both military and agricultural. At the same time, it was evident that some people were better for the nation than others, and a large population could only be viewed as positive if the majority was both productive and peaceful. The concept of surplus arose simultaneously with the census, and as the census expanded, it became clear that national strength could be determined not only through numbers but through physical and moral characteristics. The census could, and did, gather information about more than population, even as population remained central to ideas of national strength.

The relationship between quality and quantity was complicated and contradictory. In many contexts, national and racial strength continued to be defined in terms of population. As Malthusian fears of surplus ebbed in the 1840s, it became common to compare the population growth of Britain with its two greatest rivals, France and the United States. 'We have been struck', the *Manchester Guardian* wrote, 'with the different ratios of progress in the population of the three most civilised and most powerful nations in the world.'[55] According to the censuses, the American population was increasing the fastest, the French population the slowest. Since American growth was considered positive in Britain because of the perceived racial connection between the two nations, the comparison sparked unqualified feelings of superiority: the Anglo-Saxons were gaining strength while their age-old rivals on the continent were weakening. The English press, however, often made such favourable comparisons specifically between England and France, and chose to ignore Scotland and Ireland, both of which had lost population in recent years. Commentators dismissed especially Ireland as a special case that did not reflect the greatness of the nation as a whole. In this context, it was not the political entity of the United Kingdom that was important, but the English race.[56]

William Farr was especially fond of comparing British industrial and urban growth with French stagnation. In addition to the standard moral objections to birth control that were common in Britain, Farr condemned it on the grounds of national and racial strength. But Farr also recognised the possibility of improving the vigour of the nation through means other than that of population growth. People who worked with the census had the potential to turn into social engineers because of the very nature of their work. Information was being gathered not simply for the sake of knowledge, but so the society could be improved. This improvement was to be primarily social, economic, and moral, not racial. But if different groups of people were understood to have inherent traits and capabilities, it was easy to make the shift. After studying the 1851 census results on occupation, Farr mused that people who worked with animals were 'altogether a peculiar race of men; silent, circumspect, prompt, agile, dexterous, enduring, danger-defying men . . . By their habits many of the class must be well adapted to the purposes of war; they are sometimes idle, and in a militia they could be turned to account.'[57] The example suggests that Farr saw the possibility of rendering unproductive people productive, primarily through an understanding and employment of their supposedly natural capacities.

The census was also linked to conceptions of physical fitness, in part because of the public health movement and the prominence of physicians in the statistical movement. By the 1830s, the suggestion had been raised that the working classes, because of their poor living conditions, were becoming a weak and unhealthy 'race'. The fear was not only for their own welfare, but for the future strength of the country, which depended on the labour and fighting ability of healthy people. Friedrich Engels wrote in 1844 that bad food was causing the 'enfeeblement of the whole race of workers'.[58] When Hector Gavin published his survey of workers' housing in 1850, he suggested that urban men were feebler than country men, and were thus less fit to fight in wars.[59] In the 1851 census report, which was widely quoted in the press, Farr wrote that 'extensive sanatory [sic] arrangements, and all the appliances of physical as well as of social science, are necessary to preserve the natural vigour of the population, and to develop the inexhaustible resources of the English race'.[60] For Farr, disease was not a providential obstacle to overpopulation, but a precursor to racial decline and even racial extinction.[61] If deaths were reduced, on the other hand – eminently possible to Farr's thinking – then the society could 'increase the vigour (may I not add the industry and wealth?) of the population . . ., for diseases are the iron index of misery, which recedes before strength, health, and happiness, as the mortality declines'.[62] Farr urged public health on the grounds that it would 'strengthen, and . . . improve the English race'.[63]

Questions of strength also took on more explicitly racial aspects. As early as the first decade of its existence, the Royal Statistical Society was interested in the relative height, weight, and physical strength of the English, Scots, and Irish. The 1851 census showed that the 'Celtic' race was declining in Scotland and Ireland, and one observer took this as 'an illustration of the general fact, of which the slow increase of the liberated African in the United States is another illustration, that an inferior race of men can only be sustained in conjunction

[73]

with a superior race, by being taken under its especial care'.[64] As Patrick Brantlinger has argued, the notion of extinction was central to Victorian understandings of race, and the conception of the superiority of certain races relied on both quantity and quality. Farr wrote in the 1851 report that 'the character of every race of men is the real limit to its numbers in the world'.[65]

The capacity of the census to gather detailed information about both the physical and moral traits of the population was certainly recognised, although it was not put into practice to the extent that some would have liked. In 1860 the Home Secretary, Sir G. C. Lewis, spoke teasingly of 'one enthusiastic ethnographer [who] was anxious to have returns of the number of people with different coloured hair, that some idea might be formed of the relative proportion of the Saxon and Danish races'.[66] The possibility of selective breeding was also recognised. In an 1836 letter about the Poor Law, the Assistant Commissioner for Suffolk and Norfolk, Dr James Kay wrote: 'in the absence of the workhouse system, and under the encouragement of out[door relief] allowance, marriages would occur among epileptics, cripples, the victims of scrofula, and depravity – the aged and helpless would continue to marry young women, and propagate a miserable off-spring'.[67] In the midst of medical debates about the nature of hereditary disease, Farr wrote that improvements in animal breeding were related to the science of population, and that those studying human heredity could draw inspiration from those who were involved in the breeding of livestock.[68] Farr wanted a register of sick and insane people within Britain, as well as information about the physical characteristics of different races within the empire.[69] He used statistics about disabilities in order to compare the health of different regions and countries. And it was not only that the unhealthy ought not to reproduce; interracial mixing could also, potentially, harm the future of the English race. At one point, Farr reassured his readers that, 'Scotchmen, leaving their fair countrywomen behind them, marry English wives, under the English marriage law; to which no exception can be taken in England, as neither race thereby suffers any deterioration.'[70]

Racial degeneration, however, according to Farr's understanding, could occur through circumstances as well as biology. Farr believed that even strong and healthy races could degenerate in tropical climates and in other unhealthy places, presumably including unsanitary cities in Britain.[71] Like many nineteenth-century social scientists, Farr also believed that morality and level of civilisation were affected by climate. Thus, a detrimental environment joined interracial sex and the reproduction of unfit people as possible dangers to the future of the race. The premise behind all of this discussion was that manipulating racial proportions was possible, whether by controlling migration or reproduction.[72] What Farr ultimately wanted would encompass both of these things:

> the strength, the rate of increase, and the colonization now proceeding can be sustained by the marriages of only a part of the population; hence ... If by any judicious means the increase of the incurably criminal, idle, insane, idiotic, or unhappily organised parts of the population can be, without cruelty, repressed, ... the character and good qualities of the race will be immeasurably improved, without checking the tide of population or the increase of numbers. Hitherto the flower of the British youth has been in ignorance sent to the alluvial lands of the tropics, where our race cannot live, or where it is inevitably degenerated, while, in defiance of the principles of physiology, and of the doctrines that are inculcated on the breeders of the inferior animals by the Royal Agricultural Society, – convicts have been thrown broadcast over some of the healthiest colonies in the world, and may now, without due precaution, multiply at home ... and prove a leaven of social disorder and disorganisation.[73]

Since Farr specifically mentioned the possibility of cruelty he clearly understood the more sinister implications of eugenics. But Farr believed that just as the nation ought to take control of its own public health, the 'biological future' was also subject to human control.[74] Reproduction, he thought, could and ought to be controlled for social ends. Farr believed that 'to a nation of good and noble men Death is a less evil than Degradation of Race'.[75] And a wise legislature 'deems the physical perfection of the people the sole basis of their moral and intellectual greatness'.[76]

For the most part, Farr saw the information he gathered as a cause for pride rather than alarm; the pessimism of the late nineteenth century was yet to come. But Farr also believed that there was always room for improvement, and in Eyler's words, he 'essentially welcomed the competition between races as leading towards the overall elevation of humanity'.[77] Eugenics, it is clear, could be mobilised in the service of optimism as well as pessimism, and census-takers were well placed to act as agents in this process. Ian Hacking suggests that the role statistics has always played in distinguishing the 'normal' from the 'non-normal' meant that statistical reasoning was greatly implicated in the rise of eugenics. According to him, 'statistics of populations and of deviancy form an integral part of the industrial state'.[78] The census was also implicated in eugenics because of its long-standing association with surplus, productivity, and proportions. The census not only distinguished the positive from the negative, it defined these categories as proportions of the national and imperial population.

[75]

Conclusion

There were many reasons why eugenics became popular in the middle and late nineteenth century, but for the purposes of this study let us tentatively suggest that as the empire became less peripheral to British society it also became harder to deal with problem populations by simply sending them to the empire. Australians of European descent no longer wanted to be associated with a remote convict settlement; they preferred to see themselves as a prosperous and respectable colony that was mainly white and was central to the empire. Some way other than sending 'surplus' populations abroad thus had to be found to improve the British population and to deal with the undesirables. The discourse about healthy proportions in the metropole was gradually applied to the very places that had traditionally been part of the 'solution' to domestic problem populations, opening up the need for a new kind of solution in Britain.

If the census was a tool of governmental and extra-governmental power, it in some ways reached its most extreme form of that power in the colonies. Nineteenth-century British administrators often described the census as central to technological progress and modernity, and saw themselves at the vanguard of a European project to spread science throughout the wider world. Farr declared grandly that 'the English occupy, fortunately for science, a large portion of the finest parts of the world; and ... they are, like every governing race, statistical'.[79] The colonies could be used as a site for the government and others to experiment with technologies and methods that would not have been accepted in Britain.[80] Finally, there was an implicit alliance between the colonial populations and the British people, both elite and non-elite, who viewed governmental activities such as the census with suspicion. People who opposed the census during the nineteenth century did not necessarily foresee the census leading to a form of population control such as eugenics, but they did believe that the census contributed to problems of alienation and surveillance that they associated with the modern economy and state. And in hindsight, eugenics can be seen as one possible end of the road that census opponents described: they worried about the census's focus on the health of the collectivity and on its inability to devote attention to individuals.

The censuses in the colonies raised questions about racial proportions that were directly related to concerns about proportions of people 'at home'. Irish migrants in Britain, for example, came to be understood as a racialised underclass, who suggested that the borders of Britain and Britishness were becoming dangerously fuzzy. Inside the ambiguous relationship between Britain and Ireland, therefore, was the fear that the colony might colonise the metropole. At the same time, British people were leaving the metropole to settle elsewhere, in the colonies and also in the United States. In the colonies, the metropolitan concern about the threat to racial purity was translated into concerns about racial proportions, in part because certain demographic proportions were needed to ensure the future of colonial rule.

While the census did different kinds of work in Britain and in the colonies, the various sites do need to be understood in a single framework. The racial distinctions that mattered were different everywhere; the differences between English, Scottish, and Irish, for example, became far less important in a context where Europeans were trying to gain a demographic advantage over non-Europeans.[81] But the future of the 'race', whether defined in terms of its Englishness, Britishness, or Europeanness, seemed ensured by colonial settlement and reproduction both in the colonies and in the United States. As ideas of racial competition and survival became more central, both the administration and interpretation of the census reflected the ideological shift. While earlier census-takers had had a wide range of categories available to them, and were as likely to describe people by occupation or religion as by race or nationality, the censuses of the 1860s brought race to the forefront. In as diverse a configuration as the British Empire, race could play a unifying role, making the whole thing complete and recognisable, and allowing observers to focus on simple questions, such as how many British people there were in comparison to non-British people. The idea of Britishness, of course, could be defined in cultural, political, or linguistic terms as well as in racial terms. But the image of the mother country and its 'progeny' most often relied on a notion of blood ties that survived changes of place and were extended through biological reproduction. Migration was threatening and helpful for the same reason: people could move but they could not change their innate origin. It was not only the colonies, then, that were 'sprung from ourselves', but the anxieties about healthy proportions as well.

Notes

1   *The Times* (14 June 1861), p. 8.
2   On the debate between those who believe the empire was distant to most of the British public, and those who believe it was central to understandings of class and nationhood at home, see B. Porter, *The Absent-Minded Imperialists* (Oxford, 2004). Also see A. Burton's review in *Victorian Studies*, 47:4 (2005), pp. 626–8.
3   D. Cannadine, *Ornamentalism: How the British Saw Their Empire* (Oxford, 2001). A notable absence in Cannadine's book is analysis of the West Indian colonies, where racial proportions were considered more important than racial proportions in most other parts of the Empire.
4   While administrators' choices do not allow us to draw conclusions about the wider

British public's view of their colonies, the results of the colonial censuses were widely publicised in Britain. Any reader of a daily newspaper would have been aware of both metropolitan and colonial census statistics, and the great attention that major newspapers devoted to the census indicates its centrality to nineteenth-century understandings of nation and empire. See K. Levitan, *A Cultural History of the British Census: Envisioning the Multitude in the Nineteenth Century* (New York, 2011), chapter one, for more on the census and the public sphere.

5   Although I address the ways in which the census affected British understandings of imperial demographics, colonial census-taking also affected the lives and the identities of colonial subjects. Unlike in Britain, where some sections of the public played an increasingly active role in the development of the census, in most of the colonies the general population had far less control. D. Kertzer and D. Arel argue that 'what distinguished colonial from non-colonial censuses ... was that the formulation of categories in the colonies was unilaterally done by the ruling officials, while European categories of cultural nationality and language were already being negotiated, to some extent, with social groups'. D. I. Kertzer and D. Arel (eds), *Census and Identity: The Politics of Race, Ethnicity, and Language in National Censuses* (Cambridge, 2002), p. 10. In his study of the census in India, Bernard Cohn argues that the objectification of Indian culture that the censuses taken by the British represented affected the ways in which Indians understood their own history and society, and helped make Indian society objective to Indians. B. Cohn, 'The Census, Social Structure and Objectification in South Asia,' in his *An Anthropologist among the Historians and Other Essays* (New York, 1987), p. 229. Also see A. Appadurai, 'Number in the Colonial Imagination', in Carol Breckenridge and Peter van der Veer (eds), *Orientalism and the Postcolonial Predicament: Perspectives on South Asia* (Philadelphia, 1993), pp. 314–39. Scholars have also noted that colonial censuses helped to create national identities that contributed to colonial nationalist movements. See Kertzer and Arel, *Census and Identity*, p. 32.

6   As C. A. Bayly demonstrates in his book about information gathering in British India, the processes by which colonial administrators obtained data relied on local cooperation and methods. C. A. Bayly, *Empire and Information: Intelligence Gathering and Social Communication in India, 1780–1870* (Cambridge, 1996).

7   The technical difficulties of taking a census under such radically different circumstances as the British Empire represented were immense. In 1842, the government gathered a summary of the population and trade of all the 'foreign possessions of the British Crown'. The population was only counted afresh in a few colonies, however; elsewhere it was simply taken from the most recent census. The results, then, were far from standard or comparable. The National Archives, London (hereafter TNA), Alex S. Allan papers, PRO 30/2/3/14, 'Return Relative to the Population and Trade of the Colonies or Foreign Possessions of the British Crown' (1842).

8   *Census of England and Wales for the year 1861: General Report*, 3 (London, 1863), p. 72.

9   'On the Direction in which the Census Inquiry may be extended in 1861', *Transactions of the National Association for the Promotion of Social Science*, 3 (1859), p. 708.

10   *Manchester Guardian* (23 November 1853), p. 4.

11   English writers often used the words 'British' and 'English' interchangeably. While it was usually specifically the 'English', or the 'Anglo-Saxon' race that they were interested in, they often replaced these words with 'British'.

12   For the notion that certain races were doomed to extinction see P. Brantlinger, *Dark Vanishings: Discourse on the Extinction of Primitive Races, 1800–1930* (Ithaca, 2003).

13   *The Times* (29 October 1841), p. 7.

14   *Quarterly Review*, 1 (1809), p. 263.

15   *Ibid.*, p. 266.

16   See *The Times* (31 August 1857), p. 9.

17   *The Census of Great Britain in 1851 ... Reprinted in a Condensed Form* (London, 1854), p. 5.
18   *Census of England ... 1861*, p. 4.
19   See K. D. M. Snell, *Parish and Belonging: Community, Identity and Welfare in England and Wales, 1700–1950* (Cambridge, 2006) for analysis of the phenomenon of 'belonging'.
20   In 1850 one MP worried that the Irish census would not be comparable with earlier ones because more Irish would be at home in March than in July, when many of them were away harvesting in England. *Hansard's Parliamentary Debates*, 3rd series, vol. 113 (23 July 1850), col. 138.
21   *Manchester Guardian* (6 May 1861), p. 4.
22   In reality, people of many social classes travelled a great deal in Victorian Britain; the wealthy were as likely to be away from home on extended social visits as labourers were to be searching for work. But because of pervasive fears about vagrancy and crime, concern tended to focus on the working poor.
23   *The Census of Great Britain in 1851 ... Reprinted in a Condensed Form*, p. 76; *Manchester Guardian* (16 August 1854), p. 10.
24   *Parliamentary Register* (1800), p. 196. The first census-takers were concerned about foreigners because Britain was at war with France, and they were worried about Jacobins and spies entering the country.
25   *Hansard's Parliamentary Debates*, 3rd series, vol. 111 (6 June 1850), col. 871.
26   *Quarterly Review*, 76 (1845), p. 16.
27   *Manchester Guardian* (30 April 1851), p. 6.
28   *The Census of Great Britain in 1851 ... Reprinted in a Condensed Form*, p. 73.
29   Quoted in T. C. Holt, *The Problem of Freedom: Race, Labor and Politics in Jamaica and Britain, 1823–1938* (Baltimore, 1992), p. 282.
30   *Manchester Guardian* (23 November 1853), p. 4.
31   *The Census of Great Britain in 1851 ... Reprinted in a Condensed Form*, p. 77. An increased knowledge of one's own country and potentially one's empire was also coming to be understood as positive because such knowledge could create and maintain national unity. As a result of migration 'the whole of the inhabitants will gradually grow acquainted with the different parts of their native land, to which, as well as to the town or village of their birth, it is desirable that the people of the United Kingdom should be attached'. *Ibid.*
32   *Manchester Guardian* (16 August 1854), p. 10.
33   *Illustrated London News* (5 April 1851), p. 263.
34   *Ibid.*
35   'Results of the Census of 1851', *Westminster Review*, 61 (1854), p. 347.
36   *The Census of Great Britain in 1851 ... Reprinted in a Condensed Form*, p. 6.
37   'Results of the Census of 1851', p. 344.
38   *The Census of Great Britain in 1851 ... Reprinted in a Condensed Form*, pp. 42 and 52.
39   *Census of England ... 1861*, p. 5.
40   *Manchester Guardian* (14 September 1853), p. 6.
41   *The Times* (18 June 1851), p. 5.
42   *Ibid.*
43   *Ibid.*
44   Unlike the early censuses in Europe, the American census was from its origin explicitly linked to political representation, for the states acquired representatives based on their population. Slavery was written into this system via the 3/5 law, whereby slaves counted as 3/5 the population of free people. During the 1840s and 1850s the American census showed a rapidly increasing population in the North and in the new Western states, and a relatively stagnant South. During the 1850s, the census was seen as an enemy of the South because it indicated the Southern loss of power. In the new states of the West, the proportions of slaveholders and abolitionists would determine whether the state became a free or a slave state, so census results were anxiously awaited. Within the United States, the census was therefore

increasingly associated with disunity and sectional crisis. At the same time, the census was seen as a potential aid in reuniting the country. US census administrator Charles Kennedy said in 1862 that 'the truth as presented by the census, will teach us the importance of union and harmony, and stimulate a proper pride in the country and people as one and indivisible'. Quoted in M. Anderson, *The American Census: A Social History* (New Haven, 1988), p. 68. But whether the census was a symbol of division or harmony, the importance of population to understandings of the struggle between North and South can be demonstrated by a verse of Yankee Doodle, printed in 1865 in a *Times* article about popular Southern songs: 'Yankee Doodle said he found/ By all the census figures,/ That he could starve the rebels out,/ If he could steal their niggers./ Yankee Doodle, doodle-do,/ Yankee Doodle dandy,/ And then he took another drink/ Of Gunpowder and brandy. *The Times* (30 May 1865), p. 6.

45 See *Manchester Guardian* (22 February 1851), p. 5.
46 *Quarterly Review*, 76 (1845), p. 23.
47 *Leicester Guardian* (9 September 1861), cited in R. J. M Blackett, *Divided Hearts: Britain and the American Civil War* (Baton Rouge, 2001), p. 6.
48 See C. Hall, K. McClelland and J. Rendall (eds), *Defining the Victorian Nation: Class, Race, Gender and the Reform Act of 1867* (Cambridge, 2000), pp. 191–2.
49 *Ibid.*, pp. 192–204.
50 *Illustrated London News* (5 April 1851), p. 263.
51 *Ibid.* (28 June 1851), p. 624.
52 *The Census of Great Britain in 1851 . . . Reprinted in a Condensed Form*, p. 56.
53 *Ibid.*
54 *The Times* (14 June 1861), p. 8.
55 See *Manchester Guardian* (16 April 1845), p. 3.
56 *Ibid.* (28 June 1854), p. 10.
57 *The Census of Great Britain in 1851 . . . Reprinted in a Condensed Form*, p. 67.
58 Friedrich Engels, 'The Condition of the Working Class in England', in K. Marx and F. Engels, *On Britain* (Moscow, 1953), p. 135.
59 H. Gavin, *The Habitations of the Industrial Classes: Their Influence on the Physical and on the Social and Moral Conditions of these Classes . . . being an address delivered at Crosby Hall, November 27th, 1850* (London, 1851), p. 64. During the 1850s, fighting gained renewed importance because of the Crimean War (1854–56) and because of a sense that strong British soldiers were needed to protect the empire, especially after the rebellions in India and Jamaica.
60 *The Census of Great Britain in 1851 . . . Reprinted in a Condensed Form*, p. 26.
61 J. Eyler, *Victorian Social Medicine: The Ideas and Methods of William Farr* (Baltimore, 1999), p. 156.
62 Quoted in *ibid.*, p. 124.
63 Quoted in *ibid.*, p. 153.
64 *Illustrated London News* (28 June 1851), p. 624.
65 *The Census of Great Britain in 1851 . . . Reprinted in a Condensed Form*, p. 55. See Brantlinger, *Dark Vanishings*.
66 *Hansard's Parliamentary Debates*, 3rd series, vol. 160 (24 July 1860), col. 83. The International Statistical Congresses did recommend that European censuses ask about language and other identifiers of 'nationality', but British census-takers, for the most part did not see such issues as important.
67 TNA, Lord John Russell papers, PRO 30/22/2F, fol. 282, Kay to G. C. Lewis, 'On the Cause of the Efficacy of Workhouses, and on the Out-door Relief of the Impotent Poor', 19 July 1836. This was the same G. C. Lewis, the future Home Secretary mentioned above, who at this time was a leading expert on the Irish problem, and later distinguished himself as a Poor Law Commissioner between 1839 and 1847. His father Thomas F. Lewis was chairman of the Poor Law Commission (1834–39).
68 *The Census of Great Britain in 1851 . . . Reprinted in a Condensed Form*, p. 52; *Census of England . . . 1861*, p. 56.
69 Eyler, *Victorian Social Medicine*, p. 155.
70 *The Census of Great Britain in 1851 . . . Reprinted in a Condensed Form*, p. 74.

71 Eyler, *Victorian Social Medicine*, p. 156.
72 *Census of England . . . 1861*, p. 7.
73 *The Census of Great Britain in 1851 . . . Reprinted in a Condensed Form*, p. 42.
74 Eyler, *Victorian Social Medicine*, p. 156.
75 Quoted in *ibid*.
76 Quoted in *ibid*, p. 157. See *William Farr, 1807–1883. The Report of the Centenary Symposium held at the Royal Society on 29 April 1983* (London, 1983), p. 7, for an opposing view about Farr's interest in eugenics.
77 Eyler, *Victorian Social Medicine*, p. 157.
78 I. Hacking, 'How Should We Do the History of Statistics?', in G. Burchell, C. Gordon and P. Miller (eds), *The Foucault Effect: Studies in Governmentality* (Chicago, 1991), p. 183.
79 Quoted in Eyler, *Victorian Social Medicine*, p. 35.
80 The censuses in Canada, Australia and New Zealand developed differently from the censuses in places with indigenous majorities. While local populations had little control over the census in India and Africa, settler populations with representative assemblies gained increasing independence in census-taking. The Canadian census reports, for example, which were written and published by local authorities, suggest that administrators in the colonies often understood their censuses to be serving a similar nation-building role as the census in Britain served; bringing satisfaction and a sense of unity to settlers. See TNA, Colonial Office papers, CO 229/34, 'Abstract of the Census of The Population and other Statistical Returns'. Prince Edward Island, *Sessional Papers* (1861).
81 On the other hand, as Cannadine argues, some colonies saw an entirely different situation evolve, where metropolitan class hierarchies were replicated to form a complex set of alliances between colonial officials and local indigenous elites.

CHAPTER 3

Religious nationalism and clerical emigrants to Australia, 1828–1900

Hilary M. Carey

This chapter addresses one of the thornier problems in the history of emigration and colonisation to the British settler colonies, namely why did Australians remain attached to Britain for so long? Historians have rightly stressed that the nature of the relationship between Australia and Britain was one of contestation and insecurity as well as emulation and adulation, a reflection of the cultural and emotional tussle that afflicted those who sought to build a new colonial society while remaining citizens of a wider empire.[1] However, there has been less success in attempting to identify the sources for the cultural and emotional bonds to the British homeland which endured for well over a century after the Australian colonies became more or less self-governing. While it is clear that cultural institutions such as the monarchy and sport have been at least as influential as political, military and economic ones such as the constitution, Parliament, and the legal and monetary systems, we really know very little about the way in which such complex discourses were transplanted from British to colonial soil. Like the English language, it is generally assumed that adherence to Britain was part of the invisible cultural baggage that emigrants stowed away without the need for particular mechanisms of transference and control.

The plan here is to take a rather different approach to this question, focusing on one of the most important (but generally underestimated) of all British colonial institutions, namely the emigrant churches. Although the story of the dependence of Australian Catholics on Irish émigré clergy has been well studied, to the extent that the contribution of other ethnic groups to the Catholic community and of the large number of Irish who contributed to Australia's Protestant churches tends to be overlooked,[2] it is less well known that all the major churches were heavily dependent on British-born clergy until well into the twentieth century. This chapter provides an analysis of some of the consequences of this patterning of ethnicity, profession and religion, which would appear to be unmatched by few other professions or migrant groups who came to the Australian colonies.[3] It is argued that clergy were one of the key components in the transmission of a sense of British identity to churchgoing Australians, and that their role makes explicable the surge of empire-mindedness at the time of the federation of the Australian colonies in 1901. Yet, as with other cultural institutions, the influence of religion did not act entirely in one direction from metropole to colony but rather, as Catherine Hall has emphasised, drawing on the work of Frantz Fanon, colonial subjects and objects were 'mutually constituted' and to some extent create each other.[4] To what extent was religion used to reinforce the loyalty of colonists in the way that Hamish Ion has argued was axiomatic for the British defence forces?[5]

To address these questions, this chapter is divided into four sections: the first section gives an account of the historical background to religious emigration from the British Isles and the responses of the churches to the crisis of personnel created by mass migration; the second section considers the role of colonial missionary societies in promoting religion and imperial loyalty; the third looks at the characteristics of clerical migrants to the Australian colonies of New South Wales (NSW) and Victoria as their numbers peaked in the 1880s and 1890s; the final section looks at the development of colonial religious nationalism, typically ardently patriotic to Britain, as this is reflected in church periodicals in the colonies.

Emigration and the churches

Until the middle decades of the nineteenth century, it was felt that there was little urgency in providing for the religious needs of British overseas colonies. In the course of the colonisation of North America, dissenting colonists provided for themselves in scornful defiance of the established church while Anglicans made do with chaplains supplied by the Society for the Propagation of the Gospel (SPG).[6] The deficiencies of this system are one factor in the relative decline of Episcopalianism in North America, in contrast to the vigorous growth of other Protestant churches such as Baptists, Wesleyan Methodists and Independents or Congregationalists. American colonists were profoundly suspicious of religious overtures from Britain which were associated with the advance of establishment religion at the expense of colonial liberties. Officially supplied colonial clergy in both British North America and the West Indies were sometimes derided as lazy and second rate and too closely identified with settler interests on issues such as slavery, and other issues which reflected the economic self-interest of the expatriate communities. Nor was there any more official enthusiasm to provide new colonies with religious establishments. In the late eighteenth century, it required the intervention of William Wilberforce with Prime Minister William Pitt to ensure that a chaplain was provided to sail with the convict colonists bound for Botany Bay.[7] In response to local requests Catholic and Presbyterian chaplains were regularly supplied to troops stationed in India and elsewhere as a contribution to military discipline, but there was no urgency about this. While semi-official sources such as the SPG continued to advocate the cause of religious colonisation,[8] such views were not nourished with the funds which would allow the planting of any but the most basic of chaplaincy services.

It was not until the 1820s that these official attitudes begin to change. They did so partly as a result of religious reform in Britain and partly as a response to colonial conditions. Catholic emancipation in 1829 was followed by the arrival of Catholic bishops in British territory that had previously been off limits to them both at home and in the colonies.[9] Even before this, where Britain had acquired colonies in which the Catholic powers of Spain, France, and Portugal had already planted Catholic dioceses there were ready-made populations of Catholics who became British subjects and who asserted the right to practise their religion. In the case of the former French colony of Canada, now the British province of Quebec, such rights were guaranteed by the terms of the Treaty of Paris (1763). Elsewhere the practical necessity of extending religious toleration to the mixed communities of overseas Britons, in which the adherents of the established churches of England, Scotland and Ireland were challenged by the number of Catholics and dissenters, forced the hand of reform.

One of the earliest experiments in religious toleration was conducted in New South Wales by the Church Act (1836), which was introduced by Governor Richard Bourke (1777–1855) to encourage the building of churches and the maintenance of ministers of religion.[10] This effectively removed the special privileges of the Church of England and provided funding 'for the advancement of the Christian Religion [and] the promotion of good morals in New South Wales' regardless of denominational adherence. Initially support was claimed by the Anglicans, Catholics and Presbyterians; later other denominations benefited from the Act, including Baptists, Jews and Methodists. In this way the colonies became the sites for both religious reform and for sectarian competition to plant churches and attract settler devotion. Between 1842 and 1847, several years before the restoration of the Catholic hierarchy in England and Wales (1850–51), five Catholic dioceses were erected in the Australian colonies. After the establishment of the Colonial Bishoprics Fund in 1842, the Church of England also had the capacity to send out colonial bishops who had been so conspicuously absent from the first British Empire.

The other churches were just as active in planting churches, particularly the Wesleyans whose missionary expansion occurs at the same time as the expansion of the empire. Presbyterian interest in religious colonisation was stimulated by the Disruption of the Church of Scotland (1843), which led to a burst of colonial and missionary energy by the Free Church of Scotland. Colonial reforms also created opportunities for the churches overseas which were not matched by those at home. In the same year as the Disruption, widespread resentment at the economic injustice of the Canadian clergy reserves, whose revenues had been directed exclusively to the support of the Church of England, led to their abolition. While some shreds of the old establishment of the national churches of the British Isles remained in evidence, to a large extent the settler colonies were open to free religious colonisation by the churches.

This was the situation at the beginning of the 'hungry 1840s', which were followed by a fever for emigration that affected all classes and sectors of British society, not least the churches. In the aftermath of the famine, Irish emigrants profoundly altered the character of Catholicism in both England and Scotland.[11] In relation to emigration to the colonies, Edward Gibbon Wakefield's advocacy of planned or systematic colonisation, in which the moral character of the emigrant communities was strongly emphasised, may also have played a role in encouraging the churches to play a more active part in the emigration process. While, initially, the churches were concerned only with providing spiritual comforts to emigrants in transit, the scale of mass emigration soon led to more ambitious plans. This took several forms. First, at the home end, clergy were enlisted to form part of emigration committees and societies devoted to the welfare of migrants. They also played a significant role in writing recommendations and references for potential migrants who were being considered as possible candidates for assisted migration to Australia, the destination with the most carefully managed emigrant programme.[12] Second, a number of churches created emigration societies or emigrant chaplaincy services with a special mission to assist emigrants either in transit or while they were making the adjustment to life in a new country. There has been more interest in the activities of clergy ministering to Irish Catholic emigrants to the United States than to those of other faiths,[13] but all the churches were active in this work and the United States was simply one destination for British migrants during these decades.[14] Irish emigrant chaplains have also been studied in relation to the Irish emigrant communities in Britain in more recent times.[15] Third, some home churches undertook to supply clergy directly in response to requests and funding from colonial churches. For the Irish Catholic diaspora, Sheridan Gilley has illuminated this question more thoroughly than anyone else.[16] Suellen Hoy has considered the emigration of Irish religious women to the United States in the great growth era of the US churches.[17] There have been more limited studies of the colonial schemes of the Church of Scotland.[18] But overall it must be admitted that there are many gaps in our knowledge of emigrating clergy and the impact they may have had on the communities they came to serve.

The official chaplains and some higher clergy were part of the colonial establishment; they had their passages paid by the government and their salaries and positions were included in the *Colonial Office List*. Their power and salaries could be substantial. In the West Indies in 1867, the Bishop of Barbados, Thomas Parry earned £2,500 with a seat on the Executive Council and a rank and salary second only to the Governor; Anglican rectors earned £320 and even curates collected £200 as well as being provided with a residence.[19] However, most clergy were not government officials and they made their way out to the colonies either under their own steam or with the financial assistance of their churches. The financial support provided by the SPG to the Church of England began to be withdrawn as soon as the churches became more independent. In New South Wales, the Bishop of Australia, W. G. Broughton, tried hard to get the Colonial Office to continue paying the passage money for SPG chaplains, but by March 1847 the colonial secretary, Earl Grey, was advising that he was only prepared to do this on the direct instruction of the Governor.[20] This reluctance was understandable when the 'passage allowance' was as high as £150 – a year's salary for a curate. Besides, the number of clergy in the colony was rapidly increasing. From this time, most clergy who arrived in Australia were sponsored by the churches; but a good number were likely to have made their own way, ignoring the common advice that there were no opportunities there for the gentleman emigrant.

It was also possible for a clergyman to work his way to the colonies. In the 1850s the Colonial Land and Emigration Commission (CLEC) allocated free passage for clergy willing to travel on emigrant ships and provide religious instruction on the voyage to groups of migrants. In general, there were always more clergy seeking to take advantage of these provisions than there were places available. After 1858, a stream of correspondence between the CLEC and the colonial seminary of All Hallows College, Drumcondra, secured passage in this way for some newly ordained Catholic priests on their way to Australian dioceses.[21]

Another important route to the colonies was provided for a limited number of the Protestant churches as a result of the work of colonial missionary societies, organisations established by most of the churches specifically to supply subsidies for clergy, schoolteachers, churches and other support for the colonial churches. These provided the most sophisticated response to the problem of clergy emigration, which is considered in the next section.

Colonial missionary societies

Colonial missionary societies were not an innovation of the nineteenth century but had existed in some form since the foundation of the Society for the Promotion of Christian Knowledge (SPCK) in 1698, and the SPG in 1701. Under its charter, the three objects of the SPG were: first, to provide a sufficient maintenance for an orthodox clergy to live among British colonists; second, to make other provision for the propagation of the Gospel; and finally, to receive, manage, and dispose of the charity of His Majesty's subjects for those purposes.[22] A subsidiary object was the proselytisation of the indigenous Americans. At the end of the eighteenth century a second wave of missionary enthusiasm led to the formation of missionary societies, including the Baptist Missionary Society (1792), the London Missionary Society (1795), and the Society for Missions to Africa and the East, later the Church Missionary Society (1799). Unlike the SPG or the SPCK, these new societies were focused on foreign rather than colonial missions, though both the Baptist and Wesleyan Methodist Missionary Societies continued the older tradition of sending out missionaries to Christian colonists.

Colonial missions were revived as a religious object in the 1820s and at first they were largely the work of pious laypeople serving the needs of particular colonies. The Glasgow Colonial Society (1825) funded the training and supply of ministers from the Church of Scotland for Canada;[23] the Newfoundland School Society (1823) provided evangelical schoolteachers for the bleak and outer reaches of this colony which was threatened by its large Catholic population.[24] Others had more general objects, including the Colonial Missionary Society (1838), which provided support to Congregational churches in British colonies and ports throughout the empire from Canada to Shanghai.[25] Although the overall efforts of the colonial missionary societies were on a smaller scale than the societies which focused on foreign missions, they still represent a significant investment by the home churches in the settler colonies. By the end of the nineteenth century, when most were scaling down their operations in tune with the flow of emigrants, there were at least fifteen colonial missionary societies providing for emigrant and settler needs in this way.[26] Although the SPG had the benefit of annual grants from Parliament to support its work in North America (discontinued in 1834), all the colonial missionary societies were obliged to seek funds from members of their own churches to support their work; their annual sermons, missionary journals and reports provided a stream of propaganda promoting the religious objects of empire.

In relation to Australia, these points might be illustrated from the early activity of the Colonial Church Society (CCS), an Anglican society which was formed in 1835 to supply evangelical clergy to British colonists.[27] In 1851 the CCS merged with the Australian Church Missionary Society and the Newfoundland School Society to form the Colonial Church and School Society and eventually the Colonial and Continental Church Society (CCCS). Although its original activities were modest in scope, by the middle of the century the CCCS had secured royal patronage and the support of the majority of the home and colonial bishops of the Church of England. Emboldened by this support, it then launched a worldwide operation to provide for the needs of British colonists, as well as support for travellers and sojourners in Europe.[28] In the 1830s, the Anglican CCS had been equally ambitious: it would be for Christian colonists what the Church Missionary Society was for the heathen in Africa and the East, becoming the evangelical equivalent of the SPG.[29] Indeed, the first report made scathing reference to the fact that the work of evangelising the heathen was going on apace while the colonists of Great Britain were being neglected: 'connected with us by the closest ties, and retaining, wherever they settle, English opinions, habits and affections . . . more than any Heathen community . . . they claim our friendly aid'.[30]

The report went on to outline the dimensions of the problem: the British people had spread throughout the world, but their clergy had been unable to accompany them. In Newfoundland, there was a white population virtually without clergy. At the Cape of Good Hope, for 60,000 whites, many English, it was alleged that there were no more than two or three churches with two or three English clergymen. In the colony of New South Wales, eight small churches were available to serve a population of 80,000 persons.[31] The grim statistics – which are in fact wildly inaccurate – were presented in tabular form (table 3.1):

The challenge of persuading supporters of the urgency of the need to support colonial missions in the face of other competing causes was, nevertheless, met in various ways. One of the most important was the preaching of an annual sermon at which a collection would be taken up in aid of the cause and was later published in the CCCS's

Table 3.1 Clergy in the British colonies, 1836

	Area in square miles	Population	Clergy	No. of sq. mls to each minister	No. of souls to each minister	Increase of the population in 10 yrs
England	50,387					
Upper Canada	100,000	296,544	60	1,666	4,942	145,447
Newfoundland	36,000	75,000	10	3,600	7,500	Increasing
Cape Breton	3,125	30,000	2	1,562	15,000	
Lower Canada	205,863	498,605	29	7,098	17,193	Increasing
Nova Scotia	15,617	123,848	35	446	3,538	21,288
New Brunswick	27,734	119,451	28	982	3,571	Increasing
Prince Edward's Island	2,134	32,292	3	711	10,761	8,832
The Cape	128,150	60,000 whites	3 or 4			
The Mauritius	676	85.516	1 or 2			
New South Wales		80,000	Not 30			
Van Diemen's Land	24,000	32,826	Not 20			

Source: Second Report of the Australian Church Missionary Society (n.d. 1838?), p. 10. Blank spaces for missing data are original.

journal.[32] Besides providing an opportunity for such a collection, these annual sermons were also used to articulate links between religion and empire, and the key place of the colonial mission in advancing the providential purpose of Christian colonisation. For the Anglican evangelicals who supported the work of the Colonial Church Society and its successors, the planting of the Protestant faith was bound inextricably to the advancement of British culture. In his annual sermon for the Society, Rev. Edward Bickersteth (1786–1850) argued that the empire was part of a divine plan for Britain: 'God favoured our beloved country by rescuing us from Pagan and Papal darkness, giving us a truly scriptural Church. . . . Thus it may be transplanted to every one of our Colonies, with all its treasure of truth and devotion. What an empire spread over the world has God thus entrusted to Great Britain'.[33]

Somewhat muted, though similar, arguments were presented by the SPG when responding to the call to minister to the expanding British population overseas.[34] Sectarianism was also used as a weapon to secure funding by both Protestant and Catholic clergy. Broughton's urgency is easily matched from the correspondence of the first Catholic Bishop of Australia, the English Benedictine, John Bede Polding (1794–1877). In 1835, when he arrived in Sydney, there were only four priests to greet him. Against his own better judgement, he felt driven to ordain his own accompanying clerks in order to provide some relief. At this time there were over 100,000 people in New South Wales and annual musters show that 28 per cent of them were Catholic. It seemed like a golden opportunity: 'We only want priests', Polding wrote in 1836, 'to make this country Catholic.' Four years later he was still begging for clergy from his agent, Father Heptonstall, in Dublin: 'Clergy, clergy, clergy, in the name of God I do ask and entreat you to send me.'[35] Over the next few decades he may have had cause to reject the answering of his prayers as Irish clergy flowed in a steady stream to Australian dioceses to answer the call and few Australian candidates presented themselves as candidates for the priesthood. In the 1880s, Cardinal Moran attempted to establish a national seminary in the seaside Sydney suburb of Manly, but its early intake was disappointingly small.[36]

The difficulties faced by the Catholic hierarchy in New South Wales were not unique: all the colonial churches were starved of personnel and the colonial missionary societies, including the SPG, the CCCS, and the Colonial Church Society, were only ever able to make a partial response to the need. But how many clergy came? And what impact did they have?

Characteristics of clergy emigrants

Trying to calculate the number of clergy in the home and colonial populations in the middle of the nineteenth century is surprisingly difficult. There has been no religious census in England and Wales until recent times and although there was a religious census of 1851 this counted worshippers and their places of worship, but not their clergy. Using the census returns, Reader suggests that the number of Anglican clergy, Dissenting ministers and Catholic priests in England and Wales rose at a slower rate than the population in the second half of the nineteenth century and this was mostly because of the low pay and poor conditions. They did rather better in the second half of the century.[37] Like other aspiring members of the middle classes, a certain proportion of these were making their way to the colonies. It is more difficult to make effective comparisons on the clerical occupation when we look across the empire. In his report on the English Census for 1881, the statistician Dr William Ogle states that 'the most laborious, the most costly, and after all perhaps the least satisfactory part of the Census is that which is concerned with the Occupations of the people'.[38]

The evidence we have on religion and occupation is, indeed, rather patchy: it includes the religious census taken in Ireland in 1901 and twenty-eight of the British colonies. Nonetheless, it allows some comparison to be made between the home and colonial populations after the great surge of outward-bound emigration had passed.[39] Using the latter source, it would seem that the great campaigns fought by the migrant denominations in the Australian colonies to staff their churches were, by 1901, highly successful. The summary tables of the professions enumerated across the British Empire indicate that in the new Australian Commonwealth, the proportion of the population constituting the clerical profession was more or less the same, namely 0.3 per cent, as that in England, Wales and Scotland. Ireland, at 0.4 per cent had an abundance of clergy and might have had far more if the category 'nun' had been included.[40] Unfortunately, as far as the Australian Commonwealth is concerned, the figure recorded in the 1901 Census is almost certainly wrong.

If we turn, for example, to the much more precise occupation tables of the New South Wales Census of the night of 3 March 1901 prepared by the government statistician T. A. Coghlan, the number of clergy collapses dramatically from a very respectable 0.3 per cent to a mere 0.09 per cent of the population.[41] For 1894 the *Year-book of New South Wales* ranks the proportion of adherents to clergy from a high of 0.45 per cent for the Methodists (despite a 50 per cent increase in their numbers between the 1881 and 1891 censuses), 0.25 per cent for the Congregationalists, 0.21 per cent for the Baptists, down to 0.15 per cent for the Catholics and Presbyterians and a mere 0.06 per cent for the Church of England.[42] Yet even at the lesser figure of one per cent of the Australian population, the clergy represent a very significant group: they were outnumbered only by schoolteachers but there were, for example, more clergy than doctors and as many clergy as lawyers. The Australian colonies needed clergy and the United Kingdom was the major supplier of candidates.

The next problem to address is country of origin of the Australian clergy. If we are forced to rely only on the census, we are again bedevilled with difficulties. Because of the decision to destroy individual household returns for Australian censuses from 1901, as well as for most of the earlier colonial musters and census returns, it is not possible to cross-tabulate occupation and country of origin, or country of origin and religion. Colonial chaplains were servants of the crown and are listed in the colonial returns. However, most clergy were not on the government payroll but were recruited directly by colonial bishops or their agents, or migrated independently, leaving few official traces of their departure or arrival.[43] However, information on clerical education and ethnicity is available for the larger churches from year books, synod reports and clerical directories.[44] Using sources of this kind, can we confirm that the clergy of the major denominations were more likely to be British-born than their congregations? Let us try.

Turning again to the imperial census of 1901, we can see that while Australia was overwhelmingly a country of British settlement, much of that settlement was the experience of earlier generations. By 1901, over three-quarters of the population (77.23 per cent) had been born in Australia; the number born in the UK ranged from as high as 25 per cent in expanding Queensland, to as low as 11 per cent in settled Tasmania and a remarkable 95.94 per cent of the population were born in either Australia, New Zealand or the UK.[45] So were the clergy more likely to be British-born than the rest of the population? As we might expect, it is more difficult to determine the ethnicity of particular occupational groups such as the clergy than of the population as a whole. In Australia, the first systematic occupational census which included religious denomination proves to be the NSW census of 1901.[46] This confirms the strong presence of non-native born among the professions, and among religious professionals in particular. Indeed, by 1901, according to this source, of 1,623 males ministering to religion, 1,170 or 72 per cent were British-born, 488 (30 per cent) in England and Wales, 142 (8.7 per cent) in Scotland, and 330 (20.3 per cent) in Ireland.[47]

The Irish in particular benefited from clerical employment opportunities in New South Wales. According to David Fitzpatrick, 'the male occupations most heavily colonised by Irish immigrants were (in descending order [of occupational class]) religion, "independent means", refuse disposal, and road construction: a rich mix'.[48] The clergy was the only profession in which the Irish flourished where otherwise they tended to be concentrated in the unskilled parts of the labour force. On the other hand, the Catholic population, which by 1901 was of Irish descent but no longer dominated by the Irish-born, could be found working across some fifty major occupations. Like their clergy, Irishwomen also benefited by the career opportunities made available by clerical migration to Australia and, turning to Fitzpatrick again, he notes that they made their best showing as 'agriculturalists, grocers, proprietors, and nuns'.[49] This effect continued well into the twentieth century so that as late as the 1960s, the Irish-born made up 70 per cent of the diocesan priesthood, though the sisterhood of religious women were more likely by this time to be Australian.

Although more work has been done on the migration of the Irish Catholic clergy than the clergy of other denominations, Catholics were not alone in preferring clergy who spoke with the accents of their home churches. Malcolm Prentis has demonstrated the very high levels of Scottish and Irish recruitment to the Presbyterian ministry, which continued well beyond the period of colonial dependence. Scottish ministers were sought from Ulster and Edinburgh as much for reasons of prestige as out of necessity.[50] In Victoria, the colony with the strongest Presbyterian community, 65 per cent of the ministry came from Scotland, 13.5 per cent from Ireland, another 8 per cent from England and Wales, and only 10 per cent were Australian-born. Although the strongest period of recruitment was from 1850 to 1880, by 1900, 90 per cent of candidates for the Presbyterian ministry were still born overseas.

Surprisingly, in 1900 the Anglican clergy were rather more likely to have been born in Australia than either the Catholics or the Presbyterians, though still less than the general population. This is probably due to the impact of the Moore Theological College at Liverpool, founded in 1856, as a theological training college for the Anglican ministry. In 1906, half the rectors in the diocese of Sydney had been trained at Moore College.[51] Education and experience in the United Kingdom still mattered, however. If we take representative samples from the synod reports of two Anglican dioceses in New South Wales, of the 141 clergy licensed in the Sydney diocese, the largest number, fifty-one (36 per cent), had attended universities or theological colleges in the UK, while forty-nine were graduates of Moore College, and nineteen were graduates of the University of Sydney. About a quarter of the Sydney clergy had also had parochial experience in the UK.[52]

The Anglican diocese of Newcastle shows a similar pattern. In 1900–01, there were forty-six clergy licensed in the diocese. Of these, eighteen (39 per cent) were university graduates of whom fifteen, or about a third of the total, had degrees from universities in the UK; six Newcastle clergy had parochial experience in England and four were ordained by English bishops. Across the Australian colonies this pattern is likely to be much the same, though rural dioceses were more likely to be forced to recruit directly from home and retained their English accent for longer.[53] In dioceses where a particular preference was for English clergy, however, the proportion might be nearly 100 per cent. In the diocese of Brisbane, for example, Bishop W. T. T. Webber dismissed clergy he regarded as inefficient and staffed exclusively from home, securing young men for five-year terms.[54] By the turn of the century this had begun to seem retrograde.

There is rather more accessible information about the Catholic clergy, which consisted of both ordained priests as well as members of some religious orders who did not take holy orders, than for other groups. The Catholic priesthood in Australia in the period from first settlement in 1788 until 31 December 1900 was analysed by T. J. Linane, parish priest of Bungaree in Victoria and editor of the magazine *Footprints*.[55] Linane's sources included Catholic directories, with evidence of date of death taken from cemeteries, and necrology lists kept by superiors of religious orders. He calculated that during the period studied there were 1,800 priests who made some or all of their lives in Australia. Of these, 1,300 submitted death duties. Unlike the Anglican clergy, Catholic priests were unlikely to ever return to their country and diocese of origin to retire because no funds were ever provided for this purpose. While some had international careers, most came to Australia directly from their seminaries of training and pursued their calling there. In terms of their national origins, in Australia, the dependence of the Catholic Church on foreign-born clergy in the nineteenth century is self-evident, amounting to 95.5 per cent of the total. Of those whose nationality is known, 1,282 or 79 per cent were from Ireland. In rank order, the French and Australian-born come a distant second and third with eighty-nine each or 5.5 per cent; the English-born, Italians and Austrians all manage to secure more than one per cent of the total. All other nationalities, sixteen in all, contribute 3.5 per cent to the total (see table 3.2).

At nearly 80 per cent of the total, it is important to stress the importance of Ireland as a source for priests to Australian colonies

Table 3.2   National origins of Catholic priests in Australia, 1788–1900

Nationality	Number	Per cent
Irish	1,282	79.1
Australian	89	5.5
French	89	5.5
English	48	3.0
Italian	31	1.9
Austrian	26	1.6
Spanish	14	0.9
Mid-Eastern	6	0.4
Scotch	5	0.3
Belgian	5	0.3
Dutch	5	0.3
German	5	0.3
Swiss	3	0.2
Welsh	2	0.1
Polish	2	0.1
Alsatian	2	0.1
Prussian	2	0.1
Malta	1	0.1
Bavaria	1	0.1
Lithuania	1	0.1
Chinese	1	0.1
United States	1	0.1
Total known	1,621	100.0
Not known	129	
Total priests	1,750	

Source: F. J. Linane, 'Abel to Zundolovich', Footprints (n.d. [2006?]), p. 15.

before 1900. However, it is worth noting that priests from other parts of Europe were significant as members of the religious orders, the majority of whom worked as teachers in Catholic schools. Of the 1,750 priests counted by Linane, 505 came from one of eighteen religious orders of which the Jesuits, Benedictines and Marists led the way. All of these orders ran high schools in which Australian students might come into close association with Austrian Jesuits, English Benedictines or French Marist Fathers. However, these were islands of European Catholicity in an Irish Sea. For county of origin, Linane has secure information for only 515 of the 1,282 Irish in the cohort. Kerry, Limerick, Cork, Kilkenny and Tipperary account for more than 50 per cent of the total. However, the single most significant agent in the formation of Catholic colonial clergy in Australia was the missionary seminary of All Hallows, Dublin, which trained over 2,000 priests for Australia between 1842 and 1891.[56]

Before the foundation of All Hallows in 1842, other seminaries which contributed to the Australian mission fields included Maynooth, Waterford, Carlow, Thurles, and St Laurence O'Toole's in Dublin. Of these, Maynooth and Carlow were probably the most important. Two other bodies of Catholic clergy should also be considered here. The teaching orders, of which the Marist Brothers, founded by Marcellin Champagnat (1789–1840) in France in 1817, and the Irish Christian Brothers were the largest, were also a very important presence in Australia. Like the priesthood, they were initially dominated by the Irish-born with peaks for new arrivals occurring in the 1880s, and again in the 1890s, when the main national education acts removed state support for Catholic education, and Irish clerical teachers were despatched to fill the need.[57] After this date, Fogarty notes, most religious orders were able to recruit from their own daughter communities established in Australia, estimating that in 1880 more than half of all members of religious orders in Australia would have been Irish-born.[58] The third group of clerical personnel were religious women or nuns whose trajectory of arrivals follows that of the male religious orders. Women in religious orders in Australia included trained teachers, nurses and a much smaller number who chose a life of prayer and strict enclosure. They were also sourced from Ireland, France, and England to teach the schools established by orders such as the Sisters of Mercy, and the hospitals of the Sisters of Charity.[59] But even the Australian Sisters of St Joseph found it useful to maintain a house for new recruits in Ireland.[60]

Overall, despite the limitations of the evidence, it can be concluded that the ethnicity of the clergy of all the major denominations followed the pattern we can observe for Presbyterians and Catholics in that they were more likely to be born in England, Scotland or Ireland than might be expected for the colonial population of New South Wales and Victoria as a whole. Although it has generally been assumed that the Catholic clergy were dominated by emigrants from Ireland, it needs to be stressed that the Anglican and Presbyterian clergy, where figures are available, were just as dependent on emigrants. And though Ireland was a significant source of Catholic clergy who made emigrant journeys to Australia, the cohort was quite diverse and included significant numbers of French, English, Italian and other European nationalities as well. Just what impact this heavy dependence on first-generation emigrants had on religious communities is difficult to determine, but is the topic of the next section.

Importing morality and culture

The attempts to recruit clergy for Australian churches was based on the assumption that churches provided a significant contribution to morality and culture in the colonies – societies in which these valuable commodities were in short supply. Especially in the former convict colonies, statistics which seemed to indicate the improvement of the moral tone of the colony were carefully delineated. The Victorian census of 1881 prepared by the French statistician Henry Heylyn, gives some insight into the number and variety of people who made a livelihood, by one means or another, by ministering to religion in the Australian colonies.[61] By Heylyn's reckoning, this comprised a large and varied group, including at its most humble levels gravediggers and lay preachers, and extending to the most senior clergy. While the most numerous single group within this class was the 195–strong clergymen of the Church of England, the next largest was made up of the 155 women who registered themselves as nuns or sisters of charity. Many of these women were working as nurses and teachers; some would have considered themselves primarily as ministering to religion. Even if we exclude these religious women from our calculations, the Victorian census indicates that the clerical profession formed a visible and significant group in Victorian society, as in other colonies. However, in 1881 they were vastly outnumbered, by a factor of 5.5:1, by the teachers; they were also outnumbered by the medical practitioners and druggists, and the lawyers. It is obviously important, therefore, that we avoid making too many assumptions about the impact of the clergy on the wider Victorian society.

Colonial cultural rivalry may be one reason why Heylyn includes a table which compares the members of the various occupations in the

Table 3.3 The professions in the Victorian census, 1871 and 1881

	1871	1881
Clergymen and church officers	899	1,237
Law court officers, lawyers and their subordinates	1,152	1,243
Medical practitioners, druggists, etc.	1,308	1,595
Authors, literary persons	132	197
Scientific persons	232	300
Teachers	5,428	6,795
Artists	444	734
Musicians, music teachers, etc.	669	1,289
Actors	343	560

Source: Heylyn, 1881 Census of Victoria.

Table 3.4 Occupations in Australasian colonies, census of 1881

	Victoria	NSW	Qld	SA	WA	Tas	NZ
Total population	862,346	751,468	213,865	279,865	29,708	115,705	489,933
Clergymen, ministers, and church officers	1,237	725	374	469	119	203	747
Law court officers, lawyers, etc.	1,243	920	285	268	25	205	844
Physicians, surgeons	1,595	1,049	406	765	46	170	810
Teachers	6,795	–	1,365	1,661	250	860	3,437

Source: Heylyn, 1881 Census of Victoria, p. 141.[62]

Table 3.5 Occupations in Victoria, 1854–81

	1854	1857	1861	1871	1881
Ministering to religion					
Numbers	194	286	490	899	1,237
Proportions per cent	0.08	0.07	0.09	0.12	0.14

Source: Heylyn, 1881 Census of Victoria, pp. 263–4, Table 1, xviii–lxix.

Australasian colonies (table 3.4). It shows the clear advantage that the colony of Victoria enjoyed in terms of the number of its clergy across the different colonies.

It was thus apparent that Victoria had by far the largest proportion of the clergy in proportion to the population. Clergy made up 0.14 per cent of the Victorian population, but just 0.10 per cent of that of New South Wales. It was also possible to show that the proportion was increasing over the five census years (table 3.5).

This indicates that by 1861, the proportion of the clergy to the population was already as high as it was in England and Wales (where it was about 0.1 per cent) and by 1871 it had actually exceeded it. Even though the proportion of clergy did not match that of its cultivated southern neighbour, the report on the NSW census of 1900 indicates that there were 1,132 Christian clergy in New South Wales stretched across six major denominations. Of these, the Congregationalists had the highest proportion of clergy to adherents, while the Church of England, at 0.06 per cent, had the lowest. It was, of course, galling to majority Protestant opinion to realise that the Roman Catholics had more clergy among their ranks. A final table shows occupations according to 'distinct callings'.[63] This shows that the number of clergymen rose from 1871 to 1881 from 633 to 782. However, it is also significant that the number of theological students remained very small in this period, rising in number from six to twenty-two, indicating the continuing need to call on the home country for supplies.

Clergy and religious nationalism

Leaving aside these thorny statistical questions, the overall pattern is clear: the Australian clergy were distinctive as a predominately British-born group peaking in the 1880s and 1890s, and this forms a contrast with the pattern in other white settler societies, especially the United States, where theological schools and seminaries were established very early and were able to train a native-born ministry. Throughout the second half of the nineteenth century, in all the major Christian churches, Australians showed a great reluctance to enter training for the ministry. While there were differences in the overall pattern of ethnicity and clerical occupation, Methodists were rather more likely to have native-born pastors, and Presbyterians most likely to be ministered to by a native Scot or Irishman. For most churchgoing Australians, religion was something administered to you by especially imported English, Scottish, or Irish professionals. A final question for this chapter is to consider the possible effect of this ethnic conservatism in relation to colonial religious identity and imperial and national identities. Did the clergy act to reinforce empire values? Were they a kind of conservative break on the development of a more independent Australian consciousness? Of course, there is no necessary reason why clergy (or any other migrant) might be more inclined, simply by reason of their original place of birth to be more or less supportive of national movements in the Australian colonies. But what kind of role did they play in maintaining conservative traditions? As bearers of the home culture, clergy might at the very least be seen to be agents in the 'chains of memory' that the French sociologist Danièle Hervieu-Léger, has argued constitute the essential bonds that bind religions to their societies and keep people going to church.[64]

Church periodicals, of which there are at least two or three for each major denomination, are rich sources of commentary on clerical arrivals and departures. While some were written and published independently of the churches whose readers they served, mostly they reflect conservative opinion which is close to that of their churches' leading clerics. All churches shared the view that British (or, more precisely, English, Scottish, Irish, or Welsh) was better, even when all efforts to try and supply candidates for the ministry from local candidates failed. In a letter to the SPG in 1847 Bishop Broughton reflected on the difficulty of training colonial youths to the Anglican ministry. He thought it would be better to bring out young men from 'good English schools' so that there would be 'a perpetual infusion of English feelings upon church subjects', which he believed colonial youths could never supply.[65] When the first Australian-trained bishop was made Bishop of North Queensland, the Archbishop of Sydney defended himself from the charge of disloyalty for his actions: 'Does this consecration of a colonially-ordained clergyman in Sydney intimate any desire rashly to sever ourselves from the close connection with the Church in the motherland'?[66] It is hard to avoid the conclusion that there was active resistance to the development of a colonial ministry by English bishops until forced by absolute necessity to seek locally for candidates. This did not happen on a significant scale until the first half of the twentieth century, when reformers such as the bishop of Brisbane, St Clair Donaldson (1863–1935) established theological training colleges for Australian-born candidates and appointed them in their own dioceses.[67] Until then, the ideal was to attempt a reconstruction of the English parochial system in Australia and import clergy to staff them if at all possible.

If anything, the Methodists were even more eager to defend their loyalty to the empire than the Church of England. At a speech to the 1864 anniversary meeting of the Methodist Missionary Society, the Rev. William Butters (1810–1887)[68] asserted that the church in Australia was benefiting from the services of men who had no connection with England. However, this was done with a certain defensiveness: 'Our people are as loyal to English Methodism as the colonists are generally loyal to the British throne.' By the 1890s, *The Methodist* in particular was an organ for what one might term hard-core imperialist propaganda. In a talk delivered in the Leichhardt Wesleyan Hall in Melbourne in 1901 (reproduced by special request of the congregation), Rev. F. C. Boyer provided a providentialist interpretation of the establishment of the Australian Commonwealth and of its 'national' (i.e. British) expansion, the characteristic mode of Methodist historiography.[69] Only the intervention of Providence, in Boyer's view, had secured Australia for the British rather than the Catholic Spanish or Portuguese. It was a chance gale, blown by God, which drove Captain James Cook onto the east coast and ensured that the great navigator made his way to Australian shores: 'We gratefully recognize the hand of God, moreover, in the rapidly increasing strengths of the Protestant nations of the world, and in the assignment to them of so large a proportion of the world's colonies.'[70] The Melbourne *Methodist* was always a reliable source for loyal addresses on the occasion of major events such as coronations or the death of a monarch; there was rapture at news of imperial honours conferred on colonial notables, and rebukes to Republicans who questioned them. Coverage of the 100th anniversary of the Battle of Trafalgar, celebrated on 21 October 1905, had to be carried over a dozen issues with emphasis on the role of the 'God of battles' and His timely intervention on behalf of 'our island Empire and its Protestant Constitution and Throne'.[71] The Rev. James Carruthers (1848–1932), once described as the best editor the *Methodist* ever had,[72] tapped the same rich vein when he stated that Methodism and imperialism were outgrowths of the same spirit: 'We believe the Empire as it stands today is in the line of Divine Providence, It is the work of God.'[73] Such sentiments reflected the loyalty, patriotism and religious conviction of colonial Methodists throughout Greater Britain.

Conclusion

By the end of the nineteenth century, colonial churches in Australia were only at the beginning of the long process of becoming Australian, which necessarily began with creating a native clergy. While it is at all times difficult to trace the sources of national ideologies, the strength of British imperial attachment among colonial churchgoers, as reflected in their semi-official periodicals, could only have been reinforced by the habit of importing clergy from the old country. By 1900 there were beginning to be some concerns at the largely non-Australian make-up of the clerical profession, but by and large it was the Britishness of these clergy and their roots in the national or majority churches of England, Scotland and Ireland, which made them attractive to both their congregations and the appointment committees or bishops who guaranteed their employment. Even if we must reject the geographical idiosyncrasy which led Carruthers to speak of 'our island Empire', perhaps it seemed so to the patriotic colonial Methodist. In a volume which seeks to explore the networks which bound together the British World, it therefore seems essential that we consider the key role played by emigrating clergy in binding Australian Britons to the bonds of a common imperial culture.

Notes

1 For a recent synthesis, see J. Hirst, 'Empire, State, Nation', in D. M. Schreuder and S. Ward (eds), *Australia's Empire* (Oxford, 2008), pp. 141–62 and, more generally, W. J. Hudson and M. P. Sharp, *Australian Independence: Colony to Reluctant Kingdom* (Melbourne, 1988); S. Ward, *Australia and the British Embrace: The Demise of the Imperial Ideal* (Melbourne, 2001). For the complex performance of colonial nationalism and British adherence see the discussion by C. Bridge and K. Fedorowich (eds), *The British World: Diaspora, Culture and Identity* (London, 2003).

2 For Irish Catholics and Protestants in Australia, see O. MacDonagh, 'The Irish in Australia: A General View', in O. MacDonagh and W. F. Mandle (eds), *Ireland and Irish Australia: Studies in Cultural and Political History* (London, 1986), pp. 155–74; P. J. O'Farrell, *The Catholic Church and Community: An Australian History*, revised edn (Sydney, 1985); P. J. O'Farrell, *The Irish in Australia: 1788 to the Present*, 3rd edn (Sydney, 2000). For English and Scottish Catholics, see P. Cunich, 'Archbishop Vaughan and the Empires of Religion in New South Wales', in H. M. Carey (ed.), *Empires of Religion* (London, 2008), pp. 137–60; and M. D. Prentis, 'Scottish Roman Catholics in Nineteenth Century Australia,' *Innes Review*, 33 (1982), pp. 58–70 respectively.

3 Professional emigration has been little researched, though for Irish policemen, doctors and lawyers see studies in O. Walsh (ed.), *Ireland Abroad: Politics and Professions in the Nineteenth Century* (Dublin, 2003).

4 C. Hall, *Civilising Subjects: Metropole and Colony in the English Imagination, 1830–1867* (Oxford, 2002), pp. 12–14. For Fanon, the relationship was essentially violent and binary, which is not the argument taken here.

5 A. H. Ion, 'The Empire that Prays Together stays Together: Imperial Defence and Religion, 1857–1956', in G. C. Kennedy (ed.), *Imperial Defence: The Old World*

Order 1856–1956 (London, 2008), pp. 197–217. For more extensive discussion of this theme, see H. M. Carey, *God's Empire* (Cambridge, 2011).

6   J. S. M. Anderson, *The History of the Church of England in the Colonies and Foreign Dependencies of the British Empire*, 3 vols, 2nd edn (London, 1856). For religion as a primary motivation for settlement in New England see V. De John Anderson, 'Migrants and Motives: Religion and the Settlement of New England, 1630–1640', *New England Quarterly*, 58:3 (1985), pp. 339–83; C. B. Cowing, *The Saving Remnant: Religion and the Settling of New England* (Urbana, IL, 1995).

7   S. Piggin, 'The American and British Contributions to Evangelicalism in Australia', in M. A. Noll, D. W. Bebbington, and G. A. Rawlyk (eds), *Evangelicalism. Comparative Studies of Popular Protestantism in North America, the British Isles, and Beyond, 1700–1990* (Oxford, 1994), pp. 290–307.

8   R. Strong, 'A Vision of an Anglican Imperialism: The Annual Sermons of the Society for the Propagation of the Gospel in Foreign Parts 1701–1714', *Journal of Religious History*, 30:2 (2006), pp. 175–98. For the much bolder imperial vision which led to the establishment of the Colonial Bishoprics' Fund (1842), see R. Strong, *Anglicanism and Empire* (Oxford, 2007).

9   For Catholic settlement in the empire, see W. T. Southerwood, *Catholics in British Colonies: Planting a Faith Where No Sun Sets – Islands and Dependencies of Britain Till 1900* (London, 1998).

10 New South Wales Church Act (1836), preamble.

11 D. R. Gwynn, 'The Famine and the Church in England', *Irish Ecclesiastical Record*, 5th series, 69:10 (1947), pp. 896–909; J. E. Handley, 'The Famine and the Development of the Church in Scotland', ibid., pp. 910–24; O. MacDonagh, 'The Irish Catholic Clergy and Emigration During the Great Famine', *Irish Historical Studies*, 5 (1946–7), pp. 287–302.

12 H. L. Malchow, 'The Church and Emigration in Late Victorian England', *Journal of Church and State*, 24:1 (1982), pp. 119–38.

13 B. Aspinwall, 'Scots and Irish Clergy Ministering to Immigrants, 1830–1878', *Innes Review*, 47 (1996), pp. 45–68, MacDonagh, 'Emigration During the Great Famine', pp. 287–302. By 1900 there were more than thirty church agencies, from the Austrian Society to the Women's Christian Temperance Union, which provided a ministry to emigrants in the United States. For a list see J. B. Clark, 'Emigrants and Immigrants, Mission Work Among', in S. M. Jackson (ed.), *The New Schaff-Herzog Encyclopedia of Religious Knowledge* (London, 1909), pp. 119–20.

14 For the later activity of the Salvation Army see M. Harper, 'Emigration and the Salvation Army, 1890–1930', *Bulletin of the Scottish Institute of Missionary Studies*, new series, 3–4 (1985), pp. 22–9.

15 M. Kells, 'Religion and the Irish Migrant', *Irish Studies Review*, 6 (1994), pp. 16–18; W. Sloan, 'Religious Affiliation and the Immigrant Experience: Catholic Irish and Protestant Highlanders in Glasgow, 1830–1850', in T. M. Devine (ed.), *Irish Immigrants and Scottish Society in the Nineteenth and Twentieth Centuries* (Edinburgh, 1991), pp. 67–90.

16 S. Gilley, 'The Roman Catholic Church and the Nineteenth Century Irish Diaspora', *Journal of Ecclesiastical History*, 35:2 (1984), pp. 188–207.

17 S. Hoy, 'The Journey Out: The Recruitment and Emigration of Irish Religious Women to the United States, 1812–1914', *Journal of Women's History*, 6–7 (1995), pp. 64–98.

18 See the introduction to E. A. K. McDougall and J. S. Moir (eds), *Selected Correspondence of the Glasgow Colonial Society 1825–1840* (Toronto, 1994).

19 Colonial Office List or General Register of the Colonial Dependencies of Great Britain (London, 1867), p. 17.

20 Rhodes House Library, Oxford (RHL) USPG Archive, Correspondence Letters Received (CLR) 202 (Australia), fols 14–15, 19 and 51, Benjamin Hawes MP, Under-Secretary of State for the Colonies, to Reverend G. H. Fagan, SPG Executive in London, 9 November 1846, 30 November 1846, 5 March 1847 and 22 September 1847.

21   National Library of Australia, Canberra (NLA), Australian Joint Copying Project, microform: M871–874, Correspondence 1858–60, Colonial Land and Emigration Commission relating to religious instruction on board emigrant ships, All Hallows College (Dublin).

22   SPG, *The Results of 180 Years of Work, as Set Forth in Letters of Colonial & Missionary Bishops* (Westminster, 1882), p. 4. D. O'Connor (ed.), *Three Centuries of Mission: the United Society for the Propagation of the Gospel 1701–2000* (London, 2000).

23   McDougall and Moir (eds), *Selected Correspondence of the Glasgow Colonial Society*. See also M. Harper, 'Glasgow Colonial Society', in N. M. de S. Cameron (ed.), *Dictionary of Scottish Church History & Theology* (Edinburgh, 1993), p. 365.

24   P. McCann, 'The Newfoundland School Society 1823–55: Missionary Enterprise or Cultural Imperialism?', in J. A. Mangan (ed.), *'Benefits Bestowed?' Education and British Imperialism* (Manchester, 1988), pp. 94–112.

25   J. Brown, *The Colonial Missions of Congregationalism: The Story of Seventy Years* (London, 1908).

26   E. M. Bliss, *The Encyclopaedia of Missions* (New York, 1891), pp. 307–8.

27   Not to be confused with the Congregational Society of the same name.

28   The Society is now known as the Intercontinental Church Society. Its website describes it as 'an international Church of England mission agency which seeks to make known the Christ of the Scriptures to people of any nationality who speak English'. There is a history by Brian Underwood, now in its second updated edition, B. Underwood, *Faith and New Frontiers: A Story of Planting and Nurturing Churches, 1823–2003* (Warwick, 2004). This is based on his unpublished MA dissertation, 'The History of the Commonwealth and Continental Church Society' (MA dissertation, Durham University, 1972).

29   NLA, Australian Joint Copying Project, microform: M413–416 and M577–579, Records of the Colonial and Continental Church Society, Colonial Church Society, *Second Report* (1836), p. 11: 'We trust that it is not necessary for us solemnly to disclaim the spirit of rivalry with any existing institutions, devoting their attentions, in whole, or in part, to the same object with ourselves . . . If asked, why do we not rather leave this sphere to the exclusive care of the Society for the Propagation of the Gospel, we answer, that the field is very wide, the destitution immense, our Colonies already occupy territories . . . ten times as large as England, without reckoning India, Ceylon, the West Indies, or the unsettled continent of Australia, and it is our settled belief that a new Society is required.'

30   *Second Report of the Australian Church Missionary Society* (1836), p. 5.

31   The figures are essentially missionary propaganda. According to R. M. Martin, *Statistics of the Colonies of the British Empire* (London, 1839), p. 156, in Lower Canada, for example, there were not 29 but 67 Protestant clergy made up of 40 Anglican ministers with their own bishop as well as 14 Presbyterian and 12 Wesleyan ministers. The Catholic established Church had over 200 priests alone and hundreds more who were members of religious orders.

32   The Annual sermon of the CCCS was printed in their *Annual Report*, published from 1851 to the present. From 1876, the Society also published the pictorial *Greater Britain Messenger* (London, 1876–1957) with a more newsy format.

33   E. Bickersteth, 'The duty of communicating the gospel to our colonies', *A sermon preached before the Colonial Church Society* (1830). *Third Report of the Colonial Church Society with the Anniversary Sermon by the Rev. Edward Bickersteth* (London, 1839), p. 16.

34   The SPG annual sermon served a similar function. See Strong, 'A Vision of an Anglican Imperialism'.

35   Cited by J. Waldersee, *Catholic Society in New South Wales, 1788–1860* (Sydney, 1974), p. 199.

36   K. T. Livingstone, *The Emergence of an Australian Catholic Priesthood 1835–1915* (Sydney, 1977), p. 131, notes that the first intake at Manly (1885) included 90 students of whom 45 eventually graduated.

37   W. J. Reader, *Professional Men. The Rise of the Professional Classes in Nineteenth-century England* (London, 1966), pp. 208–9. Between 1841 and 1911 the number of clergy rose from 14,527 to 24,859, the number of ministers from 5,923 to 11,984. Priests rose from 2,089 in 1881 to 40,145 in 1911. From 1841 to 1881 the population of England and Wales rose 64 per cent while the increase in the number of all clergy was 63 per cent. In the next ten years, from 1881 to 1891, the population increased by 39 per cent while the clergy increased by 20 per cent.

38   *Census of the British Empire, 1901. Report with Summary* (London, 1906), xxix. Online Historical Population Reports: http://histpop/org/ (accessed 1 September 2008).

39   *Ibid.*

40   *Ibid.*, xxxi.

41   T. A. Coghlan, *Results of a Census of New South Wales Taken for the Night of the 31st March, 1901* (Sydney, 1904).

42   *Year-Book of New South Wales* (Sydney, 1897), pp. 119–22. This was a commercial directory compiled from census data and information provided by the churches.

43   Shipping lists, for example, seldom list occupation with any reliability. The Scottish Emigration Database: www.abdn.ac.uk/emigration/index.html (Accessed 26 August 2008), has records of 21,000 passengers who embarked at Glasgow and Greenock for non-European ports of whom there are only eleven passengers whose occupation is listed as 'minister' or 'minister of religion'; nine 'clergymen' (four of whom are from the Scottish Immigrant Aid Society), one 'Clerk in Holy Orders', and no priests.

44   For example, Crockford's, *Clerical Directory* (London, 1817–present), and the *Catholic Directory* (Dublin, 1836–present). *The Catholic Directory and Annual Register* was first published in 1838 and like Crockford's Anglican directory, it listed clergy in England, Scotland and Ireland as well as those in the colonies.

45   G. H. Knibbs, *Official Year Book of the Commonwealth of Australia Containing Authoritative Statistics for the Period 1901–1908 and Corrected Statistics for the Period 1788–1900, etc.* (Melbourne, 1908), pp. 157–8.

46   Coghlan, *Results of a Census of New South Wales Taken for the Night of the 31st March, 1901*.

47   *Ibid.*, 770, table xiii. Unfortunately, data for lawyers, doctors and teachers in this table is not disaggregated from the more general occupational categories of those 'ministering to' law and order, health, or education.

48   D. Fitzpatrick, *Oceans of Consolation: Personal Accounts of Irish Migration to Australia* (Ithaca, 1994), p. 17.

49   *Ibid.* Fitzpatrick bases his analysis on two doctoral dissertations: C. McConville, 'Emigrant Irish and Suburban Catholics: Faith and Nation in Melbourne and Sydney, 1851–1933' (PhD dissertation, University of Melbourne, 1984); and R. E. Haines, 'Government-Assisted Emigration from the United Kingdom to Australia, 1831–1860' (PhD dissertation, Flinders University, 1992) both which have now been published: C. McConville, *Croppies, Celts and Catholics: The Irish in Australia* (Melbourne, 1987); R. F. Haines, *Emigration and the Labouring Poor: Australian Recruitment in Britain and Ireland, 1831–60* (Basingstoke, 1997).

50   M. D. Prentis, 'The Presbyterian Ministry in Australia, 1822–1900: Recruitment and Composition', *Journal of Religious History*, 13:1 (1984), pp. 46–65; R. S. Ward and M. D. Prentis, *Presbyterian Ministers in Australia, 1822–1901. Biographical Register* (Melbourne, 2001).

51   S. Judd and K. Cable, *Sydney Anglicans: A History of the Diocese* (Sydney, 2000), pp. 76 and 215.

52   *Sydney Diocesan Directory for 1900* (Sydney, 1900).

53   *Ibid.* For the English character of Australian Anglicanism, see R. Frappell, 'The Australian Bush Brotherhoods and Their English Origins', *Journal of Ecclesiastical History*, 47:1 (1996), pp. 82–97; R. Frappell, 'Imperial Fervour and Anglican Loyalty 1901–1929', in B. Kaye (ed.), *Anglicanism in Australia: A History* (Melbourne, 2002), pp. 76–99.

54 G. P. Shaw, 'Webber, William Thomas Thornhill (1837–1903)', *Australian Dictionary of Biography*, 12 (Melbourne, 1990), p. 429.

55 *Anglican Diocese of Newcastle Year Book* (1900–present).

56 K. Condon, *The Missionary College of All Hallows, 1842–1891* (Dublin, 1986), pp. 290–364. All Hallows graduates departed for dioceses in the following countries in this period: United States 638; Australia and New Zealand 618; England, Wales and Scotland 271; Canada and Newfoundland 104; West Indies, Central and South America, and Mauritius 106; Australia ranked second only to the USA as a destination for ordinands, although its population in 1900 was more than eighteen times the size of Australia's.

57 Figures from R. Fogarty, *Catholic Education in Australia 1806–1950, 2 Catholic Education under the Religious Orders* (Melbourne, 1959), p. 273.

58 *Ibid.*, p. 276.

59 R. MacGinley, *Foundations of Australian Congregations of Religious Women: An Investigation* (Sydney, 1979).

60 Fogarty, *Catholic Education in Australia*, 2, p. 286, footnote 81.

61 H. H. Heylyn, *Census of Victoria* (Melbourne, 1883), p. 99.

62 Heylyn notes the difficulty of comparing across all classes because of the 'peculiar manner in which the occupations in New South Wales are classified'. *Ibid.*, p. 141.

63 *Ibid.*, p. 270.

64 D. Hervieu-Léger, *Religion as a Chain of Memory*, trans. S. Lee (Cambridge, 2000).

65 RHL, USPG Archives, Broughton to SPG, 9 January 1847.

66 *Church Chronicle* (1 December 1892), p. 12.

67 B. Crouchley, 'Donaldson, St Clair George Alfred (1863–1935)', *Australian Dictionary of Biography*, 8 (Melbourne, 1981), pp. 319–20 notes that Davidson established Nundah Theological College in 1907; by 1921 over two-thirds of Brisbane's Anglican clergy were Australian-trained.

68 B. Dickey (ed.), *The Australian Dictionary of Evangelical Biography* (Sydney, 1994), p. 61.

69 For the American case, see R. E. Richey, 'Methodism and Providence: A Study in Secularization', in K. Robbins (ed.), *Protestant Evangelicalism: Britain, Ireland, Germany and America c.1750–c.1950. Studies in Church History, Subsidia, 7* (Oxford, 1990), pp. 51–77.

70 *Methodist* (19 January 1901).

71 *Ibid.* (28 October 1905).

72 Dickey (ed.), *Australian Dictionary of Evangelical Biography*, pp. 66–7.

73 *Methodist* (27 May 1911).

CHAPTER 4

Resistance and accommodation in Christian mission: Welsh Presbyterianism in Sylhet, Eastern Bengal, 1860–1940

Aled Jones

It has long been recognised that the colonised peoples of the nineteenth and early twentieth centuries negotiated with imperial authorities and their interlocutors in continually shifting and often ambivalent ways. The grand Western narrative of the 'burden' of racial, moral and cultural superiority that helped mobilise support for empire thus sat uncomfortably with the lived historical experience of colonisation, where colonial strategies for the reshaping of individuals and their social systems were simultaneously absorbed, contained, resisted and subverted.[1] Rarely is this more evident than in the history of Christian foreign mission.[2] European efforts to convert people of many faiths to Christianity, particularly in areas of the world where direct imperial governance prevailed, exposed complex tensions between the ideas that drove evangelical activity and those that moulded its reception.[3] By viewing the tensions of empire through the highly focused lens of mission we may, arguably, be able to observe some of the less accessible but everyday forms of the social relations of empire in particularly fine, subjective detail. We can identify two key reasons why this may be so. First, the mission process involved both the social elaboration of otherness and its daily negotiation. Unlike the home churches that directed and funded mission activity, and indeed the broader Western audience for missionary work, European Christian evangelists on the ground were required not only to express the spiritual superiority of their belief system over others in an abstract sense, but were obliged to do so while engaging, often in ways that involved them in intimate social and personal forms of communication, with non-Christian social systems and the individuals who sustained them. These were people with whom they had established and maintained personal relationships, whose names they knew, and with whom they debated and learned from, made friendships and quarrelled with. They may also have competed or collaborated in the acquisition of food, domestic services and other resources, or the buying, selling and renting of land, the construction of buildings, or other forms of engagement with civil, legal and financial institutions. Second, mission societies tended to accumulate and store extensive archives, in manuscript, print and visual forms, which, while embodying the missionary ethos, may also contain a highly diversified range of content that often includes, for example, documents produced by those who sought to disrupt, undermine or supersede their work.[4]

Among the most significant yet least studied attributes of these sources is their transcontinental and cross-cultural dimension. The single most important function of mission was publicity. Public preaching, the staging of musical and cultural events, and the production and distribution of biblical images were organised continuously and in parallel with the more institutional activities of running schools, orphanages and medical dispensaries. Mission was literally geared to 'bringing the Good News' and the key instrument of missionary publicity was journalism. Newspaper and periodical writing served two powerful purposes: to provide support to the work in the field, and to communicate the 'good news' of Christianisation to missionary publics in the home countries.[5] In so doing, periodical print not only opened new routes of cultural transmission between distant audiences and produced new forms of knowledge,[6] but, crucially, became implicated in the construction and reconstruction of 'publics' across continents in highly specific, and thus observable, ways. One consequence of conceiving of missionary print media in this way is that it presents the possibility of exploring a historically specific communication process from a 'de-Westernised' perspective, one that constitutes and connects publics across borders without universalising one while silencing others, yet which acknowledges that they were separated by enormous disparities of power. But while missionary writing may have embodied what Edward Said termed a cultural 'restlessness' that furthered heterogeneity and interconnectedness,[7] strategies of resistance to missionary activity presented Christian evangelists with two quite separate sets of difficulties. One was how to amend or reinforce their own activity in practice when faced with opposition; the other was how to describe and explain such resistance in the discursive arena of print, and to do so continuously over many decades.[8] The historical peculiarities of missionary communication, then, may suggest ways in which other forms of trans-global media communicated and constituted, simultaneously and over time, broader 'publics' in both 'Western' and 'non-Western' worlds.[9]

The purpose of this chapter is to explore the social relations of mission in the context of a specific history, one that allows its tensions to be studied over an extended period of time and which traces the interconnections between at least three distinct sets of actors: the missionary presence, the subject population and the Western domestic audience. The case drawn upon is one that emerged over eighty or so years in the then small town of Sylhet in north-east Bengal, now Bangladesh. Sylhet occupies a particularly important place in the modern history of Wales since it was there and in neighbouring Assam that the largest concentration of Welsh Presbyterian missionaries were dispatched to Christianise Indians in a peculiarly Welsh form of Presbyterianism from 1840 to the mid-1960s.[10] In the process, the people and terrain of the town of Sylhet, and the rivers, plains and settlements that surrounded it, figured prominently in the Welsh Nonconformist imagination, fed over decades by the weekly and monthly press, travelling lantern slide shows, lectures, sermons, hymns and exhibitions, and later also by films, stage plays and novels.[11] What is of particular interest in the case of the Welsh mission in Sylhet is the manner in which this very specific historical encounter generated modes of engagement with Indian Christians and non-Christians that reveal individual and collective strategies for addressing difference. Bearing in mind the structural inequalities of those colonial and racialised relationships, the practice of mission involved an acknowledgement of their fluidity and indeterminacy, and the hybridity and interconnectedness of the civic culture in which they participated.[12]

The doctrinaire nature of Calvinistic Methodism in Wales, intimately related in the minds of many in Welsh Calvinism with the supposed spiritual 'purity' of the Welsh language,[13] clearly distinguished it not only from the far larger and better-resourced mission societies of the Anglican and Roman Catholic churches, and the English Methodist movements,[14] but also from other Welsh missionary enterprises, most notably the Baptist missions in the Caribbean. The notion of being a theologically and linguistically embattled religious community, assiduously promoted within Welsh Calvinism almost from its origins, played itself out in complex, even contradictory, ways when mission obliged it to engage with a cultural world they struggled to comprehend.

The politics of belief

At the turn of the twentieth century, and still recovering from the catastrophic earthquake of 1896, Sylhet's urban population of some 18,000 consisted of a very small number of Christians, a slightly larger group of so-called 'animists' from the Assamese Hill tracts, with the rest equally divided between Muslims and Hindus. It was also a highly cosmopolitan and ethnically diverse town, Islam having been brought by Yemenis in the fifteenth century, followed by Parsi exiles from north-west India,

Catholic Portuguese traders, Eastern Orthodox Armenian industrialists, and Anglican English adventurers, such as William Makepeace Thackeray (1749–1814).[15] It was the administrative capital of a province that included other urban areas where the mission had developed a presence, such as Sunamganj to the west, Karimganj and Silchar to the east, and Maulvi Bazaar, Habiganj and Srimangal to the south, towns joined by rivers, notably the Surma and its tributaries, or directly or indirectly by the Assam and Bengal railway, which was completed as far as Silchar, from Calcutta, in 1898.[16]

With the expansion of the Assamese tea industry from the 1850s, predominantly Hindu workers from the North-West Provinces and Bihar were transported in large numbers into the cleared forest 'wastelands', followed closely by Christian evangelists, both Protestant and Catholic.[17] The first Welsh Presbyterian missionary, the Reverend William Pryse, had established the first base in the town in 1860, thus effectively extending south to the Bengali plains the existing Welsh mission field in the Khasi Hills to the north established by Thomas Jones twenty years earlier.[18] Pryse and those who followed him quickly found that as well as competing against each other, Christian missions were also obliged to address powerful evangelical missionary activity from both Hindu and Islamic movements, and struggled for dominance among an often bewildering array of religious movements and sects. The orthodox imperial view they had imbibed at home was, as Francis Wrangham of Trinity College, Cambridge, had written in 1805, that Muslims were 'the usual composition of bigots ... a blind and bloody sect', while Hindus were 'a mild and quiet people, free from the stronger tumults of the passions, with considerable powers of intellect and some excellencies of feeling' but who were 'enslaved by a wily priesthood'. Overall, the purpose of the British presence was, as Wrangham postulated, to 'protect and enlighten India' so that India could 'enrich and strengthen Great-Britain'.[19]

Christian agencies, formal and informal, took numerous forms. Politically, they exerted pressure on government to remove state aid for Hindu and Islamic foundations, which Jackie Assayag has identified as one of the key triggers of modern Indian communalism.[20] Culturally, they explicitly sought to conquer minds through education and Westernisation. As John Macdonald, a lieutenant-colonel in the Indian Army had written in 1820, 'a communication of a knowledge of the *English language, and of a moderate portion of European literature* to the native mind, would attach them to British interests more than *one hundred thousand bayonets* ...' Mission and education thus drove what he termed an 'intellectual machine', which would ensure that Indians would 'self-convert' to Christianity, thereby ensuring the *'permanent security and stability* of British power in India'.[21] Imperial assumptions about the role of Western rationalism and industrial technologies to transform and modernise India continued to influence administrators and missionaries throughout the nineteenth century and continued well into the twentieth.[22] In practice, however, the simplicity of this analysis did not, and could not, match the tapestry of human experience, and the patterns of loyalty and aspiration that missionaries actually encountered in their daily communication with non-Christians. Additionally, the ethos of mission embodied by Wrangham, Macdonald and others, and which had been internalised by many of the mid-nineteenth century Christian missionaries in India of all denominations, led to tension, even confusion, between the priorities of Christianising Indian society and social practices, on the one hand, and the conversion of individual non-Christians, on the other. In areas such as the Assam Hill tracts where large-scale conversion of 'animist' tribal groups continued throughout the century, the tension was never as evident as in those areas, such as the Sylheti plains, where Hindu and Muslim civil and religious movements rendered individual conversions exceedingly difficult to enact, and even more so to sustain.[23]

Religious engagement

That mission involved deeper theologically oriented engagements than preaching, schooling and the provision of medical care has been known for some time. A debate strategy, in particular, brought Christian missionaries into sustained contact with scholars and religious leaders. In Sylhet, the Welsh missionary William Pryse, organised a series of theological meetings, though only after insisting that he would 'not enter into any discussion with a Mahommedan unless he were acquainted with Arabic History and Literature'. Eleven Islamic clerics (*maulvis*) met at Pryse's house in Sylhet, in the autumn of 1856, to discuss the relative merits of the two great religions.[24] These initially private discussions grew into more public events as other Muslims came to listen and, Pryse claimed, 'to show their respect to the Christian religion'.[25] A further step was to organise a series of public lectures for Christians, Muslims and Hindus on broad intellectual subjects, the first being on the Ancient History of India. He reported that 130 attended the first lecture, while subsequent events enabled inter-community dialogues to be held on subjects as diverse as biblical and Koranic comparisons between accounts of the Creation, the Fall and the Flood, the object of punishment, the omnipresence of God, the origin of sin and punishment, and the meanings of such concepts as fate, righteousness and reward. Other encounters explored the elusive nature of true happiness, the source and effect of prejudice, and what constitutes truth.[26]

The debate strategy continued under markedly different circumstances with the strengthening in Sylhet of the Bhramo Somaj Hindu reform movement. Sylhet-born Bipin Chandra Pal (1858–1932) was reported to have 'stirred up' the 'educated section' of Karimganj in 1898 with a series of public meetings.[27] Pal was born into a Bhramo Somaj family and was an early activist in the Indian National Congress. He had established and edited the weekly newspaper *Paridarshak* in Sylhet in 1886, a year before publishing a biography of Queen Victoria. He started a daily paper, *Bande Mataram*, in 1905 as a protest against the British partition of Bengal, and was imprisoned for sedition in 1907. On his release he travelled to Britain where he studied briefly at the Unitarian College in Manchester.[28] The impact of his newspaper and the legal action against it continued to be felt in Sylhet in 1909, when Elizabeth Williams, the first fully accredited female missionary to be sent to the Indian mission field by the Welsh Presbyterian Church in 1889,[29] reported the change that she had witnessed in the town since 1905.

> Pictures of the principal leaders of the unrest in India hang on the walls of the zenanas, along with pictures of the young men executed for taking lives – they hang next to images of their gods, like heroes; with 'Bande Mataram' printed in large letters on the walls and above the doors.[30]

However, in January 1913, we find her colleague Laura Evans attending a Bhramo Somaj women's meeting in Silchar, at which some thirty or forty were present, where she was well and courteously received.[31] Three years later Dilys Edmunds in Silchar also opened discussions with local members of the Bhramo Somaj, following which she reported that 'the closer I get into contact with Hindus the more I feel what grand Christians some of them would make'. She was particularly influenced by her Bengali teacher, 'a Reformed Hindu' who helped her arrange an informal meeting with other Bhramo members, whom she found to be 'not far from the Kingdom of Heaven'.[32]

John Roberts's meeting with Sir Rabindranath Tagore in November 1919 was of an altogether different nature. Tagore had been invited to stay in a mission-owned bungalow in Sylhet, and the Bhramo Somaj poet paid a visit to the Welsh Presbyterian mission compound to thank Roberts personally for his hospitality. In the conversation that followed, Roberts acknowledged that Tagore's 'indictment of the materialistic aims of Western Civilization was an overwhelming one' while 'his ideals were those we stand for, and with which every true Christian is bound to agree'. More surprisingly, he found himself in sympathy with his 'veiled antipathy' to the British Government in India since 'so many of the officers of the Govt have so little sympathy with Indians, and so little real knowledge of their aspirations, while Europeans engaged in commerce know less still'.[33]

Six years later, in April 1925, Roberts met the Anglican missionary and trade union leader C. F. Andrews on his visit to Sylhet. He suspected that Andrews had 'imbibed Indian ideas' and that his teaching was 'pantheistic in tendency', and wondered whether 'Hinduism is not once again trying to absorb its enemy'. However, having heard Andrews preach at the Welsh mission church, Roberts conceded that 'Mr Andrews is an interesting man . . . (h)e is also a power in India these days, as he is an idol of the people . . . He came to Sylhet wearing a shirt and dhuti the Indian national dress . . . He was barefooted . . . It is very rarely indeed that we see a European dressed in this way, and many Indians now wear European dress.'[34] The following year, at a public meeting in Karimganj, Dilys Edmunds spoke of her 'desire to understand the Indian point of view, her sympathy with everything Indian', while Hindus in the audience are reported to have admired Edmunds's love for her 'Guru Jesus Christ'.[35]

Political engagement

However, few among the Western missionaries in Sylhet sympathised with the broader aspirations of Indian nationalism, though in 1917 John Roberts gave a different set of reasons for his opposition that were based on references to the recent history of his own Welsh people. 'What is called the home-rule movement here has no right to such a name as it really is an attempt on the part of the Priests and Landlords to get hold of the reins of Government. The masses of the people would have no say in the matter . . . We of Wales know what the tyranny of priest and landlord is, and it would be a hundred times worse out here.'[36] Missionaries in particular responded with alarm to the politicisation of Muslims into what had largely been a Hindu nationalist phenomenon in Sylhet. By the time Gandhi visited Silchar in September 1921, Thomas Reese noted how 'the badges of the Khilafat, and the Gandhi caps, are in evidence everywhere – on the heads and shoulders of the sons of the Prophet'.[37]

Relationships with individual nationalist activists, however, were often more nuanced. In 1932 Laura Evans found that the four sons and three daughters of one of the mission teachers were Swaraj activists, The four sons were 'among the first to make bombs' and had been interned. Their mother had been educated in the mission school in Silchar. Evans took a circuitous route to visit the eldest of the sons,

Hen Babu, in hiding near Shaistaganj in what was 'clearly a hideout for volunteers'. They took tea, and when she returned to her boat Hen Babu had presented her with a bunch of roses.[38] Four years later, Elizabeth Lloyd in Silchar argued that:

> The most arresting feature in the present political movement in India is the part played by the women. Even those women who are still in *purdah* have enrolled themselves as national volunteers, and have taken an active part in organising processions and meetings, and in picketing liquor shops, and shops where foreign cloth is sold.

Significantly, she attributed the feminisation of the nationalist movement to 'the educational work of years ... Missionaries have from the beginning been pioneers of this great work of education, believing what is now maintained by all leaders of public life in India, that no true and permanent progress is possible in the life of the people unless the education of girls is carried on side by side with that of boys.'[39]

The gendering of public life, however, was a site of contestation especially in relation to Hindu as well as Islamic sensibilities in Sylhet, and played a significant part in the popular attacks on Christian mission. As early as 1864, William Pryse had reported the formal distance of personal relationships,[40] but by the end of the century the anxieties were of a different order. In June 1895, the medical missionary Dr O. O. Williams felt obliged to condemn 'the licentiousness' of Hindu and Muslim men, the consequence of which was that 'no woman speaks to a crowd of people – all men – without raising morbid curiosity', adding in a subsequently struck-out sentence that 'there ought to be men in Wales men enough to come and preach to the men here, without the pressure being such as to tempt Christian women to expose themselves to insult'.[41] Williams's disapproval of the 'morbid curiosity' of the male Sylheti crowd was, however, differently interpreted in a pamphlet of the mid-1920s published by the Islamia Press, founded in Sylhet in 1870 by Moulvi Abdul Karim.[42] Entitled *Religious Advice from (the) Bible*, by Mohd Abdul Lotif, it provided a seven-point critique of the Bible. But it was most eloquent when it spoke of the local perceptions of Welsh Christian activity, which from the turn of the century had been overwhelmingly female in composition. Abdul Lotif observed that, in Welsh Christian worship,

> many kinds of pleasure like a theatre are found. From charming throats and by the sweet sounding voices of handsome women many songs are sung with moving of hands stretching of necks like hearts. With their eyes these women drink in the men, goggling and dancing and by music and other means the weak minds of men are drawn and in these places

given to error, become infatuated . . . In the religion of Islam who ever saw such things . . . Our Christian brothers are not afraid of preaching sin.[43]

Responses such as these found expression at street level as well as in the press. In 1895 two female missionaries, one Welsh and one Sylheti, preached in the bazaar of a village that was new to them. The crowd 'tried to hustle them' and as the women fled to the safety of a rest house, clods of earth were thrown after them, one of which struck Kate Williams on the back of the head. Dr Williams, who witnessed the scene, assured the mission Secretary that, 'Rowdyism is really very rare . . . but it illustrates the state of mind of the hearers when they are preached to by women.'[44] When Florence Williams arrived in Sylhet for the first time in 1909, she confessed to being amazed at how:

very few women (are) to be seen on the streets, men, men everywhere. When we go to the bazaar to buy something, a crowd gathers round us. I suppose to see and hear us talk. I have often heard of the personal remarks they pass but now we are here it makes one feel funny when a man will shout after us. Where are you going etc. One boy was asking Miss W(illiams) this morning what was that Miss Evans had round her waist, like a chain. It was you may guess a belt. Of course we do not understand but Miss W tells us, sometimes though I know that they ask her more than she is willing for us to know.[45]

In the same year, Elizabeth Williams regretfully acknowledged that the overwhelming sense she had observed even in the most respectable of zenanas, was that missionaries were there 'on sufferance'.[46] There was in Sylhet, she reported, a 'strong feeling against Europeans, no matter who they are . . . Schoolboys . . . are the worst by far.' They would not give way to her on the street until 'the wheels of her bicycle were almost upon them', and even then they kept their opened umbrellas so close together as to make it difficult for her to pass without being poked in the eye. On another occasion, a youth had thrown a bottle of red liquid over her in the street, staining her blouse, and had taunted her with cries of, 'Jesus Christ will save us.' Another time in the bazaar she was hooted, others threw stones and shouted 'Bande Mataram' while young and older men spat and cleared their throats as she went past.[47] The social volatility intensified in the early 1920s, and in 1921 John Roberts reported that in Sylhet 'there have been a series of petty insults to Europeans as they go along the streets of the town here, and last week, a lump of mud was thrown at a planter and his wife as they were motoring'.[48] In a separate incident at around the same time betel juice had been spat on the dress of a European woman, and a half-brick thrown at a European driving through the town in a motor car.[49] The following year Dilys Edmunds noted that 'politically things seem(ed) to be settling down' in Karimganj, though 'now and then, a hostile Mohamedan expresses his feelings by spitting on the ground when we pass'. But a greater cause of alarm was the way in which the hostility of Hindus and Muslims was being augmented by tensions with the mission's own Christian converts. As Edmunds noted, parents were refusing to allow their children to attend the mission school, 'preferring to wait until a non-co-operation school for girls is opened in Karimganj, which event, they say is to take place soon'. But for Edmunds, 'the saddest part of it all' was the support the boycott received from 'one of our Christians, who has gone right off the rails . . . He refuses to attend the services, and has withdrawn his girls from our school.'[50]

This brings us to the most contested arena of all, namely the deeply problematic engagement between missionaries and those Indians they converted to Christianity. Much was written at the time about the holiness of a handful of Christian sadhus, but even then Indian religiosity seldom conformed to Western notions of the sacred.[51] Dilys Edmunds, on meeting the Sadhu Sundar Singh at the Mairang Assembly in 1923, struggled to comprehend the nature of his belief. 'Denominationalism has for the Sadhu no meaning', she noted, 'nor does he find God so easily in Churches or Chapels, as in the silences of jungles, or in the lonely hill caves of Tibhet [sic].'[52] Relations with local Christians were even more troubled, even hostile. The Anglican Church had for decades been sceptical of 'rice converts',[53] which, as Walter Bruce Davies noted in his retrospective analysis of the mission in Assam, was a phenomenon prompted as much by political advantage as by economic gain. 'Bengali Christians', he noted, 'looked down on Muslims, due to being better educated and they had the help of foreign missionaries whose influence with British officials was proverbial. And their religion was that of the ruling power.'[54] Eliza Kent has also noted that Christianity for many Hindu converts was 'a strategy for moving up within the ranked order of castes, rather than an effort to destroy or escape from the Hindu social order'.[55]

Identity and autonomy

Anglicans were also alive to the social and theological dangers of extending forms of Christianity that were distinctly unlike their own. In February 1902, the Right Reverend James MacArthur, Anglican Bishop of Bombay, had welcomed the growing number of Christians in Assam while admitting to an anxiety. 'There is no danger so alarming, so distressing in its possibilities, so fraught with risks to true progress in the future, as the danger latent in an ill-instructed and shallow profession of the religion of Christ.'[56] Conversion was evidently not an unproblematic idea for the missionary churches, and fears about its actual, unpredictable meanings were if anything more keenly felt in the mission fields than in the home churches that controlled them.[57] The danger of heterodoxy in this intellectually and theologically charged urban culture, especially as it affected European Christians, was closely monitored by the foreign mission management committee at home. In 1863, Robert Parry was ejected from the mission and obliged to take a school teaching post in Calcutta following accusations that he had adopted 'Rationalistic principles', an allegation based on an overheard conversation in which he was claimed to have told 'young Catechists here that the Bible is not to be regarded as historically true'.[58]

In other ways, too, the presence of Europeans complicated evangelical missionary work. In 1863 there were estimated to be more than two hundred European tea planters in Cachar who, William Pryse noted, gave 'assistance of their influences and purses' to the Welsh mission.[59] By 1906, however, J. W. Roberts had adopted a less benign view of their influence, regretting that 'it is only the exception that cares in the least for Christian work'. In Silchar, settlers sustained a racecourse, two clubs and a ballroom, and while 'personally kind and hospitable, are a hindrance to the progress of the Kingdom of God'.[60] In a similar vein, Dilys Edmunds reported how her Hindu Bengali teacher had asked her 'why it was that Christians do not live more in accordance with Christ's ideals. It was difficult to answer, with visions in my mind of drunken tea-planters reeling along the Silchar roads.'[61] While missionaries were often regarded as cultural intermediaries between Bengali society and European settlers, they were, at the same time, eager to distance themselves from the social and moral beliefs and practices of their fellow Westerners.[62]

While some converts were the products of mission schools and orphanages, others came voluntarily as adults. Laura Evans reported in 1919 on the 'constant stream of men' who came to the mission compound in Sylhet, including, in the space of one day, 'two Mahommedans wanting to be Christians, one because he wants to get more education, the other says that he wants to know the Truth. Two Babus wanting an English Bible Class. A young man in great distress wanting to be saved from himself.'[63] In 1935 the same missionary left her bungalow at ten in the evening on 'a lovely moonlight night' when, to her surprise she met '3 men dressed in long yellow robes' who claimed to be 'secret disciples of Jesus Christ'.[64] Reports of such voluntary approaches, however, were rare. Far more frequently, missionaries on the Sylheti plain wrote of the difficulties of breaking through the social constraints of Indian society. The medical missionary Dr O. O. Williams, writing in Karimganj in 1899, found that 'the Bengalis are not receptive and one's work seems to be confined to making a favourable impression on the *whole* community rather than on individual members. Individual members when dealt with in Bible class or dispensary never forget that they are members of a great organism, the fear of which is constantly in their minds.'[65] Williams also drew attention to that other, deeper anxiety to which the Bishop of Bombay was also to refer, namely the growth of the 'now common type' of Hindu who, 'without becoming Christians, they desire the liberty which Christians bring', in particular in relation to the breaking of caste rules.[66]

The social pressure on converts, and the isolationist responses of missionaries, created some of the more difficult, even conflictual, relationships that were established between the Welsh and the Indians with whom they came into contact.[67] The following example is not untypical of the recorded cases. In 1904 a high caste, land-owning Hindu (who, significantly, is not named in any of the reports) was baptised by the Welsh mission, along with his immediate family, in Sylhet. He pursued his new faith diligently for many months, even preaching in the *mofussil* villages. Farmers on his land in turn began to embrace the new religion of their landlord and in high excitement missionaries believed that an entire swathe of the Sylhet countryside was being successfully evangelised. 'But, but', John Roberts cautioned in 1908, they had not taken into account the social and economic complexities of conversion. Within a year, worried reports indicated that the landowner convert was losing interest in Christianity. He had been disappointed to have found Christians to be neither holy nor pure. He had also suffered in the wake of the Hindu 'boycott which followed his breaking caste, [and] ... he found it difficult to be denied the fellowship of his old friends'. Could he, he asked, 'not conform to some of the Hindu rules, and still believe in Christianity?' Later, it was rumoured that he and his family were seeking readmission into Hinduism, and that 'the price had been fixed'.

Enter at this point a Brahmin, Mohin Babu, who had also been baptised by the mission in Sylhet in 1904. He had subsequently severed his connection with the church but in 1907 had demanded readmission. Mohin Babu's repeated requests were, according to Roberts, 'spoken with half a smile, half a sneer, and an expression that seemed to suggest the guile of the serpent'. Roberts's scepticism stemmed from his knowledge that Mohin had also been making similar advances to the Roman Catholics at Badapur. Early in 1908, Mohin Babu had moved into the convert's house and began, Roberts reported, to wield 'considerable influence over him'. With significant lawsuits pending, which if decided against him might have led to the loss of a significant part of his estate, the landowner transferred all his property to Mohin Babu's name in order to avoid the seizure of his properties. All the Brahmins except one were reported to have agreed to accept the landowner back into the Hindu community on condition that he paid 300 rupees and made a pilgrimage to Benares. Roberts detected in the delay in allowing the landowner back into the Hindu fold a tactic 'to make a fool of a man who has dared to accept baptism. They with [Mohin] Babu seem set on degrading the Christian name before a whole district of people, because this matter is a topic of conversation in many many villages in that part.'

But, crucially, the most bewildering and painful element in the whole tangled affair was the realisation that the mind that 'with consummate cleverness' had coordinated the campaign with the Brahmins was a baptised Christian convert. 'Behind the scenes, keeping the Landowner's mind set against Christianity, one sees undoubted traces of [Mohin] Babu's influence.' Later, the landowner, his family and Mohin Babu travelled to Calcutta, ostensibly to 'confer with the missionaries there', but later admitted that the purpose of their journey had been to bathe in the Ganges 'at the fixed time and . . . at the advice of the Brahmins'. On their return, Mohin Babu met Roberts with a smile, denied 'all in the name of all that is sacred', and requested a house on the Sylhet mission compound 'in order to be able to attend the services'.[68]

While baptised converts presented the mission with some of its most intractable problems, those who were ambitious themselves to serve as active evangelists often generated unresolvable tensions between missionaries in the field and their managers in the home church. Much revolved around status within the local church structures, and remuneration.[69] Joy Gobinda Shome, one of William Pryse's earliest converts, had demanded the status and salary and allowances of a European missionary, and when he was refused, he began to study for the Bar and started 'to wage war against European Missionaries'. While practising as a Pleader in the Calcutta High Court, Shome joined the Free Church of Scotland and became one of its Elders. Later, he and Kali Charan Bannerjee formed their own church, the Christo-Somaj, and started the *Indian Christian Herald* as an outlet, the Welsh Church claimed, for 'Shome's spleen against Missionaries'.[70]

Joy's eldest brother, Sonaton, baptised by Pryse and allegedly 'the first of all the converts', also sustained an ambiguous relationship with the mission. Professing 'to carry on a Mission of his own' while working as a homeopathic doctor, John Pengwern Jones noted that Sonaton ran a school in Akhalia village, three miles from Sylhet, 'but he had no Christian teaching there',[71] and that in Jones's view Sonaton had 'never considered himself or any of his family' to be 'members of our church, and was accustomed to administer both baptisms and the Lord's Supper himself. He used to style himself Rev.', but attended Christmas and

Easter services at the Welsh mission chapel in Sylhet. He also insisted that 'Christians should be independent, and not Europeanised or dependent on foreign money'.[72] 'He was an exceedingly cantankerous man', Jones recalled, 'and during my first few years repeatedly gave me a good deal of pain by recounting the number of Missionaries of our Mission that had been recalled or dismissed.'[73]

Complaints by baptised converts against missionaries had been a constant theme in the history of the mission since the excommunication of its founder, Thomas Jones, in 1847, and of his successors William Pryse and Thomas Jones ('the second') in 1867 and 1872 respectively, all following vigorous protests regarding their allegedly inappropriate sexual and social behaviour. By the 1920s, however, tensions between converts and missionaries took on more explicitly politicised forms. When in 1925 John Pengwern Jones came under suspicion of having a physical relationship with a young Khasi woman on the mission compound in Maulvi Bazaar, his initial response was that the accusations had arisen:

> out of jealousy between the girls and from the Swadeshi and Nationalist feeling that is so common in India today. It is true that there is at the present time a strong anti-missionary feeling among many preachers, and mission-workers in India. Indian Christian papers often state that missionaries are unwilling for Indian workers to rise to positions of responsibility and block their way to adequate spheres of work.[74]

The instigator of the complaint, the Reverend Badshah, was, Jones informed the commission, 'full of this spirit and was dissatisfied with his status and salary'.[75] The commission of enquiry, consisting of four other missionaries, was generally unimpressed by Jones's explanations but cleared him of the specific charges on lack of evidence.

Differences between converts and missionaries were also revealed in cultural and aesthetic choices. By 1909, for example, Christian Babus in Sylhet had taken up the violin as their proselytising instrument of choice 'and they take them everywhere', eschewing the portable organs of the missionaries.[76] A year later, Elizabeth Radcliffe described the Sheikghat Chapel choir in Sylhet as being accompanied by 'a violin and two queer looking drums and some other indescribable instrument. I have never in all my life heard such a noise.'[77] At other times, missionaries were convinced that the stubbornly autonomous 'Indianness' of their converts' Christianity could only be explained by the fact that they had been administered 'a drug that deranges the mind' by relatives eager for them to return to Hinduism. 'That these kinds of drugs are known and used in India', Pengwern Jones insisted, 'is certain . . .',[78] raising the spectre of Christian conversion being regarded by both the families of the converted and the broader Bengali society as a pathological and thus also a medicalised condition treatable by a combination of social opprobrium and appropriate, if covert, medication.

But the most significant arena of contestation between missionaries, their converts and the broader Bengali society turned around the acquisition and control of property and land which brought them into direct and sustained conflict with Hindu and Islamic organisations. In the spring of 1911 the mission responded to a request for aid by local low-caste Namasudra leaders by organising a conference in Sunamganj to agitate for Namasudra rights to land and water.[79] A short time later, a Namasudra hostel was built on the Sylhet mission compound, and closer relations with the low-caste population in and surrounding Sylhet led to individual conversions and plans to build an 'independent Christian community' on which they could settle and farm by means of land purchased by the mission on their behalf.[80] Namasudras, the Welsh believed, had initially approached them for assistance because of their anxiety about the growing influence of the *khilafat* non-cooperation movement, which was led by 'intellectuals' who had 'for centuries oppressed them. Now that the struggle is between the educated Indians and the British, they have expressed their desire to side with the Sahibs, and are willing to go to the length of adopting the Sahib's religion.'[81] Caught in the local politics of Sylheti Hinduism, the mission's conversion strategy also attracted Muslim attention. 'Hindu, Mohammedan and Christian are seeking to win these people', John Roberts warned his home church, as a consequence of which the Presbyterian mission was able to make only very limited inroads into the scattered Namasudra communities of Sylhet.[82]

The overwhelmingly Muslim village of Ghorgao, near Habiganj in southern Sylhet, however, had initially presented a more promising prospect for collective conversion. However, here again the defensive Islamic response was aggressive and effective. As a settlement of some 200 houses, the evangelisation of Ghorgao also relied on the purchase of land in and around the village to distance the tenants from their Muslim landlord. Within weeks, Sylheti Muslims were raising funds to establish a madrassa in the village and to pay the salaries of Islamic teachers and spiritual leaders to reconvert apostate villagers.[83] The counter-assault also included popular cultural interventions and performances, including enactments of anti-Christian dramas, the spreading of anti-missionary rumours, and theological point-scoring. Frequent references were made in pamphlets and sermons to the polytheistic nature of the doctrine of the Trinity, the apparently contradictory testaments of Matthew and Luke, and the paucity of recorded evidence for miracles, which were 'opposed to nature and reason'. One theatrical performance, staged in the main street of Ghorgao, caricatured the baptismal service by dressing the chief actor as a European, with his face whitened with chalk, and wearing a battered hat. A bowl covered with a cloth was placed on a table to represent the baptismal font, and the missionary character, being asked where he came from, replied, 'I live in England, but not being able to gain my livelihood there, I came to this country to make you Christians' before comically begging the audience for money in return for baptism.[84] In 1930, when tensions were at their most intense, Ghorgao was visited by five Brahmins, 'all congress men', including a head teacher and a priest, who said they had come to 'attack Christianity', and especially Indian Christians.[85] Tensions remained high for at least another decade, and in 1940 sporadic violence again broke out when Sylheti Islamic leaders sought to bring a legal case against the mission's claim to landownership in the village.[86]

Conclusion

This chapter has tried to show that instances of resistance were far from being isolated events. On the contrary, as embattled missionaries themselves strenuously argued, they were systemic to the missionary process. By focusing on missionary responses to resistance, attention may be drawn both to the limits of evangelical activity and to the broader character of colonial social relations. In this particular case, the evidence suggests, above all, that individual subjectivities, cultural practices and changing political currents on the ground in India were far more complicated than the missionary project at home had trained Welsh evangelists to expect, and much missionary activity was devoted to negotiating that deficit. The actual experience of mission demonstrated that faith communities in colonial India communicated between, as well as within, their belief networks, responding organically to the interpenetration of the other into their respective religious and civic cultures. While these dialogues provided some, if limited, opportunities for Christian evangelisation, they also created space for the exercise of Hindu and Muslim counter-strategies aimed at containing, resisting and repelling Christian influence. But inter-personal religious dialogues, conducted face to face in a Sylheti 'rational public sphere',[87] also involved Welsh encounters with sadhus, Sufis, ambiguity, syncretism and, above all, the historical complexity and specificity of the actors themselves, which tended to blur the absolute distinctions between Islam, Hinduism and Christianity that underpinned each of their missionary models. Tellingly, the most enduring difficulty Welsh missionaries in Sylhet encountered was the effort to comprehend the hostility shown towards them by an Indian Christianity, even in its

Presbyterian variant, that rejected their claims to both administrative and doctrinal authority. A further complication involved the ways in which religious dialogues were represented and communicated to broader publics as cultural information transmitted across and through belief networks by sermons, letters, pamphlets and periodicals, as much in Muslim and Hindu circles as in the Christian. At the same time, the depiction of Islam in some Christian literature as a socially cohesive and dynamic form of mass devotion to God, free from alcohol and with a strong emphasis on moral improvement, chimed remarkably well with the doctrinal instincts of a Nonconformist public in Wales and beyond.

Politically, too, messages were mixed. The Welsh audience at home in the 1920s learned through its Indian missionaries that opponents to British imperial rule had acquired powerful direction in the *khilafat* and *swaraj* movements, precisely at the time that Wales itself was being convulsed by industrial unrest and tipping in its loyalty from Liberalism to socialism, and in some quarters also to nationalism. But while tensions generated by Welsh evangelists in East Bengal were overshadowed in the 1940s by the far more visceral experiences of war, famine, nationalist struggle, independence and partition, the history of resistances and accommodations between competing religious movements during the previous eighty years had left significant legacies. The Welsh in their direct experience of mission in Sylhet, and in the ways it was reported and popularised among their missionary public at home, were ineluctably involved in a long and often uneasy exploration of adaptation to difference. That process, however tentatively or reluctantly it was acknowledged, exposed the missionaries to circumstances that obliged them to make doctrinal and aesthetic accommodations to the Sylheti society they had been sent to change, but in whose complex social space they were only ever able to occupy a marginal, if highly engaged and strangely visible, position.

Notes

1 Indian resistance to the practices of Christian mission is effectively explored in I. Copland, 'The Limits of Hegemony: Elite Responses to Nineteenth-Century Imperial and Missionary Acculturation Strategies in India', *Comparative Studies in Society and History*, 49:4 (2007), pp. 637–65.

2 For a stimulating exploration of the relationship between empire and mission, see J. Cox, 'Were Victorian Nonconformists the Worst Imperialists of All?', *Victorian Studies*, 46:2 (2004), pp. 243–55.

3 B. Porter, *The Absent-Minded Imperialists. Empire, Society and Culture in Britain* (Oxford, 2004); A. Porter (ed.), *The Oxford History of the British Empire*, 3 *The Nineteenth Century* (Oxford, 1999); P. van der Veer, *Imperial Encounters. Religion and Modernity in India and Britain* (Princeton and Oxford, 2001); K. Armstrong, *The Battle for God. Fundamentalism in Judaism, Christianity and Islam* (London,

2000); A. A. Powell, *Muslims and Missionaries in Pre-Mutiny India*, London Studies on South Asia, no. 7 (SOAS, 1993); R. E. Frykenberg (ed.), *Christians and Missionaries in India. Cross-Cultural Communication since 1500* (London, 2003). A. N. Porter, 'Cultural Imperialism and Protestant Missionary Enterprise 1780–1914', *Journal of Imperial and Commonwealth History*, 25:3 (1997), pp. 367–91, provided a major impetus for this approach to the role of mission in colonial societies.

4   I wish to thank the History Department of the Presbyterian Church of Wales for permission to access the Calvinistic Methodist Archive (CMA) at the National Library of Wales, Aberystwyth (NLW) and to the Arts and Humanities Research Council for a research award that enabled me, inter alia, to examine the entire CMA archive.

5   See A. Johnston, *Missionary Writing and Empire, 1800–1860* (Cambridge, 2003).

6   B. S. Cohn, *Colonialism and its Forms of Knowledge. The British in India* (Princeton, 1996), pp. 16–56 are especially pertinent in this respect, particularly in relation to the uses of language.

7   E. W. Said, 'The Clash of Definitions', in L. M. Alcoff and E. Mendieta (eds), *Identities: Race, Class, Gender and Nationality* (London, 2003), pp. 333–5. Said argues for a 'sense of restlessness within each culture', and rejects the notion that 'there is complete homogeneity between culture and identity', p. 335.

8   H. Schwarz, 'Aesthetic Imperialism: Literature and the Conquest of India', *Modern Language Quarterly*, 61:4 (2000), pp. 563–86, discusses literary strategies for avoiding resistance to formal methods of colonialism.

9   This is also discussed in the context of mission in R. S. Sugirtharajah, 'Imperial Critical Commentaries: Christian Discourse and Commentarial Writings in Colonial India', *Journal for the Study of the New Testament*, 21:73 (1999), pp. 83–112.

10 E. Thomas, *Hanes Cenhadaeth Dramor Eglwys Bresbyteraidd Cymru. Cenhadaeth Casia. Y gyfrol gyntaf, Bryniau'r Glaw* (Caernarfon, 1988); J. Meirion Lloyd, *Hanes Cenhadaeth Dramor Eglwys Bresbyteraidd Cymru. Cenhadaeth Mizoram. Yr ail gyfrol, Y Bannau Pell* (Caernarfon, 1989); D. G. Merfyn Jones, *Hanes Cenhadaeth Dramor Eglwys Bresbyteraidd Cymru, Cenhadaeth Sylhet-Cachar. Y drydedd gyfrol, Y Popty Poeth a'i Gyffiniau* (Caernarfon, 1990). Other useful studies include J. Meirion Lloyd, *Nine Missionary Pioneers. The Story of Nine Pioneering Missionaries in North-East India* (Caernarfon, 1989), and I. W. Gruffudd (ed.), *Cludoedd Moroedd. Cofio Dwy Ganrif o Genhadaeth* (Swansea, 1995).

11 Examples include D. G. Merfyn Jones, *Ar Fryniau'r Glaw* (Swansea, 1980), and *Eryr Sylhet* (Denbigh, 1987) – two works of fiction. For a broader discussion, see B. Parry, *Delusions and Discoveries: India in the British Imagination* (London, 1998), pp. 35–77.

12 L. Sanneh, *Translating the Message: the Missionary Impact on Culture* (London, 1989) provides a valuable set of references for this approach.

13 D. Morgan, *The Span of the Cross: Christian Religion and Society in Wales, 1914–2000*, 2nd edn (Cardiff, 2011).

14 Closer connections were maintained with Scottish Calvinism into the early twentieth century, and were instrumental in establishing and sustaining the initial mission in Eastern Bengal, see for example, NLW CMA 27161, William Pryse, Sylhet, to John Roberts, Liverpool (marked 'Private'), 25 May 1863.

15 A. Jones, 'Thackeray, William Makepeace', *Banglapedia. National Encyclopedia of Bangladesh* (Dhaka, 2003): www.banglapedia.org/HT/T_0131.HTM

16 Sharif uddin Ahmed (ed.), *Sylhet. History and Heritage* (Dhaka, 1999), *passim*.

17 For a fuller analysis of the relationship between mission and the tea industry in Sylhet, see A. Jones, 'Gardens of Eden: Welsh Missionaries in British India', in R. R. Davies and G. H. Jenkins (eds), *From Medieval to Modern Wales. Historical Essays in Honour of Kenneth O. Morgan and Ralph A. Griffiths* (Cardiff, 2004), pp. 264–80.

18 D. R. Syiemlieh, 'Christian Missions and Tribes in the Hills of North-East India', in T. B. Subba, S. Som and K. C. Baral (eds), *Between Ethnography and Fiction: Verrier Elwin and the Tribal Question in India* (Hyderabad, 2005), pp. 147–56. For the Welsh presence in the Khasi Hills, see A. Brown-May, 'Collision and

Reintegration in a Missionary Landscape: The View from the Khasi Hills, India', in R. McGregor and P. Grimshaw (eds), *Collisions of Cultures and Identities: Settlers and Indigenous People* (Melbourne, 2007), pp. 141–61. See also S. D. Talukdar, *Khasi Cultural Resistance to Colonialism* (Gauhati, 2004).

19 F. Wrangham, *A Dissertation on the Best Means of Civilizing the Subjects of the British Empire in India and of Diffusing the Light of the Christian Religion throughout the Eastern World* (London, 1805), pp. 2 and 29.

20 J. Assayag, 'Passeurs de frontiers, poseurs de barriers. Chrétiens et Musulmans en Inde', in J. Assayag and G. Tarabout, (eds), *Altérité et Identité. Islam at Christianisme en Inde* (Paris, 1997), pp. 46–7.

21 Lieutenant-Colonel John Macdonald, *Some short arguments and plain facts shewing that the civilization and instruction of the Natives of India furnish the surest means of upholding the stability of our oriental empire and of the introduction and speedy progress of Christianity, without arming the superstitious prejudices of the country against that cause: with an alphabetic-cipher-table for secret correspondence and a few requisite animadversions to subjects becoming daily more prominent and commanding* (London, 1820), pp. 6–9.

22 S. Sivasundaram, 'A Christian Benares: Orientalism, Science and the Serampore Mission of Bengal', *Indian Economic and Social History Review*, 44:2 (2007), pp. 111–45.

23 L. Dena, *Christian Missions and Colonialism* (Shillong, 1988), pp. 85–90 on process of conversion and pp. 58–84 on tensions between Christian missionary movements.

24 A. Sen has demonstrated how the 'argumentative tradition' in India 'can be a strong ally of the underdog'. See A. Sen, *The Argumentative Indian. Writings on Indian History, Culture and Identity* (London, 2005), p. 37.

25 Anon. 'A Short account of the Mission Work in Sylhet from its commencement in 1849', 2 vols. No author, but written in Sylhet on the jubilee of the Sylhet mission in 1899. [Manuscript in private possession of E. L. Roberts, Saltney Ferry, Chester], 1, pp. 41–3.

26 *Ibid.* See also D. J. Hesselgrave, *Communicating Christ Cross-culturally: An Introduction to Missionary Communication* (Grand Rapids, MI, 1991). For a discussion of the 'orientalist' dimension of missionary fascination with Indian culture see F. Settler, 'Orientalism and Religion: the question of subject agency', *Method and Theory in the Study of Religion*, 14:2 (2002), pp. 249–64.

27 National Library of Wales, Aberystwyth (hereafter NLW), Calvinistic Methodist Archive, CMA 27287, O. O. Williams to Josiah Thomas, 18 July 1898. The majority of correspondence from the mission field to the home church was addressed to the following Mission Secretaries: John Roberts [Minimus] (1840–66), Josiah Thomas (1866–1900), R. J. Williams (1900–31), and Oliver Thomas (1935–48).

28 A. Chakravarti, *Bipin Chandra Pal: Nationalist Politics and Ideology* (Lucknow, 1998); M. G. Sinha, *The Political Ideas of Bipin Chandra Pal* (New Delhi, 1989).

29 NLW, CMA 27265, Elizabeth Williams file.

30 NLW, CMA 27265, Elizabeth Williams to R. J. Williams, 18 January 1909. See also Christopher Pinney, *'Photos of the Gods'. The Printed Image and Political Struggle in India* (London, 2004).

31 NLW, CMA 27274, Laura Evans to R. J. Williams, 27 January 1913.

32 NLW, CMA 27337, Dilys Edmunds to R. J. Williams, 8 October 1916.

33 NLW, CMA 27306, J. W. Roberts to R. J. Williams, 11 November 1919.

34 NLW, CMA 27307, J. W. Roberts to R. J. Williams, 28 April 1925.

35 *Ibid.*, 24 July 1926.

36 NLW, CMA 27305, J. W. Roberts to E. L. Williams, 31 October 1917.

37 NLW, CMA 27293, T. W. Reese to R. J. Williams, 14 February 1922.

38 NLW, CMA 27275, Laura Evans to R. J. Williams, 24 August 1932.

39 NLW, CMA 27304, E. M. Lloyd, Sylhet, 'School work among the girls of the Plains', n.d. (1936?).

40 NLW, CMA 27227, William Pryse to J. Roberts, 26 September 1864.

41 NLW, CMA 27287, R. J. Williams to J. Thomas, 4 June 1895.

42 For broader studies of the press in Bengal, see K. P. S. Gupta, 'The Christian Missionaries and Bengali Journalism in the first half of the Nineteenth Century', *Indian Church History Review*, 16:1 (1982), pp. 61–71, and J. Sharma, 'Missionaries and Print Culture in Nineteenth-Century Assam: The *Orunodoi* Periodical of the American Baptist Mission', in Frykenberg (ed.), *Christians and Missionaries in India*, pp. 256–73.
43 NLW, CMA 27305, J. W. Roberts to R. J. Williams, n.d. 1909.
44 NLW, CMA 27287, R. J. Williams to J. Thomas, 4 June 1895.
45 NLW, CMA 27311, Florrie Evans, Sylhet, to R. J. Williams, 4 January 1909.
46 On the role of women in mission, see A. Burton, *Burdens of History. British Feminists, Indian Women, and Imperial Culture, 1865–1915* (Chapel Hill, NC, 1994). For a detailed study of women in Welsh missionary culture, see Gwennan Mair Gruffydd Schiavone, 'Y Genhades Dramor a'r Diwylliant Cenhadol yng Nghymru 1887–1930' (PhD dissertation, Aberystwyth University, 2008).
47 NLW, CMA 27265, Elizabeth Williams to R. J. Williams, 18 January 1909.
48 NLW, CMA 27305, J. W. Roberts to R. J. Williams, 12 April 1921.
49 NLW, CMA 27306, ibid., n.d. (April?) 1921.
50 NLW, CMA 27337, Dilys Edmunds to R. J. Williams, 20 January 1922.
51 For kinship conversion patterns see S. Dube, 'Conversion, Translation and Life-History in Colonial Central India', in D. Lindenfeld and M. Richardson (eds), *Beyond Conversion and Syncretism. Indigenous encounters with Missionary Christianity 1800–2000* (Oxford, 2012), p. 30.
52 NLW, CMA 27337, Dilys Edmunds, 'Sadhu Sundar Singh – an appreciation', type-script mailed to Williams, 29 March 1923. See also C. F. Andrews, *Sadhu Sundar Singh: a Personal Memoir* (London, 1934). Sundar Singh addressed the Calvinist Methodist Exhibition at Caernarfon, chaired by David Lloyd George, in June 1929, *The Handbook of the Orient Exhibition* (Caernarfon, 1929).
53 For a recent study of this term, see M. Melanchthon, 'Persecution of Indian Christians', *Dialog. A Journal of Theology*, 41:2 (2008), pp. 103–13.
54 NLW, CMA 27219, file 5, Walter Bruce Davies, 'A Study of Christian–Muslim Relations in East Pakistan', unpublished confidential position paper, August 1961.
55 E. F. Kent, *Converting Women: Gender and Protestant Christianity in Colonial South India* (Oxford, 2004), p. 18.
56 *Statesman* (26 February 1902).
57 See for example J.-Y. Carluer, 'Missionaires gallois et protestants Bretons, les réali-tés et les ambiguïtiés d'une solidarité interceltique, 1832–1940', *Parcours Pays de Galles-Bretagne*, pp. 47–64, Triade Galles, Ecosse, Irlande 1 (Brest, 1995).
58 NLW, CMA 27227, William Pryse to J. Roberts, 25 May 1863.
59 *Ibid.*, 13 August 1863.
60 NLW, CMA 27305, J. W. Roberts to R. J. Williams, 18 December 1906.
61 NLW, CMA 27337, Dilys Edmunds to R. J. Williams, 28 March 1915.
62 *Ibid.*, 29 December 1916.
63 NLW, CMA 27275, Laura Evans to R. J. Williams, 1 July 1919.
64 *Ibid.*, Laura Evans to J. H. Morris, 20 March 1935.
65 NLW, CMA 27287, O. O. Williams to J. Thomas, 7 August 1899.
66 *Ibid.*, 18 November 1899.
67 See also R. Gray, *Black Christians, White Missionaries* (New Haven, 1991).
68 NLW, CMA 27305, J. W. Roberts, Sylhet, to R. J. Williams, 20 April 1908.
69 Other equally decisive issues surrounded ritual and text, as missions feared that converts were engaged in 'wresting control of Christian language', P. Landau, 'Language', in N. Etherington (ed.), *Missions and Empire* (Oxford, 2005), p. 202.
70 NLW, CMA 27258, file 4, John Pengwern Jones, Sylhet, to R. Morris, 5 April 1920.
71 NLW, CMA 27258, file 4, J. P. Jones, Sylhet, to J. H. Morris, 5 April 1920.
72 NLW, CMA 27305, J. W. Roberts to R. J. Williams, 6 June 1916.
73 *Ibid.*, 6 June 1916, report on the death of Shanatan (Sonaton) Shome.
74 NLW, CMA 27258, file 4, 'Report on the enquiry held in Maulvi Bazaar, November 1925'.

75 *Ibid.*
76 NLW, CMA 27311, Annie Florence Evans to R. J. Williams, 22 July 1909.
77 NLW, CMA 27319, Elizabeth Radcliffe to R. J. Williams, 8 January 1910. See Kent, *Converting Women*, pp. 199–235, for an excellent discussion of Christian sartorial style and the culture of respectability in colonial India.
78 NLW, CMA 27305, J. W. Roberts, Sylhet, to R. J. Williams, 2 September 1907.
79 *Ibid.*, 10 April 1911.
80 *Ibid.*, 6 June 1916.
81 NLW, CMA 27337, Dilys Edmunds to R. J. Williams, 20 January 1922.
82 NLW, CMA 27305, J. W. Roberts, Sylhet, to R. J. Williams, 10 April 1911.
83 NLW, CMA 27276, miscellaneous file, n.d.
84 A. Dutta, *Nineteenth Century Bengal Society and Christian Missionaries* (Calcutta, 1992), pp. 195–210. Right to property also impacted on concepts of identity and nationality, particularly in the period shortly before and after 1947, see J. M. Brown, 'Who is an Indian? Dilemmas of National Identity at the End of the British Raj in India', in B. Stanley (ed.), *Mission, Nationalism, and the End of Empire* (Cambridge, 2003), pp. 111–31.
85 NLW, CMA 27275, Laura Evans to R. J. Williams, 15 September 1930.
86 NLW, CMA 27276, Laura Evans to O. Thomas, 9 April and 22 May 1940.
87 For a postcolonial critique of the Habermasian public sphere, see R. Bhargava and H. Reifeld (eds), *Civil Society, Public Sphere and Citizenship: Dialogues and Perceptions* (New Delhi and London, 2005).

CHAPTER 5

Asian migration and the British World, *c*.1850–*c*.1914

Rachel Bright

Both writers and critics of the British World have primarily focused on the white inhabitants within it; the role of non-whites and their impact remains problematic. It is only by studying the reactions to Asian migration, however, that historians can understand why, over time, the concept of empire became less compelling to the settler colonies and why alternative imagined communities like that of a Greater Britain were called into existence. As Bridge and Fedorowich have explained, 'being British anywhere meant exercising full civil rights within a liberal, pluralistic polity, or at least aspiring to that status. "Whiteness" was a dominant element.'[1] The centrality of whiteness and Britishness, and the occasional conflict between these two identities, in part, depended on an Asian 'other' which captured settler imaginations in the late nineteenth and early twentieth centuries. Indigenous peoples were the others of the early nineteenth century,[2] but each colony had a distinct 'native problem', whereas Asian migration increasingly became *the* issue which could unite disparate parts of the Anglo-British World. At its core were contested ideas of what it meant to be a British subject: for it was 'whiteness' contrasted with 'yellowness' that came to dominate turn of the century debates on what constituted full imperial citizenship in the self-governing colonies.

This chapter explores shifting attitudes towards Asian migrants within the British World from the 1850s when European and 'free' (unindentured) Asian migration increased to the temperate zones, which were thought most suited to European settlement.[3] It will then chart how networks of people and information spread shared concepts of 'Asians' which transcended class barriers. This chapter concludes by demonstrating how the desire to limit Asian migration posed a serious challenge to the unity of the British Empire. It also considers throughout why a British World could conceptually materialise across strong

[128]

networks of people and ideology, but why wider imperial federation and citizenship remained elusive.

Creating an 'Asian' menace

In the nineteenth century, about 50 million Europeans, 50 million Chinese and 30 million Indians migrated globally.[4] Adam McKeown has calculated that, of these, almost 750,000 Chinese and 1.5 million Indians were formally indentured to European employers for use in their colonies.[5] Indentured labourers, or 'coolies',[6] were first used in the Dutch East Indies in the 1600s. In the British colonies, it was only following the 1833 abolition of slavery that plantation owners looked to Asia's sizeable and impoverished populations there.[7] By mid-century, as shipping became more organised, cheaper and speedier, indentured labour was also adopted in places without a history of slavery. Small numbers of Pacific islanders and Chinese were imported into New South Wales between 1848 and 1852, to replace convict labour and assist the European wool industry.[8] Natal too began an Indian indenture scheme in the 1860s as one of their first acts as a self-governing colony. This labour assisted colonial businesses so European settlers initially accepted it as a commodity necessary for economic success when the climate allegedly did not allow for 'whites' to do physical labour or because of a shortage of any sort of settler.

While most of this indentured labour was at first uncontroversial, 'free' Asian migration (especially Chinese) to the self-governing colonies increased dramatically from about mid-century. 'Free' is a slight misnomer; but essentially meant that they operated their own loan systems to organise and control migration, outside the direct control of Europeans. Indentured labourers too could become 'free' once their period of service had ended, and increasing numbers chose to do so. Likewise, 'free' migrants tended to follow their indentured fellow nationals, regularly working as traders or artisans either servicing 'coolie' needs or benefiting from the good reputation for work of their indentured predecessors. From 1849, a series of gold discoveries in California, British Columbia and Australia attracted these 'free' Chinese men to work, placing them in direct competition with European settlers. McKeown estimates that 135,000 Chinese migrated to Australia and California in the 1850s alone, all 'funded and arranged by Chinese capital (albeit transported on European ships) and [dependent] on Chinese mining skills.'[9] In 1851, the Chinese government repealed the law which had made migration outside China a criminal offence, punishable by death, further increasing the flow outwards.

The long European tradition of stereotyping the Orient and the

[129]

East already existed in the settler colonies. Stuart Creighton Miller, for instance, has demonstrated how stereotypes spread in America, gathered from travellers, traders, missionaries, and newspapers, before the Chinese had arrived.[10] The predominant view regarded 'China as an exotic, backward, only semi-civilized, and in some ways rather barbaric country'.[11] The place and its people were subjects of curiosity and occasional superiority, but certainly not a threat.

However, it was one thing for 'coolies' to fill manual jobs which 'whites' could or would not fill, but quite another for them to compete in the more lucrative industries of trade and gold mining. From 1849, pre-existing stereotypes about the Chinese nation were applied and adapted to the new influx of Chinese migrants. This was fostered by a common language and a steady exchange of migration and information, especially between the mines. The increasingly international business of book and newspaper publishing and dissemination, higher literacy rates and the improved speed of railway and oceanic travel only aided this flow.[12] Steamboat services regularly carried news and people along the Pacific and Indian Ocean coastlines; border control was almost non-existent. Many of the growing number of colonial papers based their international news on 'verbatim reprints from British papers that had arrived by ship'[13] or on Reuters cables from London. The Colonial Office rarely supplied information to colonies about each other and there was simply no official system for them to communicate with each other, so information networks were largely informal in nature and, in the case of Chinese stereotypes, largely bypassed Britain.

It is not surprising that places undergoing broadly similar social, economic and political upheaval stereotyped the Chinese in similar ways. One idea, in particular, was often repeated over the next fifty years to sum up feelings towards Chinese migrants: the Chinese were disliked as much for their virtues as for their vices. They had been wanted as manual labourers because they were perceived as hard-working and cheap, but they were increasingly thought to undermine 'white' settlers. 'The struggle was perceived not simply as between Europeans and Chinese, but between "white" labour and capitalists using Chinese as their pawns' to lower wages and prevent the spread of labour unions.[14] And because these things were broadly perceived to be happening throughout the self-governing colonies and in the United States, a similar imagery was evoked to describe their situations. Clearly, movement of European labour between the mining communities was important in developing a sense of commonality among the settler colonies and the United States. The increasing organisation of this labour into unions also played an important part in this process. As Andrew Thompson has shown, from the 1840s, British trade unions increasingly operated in the colonies.[15] Furthermore, as Jonathan Hyslop has explained, this was 'fuelled by the human rivers of migration' from both Asia and Europe. 'It was this conjuncture which created a context in which defining themselves and their labour market interests as "white" could seem an advantageous option to organised workers.'[16]

Exclusionary policy adopted

California was the first to implement legal restrictions on Chinese migrants through local mining codes in the 1850s, though illegal expulsions of Chinese from mining communities had begun in 1849, almost as soon as any Chinese arrived. Despite this, by 1860, the Chinese population in California was 35,000, roughly a quarter of the total mining population, and the most clearly 'foreign' looking of the diverse group there.[17] In Victoria, by 1858 the Chinese were estimated at 40,000, or 24.5 per cent of miners. When the annual earnings of each digger declined from an estimated average of $780 in 1852 to $284 in 1854, widespread complaints and violent illegal exclusions of Chinese resulted. While there were fewer violent attacks on the Chinese, in 1855 the colony passed a bill modelled on one in California which provided for a poll tax on Chinese immigrants and restricted the number of Chinese brought into the colony by any ship.[18] After similar events in New South Wales, they also passed restrictive legislation in 1861, modelled in turn on Victoria's.[19]

The appeal of Chinese exclusion was not limited to mining communities, however. Like their European counterparts, numerous Chinese drifted into factories, railway construction, and farm work. Some even established their own businesses in direct competition with the settlers. With growing numbers of European migrants also arriving and looking for work, wider sections of the settler population demonstrated antipathy towards Asian migration. The alleged intelligence of the Asian populations, their numbers and low standard of living threatened settler supremacy in the colonies in a way that indigenous populations were rarely seen to do. While employers were largely satisfied, European migrants who felt their jobs were being taken away were not. Companies several times used Chinese men to replace striking Europeans.[20] They also increasingly replaced factory workers in semi-skilled and skilled positions in Australia, the USA and Canada.[21] One Nevada union complained in 1869 that 'Capital has decreed that Chinese shall supplant and drive hence the present race of toilers ... Can we compete with a barbarous race, devoid of energy and careless of the State's weal?'[22] Republican Senator G. C. Perkins of California described the situation as a fundamental question of racial dominance:

'when two races, as radically different as the Chinese and Americans freely intermingled there were only two possible outcomes: assimilation or subjugation ... dominate or be dominated'.[23] The very idea of white colonies depended 'on the premise that multiracial democracy was an impossibility', as Lake and Reynolds have recently shown. This belief grew out of 'the great tragedy of Radical Reconstruction in the United States', and was popularised by 'the British Liberal politician and historian, James Bryce, whose *American Commonwealth* was taken up as a "Bible" by white nation-builders in Australia and South Africa', when it was published in New York in 1888.[24] These ideas were swiftly adopted to fit the more widespread threat of Asian migration and lent an intellectual justification to exclusion. Social Darwinist ideas about 'survival of the fittest' further justified these growing demands for exclusion.

Perhaps the most unifying factor of all was the fear of disease. A judge in the British Columbian Supreme Court explained in an official Canadian report in 1885 that 'the air is polluted by the disgusting offal with which they are surrounded and the vile accumulations are apt to spread fever and sickness in the neighbourhood'.[25] When there was an outbreak of smallpox in Sydney in 1880, a mob attack on the Chinese community was only narrowly averted, while an Anti-Chinese League was established as a result, which advocated the exclusion of all Asians from Australia.[26] When news of this reached British Columbia and Natal, there were several sympathetic anti-Chinese marches and newspaper articles started linking disease with Asian migrants.

As Kathrin Levitan's chapter in this volume demonstrates, one of the effects of the increasing use of censuses in this period was further to provoke anti-Asian feeling. From the 1840s, their charting of rapidly growing Asian populations caused periodic panics among the host European populations. This only increased as indentured labour spread and Asian nations like Japan and China increasingly asserted the rights of their citizens overseas. There was a reason that papers so often referred to Chinese and other Asian migrants as a '"tide", "horde" or "invasion"'.[27] The statistics, however accurate they actually were, 'proved' an increase of Asians at a time when many settler populations were stagnating or declining, particularly in Australia and Canada.[28] In Southern Africa, not only were Europeans outnumbered by native Africans, the two 'white' races were themselves divided and fighting; in Natal, Indians outnumbered all 'white' migrants, and the indigenous Africans outnumbered all other groups by a significant margin. Although Europeans were reluctant to accept such an idea, white settlers increasingly described Asian migration as an invasion by stealth, a view most famously expressed by the writer and politician,

Charles Pearson in his book *National Life and Character* (1893), which used censuses and other 'hard' evidence to prove that white supremacy could not be assumed; and that its greatest menace came from China.[29]

The Chinese were only 1.75 per cent of the entire New Zealand population in 1870, but 6 per cent of the population in Otago; in an area where the number of white settlers was already almost equal to Maori residents, the Chinese population was seen to tip the balance away from the white population. So despite the small numbers, the colony implemented a series of restrictions from 1881.[30] Even Tasmania and Western Australia, which each had fewer than 1,000 Chinese, passed legislation in 1886 and 1887 respectively, largely in solidarity with their neighbours.[31]

Such concerns spread anti-Chinese feelings beyond the working classes to the middle and upper classes which, in turn, put greater pressure on governments to take legislative action. Colonials increasingly came to feel that it was the British government itself which was preventing them from securing their democratic potential. While the majority of residents in the settler colonies were won over to the notion of Chinese exclusion, there was widespread support in Britain for a concept of citizenship which, in theory at least, was racially blind. Indeed, a great deal of the British coverage derogatorily described colonial policies as a product of democracies which allowed ill-informed and hysterically prejudiced working-class people to have political power. This reflected the lack of understanding in Britain about why the Chinese seemed so threatening to their colonial cousins. After all, until the twentieth century, Asians were simply not a physical reality in most Britons' lives. Most of the Chinese and Japanese in Britain were sailors; Indians were slightly more numerous, but were usually either from educated elites or limited to port cities.[32] Furthermore, most of the coverage of Asians, excepting that which came from the colonies, was detached from any notion of an 'Asian menace' that threatened Britain directly. Charles Dickens had introduced the image of the East End Chinese opium den in London in the 1870s, but Gilbert and Sullivan's light-hearted depiction of the Japanese in their comic opera *Mikado* was a more common view. G. M. Trevelyan reflected contemporary opinion when he wrote that there was far greater danger from the white European influx into Britain, or from French and German competition, than from any 'yellow peril'.[33] Periodically, events such as the 1857 Indian Mutiny or the 1900 Boxer Rebellion would create a brief shared concern over the 'Asian menace', but such fears quickly diffused.

Britain's reluctance to take the lead in curbing Asian migration was why so many of the colonies copied each other's legislation, or looked for inspiration from the USA, which also had to deal with a central government that often vetoed local race-based legislation. Such pacts did not signal, of course, that the colonies agreed on what course of action to take. However, there was a general acknowledgement that similar 'problems' existed in each colony, that some exclusionary measures were desirable and that a common effort was needed to implement exclusion effectively. Nor was this an indication of specifically nationalist sentiments. Most colonials still adhered strongly to their Britishness; indeed, Lord Carrington, the Governor of New South Wales, explained to the Colonial Office, that 'if these Colonies *are to be an offshoot of Britain*, they must be kept clear of Chinese immigration'.[34] Maintaining their Britishness required exclusion. This widely appealed to the working classes as well as the political elites in the colonies because, as Warwick Anderson has said about Australia: 'if Asia was viewed as the centre of a coming world conflict, it followed that Australia was at the cutting edge of the struggle for racial supremacy rather than an insignificant spot on the remote periphery of the British Empire'.[35]

Furthermore, the British government's relations with its Asian allies and colonies were of significant importance. The 1842 Treaty of Nanking protected all Chinese people and property in the empire; the 1860 Convention of Peking allowed Chinese subjects to migrate freely to any British colony if the Chinese had contracts with British individuals or firms. Britain and Japan had signed a Treaty of Commerce and Navigation in 1894, which guaranteed 'full liberty to enter, travel or reside in any part of [the] Dominions and possessions of the other contracting party'.[36] Indeed, Britain's entire global defence plan was dependent on Japanese naval support in the Pacific, a situation which made many British colonials nervous. There were also Chinese who were British subjects, like those in Hong Kong or the Straits Settlements, not to mention British Indians, all of whom were entitled to travel freely throughout the empire. Although, the imperial government was always wary of stopping colonial legislation, relying instead on the moderating influence of unofficial channels, it was inevitable that conflict would arise between the self-governing colonies' desire for Asian exclusion and metropolitan concerns.

In Canada, the problem was heightened by the very regional nature of the perceived threat; British Columbia had to accommodate the indifference or intolerance of the Canadian *and* British governments. While Canada's salmon canning industry in the 1870s and the railways in the 1880s increasingly depended on Chinese labour, 'the comparatively rapid increase' in Chinese numbers scared enough people in British Columbia into passing exclusionary legislation in 1878. However, the other Canadian provinces, relatively unaffected by Asian migration and keen to complete the Canadian Pacific Railway, refused to support national legislation.[37] It was not until reports instigated by Canada's federal government into Chinese migration and Pacific railway construction were both completed in 1884 that a bill was finally passed, placing a poll tax and cargo limitations on Chinese migrants – a measure copied from earlier Australian and Californian legislation.

This conflict of interests was also apparent in Australia when the *Afghan* attempted to land in Melbourne from Hong Kong in 1888. Plague rumours had spread and a fearful Melbourne public rioted; to calm fears, the colonial government decided to deny the boat entry. One Chinese passenger issued a legal challenge, *Chung Teong Toy* v. *Musgrove*. As had happened in British Columbia, the Supreme Court of Victoria rejected the colonial defence that they had 'a sovereign right to exclude aliens from its territory as an act of state'.[38] Eventually, the Privy Council in Britain, wary of causing further rioting in Australia, overturned the Victorian Supreme Court's verdict because 'an alien has no legal right enforceable by action to enter British territory',[39] which essentially gave British consent to the self-governing colonies to differentiate between British subjects. The government was confirming that Chinese residents remained alien, that they were a distinctive racial group who could never adopt 'Britishness' as their primary identity, regardless of whether they were from a part of the empire.

Such feelings became all the more important after the British had signed the 1894 treaty with Japan; London included an article which gave the self-governing colonies the option of ratifying it. While Queensland later did for economic reasons, the other Australian colonies agreed at the 1896 meeting of Australian premiers, 'not just to refuse the treaty, but to legislate against Japanese migrants'.[40] The New South Wales legislature then passed a bill to exclude *all* Asians and Africans in 1896. This measure was first proposed at the same Australian Inter-Colonial Conference 'as part of an Australia-wide plan to bring to logical completion the defence against coloured immigration' and in preparation for future union.[41]

However, as the legislation referred so specifically to restricting immigration on the basis of race and made no exceptions for British subjects or allies, the governor of the colony reserved it for Colonial Office approval – an exceptionally rare decision. New Zealand also tried to pass an Asiatic Restriction Bill in 1896, which would have kept out all Asians (although not without some strong objections that there was no exemption for Indians who served with the Indian Army).[42] It is worth noting that the exclusion of Africans received little coverage in Britain or elsewhere. Migration from Africa to other parts of the

British Empire was exceedingly rare, after all, so their inclusion in the legislation was somewhat academic, a reflection of the general 'white' colony identities now established in these places, rather than directed towards a specific migrant group.

The entire situation put the British government in an awkward position, however, as Chinese and Japanese officials, and even the India Office protested against the legislation. While the Colonial Office debated how best to resolve the situation, the colonial backwater of Natal came up with an ingenious, if controversial, compromise. In 1860, the Natal government had subsidised the importation of thousands of Indian indentured workers for their sugar plantations. At the end of their indenture, Indians could stay on as settlers and frequently did. 'Free', largely middle-class, Indians also migrated. By the 1890s, there were as many Indians as 'white' settlers, and both were only a fraction of the indigenous population, causing an additional sense of racial insecurity. Despite the substantial economic benefits to the colony, upon gaining responsible government in 1893, one of the Natal Parliament's first undertakings was to deny Indians the franchise and to cease government subsidies for the indenture scheme; though they stopped short of an outright halt owing to economic concerns. The British government unsurprisingly declared the franchise restrictions illegal.

The traditional image of Natal during this period is of an almost purely first-generation British population deeply loyal to Britain.[43] However, by 1897, public hysteria was so widespread after reports of plague arriving from India that locals began to threaten cessation if Britain refused to allow restrictive legislation. A 5,000–strong petition against Asian immigration was organised to inform the British government that the 'older and richer British Colonies of Australia and New Zealand have found that this class of Immigrant is detrimental to the best interests of the inhabitants, and have passed laws having as their object the total exclusion of Asiatics'.[44] They made it clear that they too planned to implement such legislation and the Colonial Office took the separatist threats seriously.

The Natal prime minister, Harry Escombe, however, wanted to avoid a revolt. He was forced to imagine a way to incorporate the existing legislative aims while taking into account the British government's refusal to sanction race-based exclusion, especially of British subjects. He copied, almost word for word, the US Immigration Act of 1891, which restricted 'classes' of migrants, such as the infirm, criminals and paupers. He also lifted from the American legislation an educational assessment first put before the US Congress in 1891, which called for a reading and writing test for all immigrants over sixteen years of age in their native language. This was itself based on earlier literacy legislation introduced in the southern United States which was meant to decrease the number of voting African-Americans. Escombe considered Indians too clever for the same sort of legislation, so he wrote that the test would be in 'any language of Europe'.[45] This would enable an immigration official to make the tests easier or harder depending on their own views of the desirability of the potential migrant.

In this legislation, the Colonial Office also recognised the need to avoid conflict. Joseph Chamberlain, Secretary of State for the Colonies, wanted to bring about closer union between Britain and its settler colonies; estranging them over immigration matters could scupper vital schemes, such as tariff reform, which had become a personal crusade.[46] He saw the colonies of white settlement, not India, as potentially the greatest asset the British Empire possessed. At the 1897 Colonial Conference to mark Queen Victoria's diamond jubilee, Chamberlain famously told the colonial premiers:

> We quite sympathise with the determination of the white inhabitants of these colonies which are in comparatively close proximity to hundreds of millions of Asiatics that there should not be an influx of people alien in civilisation, alien in religion, alien in customs, whose influx moreover would most seriously interfere with the legitimate rights of the existing labour population ... but we ask you also to bear in mind the traditions of the Empire, which make no distinction in favour of or against race or colour.

While not specifically turning down the New South Wales legislation, he proposed the Natal language test as a more acceptable model. Although neither he nor the Natal legislature denied that it was formulated to keep out Asians, he could still deny accusations that it racially targeted them.[47]

The legislation was not immediately appreciated by colonials, however. They were being asked to adopt deceitful legislation, a reflection of what Robert Huttenback has described as 'a rather undefined dedication to fair play'.[48] Nor did all colonial residents believe in the exclusion of Asian migrants. Western and Northern Australia continued to import indentured labour for their plantations, owing to the very small European local populations and extreme climate. In the New Zealand legislature, a strong lobby argued that any immigration restriction bill unnecessarily pandered to the worst prejudices of the working class and wished to have at least Sikhs exempted from restrictions, given their importance within the Indian Army.[49] Senior officials in Canada were particularly uncomfortable with the overtly racist nature of much anti-Asiatic campaigning, blaming legislative restrictions on 'democracy'.[50] Increasingly vocal Indians objected to this legislation as well. M. K. Gandhi, a newly politicised Indian in Natal at the time, argued that the British Empire should not be about making 'a white man's country; not a white brotherhood, but an *Imperial* brotherhood'.[51]

However, with Chamberlain making clear that the Natal language test was the only legislation the Colonial Office would accept, the voting public gradually acquiesced. By 1907, all of the white colonies adopted some form of the Natal language test. Indeed, it was the first major legislation passed by the Commonwealth of Australia in 1901 and one of the first passed by South Africa after union in 1910. When Deakin explained to the Australian Parliament why such acts were so essential, he claimed it was 'nothing less than the national manhood, the national character and the national future that are at stake'.[52] In adopting the Natal language test rather than the New South Wales legislation, the self-governing colonies were clearly indicating their desire to remain part of a British World. But at the same time they were also legally emphasising the difference between being part of a British (or white) world and being a part of a multi-racial British Empire. From this point onwards, successfully negotiating a single imperial identity or citizenship would be impossible, despite repeated efforts. While Chamberlain had prevented the language of racism from appearing in the legislation, the intention was clear.

In addition to these problems, all participants at the 1897 Colonial Conference had agreed that closer union was desirable and that, when possible, neighbouring colonies should 'group together under a federal union', but it had proved impossible to agree on a method. The reasons for the failure of imperial federation of the British World were made clear in 1904, when the Transvaal government gained parliamentary approval to import thousands of Chinese indentured labourers to work on the gold mines. To local officials, this was one of several initiatives to rebuild the local economy and pay back some of the crippling debts after the South African War (1899–1902). Anti-Asiatic concerns did exist but were placated by including legal requirement that all Chinese were to be limited to unskilled 'kaffir' work and repatriated to China at the end of their contracts.

The situation was complicated, however, because Chamberlain had declared from the outset that the Transvaal would be treated as a self-governing colony. However, the Transvaal legislature which approved the scheme, was appointed by the British administration there, and was not elected as in other settler colonies.[53] This led to frequent accusations that the colonial administration was working in partnership with mining magnates to undermine the position of 'white' and African labourers alike to secure cheap labour. The South African War had been fought with the promise that it could become another British labour paradise like Australia. Instead, the scheme could ruin South Africa's potential as a 'white colony'.

The settler colonies all commented publicly on the situation, reflecting the growing tradition of group decision-making, especially on matters of Asian migration, as witnessed at the intercolonial conferences. This issue, however, also highlighted the limitations of consulting with each other. The Cape Parliament passed an almost unanimous resolution in the House of Assembly which condemned the scheme.[54] The Prime Minister of the Cape Colony even warned that, in light of heightened feelings, the Colonial Office was advised not to delay approving their own anti-Asian immigration legislation or the colony might revolt.[55] The Prime Minister of New Zealand also convinced the Australian Prime Minister to jointly protest after both parliaments independently passed almost unanimous resolutions against the scheme. The petitions and the parliamentary resolutions both argued that, at the very least, such an important decision was not for an imperial government to make, only for a locally elected government. If that was not possible, they argued that Australia and New Zealand should be allowed to undertake their own investigation as to whether Chinese labour was really needed, since their experiences meant that they were better qualified to decide on the matter than British officials.[56] After all, colonial soldiers had been promised more job opportunities in South Africa after the war. Instead, the newly secured colony (and the jobs) was to be handed over to the Chinese for the economic benefits of foreign mining magnates.

Not all the settler colonies were comfortable with central government interference, however. Canadian opinion largely held that Ottawa did not have the right to intervene in a local matter and they were willing to believe the imperial government's assurances that local approval was paramount.[57] The Canadian Prime Minister, Wilfred Laurier, had most of his support from within Quebec, a province with little interest in Chinese migration or in securing specifically 'British' colonies. Nor were labour organisations powerful enough to make their campaigns against the importation politically significant. Indeed, the Laurier government's refusal to interfere also reflected the sensitive nature of anti-Chinese feelings within Canada. Several times, the judiciary and central Parliament had been at war with British Columbia over control of immigration policy. The rest of the provinces simply did not share its concerns regarding Asian immigration. Consequently, British Columbia independently sent a cable to the High Commissioner in South Africa to oppose the scheme, and some local protests occurred in Toronto and other large cities, but there was no widespread objection.

Natal's government chose an equally neutral position, though they too cabled the Colonial Office to inform them of this. As one paper explained: 'The correct attitude for Natal was laid down by our Parliament, when it declined to do anything that might appear in the nature of dictation to a neighbouring Colony.'[58] Furthermore, a large portion of Natal's income came from the goods shipped to the Transvaal mines; there could be a significant profit from the scheme for the colony. Consequently, the Natal public were largely silent and none of the petitions were seen elsewhere.

The lack of agreement demonstrated the wide gap between the imagined British (white) community of the self-governing colonies and the actual differences which separated them. Indeed, southern Africans continually reiterated their frustration with the ignorance shown of their circumstances both in Britain and the other colonies. One British miner in the Transvaal sarcastically noted: 'they seem to know a good deal more about the question in England than we do out here ... Let them attempt to stop and thwart us out here, we will have none of it.'[59] A mining magnate sitting in the Transvaal legislature made a point of congratulating Laurier, 'who declined to interfere in affairs which were purely the internal affairs of another Colony ... representations made by the Premiers of Australia and New Zealand indicated rather a profound ignorance of the conditions of this country'.[60] Clearly, this situation was not an advertisement for formalising imperial federation, although it did increase some national fervour in South Africa itself. John X. Merriman, the leader of the South African Party in the Cape, stressed his belief 'in the absolute self-government of South Africa on the lines of Australia and Canada, with no dictation from Downing Street or Fleet Street and still less from Throgmorton Street',[61] referring to the London Stock Exchange. Another Oxford graduate and liberal, Professor H. E. S. Fremantle, claimed it 'unjustifiable to leave to a non-representative Government the decision of such a question'. In a letter published in London and Cape Town, he claimed that the assumption of future federation gave all parts of South Africa the right to have a say in the matter, not just the Transvaal.[62]

The debate featured prominently within Britain as well, where colonial campaigners for the first time stirred up intense British public interest in the issue of Asian migration. Labour networks proved particularly important in spreading the debate and fostering a sense of shared purpose among British labourers globally. In 1904, there were over 5,000 Australians on the Rand,[63] and about 7,000 Cornish miners, out of an estimated 16,000 white mine workers.[64] The Australians had brought anti-Chinese feelings with them, which Cornish miners transmitted back home. One Cornish miner with experience in the Transvaal told his British readers: 'In President Kruger's time the mine-owners could only employ whites and blacks, and at good wages. That was why Kruger had to go. Twenty thousand soldiers died that Beit, FitzPatrick, Rudd, and the rest might get their work done by Chinese slaves.'[65] Another British miner in the Transvaal wrote a pamphlet specifically for British working class men:

> Each colony is self-governing, but in the strictly internal affairs of South Africa the people are not self-governing. They have no South African Government with which to govern. At present they are governed through, not by, the High Commissioner, who is not independent, but is subject to the control of the Secretary of State for the Colonies at Westminster, who again is subject to the control of the Imperial Parliament. Now, this is where you, the man in the street, come in. You elect that Parliament, and neither you nor they know much about South Africa.[66]

At a time when suffrage in the UK was finally beginning to match that in the colonies and with labour organisations increasing in strength, this was an attractive message to many. White male suffrage was depicted as the only protection against capitalist power over the government, especially among newly emerging labour organisations.[67] For example, the British Trade Union Congress wrote and published pamphlets and articles, gave speeches and signed petitions against the proposal, with officials travelling frequently between Britain and South Africa to campaign for white miners' rights.[68]

As the *Spectator* explained, the issue was not simply an empty show of union support either. For the first time, significant numbers of Britons were beginning to see that Asian migration might threaten them too: 'while a kaffir could never take the place of a skilled miner, the Chinaman will be able to do so. The opinion is freely expressed that in six months there will be plenty of Chinamen well able to replace the skilled Cornish miner.'[69] Rumours even circulated in Britain that the government was planning to import Chinese into Britain, which Lloyd George particularly emphasised on the hustings in Wales. Such concern spread with what Jonathan Hyslop has called 'a common ideology of White Labourism'.[70] The widespread acceptance in Britain for the first time that Asian migration and British imperial rule could not coexist was an important shift in attitude. For the first time, Britons felt themselves to be threatened too. Those who did not feel personally threatened as such believed the use of indentured labour tainted Britain's humanitarian credentials, already damaged after the controversial South African War.[71]

The subsequent Liberal 'landslide' required the new government to take decisive action against Chinese indentured labour. On taking office, they quickly granted responsible government to the Transvaal. The newly elected Transvaal legislature's first act in 1907 banned all future Asian migration, the next required existing Asian residents to register, and the third cancelled the labour importation scheme. Jan Smuts, then deputy leader of *Het Volk* and the Transvaal's Colonial Secretary, even bragged that this was the severest legislation 'ever passed in the British Empire'.[72] Furthermore, the restrictions proved effective. All the indentured Chinese in the Transvaal were repatriated. Fresh Asian migrants were almost entirely prevented from migrating to South Africa, a position not altered until the 1990s.

The situation had revealed deep divisions among the settler colonies and Britain but it also better integrated Britons within a shared 'white' identity, threatened by Asian migration. Opponents in South Africa had utilised their British contacts to stir up interest among the imperial electorate; the Liberals had played on these concerns to win over voters. Even the Cape, Natal, Australia, New Zealand and Canadian governments had utilised the issue for their own political ends. The scheme later became mythologised in labour histories throughout the British World.[73]

Unfortunately, it also made clear the limitations of too much involvement in each other's affairs and made the British government reluctant to further meddle in any migration policies in the self-governing colonies. While previously opposed to the 'white Australia' policy and continuing to criticise labour's political influence there, *The Times*, in 1904, wrote in support of Australia's Alien Immigration Act. Referring to the experiences in the Transvaal: 'Mistaken or not, the Alien Immigration Act represents an attempt to keep an English land for the English people', and so had to be respected. The colonies should be left alone, as long as Britain's relations with India and other foreign powers were not too badly affected.[74] The British press and public started emphasising the inclusive factors of Britishness or whiteness, as they themselves became more reconciled to the ideas of immigration exclusion and the Asian 'menace'.

The situation continued to fragment the empire in 1907, when the USA and Japan almost went to war. The Anglo-Japanese alliance of 1902, which brought Britain out of its 'splendid isolation', allowed London for defensive purposes to remove naval units wholesale from the Pacific if British security was threatened by war in Europe. Thus, Britain now relied on the Japanese to maintain its maritime interests in East Asia. Such an arrangement could theoretically mean that Japanese warships would dock in colonial ports in the Pacific and that colonial soldiers could be asked to fight alongside the Japanese against

Americans. These possibilities proved even more menacing in the wake of Japan's surprise victory over Russia in 1905 and the largely successful Chinese boycott of US goods that same year. Pearson's prediction that Asia would awaken and challenge the West seemed to be coming true. A visiting Canadian official warned the British government: 'A war between the US and Japan . . . would be the beginning of the disruption of the Canadian Dominion.' British officials assured him that their treaty with Japan would never see Britain side with Japan against 'white' people,[75] but the hysteria continued.

Australia was also worried about Britain's alliance with Japan and, angered by perceived Colonial Office snobbery towards the self-governing colonies, the Prime Minister threatened a partnership with the USA.[76] Deakin circumvented the Colonial Office and asked Theodore Roosevelt directly to send the US fleet to Australia on its voyage round the world, despite the fact that he had no right to do this. He explained to the *New York Times* that the visit was 'intended to "show England – I cannot say a 'renegade' mother-country – that those colonies are white man's country"'.[77] New Zealand followed suit, as the *Wellington Post* explained, because America was 'the champion of white ascendancy in the Pacific' and represented 'the ideals of Australia and New Zealand far better than Britain'.[78] Canada chose not to invite the US navy; their proximity to the USA complicated their relationship in a way that the other Pacific colonies did not experience.

The feeling that this was a global conflict remained, however, and it was one which seemed increasingly to put the self-governing colonies in conflict with Britain. W. L. Mackenzie King, Deputy Minister of Labour, and a future premier of Canada, made clear during a visit to Britain that Canada 'should cease to think in colonial terms and to act in any way as with a colonial status. Let her become a nation or other nations will rob her of this right.'[79] Again, the emphasis was on the difference between the British Empire, and a select British World made up of equals and united by race.

The British government's response was to exercise greater restraint in advising the self-governing colonies on immigration policy. Already by 1906, the Colonial Office had decided to focus on colonial, later imperial, conferences rather than pushing for imperial federation. In 1907 the settler colonies were given their own sub-department within the Colonial Office and were renamed the dominions (at Laurier's suggestion), to signify their equality with Britain. They were even granted the right to draw up their own treaties, largely in response to the anti-Japanese agitation. While *The Times* complained that 'the purely selfish agitation of the labour unions [in British Columbia] . . . succeeded in creating an absurd, but none the less dangerous, impression that an organised attempt is being made to convert the Pacific slope into a yellow man's country',[80] there was a growing acceptance in Britain that anti-Asiatic sentiments could not be ignored or argued away. Even one-time critics of exclusion like Richard Jebb now acknowledged that it had to be accepted or Britain would alienate the dominions.[81]

Furthermore, as Andrew Thompson has argued, in the wake of a protracted South African War, 'the empire had to be reorganised so that it could continue to compete with states like Germany and America that had huge resource bases and growing populations'. The use of Canadian, Australian and New Zealand troops in the war highlighted that drawing closer to the settler colonies might be one way of achieving this. Throughout the Edwardian era, the British government moved towards embracing the settler colonies. This policy was clearly at the expense of India, 'for in raising the profile of the Dominions, they also marginalized India and Britain's other tropical colonies in imperial debate'.[82] Indeed, despite repeated Indian requests, the fact that India was 'in the grip of serious unrest and a campaign of assassination', they were not named one of the dominions. At a time when British rule in India was facing its first real challenge since the mutiny, Canada's policy of exclusion (and Australia's even more so) effectively undermined the notion of equal rights under the crown.[83]

Instead, soon after the 1907 Colonial Conference, there was a Colonial Office investigation into Asian migration to the self-governing colonies by Sir Charles Lucas. He concluded that the introduction of the Chinese into the Transvaal had strengthened 'the bias against coloured immigration in the self-governing Dominions' and 'if we do not take the initiative, the United States may stand out on and through this question as the leaders of the English-speaking peoples in the Pacific as against the coloured races'.[84] The threat of losing the dominions, just when they had demonstrated their worth in military and economic matters, and the belief in Britain that the colonies actually would cede and join with the USA if thwarted in their exclusionary aims, cautioned future British governments against interfering. Lucas was put in charge of the new Dominions Department, where he continued to reiterate this view: 'If Britain were to confront the Dominions over the race question, they might break away and form an alliance with the United States, creating a new political organisation, "having its roots in race affinity", that would be directly opposed to the idea of imperial citizenship, which took no account of race.'[85]

This belief became the bedrock of future imperial policy; Britishness remained the primary identity for many settlers, but this fact could not be taken for granted. The notion of imperial citizenship thus lost all meaning, despite the Colonial Office continuing to advocate it and to insist hollowly that Indians and other non-whites were not second-class imperial subjects.[86] The 1911 Imperial Conference (renamed because 'imperial' sounded more like a meeting of equals) unsurprisingly failed to define imperial naturalisation, nor could the dominions agree about whether a uniform immigration policy would be needed. The dominions were happy to embrace partnership with Britain to an extent, and could envision working with each other to get this, but they were not keen to embrace the rest of the empire.[87] The British government chose to accept this and appease India in smaller, usually less successful, ways.

Conclusion

Asian migration largely ceased from 1907.[88] Only in recent decades have Asian populations been allowed to migrate to the 'white' nations within the Pacific and Indian Ocean basins in any sizeable numbers. Choosing whiteness over *British* subjects as the key entry criteria allowed for increasing migration from other parts of Europe. As Ulbe Bosma has argued, between 1890 and 1913 'migration was heavily manipulated and became also increasingly directed within empires'.[89] Colonial governments, private philanthropists and Poor Law guardians, in particular, supported recruiting efforts to better ensure that the 'right' sorts of migrants arrived; to non-white emigrants the door remained firmly shut.[90] Thus while substantial differences marked the social and economic development of each of these colonies, there was also a strong sense of community between them. Lasting networks were established, linked by shared ideologies based on 'whiteness', combined with the 'threat' of Asian migration. The entire objection to Asian labour remained a central premise of transnational (or transcolonial) labour movements, in particular through to the Great War.[91] The stereotype of the Asian invader was the 'other' needed to stimulate a strong white identity in these places.

The more the racial qualities of Britishness were emphasised through discussions of immigration policy, the more the concepts of imperial citizenship and British subjecthood – which underpinned wider imperial identities – were devalued. It was therefore unfortunate for the British government that the question of Asian immigration policy reared its head at precisely the same time that the self-governing colonies were beginning to assert their autonomy in external matters and relations. By giving ground to these colonies' desire to control entry into their territory, and increasingly to privilege European over non-European migrants, Britain was faced with the consequences of alienating other groups within the empire, such as the Indians and

Straits Chinese. Educated Indian subjects in particular drew on the exclusionary policies covered in this chapter when rejecting their existence as second-class citizens of empire in favour of being first-class citizens of an Indian nation.[92]

This analysis of settler reactions to Chinese labour thus provides a fuller understanding of how differing conceptions of Britishness developed among Britons at home and overseas. This was not simply a conflict between self-governance and empire; for the dominions, rejection of imperial citizenship was clearly not a rejection of the networks established through shared Britishness or whiteness. What it reveals is a failure for a specifically imperial identity to emerge to combat localised racism in the face of Asian migration. The British World's existence depended on the exclusionary attitudes towards Asian migration and the subsequent breakdown in imperial identity.

Notes

1 C. Bridge and K. Fedorowich, 'Mapping the British World', *Journal of Imperial and Commonwealth History*, 31:2 (2003), pp. 1–15.

2 A. Lester, *Imperial Networks: Creating Identities in Nineteenth-century South Africa and Britain* (London, 2001).

3 T. C. Holt, *The Problem of Freedom: Race, Labor and Politics in Jamaica and Britain, 1832–1938* (Baltimore, 1992), p. 236.

4 P. Manning, *Migration in World History* (New York, 2005), p. 149.

5 A. McKeown, 'Global Migration 1846–1940', *Journal of World History*, 19:2 (2004), p. 158.

6 The term 'coolie' was usually applied to indentured or unskilled workers on long-term restricted contracts for work on plantations. It became a derogatory term for all Asian migrants in the late nineteenth and early twentieth centuries. The word was probably derived from the Tamil word *kuli*, meaning 'wages'. See L. Potts, *The World Market. A History of Migration*, trans. Terry Bond (London, 1990), pp. 63–4.

7 D. Northrup, *Indentured Labour in the Age of Imperialism, 1838–1922* (Cambridge, 1995), p. 22. Also see W. L. Lai, *Indentured Labor, Caribbean Sugar: Chinese and Indian Migrants to the British West Indies, 1838–1918* (Baltimore, 1993).

8 Y. Ching-Hwang, *Coolies and Mandarins* (Singapore, 1985), p. 47.

9 McKeown, 'Global Migration', p. 175.

10 S. C. Miller, *The Unwelcome Immigrant: The American Image of the Chinese, 1785–1882* (Berkeley, CA, 1969).

11 C. Mackerras, *Sinophiles and Sinophobes: Western Views of China* (Oxford, 2000), p. 60.

12 S. J. Potter, *News and the British World: The Emergence of an Imperial Press System, 1876–1922* (Oxford, 2003), p. 20.

13 *Ibid.*, p. 14.

14 A. Markus, *Fear and Hatred: Purifying Australia and California, 1850–1901* (Sydney, 1979), p. 10.

15 A. Thompson, *The Empire Strikes Back? The Impact of Imperialism on Britain from the Mid-Nineteenth Century* (Harlow, 2005), p. 69.

16 J. Hyslop, 'The Imperial Working Class Makes Itself "White": White Labourism in Britain, Australia, and South Africa Before the First World War', *Journal of Historical Sociology*, 12:4 (1999), pp. 405–6. See also D. Goutor, *Guarding the Gates: The Canadian Labour Movement and Immigration, 1872–1934* (Vancouver, 2007).

17 Markus, *Purifying Australia and California*, p. 1.
18 *Ibid.*, p. 24.
19 *Ibid.*, p. 33.
20 A. Saxton, *The Indispensable Enemy, Labor and the Anti-Chinese Movement in California* (London, 1975), p. 62.
21 *Ibid.*, p. 71.
22 June 1869, miners' union of Virginia City & Golden Hill in an address to working men of Nevada, quoted in Saxton, *Indispensable Enemy*, p. 59. See also Markus, *Purifying Australia and California*, pp. 10 and 12.
23 Markus, *Purifying Australia and California*, xviii.
24 M. Lake and H. Reynolds, *Drawing the Global Colour Line: White Men's Countries and the International Challenge of Racial Equality* (Cambridge, 2008), p. 6.
25 Quotation cited in P. C. Campbell, *Chinese Coolie Emigration to Countries within the British Empire* (London, 1923), p. 42. See also Markus, *Purifying Australia and California*, p. 21, for Australian examples.
26 B. Kennedy, *A Tale of Two Cities. Johannesburg and Broken Hill: 1885–1925* (Johannesburg, 1984), p. 44; Campbell, *Chinese Coolie Emigration*, p. 64.
27 J. Becker, *The Course of Exclusion, 1882–1924: San Francisco Newspaper Coverage of the Chinese and Japanese in the United States* (San Francisco, 1991).
28 A. Offer, *The First World War: An Agrarian Interpretation* (Oxford, 1989), p. 166.
29 Quoted in Markus, *Purifying Australia and California*, xv.
30 Campbell, *Chinese Coolie Emigration*, pp. 80–2.
31 R. Huttenback, *Racism and Empire: White Settlers and Colored Immigrants in the British Self-Governing Colonies: 1830–1910* (London, 1976), pp. 94–5; Markus, *Purifying Australia and California*, pp. 227–8.
32 See, for instance, J. Seed, 'Limehouse Blues: Looking for Chinatown in the London Docks, 1900–40', *History Workshop Journal*, 62 (2006), p. 64; S. Lahiri: *Indians in Britain: Anglo-Indian Encounters, Race and Identity, 1880–1930* (London, 2000).
33 Quoted in C. Bolt, *Victorian Attitudes to Race* (London, 1971), p. 200.
34 Quoted in D. Gorman, 'Wider and Wider Still?: Racial Politics, Intra-Imperial Immigration and the Absence of an Imperial Citizenship in the British Empire', *Journal of Colonialism and Colonial History*, 3:3 (2002), p. 13. Italics are Gorman's.
35 Quoted in W. Anderson, *The Cultivation of Whiteness: Science, Health and Racial Destiny in Australia* (Durham, NC, 2006), p. 277.
36 Lake and Reynolds, *Drawing the Global Colour Line*, p. 144.
37 Campbell, *Chinese Coolie Emigration*, pp. 36–8. See also P. Roy, *White Man's Province: British Columbia Politicians and Chinese and Japanese Immigrants, 1858–1914* (Vancouver, 1989).
38 Lake and Reynolds, *Drawing the Global Colour Line*, pp. 40–1.
39 *Ibid.*
40 *Ibid.*, p. 144.
41 A. T. Yarwood, *Asian Migration to Australia: The Background to Exclusion 1896–1923* (Melbourne, 1964), p. 11; Markus, *Purifying Australia and California*, pp. 184–5.
42 T. Ballantyne, *Orientalism and Race: Aryanism in the British Empire* (Basingstoke, 2002), pp. 80–1.
43 J. Lambert, '"The Last Outpost": The Natalians, South Africa, and the British Empire', in R. Bickers (ed.), *Settlers and Expatriates: Britons over the Seas*, Companion Series, *The Oxford History of the British Empire* (Oxford, 2010), pp. 150–77.
44 Quoted in J. Martens, 'A Transnational History of Immigration Restriction: Natal and New South Wales, 1896–97', *Journal of Imperial and Commonwealth History*, 34:3 (2006), p. 322.
45 *Ibid.*, 334.
46 J. E. Kendle, *The Colonial and Imperial Conferences 1887–1911. A Study in Imperial Organisation* (London, 1967), p. 19.
47 R. Huttenback, 'The British Empire as a "White Man's Country" – Racial Attitudes

and Immigration Legislation in the Colonies of White Settlement', *Journal of British Studies*, 13:1 (1973), p. 111.

48 *Ibid.*, p. 108.
49 Ballantyne, *Orientalism*, pp. 80–1.
50 Offer, *Agrarian Interpretation*, p. 196.
51 *Indian Opinion*, 1 June 1907. This binary distinction was used frequently by him. See also *The Collected Works of Mahatma Gandhi*, 8 vols (Delhi, 1961), 1, p. 74; 2, p. 133; 3, p. 334; and 8, p. 200.
52 M. Lake, 'Translating Needs into Rights: the Discursive Imperative of the Australian White Man, 1901–30', in S. Dudink, K. Hagemann and J. Tosh (eds), *Masculinities in Politics and War: Gendering Modern History* (Manchester, 2004), p. 203.
53 Milner to Chamberlain, 6 April 1903, in C. Headlam (ed.), *The Milner Papers*, 2 *South Africa 1899–1905* (London, 1931), p. 461.
54 Cape *Hansard*, 2 July 1903.
55 The National Archives, London (TNA), Colonial Office papers, CO 48/572/28960, Sir W. F. Hely Hutchinson, Governor of Cape Colony, to Chamberlain, 3 August 1903.
56 HCPP, Cd.1941, *Transvaal: Further Correspondence Regarding the Transvaal Labour Question* (1904), enclosures 1 and 2 in no. 26, 19 January 1904, p. 28; Cd.1895, *South Africa* (1904) 5th Earl of Ranfurly, Governor-General of New Zealand, to Lyttelton, 20 January 1904, p. 231. See also Hyslop, 'White Labourism', p. 408; and J. Martens, 'Richard Seddon and Popular Opposition in New Zealand to the Introduction of Chinese Labour into the Transvaal, 1903–1904', *New Zealand Journal of History*, 42:2 (2008), pp. 176–95.
57 Bodleian Library, Oxford, Viscount Alfred Milner papers, MS Milner dep., reel 178, file 79, Milner to Earl Grey, Governor-General of Canada, 14 March 1904.
58 *Natal Mercury* (1 January 1904).
59 A. Jabez Strong, 'The Transvaal Labour Question. A British Workingman to British Workingmen. What it all Means to British Labourers', Imperial South African Association Pamphlet, no. 70 (1905).
60 HCPP, Cd.1941, *Transvaal Labour Question*, enclosure in no. 38, Legislative Council, Labour Importation Draft Ordinance, second reading, 20 January 1904, pp. 58–9.
61 Merriman to E. Sheppard, member of *Het Volk* and founder of the South African Labour Party, 9 December 1903, in P. Lewsen (ed.), *Selections from the Correspondence of John X. Merriman*, 3 *1895–1905* (Cape Town, 1966), p. 414.
62 'Anti-Asiatic Importation League', published letter signed by Robert Forsyth and H. E. S. Fremantle, Cape Town, 1 January 1904. In 1915 Fremantle, angered by the Union government's invasion of German South West Africa, jettisoned his liberal credentials and became one of the founding members of the South African National Party led by J. B. M. Hertzog.
63 Kennedy, *Tale of Two Cities*, pp. 1–2.
64 R. Dawe, *Cornish Pioneers in South Africa: Gold and Diamonds, Copper and Blood* (St Austell, 1998), p. 211.
65 E. S. Beesly, 'Yellow Labour', *Positivist Review* (April 1904), p. 80. The three men named were the mining magnates, Otto Beit, Percy FitzPatrick and C. D. Rudd.
66 M. C. Bruce, *The New Transvaal*, 2nd edn (London, 1908 [1905]), p. 90.
67 Thompson, *Empire Strikes Back?*, pp. 69–71.
68 E. N. Katz, *A Trade Union Aristocracy: A History of White Workers in the Transvaal and the General Strike of 1913* (Johannesburg, 1976), p. 111.
69 *The Spectator* (22 October 1904), letter from Peter Green, quoted in Simone Lisa McCallum, 'Radical Racism in the Transvaal: F. H. P. Creswell and the White Labour Movement, 1902–1912' (MA dissertation, Queen's University, Kingston, 1994), p. 51.
70 Hyslop, 'White Labourism', p. 399.
71 See E. B. Rose, *Uncle Tom's Cabin* (London, 1905), p. 12.
72 Gandhi, *Collected Works*, 8 (Delhi, 1961), p. 505.

73 Recent studies include A. Drew, *Between Empire and Revolution: A Life of Sidney Bunting, 1873–1936* (London, 2007) and J. Hyslop, *The Notorious Syndicalist: J. T. Bain. A Scottish Rebel in Colonial South Africa* (Johannesburg, 2004).

74 *The Times* (20 January 1904), p. 4.

75 Offer, *Agrarian Interpretation*, p. 192.

76 Lake and Reynolds, *Drawing the Global Colour Line*, p. 194; J. A. la Nauze, *Alfred Deakin. A Biography*, 2 (London, 1966), p. 500.

77 Lake and Reynolds, *Drawing the Global Colour Line*, p. 50.

78 Quoted in *ibid.*, p. 51.

79 Entry from Mackenzie King's 1909 diary quoted in Offer, *Agrarian Interpretation*, pp. 198–9.

80 *The Times* (9 September 1907), p. 11.

81 D. Gorman, *Imperial Citizenship: Empire and the Question of Belonging* (Manchester, 2006), pp. 146–77; R. Jebb, 'The Imperial Problem of Asiatic Immigration', *Journal of the Royal Society of Arts*, 56 (1907–08), pp. 585–603.

82 A. Thompson, 'The Language of Imperialism and the Meanings of Empire: Imperial Discourse and British Politics, 1895–1914', *Journal of British Studies*, 36:2 (1997), pp. 151–2. For Curzon's views, see D. Gilmour, *Curzon* (New York, 1994). For Milner's, see Lord Milner, *The Nation and the Empire* (London, 1913).

83 Offer, *Agrarian Interpretation*, p. 189.

84 TNA, CO 886/1/1, Dominions No. 1, confidential, 'The Self-Governing Dominions and Coloured Immigration', memo. by Sir Charles Lucas, head of Dominions Department, Colonial Office, July 1908; CO 886/1/2, Dominions No. 2, very confidential, 'Suggestions as to Coloured Immigration into the Self-Governing Dominions'.

85 Lake and Reynolds, *Drawing the Global Colour Line*, p. 233.

86 Compare this to Gorman's explanation for the demise of imperial citizenship ideology in his *Imperial Citizenship*.

87 See HCPP, Cd.5745, *Minutes of Proceedings of the Imperial Conference, 1911* (1911).

88 Huttenback, *Racism and Empire*, pp. 148–9.

89 U. Bosma, 'Beyond the Atlantic: Connecting Migration and World History in the Age of Imperialism, 1840–1940', *International Review of Social History*, 52:1 (2007), p. 122.

90 K. Fedorowich, 'The British Empire on the Move, 1760–1914', in S. Stockwell (ed.), *The British Empire: Themes and Perspectives* (Oxford, 2008), pp. 63–100, especially 83–92.

91 Hyslop, *Notorious Syndicalist*, p. 10.

92 See M. K. Gandhi, *An Autobiography or the Story of My Experiments with Truth* (New York, 1983); H. J. M. Johnston, *The Voyage of the Komagata Maru: the Sikh Challenge to Canada's Colour Bar* (Delhi, 1979); Roy, *White Man's Province*.

CHAPTER 6

Righting the record? British child migration: the case of the Middlemore Homes, 1872–1972

Michele Langfield

Introduction

Between 1869 and 1939, over 100,000 children, seen to be at risk from crime and destitution, were removed from orphanages, workhouses, families and streets of Great Britain. Many were sent to Canada and are now known as British Home Children. Others went to Australia, New Zealand and Rhodesia. Approximately fifty organisations were involved in juvenile migration schemes during this period.[1] The largest and best known is Dr Barnardo's, which accounted for about one third of British child migrants. Others included Maria Rye, Marchmont, Macpherson Homes, Fegan's Homes, Quarrier Homes, the Children's Aid Society, Liverpool Sheltering Home, National Children's Homes, Child Emigration Society (Fairbridge), Salvation Army, Middlemore Homes and numerous religious organisations, workhouses and Poor Law unions.

As Marjory Harper argues, immigration in general and child migration in particular has always been controversial.[2] Recently, however, public debate has focused on the legacy of child removal per se. This includes indigenous children removed from their families, known in Australia as the 'stolen generations', and child migrants described as 'Orphans of the Empire', 'Lost Children of the Empire', and 'Lost Innocents'.[3] Several government inquiries were held in the 1990s and early twenty-first century into the long-term effects of these schemes.[4] Some historians argue that child migrants were spared from hunger and poverty, and given a better life in the more healthy and moral environments of the dominions. Others maintain that they were shipped into servitude by a British government bent on ridding itself of a social and economic menace. Some children did well, benefiting from opportunities arising directly from their emigration; others were exploited and mistreated.[5] Critics looking back from the vantage point of the present highlight the adverse effects of institutionalisation, yet not all child migrants were institutionalised. John T. Middlemore's Children's Emigration Homes in Birmingham, which operated from 1872 to 1972, placed children as soon as possible in selected foster homes, a practice widely recommended for disadvantaged children after the Second World War. While this did not always alleviate homesickness or mal-treatment, it indicates that the Middlemore scheme was perhaps ahead of its time in attitudes to juvenile migration and child care.[6]

This chapter fits within the context of several interconnected bodies of literature. They include the history of British juvenile emigration, changing conceptions of childhood and children's rights, social welfare and social action, philanthropy, class and gender studies, and the history of British imperialism in all its racial, economic, social and religious dimensions. Jon Lawrence and Pat Starkey suggest that 'the rise and eventual fall of child migration reveals much about the stub-born persistence (as well as the inherent contradictions) of ideas of the British as a "world race" with a global civilising mission'.[7] This is dif-ficult to refute but there were other dimensions to the child migration movement, which finally came to an end in the 1960s.

In relation to the recent inquiries into child removal, Geoffrey Sherington and Chris Jeffrey call on historians to provide a balanced understanding of the circumstances in which such schemes were created and implemented.[8] Stephen Constantine too has argued against constructions of history that are ignorant of the contemporary context and cautions against imposing twenty-first century values on beliefs and practices of earlier times.[9] These historians question the construc-tions of historical narratives of child removal through recent testimo-nies given at government inquiries and to the media where the normal rules of historical methodologies of balancing and cross-checking sources appear to be neglected. These personal life histories have a special value; it is accepted that such stories need to be told, that pain needs to be healed through their telling, and that hardship and ill treat-ment must be recognised and addressed. But these historians suggest that, where compensation is in question, however legitimate, there is a tendency to construct a particular kind of historical narrative which, through media exposure, then becomes the dominant one.

The majority of the British child migration schemes emerged with the growth in philanthropic and child-saving movements in the late nineteenth century and focused on the most disadvantaged in society. How did sponsoring organisations see themselves and their work? How did British and dominion governments regard such schemes? How did the public receive them? Perhaps most importantly, how did the chil-dren view them, at the time of their emigration and later in their lives?

How have attitudes to child migration changed over time? Revisiting organisational records, with an eye for contemporary values and beliefs, but cognisant of the purposes for which they were created, sheds much light on these questions.

Several studies already exist.[10] Sherington and Jeffrey provide an understanding of Kingsley Fairbridge and examine the role of the Fairbridge Society as an imperial child-rescue movement. My own work frequently includes child migration as a key component of immigration encouragement to the British dominions but I have especially concentrated on William Booth and the Salvation Army.[11] This chapter has closely related themes and focuses on a similar but lesser-known visionary, John T. Middlemore, known as the 'Child's Friend'. The Middlemore Homes had a particular relationship after the mid-1920s with the Fairbridge Society.

Early child migration schemes

The Middlemore Child Emigration Programme was neither the first nor largest of the child migration schemes, but it is unique in that a substantial quantity of its internal organisational and personal records has been preserved intact. This vast archive, now on microfilm in the Library and Archives Canada and the National Library of Australia, together with extensive government records, provides a rare opportunity to examine the process and outcomes of transplanting child migrants when such an endeavour was seen to bring with it multiple benefits for all concerned. The following outline explains the aims of the Middlemore enterprise from its own perspective and publications, the funding and functioning of its operations, and its relationships with British and dominion authorities. Through an examination of the Middlemore 'History Books', where information on all those in its care were kept, and the settlement reports,[12] it also throws light on the lives and progress of the children themselves and the success in transplanting these juvenile migrants to Canada and Australia. Terms, such as 'progress' and 'success', are themselves loaded, varying according to the values of the time and the various participants in such schemes.

Under the auspices of the Middlemore Child Emigration Programme, over 5,000 British children were taken to Canada, initially to Ontario and later to the Maritime provinces, between 1873 and 1936.[13] After 1925, when the Canadian government prohibited the emigration of unaccompanied children under 14, approximately 260 were also taken to Australia in association with Fairbridge.[14] Most Middlemore children came from Birmingham and were between 2 and 18 years of age.[15] In the centenary publication, *One Hundred Years of Child Care* (1972), the

Middlemore Committee describes the beginnings of the organisation, placing it within the context of the social and economic effects of the industrial revolution and the transformation of labour that resulted. In the mid-nineteenth century, widows' pensions, family allowances, National Health, unemployment benefits and social security were non-existent. Working-class families relied on charity in times of crisis.[16] Children deprived of the protection of families were seriously at risk without Probation or Children's Officers. The only shelter was the workhouse, the prison or, for young offenders, industrial or reformatory schools.

The 1834 Poor Law Amendments Act provided for 'workhouse schools' for such children, separating them from the adult prison population. According to a 1861 report, these schools were poorly managed and inadequately staffed. In 1862, Parliament agreed that local authorities responsible for pauper children could seek assistance from voluntary institutions, which could receive payment from public funds. While some small cottage homes began from which children attended local schools, it was only after 1871 when the Local Government Board became responsible, that the Poor Law care of children improved.[17]

During the 1860s and 1870s, several philanthropic organisations were established and significant developments in child care occurred. Josiah Mason built and endowed an orphanage to house 300 children in 1861. Thomas Barnardo opened a boys' home in Stepney in 1867 and Thomas Crowley founded the Crowley Orphanage for poor girls in 1869.[18] Maria Rye and Annie Macpherson began to transport children to Canada in 1869 and 1870 respectively, followed by Macpherson's sister, Louisa Birt. William Quarrier opened his Orphan Homes of Scotland in 1871.[19] These pioneers, especially Barnardo, undoubtedly inspired John T. Middlemore, although Barnardo's first official party of boys to Canada did not arrive until 1882, approximately ten years after the first Middlemore party. Middlemore opened his first children's home in Birmingham in 1872 specifically to help those beyond the reach of government institutions.[20] He relied on public donations and subscriptions to fund his work. The National Children's Home and Orphanage, the Fegan Homes, the Church of England Waifs and Strays, and the Salvation Army, all began operating in the following years.

The Middlemore child emigration schemes

Dr John Throgmorton Middlemore was born in 1844 in Edgbaston, south-west of Birmingham. As the son of a Baptist businessman, he had a privileged but strict upbringing. After attending the Edgbaston Proprietary School and working in the family business until the age of

20, he was sent to work in his uncle's stationery business in Boston, Massachusetts. While there he graduated in medicine and travelled widely in the United States and eastern Canada. Back home, he became active in Birmingham's political, artistic and intellectual life but felt that he was not contributing sufficiently to society. He was conscious of the sharp contrast between the squalid living conditions in industrial England and the fresh open spaces of the Canadian countryside.[21] Like other visionaries such as Kingsley Fairbridge some years later, Middlemore believed that if he could transplant poverty-stricken children into rural surroundings, they would have a better chance in life. He began to contact influential people to enlist support.

In 1872, aged 28, Middlemore opened two small Children's Emigration Homes, one for boys in St Luke's Road, Birmingham, another for girls nearby in Spring Street. Thirty-five children were admitted in the first year. Only those mentally and physically fit were accepted and trained in the homes for a year before emigrating. In May 1873, Middlemore took twenty-nine children to Canada, travelling from Liverpool to Quebec City by ship, then to Toronto and London, Ontario, by train. Through press advertisements and letters, all were placed in foster homes within a short time, twenty-three in Toronto and six in London.[22]

In his first annual report, Middlemore explained that children brought into the Emigration Homes were mostly younger than ten, and the rest were around thirteen years old, too young for Industrial Schools or beyond the provisions of the Education Act.[23] Couples fostering children had to sign an undertaking that they would treat the children as their own, ensure they attended school and a place of worship, and communicate regularly with the Middlemore Homes as to their welfare. If it became necessary to give up the children, they would return them to the Guthrie Home, London, Ontario, after two weeks' notice.[24]

Initially, Middlemore himself accompanied the children to Canada, settled them in and visited them regularly, but as numbers increased, other staff took over. Nonetheless, he and his family remained closely involved in the practical operation of the home.[25]

Like other schemes, Middlemore's venture was not without criticism.[26] He was accused of 'taking away from England every year the backbone, the very life blood of her population'. To this he replied, 'No, I am taking away what would only be diseased tissue if it were left in England, but in Canada it grows into healthy flesh and blood and sinew.'[27] Only children considered to have the worst chances in life were included. Many had lost one or both parents through death, desertion or imprisonment. When parents were unable to care for or support their children, they often asked charitable institutions to take them for the purpose of emigration. Some were brought to the homes by relatives or friends or recommended by magistrates. Middlemore himself found others and children also presented themselves. None was taken to Canada without parental consent.[28] The popular perception that most children were 'emigrated', as the term was then used,[29] without parental consent or knowledge, is largely erroneous.[30]

Middlemore's first operational base was the Newsboys Lodgings in Toronto but in 1874, the Guthrie Home in London, Ontario, became the Canadian headquarters. From there, children were placed in rural homes in Ontario, until Guthrie closed in 1898. The aim was to place all children with farmers since towns were perceived as places of poverty and vice.[31] The rural myth was perpetuated but unlike other sponsoring organisations, Middlemore did not keep children in institutions or farm schools in Canada but sent them directly to foster homes.

Annie Macpherson managed the aftercare of Middlemore children. For the first twelve years, all were taken to Ontario but in 1885, eighteen were sent to York County, New Brunswick, the first Middlemore children to go to the Maritime provinces. By 1892, operations throughout the Maritimes were underway with Middlemore taking over the placement of British children from Louisa Birt.[32] He was dependent on the assistance of local charitable institutions, such as Miss Sterling's orphanage, Hillfoot Farm, in the Annapolis Valley. In 1898, the Fairview home opened in Halifax, Nova Scotia, becoming the 'distributing home' for Middlemore children until the Canadian programme closed in 1935.[33] From Fairview, children were placed in homes in Nova Scotia, New Brunswick, and Prince Edward Island. Between 1898 and 1935, most Middlemore children were settled in the Maritime provinces, although from 1927, not in Nova Scotia.[34]

All Middlemore children brought to Canada before 1887 spent some time in the Children's Emigration Home in Birmingham but this was temporary for training only. Before leaving England, they were medically examined and certified as in good health and fit for emigration. A Canadian agent again examined them on embarkation and certified that they were 'of a desirable class'.[35] After 1887, children from Industrial Schools and unions were included. They were recognised as Middlemore children, but listed in the History Books separately as 'workhouse children'.[36]

The Middlemore History Books reveal appalling aspects of children's lives before emigration: being left alone, drunkenness, beatings, street life, severe deprivation and various levels of crime. It was generally accepted that the solution was to remove them from harmful surroundings and negative influences. For example, 9–year-old Beatrice's father had died of pneumonia. Her mother could not support all her children, one of whom was disabled, and took Beatrice to Middlemore for a better life.[37] If there was hope, the children were considered 'too good' to be admitted. There was also a gender bias: boys with a history of stealing and lying were preferred to 'impure' girls who had experienced rape or prostitution. Records indicate a preference for boys because many foster parents wanted farm labour.[38] A newspaper article describing a couple mistakenly sent a girl instead of a boy (but deciding to keep her) became the inspiration for the novel *Anne of Green Gables*.[39] Not all children went to Canada; a minority remained in England, found jobs or attended industrial schools.[40] In 1914, for example, 110 children were admitted to the homes, of whom 97 went to Canada. In 1915, 107 were admitted and 83 emigrated.[41]

Middlemore spent much time teaching the children self-respect, morals and pride in their appearance, caring for them and ministering to their needs. Inculcating values was an important part of his work, which was non-denominational but Protestant. He read extensively to them, always prefacing his readings with ten minutes of mental arithmetic to sharpen their wits and concentration. These findings disprove the claims of recent inquiries that sponsoring organisations paid little attention to the intellectual and ethical development of the children. Older boys were placed on farms and received board, lodging and a small sum for their work. Teenage girls became domestic servants under similar conditions, while younger children were adopted, preferably into childless families. Middlemore screened the families applying for children and monitored the care and education provided. Where problems occurred, children were removed promptly. Middlemore only brought British children to Canada when the Canadian manager had received an application from a Canadian family. Thus they did not remain institutionalised in training homes in England or reception homes in Canada unless they were between situations.[42]

The foregoing illustrates how the founder and early Middlemore administrators saw their work. It is worth acknowledging the legal conditions under which British juvenile migration occurred during that period. Under the Poor Law Amendment Act 1850, Boards of Guardians were empowered:

> to procure, or assist in procuring, the emigration of orphan or deserted children under the age of 16 years with the order, and subject to the regulations, of the Local Government Board; but no emigration can take place until the child has consented before the justices and the justices have submitted to the Board a certificate showing that they as well as the child have consented to the proposal. When these consents have been obtained, the Guardians make application to the Local Government Board stating that they propose to emigrate a certain child through the Roman Catholic

emigration agency, the Waifs and Strays Society, Dr Barnardo's Homes, Miss Macpherson's Home, or one of the various well-known emigration agencies. The Local Government Board cause careful inquiries to be made as to the child's physical and mental condition, and, if the case is found to be suitable, the guardians are required to pay a fee of £10 to defray the cost of regular and systematic inspection by the immigration officers specially appointed for the purpose by the Dominion government. The home in which the child is placed is chosen through the agency through which the child is emigrated. No payment other than the cost of travelling, etc. is made by the guardians, and the child is practically adopted under a contract; at thirteen years wages are paid varying in amount according to the child's usefulness and the generosity and prosperity of the foster-parent.[43]

These provisions had advantages but also risks. If agencies found suitable foster-parents in the dominions then the aims of these schemes were realised; if poor choices were made then children were left as unprotected as they might have been in England, save for the inspector or possibly a neighbour or schoolteacher. Since almost all inspectors were male, the welfare of girls was not easily monitored. There was also criticism of the policy of sending only the healthiest children to Canada. It was argued that this was unfair to others who might be in more desperate conditions, unfair to the institutions and unfair to the home country. Several receiving and distributing homes in Canada were established, not for training children as in England, but as headquarters for running the business of the societies and receiving the children on arrival, between situations, or in case of illness. By 1910, there were eleven in Ontario, three in Quebec, one in Nova Scotia, and two in Manitoba.[44]

Although the Middlemore archives are substantial, many files are restricted owing to privacy concerns. Nevertheless, a pilot project by Patricia Roberts-Pichette provides some preliminary analysis of the first Middlemore child migrants. Like other migrants, Middlemore children had varied experiences. Most adapted to the new conditions but naturally some did not. The stress of changed circumstances manifested itself in various ways, such as resistance to authority, bedwetting or running away.

Of the first twenty-nine Middlemore children who went to Canada in 1873, Roberts-Pichette found that ten were older than 12 years, fifteen were younger than 12, with the ages of the others unknown. Fourteen had only one placement and nine had four or more. In the first year, two boys and one girl ran away causing much anxiety, a boy, aged 16, was returned to England, and two children left their places of settlement with their families and contact was lost. Later, several children ran away, were found, put in new homes, and subsequently received good reports. In 1878, one girl ran away but returned to her employer voluntarily; in 1876 her mother had come from England looking for her but she refused to live with her mother. One boy, aged 12 on arrival in Canada, secured his own place within two years and left the care of the Guthrie Home. Another, aged 9 on arrival in 1873, was earning $150 per year by 1882 when teenage boys generally earned less than $100 and girls less than $50. Some earned very little or nothing. One boy, who arrived in Canada as a 7–year-old, had four different placements and was sent to the Penetanguishene Reformatory for four years in 1882.[45]

Middlemore attributed these early failures to inexperience. Those who ran away were all teenage vagrants in England who, at their own request, were placed in towns in Canada. In retrospect, Middlemore believed that they should have been settled in the country. Thereafter, older children were sent to rural areas, placed on farms or occasionally with village shopkeepers.[46] Of 500 Middlemore children taken to Canada between 1873 and 1880, three were deaf, one almost blind, two had syphilis, and one was possibly disabled. Of these 500 children, ten ran away and were not found, three were taken to the United States, two or three left Ontario with their families, three died early, two were sent to Penetanguishene Reformatory and nine returned to England (two because they were unmanageable, the others because they wished to return).[47] Roberts-Pichette concludes that:

> perhaps the most amazing fact about the Middlemore children, was not that some ran away, or were returned to England because they were unmanageable, or were imprisoned, but, considering their origins, that the number of children with problems such as these was so small. Some of the boys who returned to England actually came back to Canada to settle. By 1883, Dr Middlemore was able to report that his first boy had become a landowner and his first girl was happily married. By the early 1890s, 2,209 children had been taken into the Children's Emigration Home in Birmingham of whom 2,049 were brought to Canada.[48]

Overall, Canadian officials looked on Middlemore's work favourably. George Bogue Smart, Inspector of British Immigrant Children and Receiving Homes in Ottawa, outlined the advantages of juvenile immigration in his 1905 annual report to the Department of the Interior:

> [It] is now generally conceded to be a real benefit not only to the children whose rescue from poverty and squalor it effects, but also to Britain's chief colony as well. Juvenile immigration assists in filling a gap in an important branch of our labour market, and numbers of farmers regard the influx of the so-called English home child as a veritable boon. It is only under exceptional circumstances that these juveniles are to be found elsewhere than with farmers. The desire of their benefactors in the old land is that as far as possible the boys should become Canadian

farmers and the girls domestic helps. That this wish has been met in a large measure is borne out by the numbers of young farmers in the older provinces and western Canada, who came to this country as children under the auspices of the various societies and have prospered. I have frequently heard of many youths and young men of this class going to our new provinces and taking up homesteads there.[49]

Despite a period of social reform following the 1906 election, little had changed by 1914 for destitute children in Britain. Poverty was at least reduced by the full employment, increased opportunities, and higher wages during the First World War.[50] Some 600 former Middlemore boys served in the war although this number may be higher as many were out of contact.[51] The number of former child migrants who served during both world wars is perhaps an indication of their continuing loyalty to Britain and the overall success of the movement.

Emigration was resumed soon after the First World War with the first group of ninety Middlemore children sent to Canada in May 1919. Matrons and either George Jackson, the General Secretary, or Robert Plenderleith, his assistant, accompanied the groups. Once in Canada, they were met by William and Ellen Ray, superintendent and matron of the Fairview Home in Halifax, who had arranged foster homes in the Maritime provinces. Children only stayed at the Fairview Home if they had further to travel or if the home in which they were placed proved unsuitable, and these stays were usually brief.[52]

Post-First World War reforms in child migration schemes

There were also significant reforms after the war in the broader context of imperial migration. The 1922 British Empire Settlement Act resulted in financial cooperation between the British and dominion governments and subsidies for approved independent and private organisations sponsoring migration. While this allowed many organisations to continue operating in the increasingly difficult economic environment of the 1920s, changes were afoot.[53]

During these years, child migration was increasingly being questioned. New attitudes to child care emphasised the advantages of keeping the family together and supporting children in familiar environments, rather than removing them to foreign surroundings.[54] In its 1924 official report, the Department of Immigration and Colonization in Canada responded to heightened criticism by outlining the advantages of child migration from the Dominion perspective:

- it added to the Canadian population a class of immigrants already trained under the best conditions, physically and morally;

- children born in Great Britain coming to Canada young, grew up as Canadians and regarded Canada as home;
- many childless couples were supplied with children;
- older boys provided farm help and older girls domestic help in both urban and rural areas; and
- it directly benefited the Motherland by providing a better distribution of Empire population, supplying Canada with labour, and benefiting orphan and needy children.[55]

The objective was to give underprivileged youth a start as farm apprentices and interest them in rural pursuits. It was, as Constantine argues, a 'back to the land' movement, at the time considered widely successful, the supply never meeting the demand.[56] Middlemore's own publications (predictably) stressed that juveniles sent to Canada were given foster homes and employment and many became successful farmers, businessmen and professionals.[57] Most Middlemore children were sent to Ontario, the rest scattered through other provinces. The majority were in good homes and situations, in good health, making progress, with good character and behaviour. It was continually emphasised that where foster homes proved unsatisfactory, the children were immediately removed.[58]

Opposition grew, however, when two Canadian orphans in foster homes committed suicide.[59] They were not child migrants but the incidents attracted adverse publicity about foster homes generally. An inspectorate was established to enable regular visits by Immigration and Colonization departmental officers, in addition to those by voluntary society personnel. In 1924, a British Overseas Settlement Delegation, headed by Margaret Bondfield, visited Canada to investigate conditions of child migration and settlement and reported to the Secretary of State for the Colonies.[60] Overall, the results were positive: children were well treated and better off than they would have been in Britain. Special mention was made of 'one Society [which] arranges to distribute its parties of children direct from the port of disembarkation to the homes provided for them. Consequently, accommodation at the receiving Home has been reduced to a minimum, it being only necessary to provide for the few children who for one reason or another, cannot be distributed immediately on arrival, and for those who return from time to time to the Home.' This obviously referred to Middlemore. The committee did not find that placements under this system were inferior to those made by other societies and expenses were lower as a result.[61]

Despite these findings, local child-care societies pressured the Canadian government to adopt further safeguards. Legislation was introduced which restricted the immigration of unaccompanied children under 14. Those travelling with parents or relatives, or being legally adopted in Canada were exempted. In 1925, only ten of fifty-five Middlemore children destined for Canada were allowed to leave. In 1926, there were only eight. Ultimately, because Middlemore children remained in the society's care until they were 21, the law was waived in their case. Local competition, however, led to regulations preventing Birmingham children from being sent to Nova Scotia.[62]

Cooperation between Middlemore and Fairbridge

Conscious of the ill effects of long-term institutionalisation, the Middlemore Committee decided in 1926 to send four young boys to the Fairbridge Farm School at Pinjarra, Western Australia, through the Child Emigration Society in London. This society depended on charitable organisations and its school at Pinjarra consisted of a large mixed farm with small cottages, each with its own house mother. The children were educated and trained as farmers or domestic servants.[63] The building of a new Middlemore home in Birmingham was delayed until the future of its own emigration work was known. In 1927, Middlemore Chairman Paul Cadbury visited Canadian officials and politicians, including the premier of Nova Scotia, Edgar N. Rhodes, who encouraged him to redraft the existing Act. Although the premier accepted Cadbury's redrafted clause, no legislative amendment eventuated. With escalating unemployment, however, it was decided that work must continue. New homes at a new site in Selly Oak were opened in 1929, replacing the old buildings in St Luke's Road.

Simultaneously, the committee strengthened its relationship with the Child Emigration Society, renamed the Fairbridge Society in 1935. In that year, Fairbridge took responsibility for the placement of Middlemore and other children, most of whom went to Australia, first to Pinjarra, and later to Molong in New South Wales and Northcote Farm School in Victoria. The few still destined for Canada mainly went to the Prince of Wales School in British Columbia.[64] Owing to continued economic depression, Fairbridge also took responsibility for several very young children. Middlemore built a special unit at Selly Oak to care for them for two to three years until they could be reunited with older siblings already at the Farm Schools. The unit opened in June 1939 but with the outbreak of war, all occupants were evacuated to Wilderhope Manor, a youth hostel in Shropshire.[65]

In September 1939, the Middlemore Homes were full. Over 170 children had been admitted and plans made to send regular parties to the Fairbridge Farm Schools in Australia and Canada. During the 'Phoney War' when no bombing occurred, some of the older children were returned to Selly Oak. In 1940, fifty children emigrated to Australia and

Canada and in 1941 a further twenty-three went to Canada. By then, much of Middlemore's accommodation had been requisitioned for war use. Work at Wilderhope Manor was discontinued and the remaining children were billeted in foster homes or returned to Selly Oak. The Fairview Home in Halifax was sold. In 1943, twenty boys and six girls came to Middlemore but none was sent overseas. In 1944, eight boys and nine girls were admitted, while there were still four boys and ten girls billeted in Shropshire. Finally, in 1945, twenty-eight children went to Canada, but by 1946, all shipping was required for the repatriation of troops.[66] Total numbers of Middlemore children from 1872 until the last sailed for Canada in 1945 were: those received into the Home, 7,643; those emigrated to Canada and Australia, 6,067.[67]

A new era in child migration

The post-Second World War period was a new era. Several acts and reports in Great Britain and the dominions had a significant impact on child migration. In the context of plans for large-scale post-war immigration in Australia, it was suggested that up to 50,000 war orphans be brought from Europe. This was later modified with a focus on Great Britain. In 1946 an Immigration (Guardianship of Children) Act was passed giving the Australian Minister for Immigration guardianship of children brought by an approved government or non-government organisation. The British government and public, however, were less supportive of child migration after the war.[68] The 1948 Report of the Care of Children Committee, established two years earlier, chaired by Dame Myra Curtis, was a landmark in the history of child care. Children could only be sent overseas with the permission of the Home Office. It recommended that local authorities be responsible for all children needing protection and advised that boarding out was preferable to institutional care. John T. Middlemore had come to the same conclusion seventy years earlier. While commending the work of the emigration societies, the report emphasised that unless dominion governments maintained close inspection and supervision, this method of child care should be discontinued.[69]

The Children Act of July 1948 accepted these recommendations, acknowledging that children should be kept with their families wherever possible. It supported the idea of boarding out over institutional care and recommended emigration in certain cases.[70] Care of children under the Poor Law ceased after three centuries. Hundreds of children immediately became the responsibility of local authorities and, in spite of the recommendations, all institutions, including Middlemore, were encouraged to assist. The committee agreed and the first children were admitted in September 1948. Notwithstanding the recommendations, the emigration side of its operations ceased. Although child migration to Australia resumed in 1947, with approximately 2,500 children emigrating between the late 1940s and the mid-1950s,[71] the last party of Middlemore children left for Australia in 1949. Over the next five years, Middlemore's operations were confined to Crowley House, a small Family Rehabilitation Centre originally built as a babies' home and opened in 1939, although aftercare in Canada and Australia continued. The committee considered various ways in which its resources and vast experience in the care of deprived children could be utilised.[72]

In 1951, a former member of the Curtis Committee, John Moss, reported to the British government on child migration to Australia. While generally supportive, he was critical of several voluntary organisations.[73] In 1956, a fact-finding mission commissioned by the Earl of Home, Secretary of State for Commonwealth Relations, and chaired by the Under-Secretary of State for the Home Office, John Ross, followed, demanding changes in the organisation of child care in Australia and reflecting the growing rift between new developments and increased professionalism in Great Britain, and the situation in Australia.[74]

By the mid-1950s, views on child welfare had undergone a major change in direction focusing on care for children within their families rather than on giving them a fresh start through emigration and foster homes. The wartime evacuation of children highlighted the dangers of breaking up families.[75] The nature of the Middlemore Homes changed in the post-Second World War era along with these broader shifts in thinking[76] and from 1955 Crowley House formed the basis of Middlemore work.[77] Despite these new understandings, Australia applied considerable pressure on the British government to send children well after the war. For political reasons, the movement was allowed to continue. Part of the rationale was racial, to bolster the British component of the postwar immigration intake, part was the related desire for security after the bombing of Darwin in 1942, and part was the need for labour and population for national development.[78]

Conclusion

The story of the Middlemore Homes is a record of a voluntary organisation that through its history had more than 8,000 children in its care. Over 6,000 emigrated to Canada and Australia between 1872 and 1949. Middlemore institutional records, like those of other such organisations, claim that with few exceptions they became good citizens. In 1872 when the movement began, the perceived solution for deprived children was to remove them from their backgrounds of slum conditions, unemployment, abuse and crime and, as Shurlee Swain and Lynn Abrams have argued, from their 'unfit' parents.[79] The history of Middlemore mirrored that of other similar organisations but there were important differences. Children were not taken to Canada without parental consent and, in general, did not spend time in institutions on arrival in the dominions. Rather, they were immediately placed in foster homes, selected prior to their embarkation from England. A century later, however, children were no longer removed from their environment at all. Instead, the focus turned to assisting their families.[80]

From the 1870s to the Second World War, child migration was seen as advantageous for several reasons. For Great Britain, it helped solve social problems related to the 'underclasses', contributed to the redistribution of the population from the crowded centre to the less populated dominions, and reinforced intra-imperial links. For the dominions, it provided much needed farm labourers and domestic servants, strengthening the white, British nature of their populations, thus reinforcing the racist and eugenic agendas inherent in nation building and providing an antidote to Asian immigration.

For the philanthropists and voluntary societies, it satisfied their aims of transforming wayward and destitute British youth into 'good' imperial citizens. John T. Middlemore was a Birmingham town councillor from 1883 and represented Nechells Ward until 1892. Politically, he was a Liberal in his youth and later held strong imperialist sentiments which influenced his work. He was a member of the British House of Commons from 1899 to 1918 and knighted in 1919 as the first baronet of Selly Oak for community service.[81] He devoted over thirty years of his life to the Children's Emigration Homes and his work was generously supported. Traditionally, the Middlemore Emigration Homes in both Birmingham and Canada relied on donors and subscribers and received many legacies. They were well endowed. It was not until the inter-war period that the organisation began to work with statutory bodies, both national and local, and received grants from public funds.[82]

For the child migrants themselves, however, it is only recently that the longer-term implications have been publicly acknowledged as seen in the inquiries mentioned, and books such as David Hill's *The Forgotten Children* (2007).[83] Many like Hill, sent to the dominions as children after the Second World War and on whom much media attention has focused, concede that they benefited from opportunities they would not otherwise have had. Yet they also have 'a continuing and profound sense of loss'.[84] It is almost too late to capture the voices of those who immigrated in earlier periods. We can only rely on the records of voluntary organisations like Middlemore, which rarely include details that reflect poorly on themselves. But we must also accept that over the last century views have changed markedly about what is safe, proper or lawful care or treatment of children, and this has important implications for the way we write the history of British juvenile emigration to the dominions.

Notes

1   W. A. Carrothers, *Emigration from the British Isles* (London, 1929), p. 38; S. Constantine, 'Empire Migration and Social Reform', in C. G. Pooley and I. D. Whyte (eds), *Migrants, Emigrants and Immigrants. A Social History of Migration* (London, 1991), pp. 67–70 and 74.
2   M. Harper, 'Cossar's Colonists: Juvenile Migration to New Brunswick in the 1920s', *Acadiensis*, 28:1 (1998), p. 47.
3   G. Sherington, 'Child Migration', in J. Jupp (ed.), *The Australian People. An Encyclopedia of the Nation, its People and their Origins*, 2nd edn (Melbourne, 2001), p. 61; A. Gill, *Orphans of the Empire* (Sydney, 1997); *Lost Children of the Empire* (London, 1989), book of the television series produced by ITV; P. Bean and J. Melville, *Lost Children of the Empire* (London, 1989); Australian Senate Community Affairs References Committee (ASCARC), *Lost Innocents: Righting the Record. Report on Child Migration* (Canberra, 2001).
4   *Bringing them Home. Report of the National Inquiry into the Separation of Aboriginal and Torres Strait Islander Children from Their Families* (1997); Western Australia Legislative Assembly. *Interim Report of the Select Committee into Child Migration* (1996); House of Commons Parliamentary Papers, HC 755, *Health Select Committee: The Welfare of Former British Child Migrants. Health Select Committee, Third Report with Proceedings, Evidence and Appendices* (1998); ASCARC, *Lost Innocents*. See J. Lawrence and P. Starkey (eds), *Child Welfare and Social Action in the Nineteenth and Twentieth Centuries: International Perspectives* (Liverpool, 2001), pp. 2–4; and Sherington, 'Child Migration', pp. 60–1.
5   Home Children – Canadian Genealogy Centre: www.genealogy.gc.ca/10/1008 (accessed 12 July 2005); J. Cumming, 'The Child Emigrant from Great Britain: the Experience of Middlemore Homes', *The Archivist*, Magazine of the Library and Archives Canada, no. 115: www.collectionscanada.ca/04/04240601_e.html (accessed 24 June 2005).
6   See similar arguments in E. Daniel, '"Solving an Empire Problem": the Salvation Army and British Juvenile Migration to Australia', *History of Education Review*, 36:1 (2007), pp. 34, 37, 44 and 47.
7   Lawrence and Starkey (eds), *Child Welfare*, p. 3.
8   G. Sherington and C. Jeffery, *Fairbridge. Empire and Child Migration* (Nedlands WA, 1998), xi.
9   S. Constantine, 'History, Telling the Truth and Giving Evidence: Child Migration to Australia after 1945', British World Conference, unpublished paper, Calgary, Canada, 10–12 July 2003.
10 Examples include R. Parker, *Uprooted: The Shipment of Poor Children to Canada, 1867–1917* (Bristol, 2008); J. Parr, *Labouring Children. British Immigrant Apprentices to Canada, 1869–1924* (London, 1980); G. Wagner, *Barnardo* (London, 1979); G. Wagner, *Children of the Empire* (London, 1982); M. Roe, *Australia, Britain, and Migration, 1915–1940: A Study of Desperate Hopes* (Cambridge, 1995); G. Sherington, 'British Youth and Empire Settlement: The Dreadnought Boys in New South Wales', *Journal of the Royal Historical Society*, 82:1 (1996), pp. 1–22; G. Sherington, '"A Better Class of Boy": The Big Brother Movement, Youth Migration and Citizenship of Empire', *Australian Historical Studies*, 33:120 (2002), pp. 267–85; B. Coldrey, *Good British Stock. Child and Youth Migration to Australia*

(Canberra, 1999); B. Coldrey, *The Scheme. The Christian Brothers and Children in Western Australia* (Perth WA, 1993); Gill, *Orphans*; A. Gill, *Likely Lads and Lasses: Youth Migration to Australia 1911–1983* (Sydney, 2005); A. McVeigh, 'A History of Child and Juvenile Migration Schemes to Australia' (PhD dissertation, Queen's University, Belfast, 1995); E. Daniel, 'British Juvenile Migration to Australia: Case Studies on the Programs of the Big Brother Movement, the Salvation Army and the Church of England between 1920 and 1960' (PhD dissertation, La Trobe University, 2004).

11 M. Langfield, 'Voluntarism, Salvation and Rescue: British Juvenile Migration to Australia and Canada, 1890–1939', *Journal of Imperial and Commonwealth History*, 32:2 (2004), pp. 86–114; M. Langfield, '"A Chance to Bloom": Female Migration and Salvationists in Australia and Canada, 1890s to 1939', *Australian Feminist Studies*, 17:39 (2002), pp. 287–303; M. Langfield, *More People Imperative: Immigration to Australia, 1901–1939* (Canberra, 1999); M. Langfield, '"Fit for the Elect of the World": Government Policy and Contemporary Opinion about the Encouragement of Immigrants to Australia, 1901–1939' (PhD dissertation, Monash University, 1990).

12 Cumming, 'The Child Emigrant from Great Britain'.

13 *Ibid.*

14 House of Commons Parliamentary Papers (HCPP), Cmd.2285, *British Oversea Settlement Delegation to Canada. Report from the Delegation Appointed to Obtain Information Regarding the System of Child Migration and Settlement in Canada, 1924* (known as the Bondfield Report); V. Knowles, *Strangers at Our Gates: Canadian Immigration and Immigration Policy, 1540–1990* (Toronto, 1992), pp. 70 and 106; Parr, *Labouring Children*, pp. 151–3; S. Constantine, 'Introduction: Empire Migration and Imperial Harmony', in S. Constantine (ed.), *Emigrants and Empire: British Settlement in the Dominions Between the Wars* (Manchester, 1990), p. 9; S. Constantine, 'The British Government, Child Welfare, and Child Migration to Australia after 1945', *Journal of Imperial and Commonwealth History*, 30:1 (2002), p. 101.

15 British Isles Family History Society of Greater Ottawa, Home Children, Middlemore's Children's Emigration Scheme: www.bifhsgo.ca/home_children_emigration_scheme. htm (accessed 1 June 2008).

16 Constantine, 'Empire Migration and Social Reform', p. 62; Harper, 'Cossar's Colonists', pp. 47 and 50.

17 Library and Archives Canada (LAC), MG28–I492, Middlemore Children's Emigration Homes fonds (R5592–0–4–E), microfilm, reel A-2090, anonymous author, *One Hundred Years of Child Care. The Story of Middlemore Homes 1872–1972* (Middlemore Homes Committee, 1972), p. 6, hereafter cited as *One Hundred Years of Child Care*; Cumming, 'The Child Emigrant from Great Britain'.

18 *One Hundred Years of Child Care*, p. 8; Cumming, 'The Child Emigrant from Great Britain'.

19 Harper, 'Cossar's Colonists', pp. 50–1.

20 P. Roberts-Pichette, 'John Throgmorton Middlemore and his Children's Emigration Homes', pp. 2–3, British Isles Family History Society of Greater Ottawa: www.bifh sgo.ca/home_children_emigration_scheme.htm (accessed 30 October 2004); www. bifhsgo.ca/home_children_background.htm (accessed 24 June 2005); *One Hundred Years of Child Care*, pp. 8–9.

21 *One Hundred Years of Child Care*, p. 5; Roberts-Pichette, 'John Throgmorton Middlemore', p. 1.

22 *One Hundred Years of Child Care*, pp. 5 and 10–11; Roberts-Pichette, 'John Throgmorton Middlemore', p. 3; Cumming, 'The Child Emigrant from Great Britain'; LAC, Middlemore Children's Emigration Fonds, Administrative History: www. mikan3.archives.ca/pam/public_mikan/index.php?fuseaction=genitem.displayItem &lang=eng&rec_nbr=107020&rec_nbr_list=107020,103458,120569,131861,131864& print_version=yes (accessed 30 June 2008).

23 *One Hundred Years of Child Care*, p. 9.

24 Roberts-Pichette, 'John Throgmorton Middlemore', p. 4; *One Hundred Years of Child Care*, pp. 11–12.

25 *One Hundred Years of Child Care*, pp. 6–7 and 13; Roberts-Pichette, 'John Throgmorton Middlemore', pp. 4–5.

26 See Harper, 'Cossar's Colonists', pp. 56–65; Langfield, 'Voluntarism, Salvation and Rescue'.

27 *One Hundred Years of Child Care*, p. 6.

28 Roberts-Pichette, 'John Throgmorton Middlemore', p. 5.

29 See L. Chilton, *Agents of Empire: British Female Migration to Canada and Australia, 1860s-1930* (Toronto, 2007), pp. 15–16.

30 See similar findings in Sherington, 'Child Migration', p. 60; Constantine, 'Telling the Truth and Giving Evidence', p. 1.

31 Canada, *Sessional Papers*, series 36, vol. 10, no. 25, Annual Report of the Department of the Interior for the year 1901. Report of the Superintendent of Immigration for the Deputy Minister, James A. Smart (Ottawa, 1902), p. 101; Constantine, 'Empire Migration and Social Reform', pp. 62–3 and 66–70.

32 Harper, 'Cossar's Colonists', pp. 52–3.

33 British Isles Family History Society of Greater Ottawa, Home Children – Background: www.bifhsgo.ca/home_children_background.htm (accessed 30 June 2008); *One Hundred Years of Child Care*, p. 11; Canada, *Sessional Papers*, series 36, vol. 10, no. 25, Report of the Superintendent (1902), p. 101.

34 Roberts-Pichette, 'John Throgmorton Middlemore', p. 5; Cumming, 'The Child Emigrant from Great Britain'.

35 Canada, *Sessional Papers*, series 35, vol. 10, no. 25, Annual Report of the Department of the Interior for the year 1900. Report of the Superintendent of Immigration for the Deputy Minister, James A. Smart (Ottawa, 1901).

36 Roberts-Pichette, 'John Throgmorton Middlemore', p. 6.

37 Cumming, 'The Child Emigrant from Great Britain'.

38 Canada, *Sessional Papers*, series 35, vol. 10, no. 25, Report of the Superintendent (1901). For the gender imbalance among child migrants, see Langfield, '"A Chance to Bloom"', pp. 297–9; Sherington, 'Child Migration', p. 60.

39 L. M. Montgomery, *Anne of Green Gables* (Canada, 1908).

40 Roberts-Pichette, 'John Throgmorton Middlemore', p. 6.

41 *One Hundred Years of Child Care*, p. 16.

42 Cumming, 'The Child Emigrant from Great Britain'.

43 Report of the Royal Poor Law Commission (London, 1909), part iv, chapter 8, p. 4, cited in Canada, *Sessional Papers*, series 45, vol. 16, no. 25, Annual Report of the Department of the Interior for the Fiscal Year ending March 31, 1910. Report of G. Bogue Smart, Chief Inspector of British Immigrant Children and Receiving Homes (Ottawa, 1911), pp. 113–14.

44 *Ibid.*, p. 114.

45 Roberts-Pichette, 'John Throgmorton Middlemore', pp. 6–7.

46 *Ibid.*, p. 8; *One Hundred Years of Child Care*, p. 12.

47 Roberts-Pichette, 'John Throgmorton Middlemore', p. 8.

48 *Ibid.*

49 Canada, *Sessional Papers*, series 40, vol. 11, no. 25, Annual Report of the Department of the Interior for the year 1905. Reports of Officials in Eastern Canada, no. 2. Report of G. Bogue Smart, Inspector of British Immigrant Children and Receiving Homes (Ottawa, 1906), p. 135.

50 *One Hundred Years of Child Care*, p. 20.

51 *Ibid.*, p. 18.

52 *Ibid.*, p. 20.

53 See Langfield, 'Voluntarism, Salvation and Rescue', p. 97; Constantine, 'Empire Migration and Imperial Harmony', pp. 9–10; Constantine, 'The British Government, Child Welfare, and Child Migration', p. 100.

54 Harper, 'Cossar's Colonists', p. 49.

55 *One Hundred Years of Child Care*, p. 20.

56 Constantine, 'Empire Migration and Social Reform', pp. 62–3.
57 *One Hundred Years of Child Care*, p. 21.
58 *Ibid.*
59 Earlier concerns were raised in the Doyle Report, 1875. See Daniel, 'British Juvenile Migration to Australia', pp. 140–3.
60 See footnote 14 above; Harper, 'Cossar's Colonists', p. 49; Langfield, 'Voluntarism, Salvation and Rescue', p. 98.
61 *One Hundred Years of Child Care*, pp. 23–4.
62 *Ibid.*, p. 24.
63 Langfield, 'Salvation, Voluntarism and Rescue', p. 93.
64 *One Hundred Years of Child Care*, pp. 24–5. British Isles Family History Society of Greater Ottawa, Home Children-Background: www.bifhsgo.ca/home_children_background.htm (accessed 1 June 2008); Roberts-Pichette, 'John Throgmorton Middlemore', p. 5.
65 *One Hundred Years of Child Care*, pp. 25–7.
66 *Ibid.*, pp. 27–8.
67 *Ibid.*, p. 28.
68 Sherington, 'Child Migration', p. 60.
69 *One Hundred Years of Child Care*, p. 29; Sherington, 'Child Migration', p. 60; Constantine, 'Telling the Truth and Giving Evidence', p. 9.
70 Constantine, 'Telling the Truth and Giving Evidence', p. 10.
71 Forty per cent were sponsored by the Catholic Church. Fairbridge and Barnardo's sent far fewer than before the war. Half went to Western Australia. Consent of parents or guardians was required. Sherington, 'Child Migration', pp. 60–1. The last children from Dr Barnardo's were sent to Australia in 1967. Constantine, 'Empire Migration and Social Reform', p. 70.
72 *One Hundred Years of Child Care*, pp. 29 and 32.
73 J. Moss, *Child Migration to Australia* (London, 1953).
74 HCPP, Cmd.9832: *Child Migration to Australia. Report of a Fact-Finding Mission* (1956), p. 3, cited in Political Science Pamphlet, no. 161, p. 9, State Library of Victoria, Melbourne; Sherington, 'Child Migration', p. 61; Constantine, 'Telling the Truth and Giving Evidence', p. 10.
75 *One Hundred Years of Child Care*, p. 30; Constantine, 'Telling the Truth and Giving Evidence', p. 9.
76 The Fairbridge Society changed similarly. Sherington, 'Fairbridge Child Migrants', pp. 53–81.
77 *One Hundred Years of Child Care*, p. 32.
78 Constantine, 'Telling the Truth and Giving Evidence', p. 10.
79 Chapters by S. Swain, 'Child Rescue: The Emigration of an Idea', and L. Abrams, '"Blood is Thicker than Water": Family, Fantasy and Identity in the Lives of Scottish Foster Children', in Lawrence and Starkey (eds), *Child Welfare*, pp. 101–20 and 195–218 respectively.
80 *One Hundred Years of Child Care*, p. 43.
81 Roberts-Pichette, 'John Throgmorton Middlemore', p. 8; *One Hundred Years of Child Care*, pp. 22–3.
82 *One Hundred Years of Child Care*, pp. 3 and 15.
83 D. Hill, *The Forgotten Children. Fairbridge Farm School and its Betrayal of Australia's Child Migrants* (Sydney, 2007).
84 National Children's Homes submission to the *Lost Innocents: Righting the Record Inquiry*, p. 2.

CHAPTER 7

Travelling colonist: British emigration and the construction of Anglo-Canadian privilege

Lisa Chilton

Over the course of several months in 1924, immigration officials along with representatives of the Canadian National Railway (CNR) endeavoured to bring closure to yet another nasty little public relations incident relating to the reception of British emigrants in Canada. Margaret Boyle, an upstanding member of British Columbia's Anglo-Canadian community, had stumbled on information concerning the transportation of British female emigrants across Canada by train that had shocked her. As an enthusiastic member of the Imperial Order Daughters of the Empire (IODE), she felt duty bound to share her thoughts with her organisation's national convenor. 'Do you know – I did not – *exactly* what a Colonist car means?' she asked. Her interview with a young woman who had just arrived in Vancouver, British Columbia, via the CNR had revealed that female travellers in the colonist cars had been expected to 'sleep *four* abreast in one section – no mattresses, no pillows, *no curtains*, one lavatory for men and women – no hot water'. Worse still, 'there were many foreign men[,] the whole trip and perhaps all the way ... Chinamen'. 'Third class travel in England is decent and comfortable', the letter explained. 'English girls expect the same thing in Canada; they know nothing else.'[1] The letter's recipient was likewise scandalised when she learned of the conditions under which British women were forced to travel when moving across Canada to their new homes, so she added her own letter of chastisement to the proper authorities. To Mabel Durham, the women's superintendent of the CNR, she railed: 'you cannot know the conditions of third class travel on this Continent or you would not advise girls travelling third class until drastic changes are made. I have stated the bald facts and please give scope to your imagination for a few minutes if you would realise the whole situation – indecent and indescribable.'[2]

In academic terms, the fun that one can have deconstructing such an enticingly loaded set of letters is endless. They offer easily digestible 'textbook' examples of gendered, racist and classist over-reactions by a fanatically uptight, over-privileged, Anglo-centric minority of Canadian society. Even at the time, most of the government and railway officials who were charged with responding to correspondence of this nature were challenged by the protesters' melodramatic and impractical demands that Britons be coddled while in transit.[3] The resource-limited, multi-ethnic world in which international migrants moved was bound to disappoint travellers who truly believed the pleasant British World, land-of-opportunity mythology served up in immigration promotional literature and British Empire school curricula. Yet, the letters of protest (and there were many) achieved significant results. The information provided by Boyle and others similarly interested in the welfare of British emigrants in transit was taken seriously by Canada's government officials, who put into motion a comprehensive system of checks and balances designed to ascertain the legitimacy of the charges, and to assess whether cross-country travel arrangements might be improved in the future. As in the other British dominions, Canada's immigration officials were working within a deep-rooted tradition of pro-empire settlement. Because of complaints filed by British emigrants and their supporters, British women were segregated, whenever possible, from racially or ethnically different travellers. Not only were they protected from interactions with foreign men, but whenever practicable they were provided with sleeping accommodation and lavatories away from foreign women in government-run immigrant buildings and on trains.

Why did British emigrants expect these sorts of privileges overseas? Why did large numbers of Canadians go out of their way to support their expectations? And why did government officials and Canada's major railway companies agree to put into place the mechanisms and structures that would make such privileges possible? In this chapter, these questions serve as a starting point for a larger discussion of the concepts of Britishness, white settler society hegemony, and British superiority in pre-Second World War Canada. This discussion consists of two interconnected sections.

The first section asserts that it was possible for these sorts of attitudes of superiority to remain intact in Canada (arguably, throughout the twentieth century) because Anglo-Canadians developed a clear sense of ownership; a belief in British entitlement necessarily went hand in hand with the understanding that Canada was, at base, a British nation by virtue of the fact that British bodies numerically dominated the Canadian landscape. A large corpus of literature on the construction of whiteness has taught historians to think carefully about the power of seemingly normative categories of identity. As

Adele Perry notes, 'Interrogating whiteness as a race challenges the assumption that whiteness is normal and brownness, blackness, and redness the problematic "others" in need of explication'.[4] Clearly, the term 'British' ought likewise to be interrogated. Carl Bridge and Kent Fedorowich remind us in their introduction to *The British World: Diaspora, Culture and Identity* that people of ethnic backgrounds other than British sometimes sought to adopt a British identity in order to accrue privileges that came with British status.[5] The review of Canada's immigration history that follows suggests that in order for Canadians to be convinced of Canada's Britishness, perceptions of what it meant to be British had to be flexible. Depending upon the context, the terms 'British', 'Anglo', and 'English' were (as they continue to be) used interchangeably to indicate various meanings ranging from place of origin to a remarkably broad concept of ethnicity. For the purposes of projecting a sense of cultural domination over various others (French Canadians, Aboriginal peoples, or other, less desirable immigrants of East European, Asian, West Indian, or African-American background) a significant proportion of Canada's multi-ethnic population had to be counted into the Anglo-Canadian norm.

The second part of the chapter offers a close reading of correspondence relating to Britons in transit in the period following the First World War in order to detail some of the ways in which a discourse of British superiority was used to both justify and increase privileges accorded to British-Canadian immigrants to the detriment of other immigrant groups. This study illustrates that for British migrants, as for a large proportion of settled Anglo-Canadians, ethnicity was classed. In the abstract, when considering immigrant populations, Britons were typically considered a class above – regardless of their own class positions coming out of British society.[6] The chapter shows how British emigrants and their supporters worked, consciously and unconsciously, to create perceptions of social distance from other immigrant groups. As the example cited at the beginning of this chapter demonstrates, this sense of British superiority was channelled through gendered understandings of Britishness and foreignness.

The two strands of this chapter – one which asserts that a wide range of ethnic groups were purposefully absorbed into the normative, dominant category of 'British', and one which argues that British emigrants and their Canadian supporters worked to emphasise the social distance between newcomers from Britain and other immigrants – seem to work at cross purposes. Yet, it is evident that together, the practice of selectively including Canadian immigrants of various social, cultural and ethnic backgrounds into the category of 'British', and the practice of asserting Britons' elevated cultural status, ensured that

Anglo-Canadians could feel justified in claiming, and receiving, special privileges in Canadian society. The effectiveness of these practices may be seen in the numerous examples of preferential treatment given to British immigrants in transit, individually and as a group, during the inter-war years, and in the fact that it was more than two decades after the end of the Second World War before Canada's immigration policy was altered such that, at least on paper, it would no longer give preference to British immigrants over all others.[7]

Canada: an Anglo-British nation

At the heart of British imperialism was the idea that Anglo-Britons were superior, by nature, to any of the empire's subject populations – be they Celtic Britons, Aboriginal peoples, or previously settled inhabitants originally from other European societies. As Lord Durham succinctly put it when reporting on the Canadian situation at the middle of the nineteenth century, English dominance would inevitably prevail, because the English had 'already in their hands the majority of the larger masses of property in the country; they have the decided superiority of intelligence on their side; they have the certainty that colonization must swell their numbers to a majority; and they belong to the race which wields the Imperial Government'.[8] Sentiments similar to those of Lord Durham may be found in the correspondence and publications of government administrators and members of the public in Britain and in the colonies.

In much of the writing about colonial settlement and expansion, there was a sense of inevitability about English dominance. At the same time, underneath the confidence conveyed in Anglo-Britons' communications on this subject there was an evident tension, because again and again, in various contexts, the inevitability of English dominance (along with their evident superiority) was held up to question. Lord Durham's pronouncements about the path that the Canadas *would* follow were made in the immediate aftermath of violent protests against the colonial system of government by French *Canadiens*, along with some Irish Catholic supporters, against the right of the English to dominate the Lower Canadian political scene, and in the context of growing nativist and pro-American movements in Upper Canada. Durham believed that the English would prevail, but he also felt that a more solid plan of assimilation and government control had to be enacted. In other words, English dominance was inevitable, but the government had to be strategic in its management of both the context (social, economic, and political) and its people in order to ensure that the inevitable would, in fact, occur.

In this context it is clear why, from the beginning of Britain's formal takeover of New France, colonisation by English-speaking Protestants was considered by colonial governors to be the most appropriate way to ensure continued Anglo-British control in the region. It was important that numerically they competed well with other immigrant groups, while in terms of cultural, economic and political performance they were expected to outshine their rivals. On neither score did Anglo-British immigrants prove to be consistently satisfactory. They did not settle in Canada in the numbers desired by British emigration promoters, and the fact that British emigrants were not necessarily always desirable immigrants was the focus of regular attention, even within pro-empire circles, throughout the nineteenth and early twentieth centuries.[9] In fact, concerns about the poor quality of British immigrants (defined in terms of health, class, morals, political perspectives, and work-related skills) featured regularly in official correspondence regarding migration and in the press until the Second World War. There was an obvious disconnect between imperial rhetoric and the reality of Canadian immigration.

A brief review of immigration to British North America underlines this point. Relatively few people migrated from the British Isles to British North America in the half century following the conquest of New France in 1763. The British government was unwilling to encourage large-scale emigration for a variety of reasons, and for the most part landlords only became interested in promoting and facilitating emigration after 1815.[10] Hostilities during the American Revolution and then the Napoleonic Wars made migration to British North America both unattractive and dangerous. For these reasons, British North America's earliest colonial administrators solicited prospective immigrants situated outside of Anglo-Britain to secure the British North American colonies to the British Empire. The result until 1815 was a heterogeneous incoming population.[11]

The large-scale emigration from the British Isles to British North America that began after 1815 was hardly more ethnically homogenous. The history of the migration, settlement, and evolving ethnic identities of these newcomers has been well documented.[12] Throughout the nineteenth century there were public displays of antipathy between people of Irish and people of English background, and when religious difference was a part of the package, the 'othering' that occurred between these groups was extensive and at times violent.[13] As James Jupp has noted for the Australian context, it is not enough to consider only the classic English/Scottish/Irish/Welsh divides when considering British emigration and ethnicity. Regional differences within these separate nations could result in 'othering' as meaningful for those involved as across

[173]

the national divides.[14] Angela McCarthy's explorations of twentieth-century cultural identities among Scottish emigrants underline that this was not a sense of difference that disappeared after the First World War.[15]

The challenges associated with British emigrants' lack of ethnic homogeneity posed a set of problems that would be addressed through formal and informal processes of re-education; asserting Anglo-British dominance of Canada through sheer numbers posed a separate set of problems. Census information about citizens' 'origins' can tell us much about the social politics of the time, but it needs to be carefully inter-rogated before being used as hard data to indicate ethnic or cultural identities that can be pinned down. The wording of a Statistics Canada chart of immigrant origins for the period 1871–1971 offers a case in point. The breakdown of immigrants into three possible categories: 'Canadian-born', 'Other British-born', and 'Foreign-born', clearly sug-gests an assumption (the result of citizenship considerations) that birth in Canada made a person 'British'.[16] A brief review of immigrant numbers by ethnicity is important, all the same, because the idea that Canada became an Anglo-British nation at least in part on the strength of numbers was (and is) powerful.[17]

Unlike in Australia, at no point in Canadian history did English-origin Canadians make up more than a third of the whole population.[18] It was not until 1854, the first year in which colonial rather than British authorities dominated the management of immigration to Canada, that the number of immigrants arriving from English ports outnumbered those coming directly from Ireland. Previously, Irish immigrants had outnumbered those from England, usually by a significant margin, every year. During the quarter century before 1854, the number of Irish port immigrants were usually at least double that of English port immigrants (some of whom would have been of Irish origin), while immigrants from Scottish ports constituted about a quarter of those from England.[19] In other words, English emigrants constituted only a minor fraction of the people of British origin who travelled to Canada during this period. The fact that in the 1871 census, there are 706,369 self-identified people of English background to 846,414 people of Irish origin probably says a lot about the process of self-identification for census reports, as well as about Irish patterns of emigration out of Canada into the United States.

But even when the census reports for the last decades of the nineteenth century are taken at face value, it is clear that people of English background continued to be a minority; between 1871 and 1901, people who had self-identified as being of English origin made up approximately one-third of Canadians of British background. When thinking about all people identified in the census as 'of British origin' (a category that would have included English, Welsh, Scottish, Irish, English-speaking Americans, as well as the offspring of Loyalists, late Loyalists, and anyone of mixed heritage identified as British), it becomes evident that British Canadians constituted only slightly more than a half of the Canadian population during the first three decades of the twentieth century,[20] after which their numbers relative to people of alternate origins decreased. Clearly, Anglo-centred British imperialism did not occur solely as a result of the overwhelming numbers of English-origin Protestant Britons and their progeny in the nineteenth and early twentieth centuries.[21]

It is also evident that Canada's adoption of a British identity was not a result of its domination by people who were perceived to be 'quality' British emigrants. The poverty-stricken migrants associated with the Scottish Highlands clearances, the Famine Irish, the English Poor Law removals, and home children, received much negative attention from their contemporaries.[22] The French Canadian inhabitants in Lower Canada (Quebec) were not impressed by the immigrants who were supposed to colonise them; they assumed that it was more likely that they were being purposefully infected with mortal diseases through the importation of Britain's disease-ridden off-casts.[23] Concerns about the quality of British newcomers did not go away after Confederation. In the late nineteenth and early twentieth centuries, problems associated with British emigrants were the focus of much private and public anxiety.[24] A particularly striking set of complaints are those registered by the Albertan Frank Oliver, an actively pro-British Canadian Minister of the Interior (1905–11) who reported that a significant percentage of the British immigrants who had arrived during 1907 were not only unemployed, but might be considered: '[a] drug on the labour market from misfortune, incompetence or indifference'.[25] According to Mabel Timlin, concerns were raised by Canadians that British charities and government agencies were still endeavouring to use emigration to Canada as a way to solve their own problems of poverty and vice in the early twentieth century. During 1907, she writes, 'the provision "no English need apply" multiplied in Canadian advertisements for labour. In that year there was an unusually large number of exclusions and deportations of persons coming from the British Isles. In 1908 matters became worse: out of nearly 1,800 deportations that year nearly 1,100 (or 70%) were returns to Britain.' The changes in immigration laws that were made during 1908 and again in 1910 were, in part, a response to this period of British emigration.[26]

There is much evidence that British immigrants were not all seen as shining examples of the exemplary immigrant. There is also plenty of evidence that whenever possible, government officials and empire-promoting individuals and organisations in the Canadian context tried to separate their knowledge of specific British immigrants' inadequacies from their larger understanding of the sort of immigration that was desirable for the country's growth.[27] In her work on deportation, Barbara Roberts provides examples of how British and non-British troublemaking immigrants were purposefully disassociated from each other in government reports. For example, labour activists were routinely represented as foreign, or alien, in spite of the integration of Canadian-born and British activists into labour organisations. The International Workers of the World (IWW), which had been successfully recruiting English-speaking workers in northern Ontario, was represented by government officials as full of 'Finns, Polacks, Austrians and Hungarians and some Irish',[28] all eminently deportable with a minimum of public fuss. IWW sympathisers of British origin could then be labelled deviants from the much more sensible British norm.[29] It is worth noting that, as this example demonstrates, Irish Canadians were still being included or excluded from the category 'British' in the inter-war period depending on the observer's politics and the specifics of the case.

In the correspondence and debates among Canadian government officials concerning immigrant recruitment, the ability of prospective immigrants to contribute economically to the host society remained central throughout the period reviewed here. However, the ability to be a productive member of the host society was never the sole determinant of immigration policies and practices. Economic factors always worked in combination with racial and cultural markers that were usually less easy to pin down.[30] The concept of cultural worth tended to be subsumed into imprecise descriptions of moral fibre and social ethics, virtues that could, in theory, be held by non-Anglo-British immigrants of the right sort. Definitions of what constituted the 'right' sort of immigrant were determined by the socio-political context of the moment (so that Americans, Catholic Irish, northern and even central European immigrants could be considered almost on a par with Protestant Anglo-Britons) – although the imaginary, perfect, Anglo-British Protestant immigrant was assumed by most government officials and by imperially minded members of the public to provide the benchmark for immigrant quality.[31]

In order for Canada to become and then remain comfortably a part of the British World, the ambiguities and contradictions embodied in these understandings of Canadian immigration had to be rationalised. It was essential that all sorts of immigrants who should not have fitted into the category of appropriate British colonists be counted as such in order to support the perception of an overwhelming British dominance, and it had to be possible to claim consistent Anglo-British superiority in the face of extensive evidence to the contrary.

Creating and defending colonists' rights

A deeper understanding of how the concepts of Britishness, white settler society hegemony, and British superiority played out in the context of pre-Second World War Canada can be gained from an exploration of how British emigrants understood their own place within the context of Canadian immigration, and of how Canadians (especially Canada's migration managers) represented and treated British migrants in relation to their other-ethnic fellow travellers. Government-regulated sites at which immigrants congregated while in transit in Canada offer particularly good entry points for discussion, because they were the focus of extensive commentary and documentation. Ports, immigration buildings, railway stations, and trains were public spaces where immigrants necessarily rubbed shoulders with each other. Immigration buildings and trains are especially interesting locales to explore as in these relatively cramped spaces immigrants were forced to eat, sleep, use the toilet facilities, and bide their time, sometimes for several days in a row, in the company of unfamiliar others.

Even a superficial reading of the complaints and investigations concerning the unpleasant physical realities of travel and reception facilities for newcomers is instructive. Sights, sounds, smells, conversations, conflicts, assumptions, personalities, and identities emerge from the correspondence contained in the immigration department's files on the transportation and reception of immigrants. When this correspondence is read for what it can tell us about the social politics of immigration during this period of Canadian history, an intriguing set of dynamics becomes apparent. A recurring theme is that the filth and discomfort (physical and psychological) associated with travel in Canada was frequently linked by British emigrants and their supporters to the fact that they could not avoid encountering other immigrants en route. Through the pens and typewriters of Anglo-Canadians and British emigrants, the assaults to the senses (filth, loud voices, odours), the unhealthy conditions of travel (disgusting sinks, overflowing toilets), and the unsettling challenges to normative social conditions (invasions of space, a lack of privacy), were again and again made the products of the immigrant others' behaviour.

Concerns raised about the Canadian government's management of immigration came in a variety of styles and from a variety of sources in the early decades of the twentieth century. When reviewed together, the gendered nature of the concerns raised and the manner in which they were shared is striking. The most common form of official complaints from British emigrant men were those registered by individuals who were having difficulties establishing themselves and their families economically, and who felt that they had been misled by promotional campaigns that emphasised the opportunities for financial security and advancement to be had in Canada. The fact that the Canadian context had somehow undermined men's abilities to support themselves and their families through their own efforts was seen as a serious problem. By contrast, grievances filed concerning conditions of travel were far more likely to be those which related to the experiences of women. The fact that while in transit migrants were forced to endure living in spaces which were, concurrently, both private and public ensured that anxieties would be most emphatically voiced around women's sensibilities, identities, and safety.

Over the course of the second half of the nineteenth century, immigration buildings were constructed at all of Canada's major ports of entry, railway terminuses, and destination centres, where newcomers were officially screened, processed, fed, and accommodated, as needs be, before they were sent on their way. These institutions were widely used by immigrants because they provided valuable services for travellers seeking advice, employment and supplies. They also offered free accommodation while newcomers tried to make plans for their next move, thus limiting the extra costs that would have to be incurred during the process of migration. Immigration officials were mandated to receive all bona fide immigrants at these buildings, and periodically official communications were sent out to remind them that they were expected to welcome and treat *all* newcomers with respect. 'I wish to impress very strongly upon you the importance of giving these people the very best impressions of our country and of showing them that the desire of the Government is to treat them most courteously and do anything it can to advance their interest', reads one such memorandum from the Deputy Minister for Immigration. 'I would therefore ask you to be sure in all cases, in dealing with individuals as well as large numbers of immigrants, to exercise the utmost patience and judgement, and always make it a pleasure to give advice to all newcomers to our country.'[32]

Although all immigrants were supposed to be treated with respect by immigration officials, there was also a shared understanding of the relative value of various immigrant types firmly in place, and government officials did not pretend that all immigrants would be treated in exactly the same way. First- and second-class immigrants who had to undergo medical examinations at the immigration buildings expected – and if at all possible were allowed – a separate examination room so that they would not have to suffer the indignity of examinations in close proximity to members of the lower class.[33] Similar privileges were granted along lines of ethnic origin, resulting in the segregation of all British immigrants from 'foreigners or continental immigrants' during medical inspection.[34]

The living quarters at the immigration buildings were likewise divided along a British–foreign divide (first- and second-class travellers would have found accommodation elsewhere). When, in 1926, the British women's dormitory at the St John immigration building in New Brunswick was needed for a new nursery, the dormitory currently in use by women of non-British background was divided by an eight-foot high wall in order to create a separate space for the British. So that they would not have to share toilet facilities with the foreigners, 'three of the toilets in the Foreign Women's Quarters [were to be] kept under lock and key for the use of the British Women'. Special care was given to the furnishings in the British women's space: 'In the British Women's Dormitory, there will be comfortable white iron beds, chairs, and a few small tables and blinds on the windows', reads a memorandum outlining the new arrangements.[35] The needs of British women and foreign women were assumed to be different to the extent that the officials in charge of this particular immigration building had considered the installation of doors on the foreign women's dormitory an unnecessary expense. It was only after someone in the women's branch of the immigration department had pointed out that if the foreign women's dormitory had no doors, the immigrants would not gain an accurate impression 'of privacy and decency in Canadian life', that a move was made to install grey blankets as curtains across their doorway.[36]

British emigrants continued to be considered Canada's most desirable immigrants throughout the period under review here, and large numbers of leading Anglo-Canadians were explicit about the negative impact that too much contact with 'foreign types' would have on British immigrants' reports back home. Widespread agreement on this subject meant that segregation was considered a viable option whenever possible. As the spokesperson for North Battleford's Board of Trade, hopeful that the federal government might be convinced to pour more money into their local immigration building, put it: 'it gives the new arrival a very bad impression of any town if, when stepping off the train, the immigration agent takes the party to the immigration hall where they have to spend the night with Doukabours and Galicians'.[37]

Living arrangements at the immigration buildings caused concern for immigrants and for immigration officials. However, accommodation arrangements on trains received far greater public scrutiny. Because the experiences of the young female colonist that scandalised members of the IODE in 1924 (discussed in the introduction) were hardly unique, the files of the Canadian federal government's immigration agencies are littered with similar complaints. Whatever thrills the novelty of being in transit might have had for Canada's west-bound immigrants during the early twentieth century, they would have worn off by the time the migrants had reached Montreal. For travellers heading into the Prairies or British Columbia, moving across the country third class, or 'colonist', by train was invariably a trial of patience. In spite of the best efforts of the railway managers and Canadian government officials, there were frequently lengthy delays and shortages of necessary supplies (like food and water), and the sleeping arrangements were rustic at best. Cleaning facilities were rudimentary (travellers described sinks that had to be used for cleaning infants and their soiled clothing, as well as for eating utensils and faces), and the lavatories presented a constant challenge to passengers and trainmen alike.[38] For travellers in the colonist cars, privacy was unobtainable. In winter, cold was a problem; in the summer the heat and odours could become unbearable. But the challenge faced by British immigrant train travellers that was most persistently noted in protests to immigration officials related to British women's shocked and wounded pride.

The correspondence collected in government files relating to British women in transit provides ample evidence of the sorts of stereotypes associated with non-Anglo men that has been uncovered in previous studies of early twentieth-century Canada.[39] Veiled references to men of different ethnic and racial backgrounds as politically, physically, and sexually dangerous are well represented in these documents. However, it was the perceived poor hygiene and social behaviour of foreigners that received the most direct comments. A lack of appropriate manners was frequently cited by travellers and immigration agents alike as a clear indicator of social difference. Undignified, uncivilised, and generally uncouth – foreigners, apparently, just did not know how to behave. A letter sent home by a young British woman who had emigrated to Canada under the terms of the Empire Settlement Act reveals the compelling mix of scandalised embarrassment, voyeuristic curiosity, and nurtured sense of superiority that drove British observers to share their observations of foreigners with like-minded people back home, who then forwarded the letters to Canadian immigration and railway officials: 'The colonists apartments were filthy and the foreigners, including 26 Finlanders, got quite drunk and layed [sic] down with their girls or wives or what ever they were and slept and snored nearly all night. What an experience.'[40]

Reports like that of conductress F. M. Winfield concerning a trip from Montreal to Winnipeg similarly emphasised social distance: 'The

Foreign men in this train were particularly rough and were annoying to the other passengers. It was reported to me that some of them were seen stealing cigarettes and Post Cards at the Restaurant at Chalk River. Also at Chalk River a Foreign man knocked an English woman so violently that her companion behind her had to catch her to keep her from falling. Other similar offenses were reported but none of the offenders were identified at the time.'[41] In another report, conductress D. M. Binning emphasised the breadth of the cultural gap between British emigrants and foreigners. On this particular trip, she had had charge of two train cars carrying unaccompanied women and children: one car was reserved for Britons, the other for foreigners. Binning wrote that: 'Owing to the First-class Day Coach being on the end of the train and my car being next to it, this meant all the Britishers had to go through the cars of the Foreigners to get to the Dining Car and on this trip the Foreigners were so dirty, throwing everything on the floor, the smell of the cars were [so] dreadful that naturally the Britishers complained about it . . . At Toronto the passengers were very disgusted as the Foreigners got mixed up with the Britishers but the Station Master said he would have the Conductor put all the Britishers together'.[42]

References to Asian travellers on trains carrying British immigrants took a noticeably different form. Whereas discussions about European immigrants usually provided some detail about the nature of the Europeans' behaviour – some explanation for the distaste that their presence elicited in the British migrants – there seems to have been no need to do so when it came to Asians. The mere mention of their presence on the train was assumed to provide enough information to satisfy the readers' requirements. Young women, even in substantial groups, registered alarm on discovering that Asians would be travelling in their cars, and their matrons (in the employ of the Canadian government) tended, if anything, to fuel their fears. Detailed descriptions of Chinese travellers and their behaviour are conspicuous by their absence; it is as if the fear-engendering stereotype was so familiar that nothing more than a racial identification was necessary for the whole picture to be understood. As the following conclusion to a lengthy discussion about the likely impact of allowing Asians to travel in the same car as British female immigrants makes clear, it really did not matter what sort of behaviour the Asian travellers might display:

the fact that these girls had to share a car along with the Chinese gives them ground for complaint and if they took occasion to advise their relatives and friends in the Old Country of the conditions under which they travelled inland it would not be good advertising either for our work or the railway company of which they travelled. Would it not be possible

[181]

for some arrangement to be made which would obviate any possibility of complaints arising out of travelling conditions such as above set forth?[43]

The response of CNR manager C. W. Johnston to this request is further revealing. Johnston noted that the women in question had been provided with their own section of the car, which had been curtained off from the rest of the passengers, and that they had been given their own washroom and toilet facilities. They thus had no need to share any physical space with the Asian migrants. 'The train habits of the Chinese are not objectionable,' wrote Johnston. 'They have no occasion to, and do not intrude upon space assigned to other passengers. If they attempted to do so, the guards travelling with them, as well as train crew, would no doubt be able to control matters.' Yet he acknowledged that in spite of all of the protective strategies that the CNR had put in place, certain British immigrants and their supporters would not be satisfied if Asian immigrants were permitted to travel in their general proximity. He wrote that:

> While they are not objectionable in their habits, and usually are quiet and well behaved, it is recognized that a number of occidental passengers object to riding in the same car with them. We believe, however, we can keep risk of serious complaint down to a minimum by keeping Chinese out of cars occupied by women immigrant passengers, where this is possible, and, if at any time this is not practical, special effort will be made to consult the lady conductress or whoever is in charge, and see that proper explanation and assurances are given, in order that passengers may, in this way, be reassured.[44]

The vulnerability of British women was emphasised again and again in the letters that circulated around the issue of their migration experiences. Exposure to 'less civilised' migrants than themselves proved to be remarkably taxing. One particularly angry letter, written by 'the Lady-in-Charge' of the Queen Charlotte Coronation Hostel, Vancouver, made it clear that the association (as distant as it might be) between other ethnic immigrants and the comparatively refined British migrants was harmful: 'They are in a car with Russians, Czechs, the scum of Europe, and Chinese,' she wrote. 'The conditions are so appalling that the girls arrive here in a state of exhaustion and we put them to bed for a couple of days to recover.' The only possible solution to the problem, according to this writer, as with many others who voiced their concerns to the immigration authorities, was to orchestrate a situation as close to complete segregation as possible. They argued that in instances where British female travellers were found by train conductors to be accommodated with large numbers of 'foreigners', Asians or blacks, they ought to be moved to tourist-class or first-class cars without extra charge. Alternatively, where two or three British emigrant women were travelling together, 'the Colonist coaches should be curtained off at one end, say to accommodate six, and this be for British women only'.[45]

Bolstering the fiction that British-Canadians were, by definition, more 'refined' sometimes posed a serious challenge for the immigration agents who worked with them.[46] Not all British emigrants behaved like ideal immigrants. Moreover, examples of British females' 'preciousness' (such as the one related above) could backfire and actually undermine their promoters' arguments about their suitability for immigration.[47] But most of the government agents and politicians involved in immigration matters during the first half of the twentieth century could trace their own heritage back to British sources, and for many of them, the British imperial connection was a compelling reason to favour British immigration. Personal affinity oriented immigration officials towards supporting an increase in the size of Canada's British population, so that there was plenty of incentive, beyond public pressure (of which there was much), to pay extra attention to the needs of British immigrants. The fact that British immigrants and most government officials shared the English language also ensured that this group of immigrants would be able to have their wants and needs met with greater ease than immigrants from elsewhere. All of these factors, combined with the larger context of Canada's continued imperial affiliations, predisposed the men and women who worked with immigrants on behalf of the Canadian government to accept arguments that ethnicity worked like class, and that Britons were a class above.

Terminology relating to immigrants became loaded with meaning during the course of the late nineteenth and early twentieth centuries, as large numbers of immigrants from eastern and southern Europe moved into the Prairies, and as large numbers of Asians migrated to the Canadian west coast. Members of the white host community (having convinced themselves that the Aboriginal and Métis inhabitants of Western Canada no longer counted), assumed the position that the culture of the Canadian West was threatened by invasion.[48] In the words of Canadian Prairie historian Gerald Friesen: 'As a community of immigrants was created in the opening decades of the twentieth century, phrases such as "New Canadians", "strangers within our gates", "foreigners", and "ethnic groups" gradually became part of the Canadian vocabulary.'[49] Naturally, these terms were used to signify newcomers other than those of British origin. In the files collected by Canadian immigration bureaucrats, the same use of terminology may be found, although a further distinction appears necessary. The term 'foreigner' seems to have been favoured in most of the correspondence relating to matters of migration, and it was used interchangeably with 'continental Europeans'. Thus we find newcomers from Britain disparagingly referring to 'foreigners' (who might have been living in the region for many years) as taking jobs that ought, by right, to have been theirs.[50] However, in the correspondence collected by government officials, this term did not automatically include Asians and blacks; Asians and blacks were generally referred to as separate categories of migrants. Migrants in transit were thus differentiated by coded language: colonists were British emigrants; foreigners were Europeans (although northern/western Europeans were sometimes honoured with non-foreigner status); Asians and blacks were othered more thoroughly still. Not surprisingly, then, the Colonist cars of CNR and Canadian Pacific Railway trains were considered the rightful space of British immigrants; all other categories of immigrants were easily represented as inferior interlopers.

Writing emigration/immigration history

An online search for a definition of the term 'Anglo' offers a window into contemporary American social politics:

> Anglo is used primarily in direct contrast to Hispanic or Latino. In this context it is not limited to persons of English or even British descent, but can be generally applied to any non-Hispanic white person. Thus in parts of the United States with large Hispanic populations, an American of Polish, Irish, or German heritage might be termed an Anglo just as readily as a person of English descent. However, in parts of the country where the Hispanic community is smaller or nonexistent, or in areas where ethnic distinctions among European groups remain strong, Anglo has little currency as a catch-all term for non-Hispanic whites.[51]

The terms 'Anglo' and 'British' have worked in similar ways in Canada. Understandings of who might be considered British, Anglo-Canadian, or 'mainstream' have changed according to the context, and especially according to the nature of the perceived 'others' of the moment, just as discourses relating to whiteness, civilised society, and respectability have changed to suit different situations.

A survey history of Canadian immigration unsettles rather more than it confirms the idea that Canada became an Anglo-British nation through large-scale colonisation by Anglo-Protestant Britons in the years after the Conquest of New France. The playful reflections of William Lyon Mackenzie (soon to be one of Canada's most famous/ infamous rebels, and grandfather of Prime Minister William Lyon Mackenzie King) on the heterogeneity of an election crowd at Niagara in 1824, underscore the challenges involved in making sense of the term 'British' in the nineteenth century. Mackenzie writes:

> There were Christians and Heathens, Menonists and Dunkards, Quakers and Universalists, Presbyterians and Baptists, Roman Catholics and American Methodists; there were Frenchmen and Yankees, Irishmen, and Mulattoes, Scotchmen and Indians, Englishmen, Canadians, Americans and Negroes, Dutchmen and Germans, Welshmen and Swedes, Highlanders and Lowlanders, poetical as well as most prosaical phises, horsemen and footmen, fiddlers and dancers, honourables and reverends, captains and colonels, beaux and belles, wagons and bilburies, coaches and chaises, gigs and carts; in short, Europe, Asia, Africa, and America had there each its rep among the loyal subjects of our good King George, the fourth of the name.[52]

As the works of Linda Colley and others have demonstrated, a wide range of people in the British Isles adopted Britishness as a part of their identity over the course of the eighteenth and nineteenth centuries.[53] Clearly, a similar process occurred among specific populations throughout the British World. As Andrew Thompson suggests, 'Britishness was conceived of as a broad church, capable of accommodating a variety of settler and non-settler groups'.[54] A recently published think-piece by John Darwin on 'Empire and Ethnicity' suggests the usefulness of the concept of a shared 'imperial ethnicity' – an identity that came into existence across the British Empire by the second half of the nineteenth century, and that was most obvious and effective in the dominions of Canada, Australia and New Zealand.[55] But what *being* British (or Anglo) meant to people who self-identified as such in the context of white settler societies requires more historical analysis than it has received to date.[56]

As Lord Durham noted in 1840, people in Canada of Anglo-British extraction did indeed hold the reins of power in British North America, as they would continue to do through most of the twentieth century. There were effective governmental, military, and economic structures put in place in the aftermath of the Conquest to ensure that this would be the case. Moreover, in terms of sheer numbers, immigrants from the British Isles did dominate the Canadian scene for most of the nineteenth and early twentieth centuries. Yet there was much cultural work to be done before Canadians from heterogeneous backgrounds could identify themselves as Anglo- or British-Canadians. Central to the discourse that Canada was a culturally cohesive Anglo-British entity, a 'better Britain' that had to be protected as such, was the work of empire-wide networks of empire promoters; people who consciously and unconsciously worked to circulate images of Anglo-Britons that would shore up their claims for cultural superiority.[57] A large body of literature outlines the making of a British imperial identity – both for Britons in Britain, and for colonials.[58] Part of the effort to manage the discourse of imperial worthiness involved schooling Britons in their own superiority – a process of education that often became intensified after individuals decided to emigrate.[59] The schooling that British emigrants received was very effective, if not always in conditioning their behaviour, at least in terms of contributing to their sense of superiority and entitlement. What was established, or at least confirmed for people who might consider themselves British-Canadian, was their place at the top of a definite social hierarchy. From the 1890s, if not earlier, English-speaking immigrants to Canada, who expected to be treated better than other immigrant groups, demanded special consideration from government officials at all points of their journeys.[60] As this study shows, they often got what they wanted.

The Anglo-British identity that migrants laid claim to (or were assigned by imperially oriented observers) in order to secure more comfortable travelling conditions was fundamentally a gendered identity. The fact that it was female travellers who became the focus of efforts to reform the in-transit elements of the British emigrant's experience underlines the point. Claiming that public/private spaces managed by immigration authorities and their railway associates needed to be cleaned up for the sake of British women was significantly more effective than any less gendered arguments would have been. Likewise, the ways in which 'foreign' men and women were depicted as less cultured and less sensitive than their British counterparts in the correspondence among British emigrants, Canadian imperialists, and government and railway officials typically drew upon gendered understandings of degrees of civilisation. There was nothing benign about how the spaces in immigration depots and trains were supposed to be used. Heavy pressure was placed on women who might be considered representatives of imperial feminine virtue to carry themselves with decorum and dignity throughout their travels, regardless of their circumstances. For women who did not obviously fit the British/Anglo-Canadian mould, it was clear from whence their models ought to be drawn.

Prior to the 1960s, Canadian immigration policies and practices fit comfortably within the larger British imperial context of explicitly racist attitudes around entitlement and privilege that has been the focus of much study in the past few decades.[61] Increasingly nuanced and complex readings of the concepts of whiteness, race-relations, ethnicity, and power (among others) have challenged us to think about the interactions of people in Canada's past in new ways. Historians of imperialism and colonisation in Canada have done much to deconstruct the processes by which Anglo-Britons achieved cultural, economic, and political power in Canada.[62] But historians have also played an important (often unintentional) role in the legitimation of this power by asserting or assuming Canada's fundamental, homogenous Britishness in their writing.[63] These earlier understandings of an Anglo-Canadian mainstream, so natural and uninteresting as to almost render it invisible, continue to affect the writing of Canada's history, and particularly Canada's immigration history.

The perception that people of British origin effectively made Canada an Anglo-British nation has also been heightened by the fact that British emigration has been routinely studied in isolation. The larger context of a world in which millions of people of origins other than British were also moving, settling, and informing new societies is largely absent from British World histories. Certainly, this is the case in the Canadian historiography. One could easily come away from an exploration of English, Scottish, Welsh, or Irish immigrants – or of British immigrants more generally – with no real sense that Canada also contained many thousands of Germans, Austrians, Netherlanders, Russians, Scandinavians, Ukrainians, Poles, Italians, Chinese, Jews, and African Canadians by the turn of the twentieth century. In many respects, this is no different to how other Canadian ethnic histories have been written. However, the writing of other ethnic histories has been revolutionised since the beginning of the twenty-first century, such that there has been heavy reliance across ethnic divides for ideas, frameworks, and inspiration. Moreover, histories of Italian (and Greek, and Mennonite, and Icelandic, etc.) migrants are included in Canadian immigration history readers, where comparisons are made explicit.[64] The same cannot be said for histories of British emigrants.[65] The lack of comparative analysis, or larger, multi-ethnic context, for British immigration tends to shelter the concept of an Anglo-Canadian norm from the rigorous deconstruction and analysis that it ought to receive from historians in the field.

Notes

1   Library and Archives Canada, Ottawa (LAC), RG 76, vol. 139, file 33175, part 1, Margaret L. Boyle, British Columbia Convener of Immigration, IODE, to a Mrs Petry, Convener National Committee on Immigration, IODE, 1 February 1924; Durham, Superintendent of the Women's Branch, CNR, London, to Boyle, IODE, 24 March 1924.
2   *Ibid.*, Petry to Durham, 8 February 1924. For discussion on the IODE, see K. Pickles, *Female Imperialism and National Identity: Imperial Order Daughters of the Empire* (Manchester, 2002).
3   R. Mancuso, 'Work "Only a Woman Can Do": The Women's Division of the Canadian Department of Immigration and Colonization, 1920–1937', *American Review of Canadian Studies*, 35:4 (2005), pp. 593–620; R. Mancuso, 'For Purity

and Prosperity: Competing Nationalist Visions and Canadian Immigration Policy, 1919–30', *British Journal of Canadian Studies*, 23:1 (2010), pp. 1–23.

4   A. Perry, *On the Edge of Empire: Gender, Race, and the Making of British Columbia, 1849–1871* (Toronto, 2001), p. 5.

5   C. Bridge and K. Fedorowich, 'Mapping the British World', *Journal of Imperial and Commonwealth History*, 31:2 (2003), pp. 1–15. Further discussion of this subject may be found in A. Thompson, 'Afterword: Informal Empire: Past, Present and Future', *Bulletin of Latin American Research*, 27:1 (2008), pp. 229–41.

6   A thoughtful discussion of the complexity of this subject across various British imperial locations may be found in P. Levine's survey history, *The British Empire: Sunrise to Sunset* (Harlow, 2007).

7   For discussion about the move towards a new, non-Anglocentric immigration programme, see J. E. Igartua, *The Other Quiet Revolution: National Identities in English Canada, 1945–71* (Vancouver, 2006), pp. 53–62; V. Knowles, *Strangers at Our Gates: Canadian Immigration and Immigration Policy, 1540–2006* (Toronto, 2007), pp. 187–98.

8   Lord Durham, 'To Lord Glenelg', quoted in T. Thorner (ed.), *A Few Acres of Snow: Documents in Pre-Confederation Canadian History* (Toronto, 2003), p. 185.

9   For examples of pro-empire responses to this problem, see: L. Chilton, *Agents of Empire: British Female Migration to Canada and Australia, 1860s–1930* (Toronto, 2007); J. Cavell, 'The Imperial Race and the Immigration Sieve: The Canadian debate on assisted British migration and empire settlement, 1900–30', *Journal of Imperial and Commonwealth History*, 34:3 (2006), pp. 35–67.

10 H. I. Cowan, *British Emigration to British North America: The First Hundred Years* (Toronto, 1961), chapters 1 and 2; M. Harper, *Emigration from North East Scotland: Willing Exiles*, vol. 1 (Aberdeen, 1988); Knowles, *Strangers at Our Gates*, chapter 3.

11 J. M. Bumsted, *The Peoples of Canada: A Pre-confederation History* (Toronto, 2003), chapter 11; N. Knowles, *Inventing Loyalists: The Ontario Loyalist Tradition and the Creation of Usable Pasts* (Toronto, 1997); C. Moore, *The Loyalists: Revolution, Exile and Settlement* (Toronto, 1984); J. Potter-MacKinnon, *While the Women Only Wept: Loyalist Refugee Women in Eastern Ontario* (London, 1995). Elizabeth Vibert's current work on this subject adds further complexity to our understanding of who the Loyalists were. E. Vibert, 'Loyal Men and Needy Families: Black settler petitions in 1780s London', unpublished paper presented at the annual conference of the Canadian Historical Association, 'Authority in the Past, Authority of the Past', 25 May 2009.

12 D. H. Akenson, *The Irish in Ontario* (Montreal and Kingston, 1999 [1984]); W. Cameron and M. McDougall Maude, *Assisting Emigration to Upper Canada: The Petworth Project, 1832–1837* (Montreal and Kingston, 2000); B. S. Elliott, *Irish Migrants in the Canadas: A New Approach* (Montreal & Kingston, 1993); E. J. Errington, 'British Migration and British America, 1783–1867', and M. Harper, 'Rhetoric and Reality: British Migration to Canada, 1867–1967', in P. Buckner (ed.), *Canada and the British Empire* (Oxford, 2008), pp. 140–59 and 160–80; M. Harper, *Adventurers and Exiles: The Great Scottish Exodus* (London, 2003); M. Harper and S. Constantine, *Migration and Empire* (Oxford, 2010), chapter 2; B. J. Messamore (ed.), *Canadian Migration Patterns from Britain and North America* (Toronto, 2004); P. Thomas, *Strangers from a Secret Land: The Voyages of the Brig 'Albion' and the Founding of the First Welsh Settlements in Canada* (Toronto, 1986).

13 R. Bleasdale, 'Class Conflict on the Canals of Upper Canada in the 1840s', in L. Sefton MacDowell and I. Radforth (eds), *Canadian Working-Class History*, 3rd edn (Toronto, 2006); H. C. Pentland, *Labour and Capital in Canada 1650–1860* (Toronto, 1981); S. See, 'The Orange Order and Social Violence in Mid-Nineteenth-Century Saint John', *Acadiensis*, 13:1 (1983), pp. 68–92.

14 J. Jupp, *The English in Australia* (Cambridge, 2004), pp. 7–8.

15 A. McCarthy, 'Scottish National Identities among Inter-War Migrants in North America and Australasia', *Journal of Imperial and Commonwealth History*, 34:2 (2006), pp. 201–22.

16 Statistics Canada, series A260–269, 'Population, Canadian, other British and foreign-born, by sex, census dates, 1871 to 1971', found at: www.statcan.ca/english/freepub/11–516–XIE/sectiona/sectiona.htm#Interprovincial%20&%20International%20Migration (accessed 10 June 2008).

17 An alternative interpretation of similar statistics is offered in P. Buckner, 'Introduction: Canada and the British Empire', in P. Buckner (ed.), *Canada and the British Empire*, pp. 1–21.

18 For discussion of the significance of this difference, see Jupp, *English in Australia*.

19 Cowan, *British Emigration to British North America*, appendix B, table ii.

20 As a portion of the total enumerated Canadian population, those registered as British constituted 57 per cent in 1901; 55.5 per cent in 1911; and 55.4 per cent in 1921. Numbers calculated from Statistics Canada, series A125–163: 'Origins of the population, census dates, 1871 to 1971', found at: www.statcan.ca/english/freepub/11–516–XIE/sectiona/A125_163.csv (accessed 10 June 2008).

21 The statistics on religious affiliation make a similar point. See: www.statcan.ca/english/freepub/11–516–XIE/sectiona/A1.csv.

22 Bumsted, *Peoples of Canada*, chapters 13 and 18; Knowles, *Strangers at Our Gates*; M. O'Gallagher, *Grosse Isle: Gateway to Canada 1832–1937* (Quebec, 1984); J. Parr, *Labouring Children: British Immigrant Apprentices to Canada, 1869–1924* (Toronto, 1980). In the literature on this subject, the extent to which these migrants were, in fact, as impoverished and as uneducated as many of their contemporaries thought, is questioned. For example, see Akenson, *Irish in Ontario*.

23 G. Bilson, *A Darkened House: Cholera in Nineteenth-Century Canada* (Toronto, 1980); and Knowles, *Strangers at Our Gates*, p. 61.

24 A clear example may be seen in the correspondence contained in LAC, RG 76, vol. 498, file 774753, and *ibid.*, vol. 478, file 741316, concerning English immigrants living in Chatham, Ontario in the early twentieth century.

25 Frank Oliver, quoted in M. F. Timlin, 'Canada's Immigration Policy, 1896–1910', *Canadian Journal of Economics and Political Science*, 26:4 (1960), p. 523.

26 *Ibid.*

27 See Chilton, *Agents of Empire*; K. Fedorowich, *Unfit for Heroes: Reconstruction and Soldier Settlement in the Empire between the Wars* (Manchester, 1995); D. Goutor, *Guarding the Gates: The Canadian Labour Movement and Immigration, 1872–1934* (Vancouver, 2008); B. Roberts, *Whence They Came: Deportation from Canada, 1900–1935* (Ottawa, 1988); M. Valverde, *The Age of Light, Soap, and Water: Moral Reform in English Canada, 1880s to 1920s* (Toronto, 2008).

28 Lieutenant-Colonel R. W. Leonard, 30 July 1917, quoted in Roberts, *Whence They Came*, p. 75.

29 Roberts, *Whence They Came*, chapter 5. Further discussion and examples may be found in D. Glynn, '"Exporting Outcast London": Assisted Emigration to Canada, 1896–1914', *Histoire sociale/Social History*, 15:29 (1982), pp. 209–38; and P. Berton, *The Promised Land: Selling the West, 1896–1914* (Toronto, 1984).

30 In the Canadian context, discussions about the relationship between economic and cultural factors in determining immigration policies around Asian immigration have been especially rich. A good introduction to this subject may be found in P. E. Roy, *The Oriental Question: Consolidating a White Man's Province, 1914–41* (Vancouver, 2003).

31 Clifford Sifton, Minister of the Interior (1896–1905), publicly questioned this order of things with his implementation of an immigration programme that privileged work experience and farmer skills over British heritage in the late 1890s – to the intense discomfort of people who saw themselves as a part of a British-Canadian mainstream. For a brief discussion of Sifton's ideas and policies, and the response that they elicited, see Knowles, *Strangers at Our Gates*, chapter 5.

32 LAC, RG 76, vol. 189, file 33175, part 1, memo from J. A. Smart, Deputy Minister of the Interior, 19 May 1903. References to similar 'reminders' may be found throughout the file, which covers the period 1897–1924.

[189]

33 *Ibid.*, vol. 666, file C1595, part 1, J. B. Pagé, Department of Health, Ottawa, to W. R. Little, Commissioner of Immigration, Ottawa, 4 December 1922.

34 *Ibid.*, vol. 666, file C1595, part 1, memo, J. V. Lantalum, Dominion Immigration Agent, Saint John, to Little, 24 November 1923; *ibid.*, part 2, J. S. Fraser, Division Commissioner of Immigration, Eastern Division, to a Mr Connell, port agent, 17 December 1925; *ibid.*, vol. 138, file 32997, part 14, Little to J. C. Mitchell, Dominion Immigration Agent, 26 November 1921; *ibid.*, Lantalum to Little, 14 December 1921.

35 *Ibid.*, part 2, memo by T. B. Willans, immigration inspector, to Fraser, 14 June 1926.

36 *Ibid.*, vol. 138, file 32997, part 12, memo, Women's Branch to Little, 2 April 1921.

37 *Ibid.*, vol. 666, file C1595, part 1, correspondence for 25 January 1913. Incidentally, the response of the government indicated complete agreement in principle on the matter of British 'isolation', even though they would not go as far as investing large new sums of money into the permanent structure at that location. See correspondence for 20 and 23 February 1913.

38 A particularly colourful complaint about the lack of appropriate cleaning facilities is contained in a letter to Mrs MacKay, 'Lady-in-Charge', Queen Mary's Coronation Hostel, Vancouver, from a 'student in training', 6 October 1928, a copy of which may be found in LAC, RG 76, vol. 140, file 33175.

39 Chilton, *Agents of Empire*, chapter 2; Valverde, *Age of Light, Soap and Water*; K. Dubinsky, *Improper Advances: Rape and Heterosexual Conflict in Ontario, 1880–1929* (Chicago, 1993); C. Strange, *Toronto's Girl Problem: The Perils and Pleasures of the City, 1880–1930* (Toronto, 1995).

40 LAC, RG 76, vol. 140, file 33175, extract from emigrant's letter, contained in M. V. Burnham, supervisor of Women's Branch, Department of Immigration and Colonization, to Dr W. J. Black, CNR Director of Immigration, 14 August 1928. Black had been a former deputy minister of the Department of Immigration and Colonization before crossing over to the private sector in the early to mid-1920s. He returned to government service in early 1929 with the reorganisation of several government portfolios including immigration and agriculture (see footnote 43).

41 *Ibid.*, extract from Winfield's report, 31 July 1927.

42 *Ibid.*, extract from Binning's report, 4 March 1928.

43 *Ibid.*, Fraser to W. J. Black, Director, Department of Colonization, Agriculture and Natural Resources, 18 March 1929.

44 *Ibid.*, Johnston, Assistant General Traffic Manager, CNR, to Black, 8 April 1929.

45 *Ibid.*, extract from a letter received by Burnham from MacKay, Queen Mary's Coronation Hostel, Vancouver, 20 August 1928.

46 Entertaining examples may be found in the following correspondence: LAC, RG 76, vol. 140, file 33175, Burnham to Black, 14 October 1927; Black to Burnham, 8 December 1927; and extract from Binning's report, 3 November 1929.

47 Examples and discussion of this subject may be found in G. Binnie-Clarke, *Wheat and Women* (Toronto, 2006 [1914]); and Chilton, *Agents of Empire*.

48 For an interesting discussion of invented tradition relating to Anglo-Canadians as the original inhabitants of the Canadian West, see Valverde, *The Age of Light, Soap, and Water*, pp. 107–8.

49 G. Friesen, *The Canadian Prairies: A History* (Toronto, 1987), p. 244.

50 For example, see the correspondence during July and August, 1905, concerning immigrant Percy J. Valentine in LAC, RG 76, vol. 140, file 33175.

51 http://education.yahoo.com/reference/dictionary/entry/Anglo (accessed 25 June 2008).

52 Jean R. Burnet with Howard Palmer, *Coming Canadians: An Introduction to History of Canada's Peoples* (Toronto, 1988), pp. 18–19.

53 L. Colley, *Britons: Forging the Nation, 1707–1837* (London, 2005 [1992]). The 2005 edition of this book includes a new introduction that provides an overview of the literature on this subject.

54 Thompson, 'Afterword', pp. 239–40.

55 J. Darwin, 'Empire and Ethnicity', *Nations and Nationalism*, 16:3 (2010), pp. 386–7.

56 An interesting exploration of this question in a different context: S. Dubow, 'How British was the British World? The Case of South Africa', *Journal of Imperial and Commonwealth History*, 37:1 (2009), pp. 1–27.
57 J. Bush, *Edwardian Ladies and Imperial Power* (London, 2000); Chilton, *Agents of Empire*.
58 *Ibid.*; L. Colley, *Captives: Britain, Empire and the World 1600–1850* (London, 2002); C. Hall, *Civilising Subjects: Metropole and Colony in the English Imagination, 1830–1867* (Cambridge, 2002); and her (ed.), *Cultures of Empire. A Reader: Colonizers in Britain and the Empire in the Nineteenth and Twentieth Centuries* (Manchester, 2000).
59 British emigrants who used the services of some of the more imperially motivated emigration societies were instructed about what they should expect on their arrival overseas, how they should comport themselves as representatives of their race, and how they ought to understand their migration experiences. Chilton, *Agents of Empire*.
60 See, for example, LAC, RG 76, vol. 368, file 486288, part 1, on the management of the immigration building at North Battleford, Saskatchewan (1913).
61 Two useful explorations of this subject are: M. Lake and H. Reynolds, *Drawing the Global Colour Line: White Men's Countries and the International Challenge of Racial Equality* (Cambridge, 2008); and D. Pearson, *The Politics of Ethnicity in Settler Societies: States of Unease* (New York, 2001).
62 Of particular note in this respect are studies that have foregrounded gender and race as frameworks of analysis. For example, Perry, *Edge of Empire*; S. Carter, *Aboriginal People and Colonizers of Western Canada to 1900* (Toronto, 1999); K. Pickles and M. Rutherdale (eds), *Contact Zones: Aboriginal and Settler Women in Canada's Colonial Past* (Vancouver, 2005); and S. Razack, *Race, Space, and the Law: Unmapping a White Settler Society* (Toronto, 2002).
63 K. Corlett offers a very interesting discussion of this subject in 'A Dream of Homogeneity: Arthur Lower's National Vision and Its Relationship to Immigrants and Immigration in Canada, 1920–1946' (MA dissertation, Queen's University, Kingston, 1995). See also K. Korneski, 'Britishness, Canadianness, Class, and Race: Winnipeg and the British World, 1880s–1910s', *Journal of Canadian Studies*, 41:2 (2007), pp. 161–84.
64 See, for example, F. Iacovetta with P. Draper and R. Ventresca (eds), *A Nation of Immigrants: Women, Workers, and Communities in Canadian History* (Toronto, 1998).
65 Irish immigrants are a notable exception. Again, the Irish seem to have an identity that can go either way. Thus, for example, we find two articles on the Irish (though none on English, Welsh, or Scottish immigrants) in Iacovetta *et al.*, *Nation of Immigrants*.

CHAPTER 8

'Dear Grace . . . Love Maidie': interpreting a migrant's letters from Australia, 1926–67

Stephen Constantine

Some years ago I gave a paper in London to the first British World Conference. I chose the occasion to question the frequent use of the word 'diaspora' in historians' writings about British migration from the United Kingdom to the British Empire. The term was rarely defined, and all too often seemed to be just an alternative to the neutral term 'migration' or the historical term 'empire settlement'.[1] It troubled me especially that diaspora was being used even about British migrants who were, in the contemporary parlance of the later nineteenth and early twentieth centuries, merely moving from one part of Greater Britain to another, from Britain to another place almost as rich in Britishness, British values, British loyalties and links to Britain. Although etymologically the word, derived from Greek, only means 'a scattering', I argued that if we were to use the term 'diaspora' it was as well to pay attention to the connotations of words.[2] Especially we should be alert to the notion of loss, exile and alienation conventionally associated with the Jewish diaspora. I argued this because, if all British migration was being described as a diaspora, historians might miss what I suspected was a real change in the experiences of migrants and the effects on their personal, cultural and national identities in the shift from the nineteenth century into the twentieth century, especially by the second half. British migrants had been empire settlers in Greater Britain, but I suggested they were becoming just another stream of immigrants into communities made up overwhelmingly of native-born Australians, New Zealanders and Canadians, alongside immigrant arrivals from other European and extra-European sources. The native-born even of British extraction were people who were probably less likely to refer to Britain as 'home', who had constructed distinctive lifestyles and forged different sets of values, and who might even be resentful of British immigrant claims to special status. As late as 1891, 31 per cent of the non-aboriginal Australian population had been born overseas, but only 10 per cent by 1947 – and less than 7 per cent had been born in Great Britain. In New Zealand, the overseas-born fell from around 55 per cent of the non-Maori population in 1881 to around 15 per cent by 1961. By 1996 only 15 per cent of the Canadian population identified even their ancestry as British only.[3]

I later searched for information about more recent public performances by British and particularly English immigrants in these Commonwealth countries. I was looking for evidence which I might interpret as characteristic of diasporic communities, and this was embedded in a subsequent journal article.[4] I found a clustering of English immigrants in particular, and usually suburban, parts of such Commonwealth cities as Adelaide and Perth, Auckland and Winnipeg. I located an efflorescence of monarchical clubs in Australia and Canada. I traced the often quite recent foundation of English provincial associations, crown green bowling clubs and Morris-dancing societies across these former British white settler societies. All this looked like evidence of cultural expressions of Englishness by recent English immigrants and/or their children. They seemed to be emulating the public performance of identities characteristic of immigrant Greeks, Italians, Maltese, Chinese and other minorities. They were badging themselves as English, in competitive, multicultural, no-longer-British societies. The essay was admittedly defined as 'highly speculative', and it has prompted at least one cautionary corrective.[5]

But in any event what I did not have was the voice of the twentieth-century English migrant, as a potential source for the private expression of identity and of personal engagement with the people and place of settlement. Archived letter collections written by migrants from the British Isles, often reflecting on journeys, reception and experiences, tend to be limited to the nineteenth century.[6] With the exception of letters – usually of complaint – in official files, only a few collections dating to the twentieth century are yet publicly available and fewest of all from English migrants; and few indeed from women.[7] It is possible that such letters in private hands are thought to be too recent to be historically valuable, but more likely such correspondence is regarded by families as too personal to be yet deposited in public archives. Fortunately, oral testimony relating mainly to migrant experiences after 1945 has been collected and this has been well used, although it is of course retrospective testimony.[8]

Then, unexpectedly, I was contacted by Mrs Ann Dawes concerning a collection of letters which her late husband, Mr Derek Dawes, had inherited.[9] They had mainly been written to family in England by his Aunt Emiline – usually known as Maidie – who had emigrated to Australia with her husband Jack Viccars in 1925. I was granted access to the private voice of a twentieth-century English migrant woman, and was not just witnessing public performance.

Their interpretation is not straightforward, and hence this chapter points to their ambiguities and complexities. The problematics of interpreting these letters are perhaps common to grappling with other such collections of family correspondence.[10] There is a tension between reading these letters on the one hand as indicative of the public performance of an identity (that is, as an English migrant living overseas) and on the other as truly private correspondence expressing a personal sense of self, full of signs and signals expressed in a code meaningful to the family but less easily read by an eavesdropper, the historian.

The collection adds up to 74 pieces, running from 18 April 1926 to 13 July 1967. They include 72 letters, all handwritten until late in the sequence, and two telegrams, one of them sent from Australia on the outbreak of war in September 1939. During the war and after, all correspondence was by lightweight 'aerogrammes' or 'air letters', plus five 'airgraphs' despatched in 1943–44 – one-page letters, photographed and reduced by the postal authorities to one-quarter size, five inches by four inches, as a war economy measure to save space in transport. Four letters had been sent to Maidie in Australia by her sister Grace, but these had been returned to England in 1946 because Derek, their nephew, was collecting postage stamps and hence fortuitously they survived.[11] The other 70 pieces had all been posted from Australia: 67 were written by Maidie and three by Jack. Of the 70 letters and telegrams from Australia, seventeen had been sent to Maidie's mother, two were addressed jointly to her mother and father, six to all the family but via her mother, and six to her brother Jim after mother's death. But the bulk, 39, went principally to Maidie's younger sister Grace. It is only because Grace 'never threw anything away' that any of this material has survived.[12]

In spite of the large number, there are obvious problems. First, the correspondence is incomplete. More letters were written from Australia than have survived. Maidie and Jack sailed for Australia late in 1925. The earliest surviving letter of 18 April 1926 was written shortly after arrival: the Immigration Department in Melbourne is given as their postal address. But it is not a report on a departure, a journey and an arrival. It implies earlier correspondence after getting to Australia, and it comments on a letter already received. The 'first encounter' letter is therefore missing. So are some later ones. For instance, there is no preserved letter from Maidie following the death of her father in, probably, 1937. It is impossible to believe she did not write. Nor is there any letter referring to the death of Jack's parents, about the same time. Also one can tell from references in some of the wartime letters that others that had been posted had not been delivered, and were probably lost in transit. Parts of the narrative are therefore known to be missing.

Second, this is a one-sided epistolary conversation. Virtually all the letters are *from* Maidie. As noted, there are only four letters *to* Maidie, all from Grace, all in 1945; and yet Maidie's letters indicate that there had been many other letters from Grace over the years, and indeed from her mother, from brother Jim, and from Jack's mother. Interpreting a one-sided story is a problem. We get a partial and potentially misleading representation of the relationships between Maidie and the family, and between an 'English' home and an 'Australian' home.

Third, Maidie's letters to Grace are full of references to letters she wrote to other people, to Jack's mother, for instance, to friends in England, and indeed to contacts Maidie had made in Australia. None of those letters seems to have survived. So we only get from the letters the impressions of Australia and of herself which Maidie chose to present, consciously or not, to her immediate family. Was she writing to other people of other things, or describing them differently in those letters?

Fourth, there are the silences. Interpreting silence is acutely difficult. What are we to deduce from the irregularity in the dates of the surviving letters and telegrams from Australia? Seven were written in 1926, six in 1927, four in 1928, five in 1929, three in 1930, four in 1931, four in 1932, and three in 1933. Maidie often comments on how difficult it was in a busy day to find time to write letters. But there is only one letter in the collection dating from 1934, none from 1935, just two from 1936, three from 1937, none from 1938 and two (one a telegram) from 1939. During the war years, the surviving correspondence is reduced to one sent in 1940 and two in 1941, but none dated 1942; and only two were written in 1943, followed by four in 1944 and just two in 1945. However, eleven letters are dated 1946 (this following Mother's death). But after that the collection contains only one piece from 1955, one from 1956, and then nothing until one posted in 1962, the last from Maidie. This was followed by a final letter in 1967, from Jack, a sad one, written shortly after Maidie's death. Are the irregularities and gaps due to accidents of survival, or eloquent silences, and if eloquent, what are they saying? What does an absent record imply, if anything, about Maidie's circumstances in Australia, her attitude to England, and her relationship with her family?

Finally, there are the silences in the letters themselves: what is not said, not reported, not expressed. Of course, it is not proper to assume that what is written in a letter is a complete and comprehensive account of all matters of importance to the writer, even when written to family; indeed perhaps especially when written to family. For instance, it becomes apparent from letters written in 1946 that the financial circumstances in which Maidie and Jack had found themselves during the early 1930s had been disguised in the letters written at that time. Perhaps more than with any other form of literary production, writers of private letters are conscious of their intended readers and alert to the effect their correspondence will have.[13] As argued later, this makes it difficult to read realities straight off the page. However, the narrative substance in the letters is probably reliable, and so we may begin by telling the story as Maidie (mainly she) tells it, letter by letter, over 40 years, amplified by other documentary sources.[14]

Migrating and settling

Emiline Mary Viccars, née Dawes, usually known as Maidie, was born on 7 May 1901 and died on 25 June 1967. She was the eldest child of Frederick George Dawes and Annie Louisa Dawes. Maidie had a sister, Grace, born 4 December 1903, and a brother James (Jim), born 14 November 1905 – the father of Derek Dawes to whom the letters had descended. Maidie's father was a mechanical engineer, and Maidie's mother and certainly her grandmother were costumiers and skilled needlewomen, with talents that Maidie acquired.[15] The family probably lived for a while in Swindon, Wiltshire – Maidie's birth was registered there – but before the birth of Grace they had moved to Dorking in Surrey, 12 miles east of Guildford. Soon after Maidie's emigration, the family moved again, to 25 Costons Avenue, Greenford, in Middlesex, a large semi-detached house with a substantial garden in an agreeable suburb, in those days close to green fields.[16] The family were Quakers. Indeed, Maidie went to a Quaker girls boarding school founded in 1842 at Sibford Ferris (and the name needs to be remembered), in a pleasant rural environment of wooded hills and open fields near Banbury in Oxfordshire. The school registers show that she was there from August 1913 until June 1916, from the age of 12 to 15.[17] This private schooling itself indicates that the family was socially and usually financially secure, though Mr Dawes had periods out of work during 1931–32 and perhaps thereafter.[18]

Jack Gregory Viccars was born on 22 August 1896 and died on 13 January 1972. He was the second son of John Gregory Viccars, a butcher, and Maria Viccars. The family moved when Jack was very young from Godalming in Surrey, a few miles south of Guildford, to Woking, about the same distance to the north. At the age of 18, on 25 February 1915, he joined the British army as a volunteer and served in France, first in the Coldstream Guards but mainly in the Royal Engineers. He was transferred to the reserves on 16 January 1919, collected his service medals, and really only then began his civilian adult life, at the age of 22.[19] Since Woking is only about twenty miles west of Dorking and both are close to Guildford, it was probably then and thereabouts that he met Maidie. They were certainly a 'couple' in May 1922, since Jack bought her a handbag for her 21st birthday.[20] They may even have met in Godalming. They married on 19 September 1925, at the Friends' Meeting House in Godalming, which the Dawes family certainly attended, and Godalming is recorded as their place of residence, he at 35 High Street and she at 20 Charterhouse Road. These could be accommodation addresses prior to their marriage, though Jack's father might by then have returned to Godalming to open up a business in the centre of town.[21]

There is nothing self-evident from this background or in the early correspondence to explain why the newly married couple, she a 'clerk', he an 'engineer', almost immediately emigrated, though we return to this matter later. But they did migrate, when he was 29 and she was 24. Given the bureaucratic hoops through which they would have had to jump, this was something they would probably have begun to arrange before their marriage. Three months later, on 17 December, they sailed from the port of London on the SS *Largs Bay*, Australian Commonwealth Line, 13,850 tons, 765 passengers, calling at Fremantle and Adelaide before disembarking at Melbourne. The cover of the company's brochure for May–December sailings in 1925 enticingly described Australia as 'The Land of Opportunity'.[22] Immediately after the war, Jack had evidently not been attracted by the scheme the British government launched in 1919 to provide free passages for ex-service personnel wishing to migrate to the white settler societies of the empire. However, now with Maidie on his arm, they took advantage of the heavily subsidised assisted passage schemes funded jointly by the British and Australian governments under the 1922 Empire Settlement Act, paying £16 10s 0d each for a ticket instead of about £40.[23]

The letters indicate that they were participants in Australia's over-ambitious post-war rural settlement schemes, funded by loans raised by state governments, in their case by the State of Victoria, but with interest payments subsidised by the Australian and British government.[24] This was an attempt to develop farms in rural areas to the north and east of Melbourne, by settling Australian ex-servicemen and their families there, and also British migrants with appropriate qualifications. Jack and Maidie had the qualities of youth and health, and Jack had the additional virtues of war service, some connection with farming (his father being a butcher), and, judging from his entry on his marriage certificate and on the passenger list, some skill as an engineer (perhaps derived from his experience in the Royal Engineers). Recruiting for the Victoria scheme took place from 1923 to early in 1927. Jack would have been one of only 814 men from the UK who were selected, and indeed one of only 627 married men, and, moreover, one of the mere 361 who ever took up land under the scheme.[25] The expectation was that new settlers would be provided with a twelve-months training course at an agricultural college or farm before acquiring their own land, plus loans for the purchase of stock, equipment, and housing materials. In 1926, soon after arrival, Maidie described the courses they attended (more so Jack, at Dookie College).[26] Early on, Jack was also absent working on farms near Shepparton, 114 miles north of Melbourne, and at the neighbouring small settlement at Toolamba. There, for a period in 1926, Maidie also lived.[27] However, the couple were initially often separated. Maidie lived in a hostel and worked for a while in Melbourne, while Jack was away.[28]

The letters speak of their frustration, waiting fifteen months for their so-called 'settlement house' to be built on their own plot of land.[29] But from October 1927 until late in 1934, Maidie and Jack were farming, first 10 acres and eventually 40 acres, at Berwick, 27 miles south-east of Melbourne. Now bisected by Princes Highway, Berwick has become in effect a suburb of the city, but in the 1920s it was an underdeveloped rural area. Their address was Closer Settlement Estate.[30] Typically for the area, they ran a commercial market garden, with orchards of fruit trees, a nursery for flowers, and a poultry farm, selling eggs. Their transport was by horse and jinker.[31] From May 1930, with more land, they were also farming dairy cattle. The letters of these years are indicative of the tough economic times suffered by most of the new settlers, with low prices for their produce. In January 1933, one of their neighbours in Berwick, another English 'Oversea Settler', was 'returning home – a failure'.[32] Jack would be one of the mere fifty UK settlers who, it is said, succeeded. The entire scheme cost the State of Victoria something like £5 million.[33] Jack and Maidie survived the bad years by hard work and strict economies – and with some financial help from Jack's mother.[34]

Then, late in 1934, Maidie and Jack moved to the farming district around Sale in the Central Gippsland district of Victoria. This was further east, still on what is now Princes Highway but nearly 140 miles from Melbourne.[35] 'You will notice the new address', Maidie writes, half way through a letter, 'we've only been here a few weeks'. She had given no prior indication of any intention to move: one of those curious silences in the letters. Although they still had hens and fruit trees and grew vegetables, this was principally a dairy farm, of 80 acres, with another 'settlement house' for a home. They were aiming to build up a herd of forty or fifty cows, and acquired a pure-bred Jersey bull. The stock was bought for them, she explained, by the government of Victoria, repayable over a period of years.[36] They did not like this farm as much as the one at Berwick, because the land was flat and they missed the hills. Also the people of Sale were 'terribly smug and self-satisfied'.[37] But Maidie and Jack were at least and at last making money, though they were sometimes still financially assisted by family. Jack also inherited money after his parents died. Certainly there was eventually enough for them by 1937 to send money home to Maidie's mother, to hire labour, and to buy a car – though ten years old, Maidie says, and 'very secondhand [sic]'.[38]

There follow the war years, when letters contain information on production, prices, rationing, charitable work, and their employment of a prisoner of war (almost certainly Italian) as a farm labourer.[39] Before the war, Maidie had been sending to the family in England some of their produce – dried fruits – probably as evidence of their achievements;[40] but during and after the war they were posting off food parcels as relief supplies to the family in war-torn Middlesex.[41]

Then, in March 1946, Mother died. After a flurry of messages, the correspondence, even with Grace, virtually ceased. There follows in the letters the enigmatic break. There are only three more from Maidie to Grace – or is it just three surviving letters? – one each in 1955, 1956 and in 1962. They contain very little information about post-war life in Australia in general and in Sale in particular. The address of the last two of these letters is given as 142 MacAlister Street, very much in the heart of Sale, indicating that at some time after the war Maidie and Jack gave up the farm, but there is no reference to this move in the letters. Moreover, each is no longer signed with the familiar 'Maidie', but the more formal 'Emiline'.[42] What should we read into this shift and this silence? We know from Jack's letter – the last – in July 1967, of one deliberate concealment. Maidie, he wrote to Jim, had not wanted the family to know the extent to which her health had been failing.[43] She was only 66. After Maidie's death, Jack visited England, but returned to Australia, and eventually remarried. He died in 1972, when he was 75.

And so in the letters we can trace the lives of an English migrant couple. The letters are undoubtedly of historical value. After arriving and a period of frustration, they get established on land settlement farms, survive hard times in the depressed years of the late 1920s and early 1930s, and then come good, or pretty good, from the mid-1930s. Maidie never returned to Britain, and Jack only popped back as a visitor. This, in outline, amplifies with important personal details what may be expected from the public history.

Representations and identities

The problems start if one tries to use a migrant's letters as evidence either of a transfer into a still British culture, or of assimilation into something 'Australian', or of resistance to such an accommodation. In simple language, one wants to see whether Maidie, in her forty years or so as an immigrant, adopted a new identity. Was she an 'empire settler', merely moving into another part of the British World, or part of a diaspora, self-consciously engaged in public performances of her Englishness in an alien Australia, or did she unshackle herself from her Englishness, become assimilated and create or absorb an Australian identity and new loyalties? Were these identities – in the 1920s to 1960s – incompatible alternatives? Was the trajectory inevitable, and one way, brought on by the passage of time? In any event, was the retention of Englishness or the adoption of an Australian identity really of sole or even primary importance to migrants like Maidie? After all, she was not just by birth English and by relocation Australian. She was a woman, a daughter, a sister, a wife, an entrepreneur, a gardener, and indeed a Quaker. All these, one might argue, informed her sense of self, and might at times be her priorities. Does an inquiry about diaspora and national identity reflect the principal concern of the migrant, or only the preoccupation of the historian? Do we risk distorting migrants' lives by plundering such treasures as Maidie's correspondence just for the bits of gold that catch our eye?

Earlier it was suggested that later British migrants to Australia and other white British settler societies might have found themselves increasingly breathing a culture no longer British, but (in this instance) Australian. Demographically, the percentage of the population made up of first-generation British settlers was diminishing; and native-born white Australian culture and values were likely to be predominant. British immigrants might have felt more conscious of their Britishness in such an environment.[44] But the problem of demonstrating this shift becomes acute when personal correspondence written to family members is squeezed for the evidence it contains.

By selecting episodes and phrases from the letters it is certainly possible to suggest that Maidie was conscious of and determined to retain her 'Englishness'. She writes at times as if she is an alien in a strange land, sometimes repelled by Australia and Australians. There is, for instance, much of the usual stuff about the climate.[45] In the state of Victoria, in the neighbourhood of Melbourne, she got the lot, from baking heat to freezing cold, from drought to flood. 'Talk about the variety of the English climate', she writes in November 1926, during the Australian summer. 'This place beats all I've struck before. One day it's enough to roast an ox – 96° or so in the shade, the next down to 56° or 60°, with a biting South Wind. The next, dust clouds so thick they blot out the whole landscape.' 'Gee, but we've had some weather lately. Up to 101° and 102° in the shade, & then suddenly it went down (at midday) to just over 60°.' 'It's rained, & rained, & rained, & it still rains' – this in 1927. In the New Year of 1928, she grumbles about 'A beastly day – hot, thick dusty north wind . . . which suddenly changed at midday to a cold wind with spasmodic drizzly rain.' In 1931, after five years in Australia, she is writing of 'an awful winter, about four times as much rain as last year . . . there have been dreadful floods in places'. Three years later, she was again writing about 'terrible floods' and in the same letter of the heat, 101°. In December 1962, in her very last, brief and poignant letter to Grace, and with a shaky hand, she writes: 'I cannot write much now as the temperature is 104° in the shade.'[46] Her encounters with Australia's insect life make for vivid reading.[47] It is important to bear in mind these engagements with the environment. The inclusion of these passages in her letters, it is suggested, is not necessarily to distance herself from the unacceptable face of Australia and to project her Englishness.

Likewise, it is possible to read too much into Maidie's grumbles about Australian governments and the administrators of the land settlement scheme. In Toolamba, in May 1926, she refers to her loneliness and the failure of even the estate manager's wife to call and see if they were comfortable. She complained in 1927 about the postal service: 'That Australian Government crowd want a bomb behind 'em.' Six months later, trying to sort out their transfer to Berwick, she is 'dashing about from Government slumber chambers to Immigration Bureau'.[48] By 1930, Jack was secretary of the local branch of the British Overseas Settlers Association. This got him involved in the complaints about the administration of the land settlement scheme and the dispatch of a petition to the King, George V, asking for an independent inquiry.[49] Had this English migrant couple become 'whinging poms'?

Are we on safer ground in discerning elements of English identity in Maidie's critical comments on Australian accents and Australian 'English'? She writes to Grace in 1927, after barely a year away: 'I find myself slipping into the slovenly Australian mode of speech, not in speaking but in writing. They leave out such words as "in", "on". "I'm going Thursday" instead of "on" Thursday . . . I'm fighting all I can to prevent the habit getting a hold.' Even more emphatically, she goes on to say that 'A girl in the hairdressers . . . said she knew I was a "new chum" but couldn't trace my accent.' Apparently the girl thought Maidie '"sounded like a well-educated, travelled Australian" . . . I replied that I was a normally well-educated *English* woman,

& hoped to remain so.'[50] Ten years later, she reports to her mother that when visitors from England called she was pleased 'to hear the nice English voices'.[51] Even in 1944, Maidie writes critically of Prime Minister John Curtin (whose name she spells 'Curtain'), and 'as for his *awful* Australian accent – well! you could cut it with a knife'.[52] And in 1946, this time writing to Jim, she half apologises for using the word 'blast' in an earlier letter, but goes on: 'Just be very glad I don't use the great Australian adjective "bloody" or the equally infamous "bastard". They're used here as ordinary conversation.'[53] Are these observations indicative of her retained Englishness surrounded by a swamp of Australian vulgarity?

Supportive of such a judgement might be her delight at the victory of the visiting English cricket team in 1926. She writes in triumph: 'Who said Australia could play cricket?'[54] (The support given by immigrant communities in England to visiting cricket teams from south Asia supposedly indicated that in 1990 they had not been assimilated and become British.)[55] Australian trade unionists came in for a slating, and according to Jack not even 'Australian humourists' were much good.[56] Then there are Maidie's references to the visit of the Duke and Duchess of York to Melbourne in 1927; the traditional English Christmas pudding and mince pies she and Jack consumed in December 1928; her lust in 1932 for English-made shoes ('Aussies are no good'); her reading of the magazine *The Queen*; Jack's attendance at the memorial service following the death of 'our sane and humble George V' in 1936; and in 1937 her pleasure at receiving from the family a book on *Highways and Byways* (almost certainly about an English county) and one on Surrey.[57] Even her lounge came to be decorated with pictures of England, including three scenes of the tiny Cornish port of Looe.[58]

She also maintained contact with her old school at Sibford, subscribing to its newsletter, contacting another Old Sibfordian who had moved to Victoria many years earlier, and welcoming a visit from a member of the school's governing body.[59] Her school, it will be recalled, was at Sibford Ferris. The first home Jack and Maidie had, at Berwick, they called Ferris Gardens; and at Sale they (or was it she?) went the whole hog and called their farm Sibford Ferris. Moreover, in her letters, Maidie several times refers to England as 'home', not just on arrival in 1926 but as late as 1940.[60] 'How I want to read the English news so', she writes in 1927.[61] In addition, in the letters during and after the war, there are references to her intention to contrive a visit back to England.[62]

But it is still more tempting to equate with 'Englishness' Maidie's passion for cultivating English flowers. The letters demonstrate that she was a keen and knowledgeable gardener. This was an enthusiasm shared by all the Dawes women, and also by Jack's mother. And what could be more indicative of Maidie's 'Englishness' than her planting of English seeds in that alien environment?[63] Even before Maidie had a plot to sow, she could write in rhapsodic fashion of the 'English' plants in Melbourne's public gardens: 'Some of them were Dahlias, Delphiniums, . . . snap-dragons, Love Lies Bleeding, heliotrope, sun-flowers, chrysanthemums, carnations, roses, phlox, pansies, begonias, geraniums . . ., "Soldiers", "Gay-ladies", gladiolli, sweet peas, plum-bago, water iris, & periwinkle . . .'[64] This is poetry, mouth music. Even when funds must have been tight, in 1926, Maidie bought cut flowers for the house, and they were familiar ones – violets, marigolds and carnations.[65] With a garden of her own, she expressed repeatedly her delight in the receipt of cuttings and seeds from mother, sister and mother-in-law – primroses, violets, honeysuckle, hollyhocks, sweet williams, sweet peas, and so on.[66] In the letters she takes great pleasure, and great length, to report progress in her gardens.[67]

In among the correspondence there are just a few photographs, and one is of her brugmansia outside the kitchen window at Sibford Ferris.[68] Moreover, it is also possible by selective quotation to suggest she was even aware of her gardening as a metaphor for her English identity. In 1928 she writes: 'We discovered a very meagre quantity of stunted but none the less *real* English Buttercups, growing on what is planted as a lawn.'[69] And in 1940: 'All those English things which grow so well at Home, have to be coddled through the hot weather here, particularly primroses, crocuses and bluebell.'[70] Here, cumulatively but surely, is the evidence we need, of a migrated Englishwoman, clutching the icons of her transported but not transmuted identity – the naming of her homes, her accent, her schooling, her shoes, her royal family, her garden. She was an English rose in an Australian desert.

But how far is this interpretation derived from finding in the letters what one set out to find? Is this truffle-hunting among Maidie's obser-vations, rooting out choice remarks, ripping them out of context? The context makes them much more ambiguous. The most obvious context is that all the letters from Maidie were written back to her family in England. She was, it may be suggested, sensitive to their expectations, and perhaps especially her mother's, that she was and should remain English. Hence those gifts of Englishness from them to her: the flower seeds of English stock they sent, the books about English counties, and the news of 'home' in the letters posted to her. Though few of those letters are preserved, we know there were many.

Even with reference to the flowers and her garden, it has to be recalled that the context for much of this was business – her market gardening. True, she designed and cultivated private gardens around her two Australian homes. But the thousands of bulbs and seeds she planted were to produce stock for market, adjuncts to the fruit trees in the commercial orchards, to the hens, and to Jack's cattle.[71] The assumption that her 'English' flowers were aliens in 'Australian' horticulture, marking her off as different from true 'Australians' is weakened by that very commercialism. Maidie was producing to satisfy an Australian market demand for English flowers. She writes: 'Got 6/- clear on 3 doz bunches of flowers – pansies, roses, lupins, foxgloves, sweet williams.'.[72]

Moreover, the metaphorical issue of allegiance and identity is muddy. Maidie also began to grow native Australian plants and shrubs – or at least plants long since indigenised in Australia – and she sent Australian seeds back to family with instructions for their planting in Middlesex. 'I am sending a few seeds of Dolichos', she writes as early as January 1927. 'It is a climbing plant, grows very quickly, is evergreen (out here) . . . It would make a nice cool shade outside a verandah or summer house . . . I'm saving some for our own house.'[73] Later, settled in Berwick, she was planting Australian wattle, as well as oak and pine, alongside her front drive,[74] and in 1930 she was sending back to Middlesex the seeds of Australian or indigenised native shrubs – hakea and watsonia.[75] This is pretty impressive. Native plants were certainly being used in Australian gardens even in the nineteenth century, but designers were not defining a local garden style until the 1930s. The first society dedicated to the preservation and propagation of native Australian species was not established until 1957, in Melbourne.[76] Those horticultural gifts paralleled other tributes sent back to Britain, such as books and magazine articles on Australia.[77] If we continue to employ gardening metaphors, Maidie would seem to have put down local roots.

Politically, too, Maidie and Jack need not be thought of as peculiarly English in their protests against government. Australian land settlers were equally enraged, when ecological and economic realities savaged expectations and wrecked the rural dreams of Australian as well as British settlers.[78] Like many native-born Australians, Maidie and Jack consequently identified with the Country Party in Victoria's elections in 1932, rejoiced in Labor's roasting, and denounced that dreadful Labor man, Jack Lang, for

> doing his best to ruin us all . . . We country folk are sick to death of labour and communistic parliaments, who do nothing but stick on impossible-to-pay taxes and duties, help the artisans, and rob, or entirely neglect, trades people and primary producers, forgetting that it's on wheat & wool & fruit & dairy produce that Australia depends for her very existence.

That word 'we' is strongly indicative of Maidie's alignment with a substantial section of Australian political opinion. Moreover, and perhaps only half in jest, her political engagement was such that she even threatened to stand as a candidate in the state elections: 'They've never had a woman member yet – they seem scared of [them] being candidates. Or is it that they won't be party to the roguery & rottenness that make up the government here [?].'[79] In August 1940, Maidie was again denouncing squabbling Australian politicians in wartime for not putting first the 'welfare of the Nation' – and it is apparent to which 'nation' she was referring.[80]

Moreover, a couple of times Maidie at least mentioned the prospect of her mother migrating to Australia to join her, as early as 1927 and as late as 1940.[81] In 1940 she nominated her two nephews, Jim's boys, for migration to Australia, to escape the war in Europe. Australia was, she then declared, a 'far, far, better land'.[82] Nothing came of that, but neither did she ever return to England. Was that project only frustrated, as she claimed, first by the outbreak of war and afterwards by the huge expense of travel?[83] Or was there a reluctance anyway even to visit? In 1956, Maidie was adamant in a letter to Grace: '[W]e have not the slightest intention of coming back to live in England for good. Almost everyone who has arrived here in the last few years says that Australia is a much better place for living, health and freedom than England.'[84]

This is where it becomes still more tricky. The motives for migrating and for sticking it out were not at all apparent from the initial letters in 1926, but embedded in the sequence are those of 1946 written to brother Jim following the death of Mother. From them we learn something, though not enough, about the circumstances in 1925 which at least partly prompted Maidie to leave for Australia. Perhaps we might also learn why there was an additional incentive to stay in Australia, whatever English longings Maidie may ever have felt. The truth is, the relationship between the sisters seems to have benefited by putting half the world between them. In one of the letters to her brother in England, Maidie records that what drove her to emigrate twenty years earlier was 'bickering'.[85] It is surely not sufficient to account for emigration, but it seems to have been a factor – and a highly personal one. This uncomfortable relationship resurfaced with a vengeance after Mother died, without leaving a will. Maidie interpreted Grace's demands upon the inheritance as symptomatic of the grasping and selfish character which had long ago prompted her emigration.[86] Maidie spoke of her sister's capacity to be 'pretty poisonous'.[87] Very possibly, the after-effects of the dispute account for the limited number, more formal style, and restricted substance of the later correspondence. Mrs Ann Dawes, who had known the family in Middlesex from when she was 11 years old, had uncomfortable memories of Mother and regarded Grace as 'odd' and 'rather spiteful'.[88]

All this underlines the problems of interpreting migrants' motives for going and staying from fragmentary sources. But there is a further problem when the historian of migration endeavours to employ extracts from letters to answer large issues concerning, in this case, settlement, assimilation, Englishness and Australian identity. Reading the entire surviving correspondence in the knowledge of what pops out in the bitter observations of 1946 suggests that Maidie was not only or even primarily concerned in this set of letters – and they are all we have – with negotiating between an English or an Australian identity. What seems to have mattered to her most in the correspondence was to demonstrate to her mother and her sister her personal qualities. She inscribed in her letters a self-image. She projected her resilience, tough-ness, capacity to cope, her ability to make do, to survive and manage. One suspects that this was in part a conceit to prove that the decision to migrate was correct. But it also sets up a contrast between herself and one prompt to her migration, her sister Grace.

For example, Maidie repeatedly plays the role of educated elder sister, asserting herself over her younger unmarried sibling. This oper-ated even on the most trivial of levels, such as correcting the spelling in her sister's letters. 'By the way', she writes in the first letter, 'occasional is spelt with an "s" not a "t"'. On subsequent occasions we get these: 'Raspberries, my good sister, are spelled with a "p" and not without'; 'My dear – spell manage with one *n* please, and damage with one *m*. *Sofa*, not soffa'; 'Noticed *not* notest! And medicine, not medi*cons*.' 'You should be more careful of grammatical sequence.' She is still doing it ten years later: 'Linen not lin*n*en, convalesce not conv*e*lesce, dahlia not dalia . . .'[89]

Judging from Maidie's replies, Grace must have complained of, or at least have referred to, her bouts of ill-health.[90] Sometimes Maidie seems less than sympathetic: 'You seem to be getting enough atten-tion from the medical profession. Let's hope it does you good.'[91] Grace had mentioned her medicines. Maidie responded: 'The doctor man certainly is stuffing you up with the muck. I think you'd be a jolly sight better off if you gave them all up, did a 4 or 5 mile *walk* everyday. *Walk* I mean, not crawl.' She went on, 'I only wish I had more time for it.'[92] Maidie hoped that Grace would be well enough to get a proper job, but mostly all she seems to have managed, at a low wage, was to decorate chocolate eggs at a Lyons factory at Greenford.[93]

That leads on to the very contrasting representation which Maidie gives of herself. In this context, Maidie's descriptions of the rigours of the Australian climate take on a different meaning, not evidence of alienation from Australia and a longing for the mildness of Britain, rather as challenges confronted, and handled – similarly, the troubled state of the Australian economy. Maidie's letters make much of such matters, perhaps not by way of complaint but as indicators of her (and Jack's) abilities to cope – something Grace was failing to do with what Maidie depicted as lesser difficulties. Maidie repeatedly described her capacity for hard work. She writes of fetching water at Toolamba in 1926: 'How would you like it[,] I wonder. Every drop has to be carried from tanks outside, & all but bath and laundry water taken out again in buckets & tipped down a gully at the back of the house.' Or this on managing the farm at Berwick in 1929: 'We work *hard* from sunrise to dark.' Or on making butter in 1931: 'it keeps me busy from 5.30 until nearly 8 every morning & from 6–7.30 evenings'. She signed off one letter: 'Well – 10 p.m. & Jack says its bedtime. We're up before 6, & hard at it all day, so 10 is quite late enough.' In 1943 she writes: 'And so the year of hard solid work [will be] round again'; and in 1944 'we're working about 15 hours a day'.[94] She emphasised her ingenuity in home management: in making her clothes,[95] in decorating the house at Sale,[96] and, rather splendidly, in making a chest of drawers from kerosene cases in her temporary quarters in Toolamba.[97] She also designed her first settlement house at Berwick, and sent home the plan.[98]

And there was more. Maidie wrote in 1934: 'Woman's job may be in the home, but it's no excuse for never doing anything else.'[99] Nominally, and in Maidie's case by conviction and practice, the Dawes were a Quaker family. Maidie moved from the Quaker community in England to Quaker connections overseas. Indeed, Quakers in Melbourne might have provided the initial point of reception, since the Meeting House was for a while her postal address.[100] In Australia she was remarkably active. The Quaker connection evidently provided that network of supporting contacts which other migrants often derived from kin, ethnicity or church.[101] In 1926 she spent a pleasant weekend with the family of the clerk to the Melbourne meeting; in 1927 she went camping with Young Friends; in 1928 she was attending musical evenings with Friends; in 1929 at a monthly meeting she was debating the sale of the Quaker Meeting House in Melbourne; in 1930 she was a Melbourne representative at a General Meeting in the mountains at Healesville; in 1931 she became secretary of Melbourne Young Friends, was involved in fund-raising for a Quaker school in Hobart, and attended the General Meeting in Sydney; in 1932 she played host to a Young Friends' meeting in Berwick; in 1933 she was at the Friends' reception for an English delegation, come to commemorate the centenary of Quakerism in Australia, and she organised a camp; in 1934 she was at the General Meeting in Adelaide; and she was still busy with Quaker activities through the war years.[102] One explanation of all this public activity may have been that Maidie and Jack had no children, but nor had Grace. Moreover, Maidie enhanced her child-free status by learning to drive. On one occasion she took two visiting Quaker friends on a tour by car of over a thousand miles.[103] As evident from the letters, she also taught herself to type. She represents herself as active, resilient, engaged, independent, a partner for Jack and not merely his wife. This identity and sense of worth seem at least as important to Maidie as any residual diasporic Englishness or adopted Australianness.

Conclusion

Of course, this in itself is no more than one reading of an incomplete and singular set of letters, with little outside verification of interpersonal relations possible. But this correspondence is more extended and more complete than many. Yet historians, of necessity, have been prone to use what they can find. Undoubtedly, these letters appear to show an English migrant woman navigating between her past and her present, as all migrants do, and between English and Australian identities and associations.[104] They are also illuminating of the tensions as well as consolations felt by those who retain an epistolary connection with family back home, more particularly at a time when faster, safer and relatively cheaper transport over long distances made chain migration or return migration more possible, less daunting.

Nevertheless, we may be looking too much for that which we judge is in the public domain significant, concerned with public identities and performance. The risk is selecting fragments from the partial to fit a hypothesis, and over-interpreting the pieces to suit our agendas. And we may be ignoring how that which is represented in private correspondence is indeed that – private – with private representations in a language deliberately coded by the sender and only with certainty decoded by the recipient.

Notes

1 See for example several of the essays in *The Diaspora of the British: Collected Seminar Papers No.13* (London, 1982).
2 R. Cohen, *Global Diasporas: an Introduction* (London, 1997) adopts a purist interpretation of the word, and then analyses a plurality of types by making adjectival additions, such as 'victim', 'labour', 'trade', and 'cultural'. On the appropriateness of the term to describe British overseas settlement see also E. Richards, *Britannia's Children: Emigration from England, Scotland, Wales and Ireland since 1600* (London, 2004), pp. 7–9.
3 For data see M. Harper and S. Constantine, *Migration and Empire* (Oxford, 2010); J. Jupp, *Immigration*, 2nd edn (Melbourne, 1998), pp. 191–2; A. H. McClintock (ed.), *An Encyclopaedia of New Zealand*, 2 (Wellington, 1966), pp. 138–9; Statistics Canada: www.statcan.ca/Daily/English/980217/d980217.htm#ART1, combining

data on English and Scottish (no figures for Welsh). This and subsequent websites accessed 22 November 2011.

4 S. Constantine, 'British Emigration to the Empire-Commonwealth since 1880: From Overseas Settlement to Diaspora?', in C. Bridge and K. Fedorowich (eds), *The British World: Diaspora, Culture and Identity* (London, 2003), pp. 16–35.

5 A. J. Hammerton, 'A Postwar British Diaspora? Late 20th Century British Emigrants and the Mobility of Modernity', paper given to the British World Conference, Auckland, 2005.

6 For some among many examples of their use see C. Erickson, *Invisible Immigrants: the Adaptation of English and Scottish Immigrants in 19th Century America* (Leicester, 1972); P. O'Farrell, *Letters from Irish Australia, 1825–1929* (Sydney, 1984); K. A. Miller, *Emigrants and Exiles: Ireland and the Irish Exodus to North America* (New York, 1985); D. Fitzpatrick, *Oceans of Consolation: Personal Accounts of Irish Migration to Australia* (Ithaca, 1994).

7 Angela McCarthy used 135 letters sent from New Zealand in *Irish Migrants in New Zealand, 1840–1937* (Woodbridge, 2005), but only six from the 1920s and none from the 1930s. In her essay 'Ethnic Networks and Identities among Inter-war Scottish Migrants in North America', in Angela McCarthy (ed.), *A Global Clan: Scottish Migrant Networks and Identities since the Eighteenth Century* (London, 2006), pp. 203–26, she drew on twenty-three letters, written by a male Scottish migrant in Canada, 1925–31. In 'Personal Letters, Oral Testimony and Scottish Migration to New Zealand in the 1950s: the Case of Lorna Carter', *Immigrants and Minorities*, 23:1 (2005), pp. 59–79, she used an archived collection of 136 letters, 1951–53, but written by a Scottish woman who was only a temporary migrant.

8 A. J. Hammerton and A. Thomson, *Ten Pound Poms: Australia's Invisible Migrants* (Manchester, 2005) provides the best example of the sensitive use of oral testimony; and see also R. Appleyard, *The Ten Pound Immigrants* (London, 1988); B. Zamoyska, *The Ten Pound Fare: Experiences of British People who Emigrated to Australia in the 1950s* (London, 1988); and M. Hutching, *Long Journey for Sevenpence: An Oral History of Assisted Immigration to New Zealand from the United Kingdom, 1947–1975* (Wellington, 1999). McCarthy, 'Personal Letters, Oral Testimony and Scottish Migration', demonstrates the value of combining emigrant letters with oral testimony.

9 I am pleased to record here my immense gratitude to Mrs Dawes for allowing me to read and cite these letters in what follows. Enquiries about their current location and availability should be directed to the author of this essay.

10 Methodological issues are discussed in B. S. Elliott, D. A. Gerber and S. M. Sinke (eds), *Letters Across Borders: the Epistolary Practices of International Migrants* (New York, 2006).

11 Maidie to Jim, 22 December 1946.

12 Private correspondence with Mrs Ann Dawes.

13 This issue, and the silences, are perceptively discussed in D. A. Gerber, 'Epistolary Masquerades: Acts of Deceiving and Withholding in Immigrant Letters', in Elliott, Gerber and Sinke (eds), *Letters Across Borders*, pp. 141–57.

14 Especially census and other official data, plus private correspondence with Mrs Ann Dawes.

15 There are many references to dressmaking in Maidie's correspondence. For her entertaining account of how she unpicked, remoulded and refashioned a hat see Maidie to Grace, 2 October 1933.

16 Maidie to Mother, 8 September 1926; to Grace, 13 December 1926; to Jim, 17 March 1946. The garden was sufficiently large for apple trees and for hens to be kept during the war: Grace to Maidie, 11 March, 27 April, and 2 October 1945.

17 Information kindly provided by Mr Mike Finch, Sibford School archivist.

18 Maidie to Mother, 16 March, 27 July 1931, 16 May 1932; also 17 May 1930 may imply unemployment earlier. Born in 1875, his prospects of secure re-employment in the 1930s when he was already in his late 50s would not be good.

19 The National Archives, London (TNA), War Office papers, WO 372/20, medal card

for Jack G. Viccars. Jack's service record is missing, almost certainly destroyed in the 1940 Blitz.

20 Maidie to Grace, 2 October 1933.
21 General Register Office, marriage certificate. It is possible that Jack's father had opened a shop in the High Street and that it was from there that Jack was married. There is nothing in the letters to suggest that Maidie had left home when unmarried, which at that time with her background was in any event unlikely, and there is no hint that the family ever lived in Godalming.
22 Passenger Lists, online, TNA, Board of Trade papers, BT 27; Maidie to Grace, 18 April 1926. For the ship see: www.clydesite.co.uk/clydebuilt/viewship.asp ?id=4636, and for the brochure – which also describes the ship interiors and 'typical menus' – see: www.timetableimages.com/maritime/images/auscl.htm.
23 On government migration schemes see S. Constantine (ed.), *Emigrants and Empire: British Settlement in the Dominions between the Wars* (Manchester, 1990); K. Fedorowich, *Unfit for Heroes: Reconstruction and Soldier Settlement in the Empire between the Wars* (Manchester, 1995); M. Roe, *Australia, Britain, and Migration, 1915–1940: A Study of Desperate Hopes* (Cambridge, 1995). For passage rates in 1925 see House of Commons Parliamentary Papers (HCPP), Cmd.2640. *Report of the Oversea Settlement Committee for the year ended 31st December 1925* (1926), p. 31. In 1925, a top workingman's wage was about £250 a year.
24 HCPP, Cmd.2383, *Report of the Oversea Settlement Committee for the year ended 31st December 1924* (1925), p. 30; Cmd.2640, *Report ... for the year ended 31st December 1925*, pp. 27–8. For a description of the scheme and the hardships of the settlers and its failures see G. F. Plant, *Oversea Settlement: Migration from the United Kingdom to the Dominions* (London, 1951), pp. 96–7 and 103–5; and especially M. Lake, *The Limits of Hope: Soldier Settlement in Victoria 1915–38* (Melbourne, 1987).
25 Plant, *Oversea Settlement*, pp. 104–5.
26 Maidie to Grace, 18 April, 16 May, 29 August 1926. Dookie Agricultural College, founded 1886, became part of the University of Melbourne in 1910 and had provided courses for Victoria's soldier settlement scheme: www.dookie.unimelb.edu.au/about/history.html. 'Jack had a very interesting course . . ., although he says one or two of the classes were a bore': Maidie to Grace, 29 August 1926.
27 Maidie to Grace, 16 May 1926. Australian Bureau of Statistics, '2006 QuickStats: Toolamba State Suburb', records a population even by then of only 873.
28 Maidie to Grace, 14 November 1926, 2 January, 21 and 30 March 1927; to Mother, 19 July 1927.
29 Maidie to Mother, 8 September 1926; to Grace, 30 March 1927.
30 Maidie to Mother, 4 December 1934; Jack to Grace, 21 October 1927; address on telegram, 1932. For local histories see: www.berwicksc.vic.edu.au/lib/City_of_Casey_history.pdf and http://web.archive.org/web/20041119085059/http://www.arts.monash.edu.au/ncas/multimedia/gazetteer/list/berwick.html
31 For a picture of such a vehicle see: http://nla.gov.au/nla.cs-pa-http%253A%252F%252Farrow.monash.edu.au%252Fhdl%252F1959.1%252F3856
32 Maidie to Mother, 24 January 1933. For an account by a 'failed' migrant who returned from Victoria see R. A. Pepperall, *Emigrant to Australia* (London, 1948). A. McCormick, 'Drought, Dust and Despair', *The Historian*, 111 (2011), pp. 13–18, describes settler experiences, 1923–36, in the even more challenging environment of Millewa, 300 miles north-east of Melbourne.
33 Plant, *Oversea Settlement*, p. 105.
34 Maidie to Grace, 26 March, 3 September 1928 and 29 April 1929; to Mother, 5 July, 11 November 1929, 17 May 1930, 16 March and 19 November 1931; to Mother and Dad, 8 November 1932; to Mother, 1 March 1933; to Jim, 10 April 1946.
35 P. Synan, *Gippsland's Lucky City: a History of Sale* (Sale, 1994).
36 Maidie to Mother, 4 December 1934 and 8 December 1937.
37 Maidie to Grace and everyone, 20 October 1936; to Grace, 28 January 1936.

38 Maidie to Mother, 17 March and 8 December 1937; to Mother, 20 August 1940; to Mother and Grace, 28 July 1941; to Jim, 10 April 1946. One of the workers they hired, a lad of 17, left them to work elsewhere on a sheep farm, where he shot one man dead and badly wounded another: Maidie to Grace, 7 December 1937. Another hired hand was a German national, nominated by Maidie as an assisted immigrant, who arrived in Sydney from Ireland in October 1938 aged 17, and became a naturalised Australian citizen in 1944: see the National Archives of Australia: www.naa. gov.au/collection/using/search/index.aspx and search for 'Viccars' and 'Hollaender'.
39 Throughout the Second World War, Australia was home to thousands of civilian internees and POWs. Victoria saw some of the largest facilities established within its borders for Italian and German prisoners as well as enemy civilian internees. German POWs were never billeted to local farmers, so the reference here is probably to either an Italian POW or an Italian civilian internee, who were an invaluable but problematic source of labour during the war. See B. Moore and K. Fedorowich, *The British Empire and its Italian Prisoners of War, 1940–1947* (Basingstoke, 2002), pp. 72–91 and 188–204.
40 Maidie to Grace and everyone, 20 October 1936.
41 See references in letters from 28 July 1941 to 1 July 1946.
42 Emiline to Grace, 9 May 1955, 6 May 1956 and 3 December 1962.
43 Jack Viccars to Jim Dawes, 13 July 1967.
44 For a brief consideration see Harper and Constantine, *Migration and Empire*, pp. 68–72.
45 For equivalents see Fitzpatrick, *Oceans of Consolation*, pp. 587–9; A. McCarthy, '"A Good Idea of Colonial Life": Personal Letters and Irish Migration to New Zealand', *New Zealand Journal of History*, 35:1 (2001), pp. 13–14.
46 Maidie to Grace, 14 November and 13 December 1926, 21 March 1927, and 8 January 1928; to Mother, 27 July 1931 and 4 December 1934; to Grace, 3 December 1962.
47 Maidie to Grace, 26 March 1928; to Grace and Jim, 9 November 1931.
48 Maidie to Grace, 16 May 1926 and 21 March 1927; to Mother, 19 July 1927.
49 Maidie to Mother, 17 May 1930.
50 Maidie to Grace, 30 March 1927, and see also 1 July 1928.
51 Maidie to Mother, 8 December 1937.
52 Maidie to Mother, 2 May 1944.
53 Maidie to Jim, 22 February 1946.
54 Maidie to Grace, 29 August 1926, and see also 14 November 1926.
55 According to Norman Tebbit, a former Conservative government minister: *The Times*, 21 April 1990.
56 Maidie to Grace, 2 January 1927; Jack to Grace, 6 September 1926.
57 Maidie to Grace, 30 March and 21 May 1927, 8 January 1928; to Mother, 16 May 1932; to Grace, 28 January 1936; to Mother, 17 March 1937; to Grace, 7 December 1937. Several volumes in a *Highways and Byways* series were published in or before 1937: see British Library Integrated Catalogue.
58 Maidie to Mother and Dad, 8 November 1932.
59 Maidie to Mother, Dad, Jim and Grace, 11 November 1930; to Mother, 27 July 1931, 17 March 1937. She was invited to contribute an article on life in Australia to the Sibford Old Scholars magazine, though this has not been traced.
60 Maidie to Grace, 14 November 1926; to Mother, 20 August 1940; and see similar in letters to Mother and everyone, 11 November 1929, and to Mother, 17 May 1930; to Grace, 20 October 1930; to Mother, 8 December 1937, 3 September 1939.
61 Maidie to Mother, 19 July 1927.
62 Maidie to Mother, 3 September 1939; to Grace, 31 May 1945; to Jim, 22 February, 21 March and 1 July 1946; to Grace and Jim, 16 March 1946.
63 For the cultural significance of colonial gardening see, for example, Katherine Raine, 'Domesticating the Land: Colonial Women's Gardening', in B. Dalley and B. Labrun (eds), *Fragments: New Zealand Social and Cultural History* (Auckland, 2000), pp. 76–96.

64 Maidie to Grace, 18 April 1926, and 29 August 1926 for another rhapsody on familiar spring flowers in Melbourne gardens.
65 Maidie to Grace, 18 April and 16 May 1926.
66 Maidie to Grace, 18 April and 14 November 1926, 30 March 1927, 8 January and 3 September 1928; to Mother, 16 May 1932.
67 Maidie to Grace, 8 January and 1 July 1928, 5 July 1929; to Mother, 5 July and 11 November 1929, 16 March 1931; to Grace and Jim, 9 November 1931; to Mother, 12 April and 16 May 1932, 8 December 1937, 20 August 1940.
68 Maidie to Mother and Grace, 28 July 1941.
69 Maidie to Grace, 1 July 1928.
70 Maidie to Mother, 20 August 1940.
71 Maidie to Grace, 8 January and 1 July 1928; to Mother, 17 May 1930.
72 Maidie to Mother, 19 November 1931.
73 Maidie to Grace, 2 January 1927, and see also 30 March 1927 and 24 January 1933. The *dolichos lablab*, or lablab bean or hyacinth bean, was originally indigenous to Asia: www.floridata.com/ref/d/doli_lab.cfm.
74 Maidie to Grace, 26 March 1928.
75 Maidie to Mother, Dad, Jim and Grace, 11 November 1930. For *hakea* see: http://asgap.org.au/hakea.html and for *watsonia* see:http://members.ozemail.com.au/~davcooke/watsonia.htm.
76 For the history of the Society for Growing Australian Plants see: http://asgap.org.au/history.html.
77 Maidie to Grace, 30 March 1927; to Mother, 12 April 1932; to Jim, 19 June 1946.
78 Lake, *Limits of Hope*, esp. pp. 195–228; Roe, *Australia, England, and Migration*.
79 Maidie to Mother, 16 May 1932, and see also criticisms of the Australian Labor party, 20 August 1940.
80 Maidie to Mother, 20 August 1940.
81 Maidie to Mother, 19 July 1927, 8 December 1937 and 20 August 1940.
82 Maidie to Mother, 20 August 1940.
83 Maidie to Mother, 3 September 1939; to Grace, 31 May 1945; to Jim, 22 February and 1 July 1946.
84 Maidie to Grace, 6 May 1956.
85 Maidie to Jim, 21 March 1946.
86 Maidie to Jim, 17 March, 21 March, 10 April, 19 June and 1 July 1946; to Grace, 6 and 25 April 1946.
87 Maidie to Jim, 1 July 1946.
88 Private correspondence with Mrs Ann Dawes.
89 Maidie to Grace, 18 April, 29 August 1926, 2 January and 21 March 1927, 8 January 1928, 10 October 1936, and see also 3 September 1928. Unlike her older sister, Grace was not sent to the Sibford Ferris boarding school, but nor was brother Jim.
90 Maidie to Grace, 16 May 1926, 8 January 1928; to Mother, 16 March 1931.
91 Maidie to Grace, 2 January 1927.
92 Maidie to Grace, 21 March 1927.
93 Maidie to Mother, 19 July 1927; to Grace, 1 July 1928 and 29 April 1929; Grace to Maidie, 2 October 1945; Maidie to Grace, 26 February 1946; to Jim, 19 June 1946; private correspondence with Mrs Ann Dawes.
94 Maidie to Grace, 16 May 1926 and 29 April 1929; to Mother, 16 March and 19 November 1931; to Mother and Grace, 6 July 1943; to Mother and family, 13 December 1944; see also to Mother, 17 May 1930 and 4 December 1934; to Grace, 7 December 1937.
95 Of many examples, Maidie to Grace, 30 March 1927 and 31 May 1945.
96 Maidie to Grace, 8 December 1937.
97 Maidie to Grace, 16 May 1926 – including a drawing of her handiwork.
98 Maidie to Mother, 8 September 1926.
99 Maidie to Mother, 4 December 1934.
100 Maidie to Grace, 13 December 1926 to 21 May [1927?]; to Mother, 19 July 1927.
101 See, for example, several essays in L. Fraser (ed.), *A Distant Shore: Irish Migration*

and New Zealand Settlement (Dunedin, 2000) and McCarthy (ed.), *Global Clan.*

102 Maidie to Mother, 8 September 1926; to Grace, 30 March 1927 and 26 March 1928; to Mother and everyone, 11 November 1929; to Grace, 20 October 1930; to Mother, 27 July 1931; to Grace and Jim, 9 November 1931; to Mother, 12 April 1932, 24 January and 1 March 1933, 4 December 1934, 20 August 1940; to Mother and Grace, 28 July 1941; to Mother, Grace and Jim, 10 February 1944.

103 Maidie to Mother and everyone, 11 November 1929; to Mother, 17 March and 8 December 1937.

104 On this ambivalence see the perceptive analysis in Hammerton and Thomson, *Ten Pound Poms*, pp. 325–57.

CHAPTER 9

Staying on or going 'home'? Settlers' decisions upon Zambian independence

Jo Duffy

In 1960 the white population of the Central African Federation (CAF) was estimated at 308,300: 76,000 of these 'white settlers' lived in Northern Rhodesia (now Zambia); 223,000 lived in Southern Rhodesia (now Zimbabwe); and 9,300 lived in Nyasaland (now Malawi).[1] At Independence (29 October 1964) the settlers had to decide where their future lay. Would they stay on, move elsewhere in Africa, move elsewhere in the world, or return 'home' to Britain. This chapter focuses on a small number of individuals who remained in Zambia after Independence, and tries to capture their motivations for staying on.

The settlers who stayed on in Africa after Independence have not received much scholarly attention. An examination of journal articles, monographs and textbooks reveals that this group is rarely mentioned, if at all (with the notable exception of white farmers in Zimbabwe). Although their numbers were small this lack of attention is extraordinary. Africa's colonial legacy is often discussed in terms of underdevelopment, dependency, economic influence and neo-colonialism, focusing on the relationship between independent African states and the former colonial powers, not between whites who stayed on and African regimes. In saying this, it certainly does not mean to suggest that nothing has been done in this area, but rather that very little systematic research has been done. Settlers are touched on in other contexts, but rarely studied for their own sake.[2] There is an exception to this pattern, since there has been some popular historical (and travel) writing about whites who have stayed on.[3] In general, however, this genre treats them as an anachronistic historical curiosity, as evidenced by the title of one of these books – *Last Days in Cloud Cuckooland*. Settlers are seen as a 'dying tribe' or as 'human debris [much of which] was borne by the winds of change to South Africa.'[4]

In reality, however, the picture of the settlers who stayed on is far more complicated. The southwards drift towards South Africa is only one part of the story, as is the contemporary Zimbabwean situation. Decolonisation was not a clean break, but rather a complex and ongoing process. The immediate independence period saw attempts at Africanisation frustrated by a lack of suitably qualified African graduates and the need to retain the valuable experience of expatriates, both within the civil service and within private industry.[5] The post-independence period saw a number of whites take on prominent roles within the political or judicial spheres, often as members of African political parties.[6] One way in which the role of stayers on can be assessed is to read the extensive Africanisation literature 'backwards' – that is to say, reading it as the decline in the numbers of expatriate staff instead of as an increase in the numbers of African staff. Of course, this chapter is concerned specifically with settlers, and not with the colonial civil servants who are often the focus of such studies, but there are some parallels that can be drawn between the two groups as well as obvious dissimilarities. Colin Baker writes of expatriates within the Malawian Civil Service that: 'The reasons why an officer left or stayed were intensely individual; but whether financial, personal, domestic, political or professional, they varied broadly with age.'[7] This chapter should go some way to revealing whether the same may be said for the settler population.

There is some resonance between this picture and the themes of the most notable fictional treatment of settlers who stayed on, albeit in a different context. Paul Scott's Booker Prize winning novel, *Staying On* (1977), tells the story of Tusker Smalley and his wife Lucy who remained in India after Independence, living in the small hill town of Pankot. Many years later Tusker outlined his reasons for staying in a letter to Lucy, who would have much preferred to return to what she thought of as 'home' – Great Britain. 'I know for years you thought I was a damn' fool to have stayed on, but I was forty-six when Independence came, which is bloody early in life for a man to retire but too old to start afresh somewhere you don't know. I didn't fancy my chances back home, at that age, and I knew the pension would go further in India than in England.'[8] Instead, Tusker Smalley took up an invitation to stay on and work for the Indian Government, and following the end of his contract a couple of years later he took a commercial job. By the 1970s, when the book is set, he and his wife are the last British couple living in the town, trying to come to terms with the changes in the India they once knew.

The lack of academic focus on settlers who stayed on is not surprising. The histories of decolonisation and the independence struggle have been written either from a metropolitan perspective, or from a broadly nationalist perspective. Thus, settlers are all too often treated as a monolithic group, with an assumption of a single settler perspective. Alistair Ross has argued that, in the case of Tanganyika, the 'European group' was 'more heterogeneous in its response to the demands of African national-ists than the monolithic school would allow'.[9] It is this heterogeneity that is a central theme which this chapter seeks to draw out in since, although not new, this view has failed to filter out into broader decolo-nisation and postcolonial studies. Nationalist historians have 'tended to support the concept of a uniform European attitude of hostility of inde-pendence demands'.[10] Some of the work on white settlers in the decolo-nisation period does grapple with divisions within the European settler population, but much of this writing has been focused on settler elites and political parties, rather than on non-elite individuals. For instance, Phiri's work on the Capricorn Africa Society describes divisions between conservative liberals and radical liberals in the Northern Rhodesian settler community, while Kennedy's work on Mau Mau indicates the 'powerful crosscurrents that moved white opinion in Kenya in divergent directions – progressive as well as reactionary'.[11]

Insights from the BECM Oral History Collection

Tantalising glimpses of settler views on the decisions that they made at Independence about where to make their home do, however, exist within the archives. The British Empire and Commonwealth Museum's (BECM) oral history collection contains a small number of interviews which touch either directly or indirectly on this issue.[12] There are obvious frustrations in using an oral history collection where the interviews have been collected for a purpose other than one's own, since the interviewer will almost invariably ask different questions from the ones that you want answered, and will pick up on and pursue other threads and lines of enquiry than you would have done. An interviewer may not be skilled in the art of oral history, and might impose their own views and ideas, plant thoughts in the interviewee's head, and direct the flow of the conversation in a heavy-handed way. When undertaking one's own interviews it is at least possible to be alert to this possibility and take care to avoid these problems, although no interview is ever perfect from that point of view.

There is, if you like, no such thing as 'pristine subjectivity' to be found within an interview – interviews are conversations – mediated and influenced by the interviewer and, as such, the subjectivities of interviewer and interviewee are in constant interaction. One advantage of conducting one's own interviews is that you can reflect far more fully (and self-reflexively) on your own subjectivity than it is possible to do if the interviewer is someone else, and moreover someone whom you do not know well. In addition, some individuals will have been interviewed several times before, while others will not have been.

Sometimes questions will provoke well-rehearsed answers, and other times they will lead the interviewee to think about something for the very first time. This *does* matter, and it is not always possible to know which is the case, especially when one is not conducting the interview oneself. Nonetheless, taking all these caveats into account, such oral history collections can be an incredible resource for the historian. It is worth remembering that rarely (if ever) does a document in an archive answer all your questions either. The quality of the BECM oral history collection is generally quite high, as the overriding aim of the oral historians involved had been to allow the interview subjects to speak for themselves, and to tell their own stories.

The BECM collection yielded twenty-two interviews with relevant material – interviews with a range of settlers and former colonial civil servants who had lived across British East and Central Africa (thirteen of the interviewees were living in Kenya in the run-up to Independence, four in Uganda, four in Tanzania and one in Southern Rhodesia/Zimbabwe). Around a third of the relevant BECM interviews were with 'settlers' while about two-thirds were with members of the Colonial Service (although the distinction between these categories is discussed in more detail below). Six of the interviewees were women, and the remainder were men. Eleven of the interviewees had stayed on for relatively short periods after Independence (less than two years), and six had stayed on for longer periods (ranging from four to twenty-eight years). The remainder of the relevant interviews were with individuals who had left at Independence, but who had discussed their reasons for doing so in their BECM interviews. Unfortunately, the biographical information about the BECM interviewees varies in quality and level of detail, and usually takes the form of a brief biographical sketch which picks out those elements of the individual's life deemed interesting by the interviewer/cataloguer. In particular, information about place and date of birth, early life and career has not been systematically collected and recorded, and can only be partially reconstructed by listening to the relevant interviews.[13] This lack of context can be frustrating when using a pre-existing oral history collection, and is something that can be addressed when conducting one's own interviews.

Although not all of the interviews referred explicitly to people's reasons for staying on or for leaving, a series of interlinked and overlapping themes emerge.[14] Many of those interviewed as part of the BECM collection talked about the fact that although they knew that Independence was on the horizon they did not expect it to come so quickly. For some, their age at Independence was a crucial consideration – would their age and experience make it easier or harder to find another job elsewhere in the world? Was the best option rather to stay put? For others, age only became a consideration much later in their lives, and it was anxieties about who would care for them in their old age and declining health that made them consider leaving Africa. Whether or not an individual had children was another important consideration. If they did have children their age and educational needs were a huge part of the decision. Other family commitments could also prove crucial, either as an anchor or as a reason to leave. For instance, if an individual had elderly relatives back 'home' in Britain this could be a reason to return; but if one's entire extended family was rooted in Africa it might be a reason to stay, rather than split the family.

Another key theme to emerge from the oral testimonies was the impact of Africanisation on the decision people made about whether to stay on. For some of those interviewed it was ultimately corruption and the nature of political life in post-Independence Africa that influenced their decision to leave. However, not all of those interviewed were so negative, with a number of interviewees expressing some pride in the achievements of the British. Many of the colonial civil servants in this small sample also expressed feelings of regret at leaving Africa. Another theme that emerged strongly from the interviews, and seemed to be an influence on decisions to stay or leave, was their positive feelings about the founding nationalist presidents in some countries. Some of the interviewees were indeed asked to stay on. Even those who did not stay on in Africa after Independence, or who stayed for only a short period, often found themselves returning to Africa later in their lives. This linked into notions of a lifestyle that was too good to abandon, or in some cases nostalgia for an African childhood. Only one of the BECM interviewees discussed the issue of what to do about citizenship and the importance of having access to 'the right passport'. This was an extremely important issue, but does not emerge from the BECM interviews since they were not explicitly looking at the issue of 'staying on'. However, some of the interviewees did talk about the more abstract notion of feeling divided loyalties during the Independence period – both to Britain and to the new emerging states in Africa. The last of the themes arising from the interviews was a lack of immediate change at Independence. For many of those interviewed Independence was not a sudden dramatic break, but rather a process and the changes associated with Independence developed over time.

The diversity of 'settler' experience: interviews with stayers-on living in Lusaka

These themes and insights gleaned from the BECM oral history collection informed a series of interviews conducted in Lusaka in April 2005 and August 2006 with a small number of individuals who stayed on in Zambia after Independence. They were asked about their lives before and since Independence, with particular reference to their identities and their decisions about whether to stay. What had they expected to happen? What considerations did they take into account in making their decisions? Was age a factor (as posited by Colin Baker)? What of family circumstances? Did they consider how Independence would affect their career prospects? What were the attractions in staying, and what were the disadvantages? The settler who stayed on in Africa occupied an intermediate position – no longer tied to the colonial power, but not strictly African either. How did they negotiate this position? How did they insert themselves into postcolonial African politics and society, and how did this change over time? What were the implications in terms of their identity, loyalties and conceptions of self? Did settler conceptions of 'home' change at independence? Did they consider themselves to be British or African?

The BECM and Lusaka interviews differed in some respects. While the purpose of the BECM interviews was to provide a general over-view and flavour of the individuals' experiences of Empire and what their lives were like – and in that respect were broad and narrative in their scope – the Lusaka series of interviews was much more targeted towards questions of identity and self-perception. One of the key char-acteristics of the Lusaka interviews was an attempt to ask two very different kinds of questions. The first type of question was the obvious sort, which people would have been asked time after time in the course of their everyday lives (even if they had never been interviewed by an oral historian before), such as why they decided to stay on in Zambia after Independence. These 'obvious' questions were likely to produce answers which the individual had given on numerous occasions and were in some way 'rehearsed'. The answers to this first type of question would be part and parcel of the individual's lifetime narrative, which, looked back on, would make good sense in light of where their life had taken them. The second type was the 'thinking question' – something which the individual had probably not been asked before, and which required them to think out loud and work towards an answer during the course of the interview, rather than giving a 'pat' answer. The answers to such questions tend to be somewhat more telling since they are more instinctive, and reveal the thought processes at play. A good example is asking individuals how they would define themselves – as settlers, sojourners, or expatriates. Another 'thinking question' is to ask people how they would describe how they fit in postcolonial Zambia – what their role might be, what they feel in terms of their national identity.

This section begins with short biographies of each of the eight interview respondents in order to reveal the diversity of experiences represented within the Zambian 'settler' community.[15] The bulk of the study draws extensively on the testimony of the interviewees and concentrates on a number of themes that emerged from the interviews.[16] The concluding section is somewhat more theoretical, and focuses on the definition of the term 'settler' and asks whether it is a useful concept.

Gabriel, aged 75 at the time of interview in April 2005, was born in Northern Rhodesia to a settler family. Her father had had a career as a colonial civil servant beginning in China and ending in provincial administration in Northern Rhodesia when he volunteered for service in the First World War. He then took up farming, and later had a succession of jobs in the mining industry. Gabriel's husband was British and had gone to Northern Rhodesia as a policeman, eventually ending up in the Secretariat. Gabriel was also employed in the administration, and interestingly, was closely involved with planning the Independence ceremony.[17] She is now an artist and writer, and still designs many of Zambia's postage stamps. At the time of the interview she was recently widowed. She has no children. Gabriel has one sister, who lives in South Africa.

John, interviewed in 2005, was born in Northern Rhodesia in 1930, one of two brothers. His father migrated to join the British South Africa Company administration, transferred to the Colonial Service in 1924, and eventually rose through the ranks to become Secretary for Native Affairs before retiring to England. John followed in his father's footsteps. Having been educated in Southern Rhodesia and South Africa, he took his degree at Oxford, completed the Colonial Service course at Cambridge, and returned to Northern Rhodesia as a District Officer. He married an Irishwoman in 1956, and they went on to have three children (two sons, who now live in the UK, and a daughter who lives in Kuwait).[18] John's brother now lives in the UK.

The last of the stayers-on interviewed in 2005 was Donald, who had settled in Northern Rhodesia with his wife in 1947 after serving in the Far East during the Second World War. He has no children, but has one brother, who is living in the UK. Donald worked in the legal sector throughout his time in Zambia, and was still working as a legal executive at the time of the interview, despite being 85 years old!

Ken, interviewed in 2006, was born to British parents in Broken Hill, Northern Rhodesia (now Kabwe) in 1947 where his father worked on the mine. He was educated in South Africa from the age of 10, and has spent his entire working life in Zambia – first for a bank, later for a British multinational company, and eventually for a Japanese multinational. He retired in 2003 but continued to work for his former employers as a consultant. Ken has three brothers, two of whom live in the UK, and one of whom migrated to South Africa. Ken's wife Nikki was born in Lusaka in 1949. Her father was also born in Lusaka, and her mother had emigrated to Northern Rhodesia from South Africa, aged 3. Nikki grew up on her parents' farm, 30 kilometres outside of Lusaka, and was educated mostly in Northern Rhodesia, although she spent the last three years of her school career in South Africa. Ken has a daughter who now lives in the UK, and Nikki has a son who lived in South Africa for a spell before returning to Zambia.

Linelle migrated to Northern Rhodesia in 1957 at the age of 16. She had grown up in Durban, South Africa, but her father died and her mother remarried a Northern Rhodesian who worked for the Public Works Department in Lusaka. One of six sisters, she has lived in Lusaka throughout her time in Zambia. She is married and has two daughters, both married to Zambian-born husbands. One of her daughters has two children, a son and a daughter, both of whom hold Zambian passports.

Alfred was born in Northern Rhodesia in 1940. His grandfather on his mother's side had emigrated to South Africa from Scotland in the late 1800s, and later moved to Livingstone, Northern Rhodesia, where he was involved in the construction of the Victoria Falls Bridge. His mother was born and brought up in Livingstone, and that was where she met his father, who had emigrated from England in the late 1920s to join the British South Africa Police in Southern Rhodesia, and late the Northern Rhodesia police. Alfred is one of four brothers, all of whom were born in Livingstone. The family later relocated to Lusaka, where he has lived ever since. Alfred was educated in Northern Rhodesia, although his elder brother was educated in South Africa and his two younger brothers went to school in England. When Independence came Alfred was doing articles to become an accountant. He worked for a multinational accountancy firm until he retired a few years ago, and describes himself as 'the last white face to leave'. He and his partner now own an accountancy firm of their own. Alfred's three brothers left Zambia – two now live in Australia, and the third is in the UK.

The last of the 2006 interviews was with Margaret, who went to Northern Rhodesia with her husband in 1957 – an economist, chartered accountant and businessman. They initially spent three years on the Copperbelt, where her husband was setting up the offices of a multinational accountancy firm. Once the contract expired he was offered a job by the Northern Rhodesian government starting up a parastatal and acting as Finance Director. After Independence he became bored with this job, and took another job within the parastatal sector. His job was Zambianised during his two-year contract, so he left before it ended, although he continued to be paid. The rest of his career was split between his own company of chartered accountants in Lusaka, and the multinational accountancy firm he had previously worked for on the Copperbelt. Margaret's husband was also a director of several companies, and the couple owned a cattle ranch. Since 1976 Margaret, who is also a trained economist, has been very involved with the Lusaka Agricultural Show Society. She was widowed shortly after her husband's retirement. The couple had two daughters, both of whom still live in Zambia. Throughout their time in Northern Rhodesia and Zambia, Margaret and her husband spent six weeks a year in the UK where they always owned at least one property. Margaret still spends a month of each year in the UK.

'Home', identity and the experience of the postcolony

Several themes emerge strongly from the testimony of the Lusaka interviewees. The first of these is the question of home and identity, which are inextricably linked. Early on in his interview, John volunteered that for him Northern Rhodesia was home, and that after his four years at university in Britain 'I got back as quickly as I could!' When asked about his identity now, he gave the following answer:

> I never actually got a Zambian passport, I still have a British passport. I was, at Independence, I'd held a Federal passport, British Passport – Federation of Rhodesia and Nyasaland, and I went along to the British High Commission which was newly set up and said I would like to change this for a British passport. And the reaction I got was as neither my grandfather, nor my father, nor myself had been born in the country which was now British I was not entitled to one, which I felt was quite hard after 13 years in the Colonial Service, at times in physical danger. So I thought about getting a Zambian passport, but at about that time there was an incident at the Chilanga cement factory, where a white foreman who had taken out Zambian citizenship had a difference of opinion with a few of the local party or the local works committee. He was not only sacked, but also had his Zambian citizenship cancelled, and was left stateless. So I thought, well, if this is the sort of thing that's going to happen here I'd better stick to my British passport, and eventually managed to get one, purely on the technical grounds that my father had registered his citizenship in London when he was in the Colonial Office, and er, so was entitled to a British passport.[19]

Gabriel's decision about citizenship and identity was a different one, and she was one of the first white people to take out a Zambian passport. She says: 'Well, you had to take either your British one or your Zambian one. You couldn't have dual citizenship, and it was logic for me to take a Zambian one, the same as it was logic for [my husband] to keep his British one.' The decision about citizenship was not just an abstract one, as Gabriel's later experiences showed. When the Civil Service was Zambianised – not, in this case Africanised – Gabriel, as a Zambian, was able to retain her job, while her husband, as a British subject, lost his, and had to find another. On the subject of home, she explains: 'I think if they came from Britain, probably some of them [settlers who stayed] feel that their ... Britain is home, but I think for most people born here, this is ... this is home.'[20] For Donald, too, the issue of identity is a complex one. 'Well, I've still got a British passport. I consider myself now English, not British. [...] If people ask me my nationality, I say English now. The Welsh have gone their way, the Scots have gone their way, so why shouldn't we go ours? But I would consider myself almost an adopted Zambian, I mean, it's my home.'[21]

As children, Ken and Nikki both identified very strongly as Northern Rhodesians, although Nikki went on to say that they did think of themselves as 'probably British second'. When Independence came, like Gabriel and her husband, Ken and Nikki ended up with different nationalities. Ken was able to retain his British citizenship, which he has kept up until today, whereas Nikki took out Zambian citizenship, since both she and her father had been born in Northern Rhodesia, and she was not therefore entitled to a British passport. During the interview Ken mentioned the possibility of Zambia introducing a system of dual nationality in the near future. If that were to happen he would probably go for dual citizenship, but said that he would never give up his British passport. Asked to describe their identities, the couple gave interesting answers. Ken said: 'Oh, generally I'd say I'm British, you know. But when a Zambian, new Zambian people that I meet, when they know I'm born here, know that I've never left, I've lived here ... they say "Oh, you're a Zambian!" ... so, to all extents and purposes, I think I am Zambian and British, if you know what I mean!'[22] Nikki, who holds a Zambian passport, answered. 'Well, I guess my identity is with the British. Now. Because we're *not* South African, we're *not* truly indigenous Zambians, so yes, we're British!'[23]

When asked how she would describe herself, Linelle responded: 'Well, I suppose at sixteen I was a South African living in Northern Rhodesia, but ... over the years I'd say I'm more Zambian than anything else.'[24] Both she and her husband, who arrived in Northern Rhodesia in 1954, have permanent residents' permits, although both of her grandchildren hold Zambian passports. For Alfred, his identity before Independence was that of a Rhodesian with an English background. He described the sense of being part of something bigger, saying: 'It was an Empire – we realised that we were here, and there were others in Canada, there were others in New Zealand, others in Australia ...' These days he describes himself as a 'white Zambian' although he continues to hold a British passport. 'Well,' he said, 'I think we've always been a white something . . . We've been white Rhodesians, now we're white Zambians.'[25] Margaret's identity is probably the most explicitly British. She told me: 'England is where I was born and brought up – that is my home. Alright, I'm very comfortable living here, and so on, but if my daughters didn't want to stay here I wouldn't. Simply because there wouldn't be much reason for me to stay, and all my close family still live over there and I still have lots of friends there as well.'[26]

In the 2006 interviews, informants were asked specifically about how they would term their situation in Zambia – were they 'settlers', or 'expatriates' or 'sojourners' or something else entirely? None of these terms really seemed to fit with how these people see themselves. Linelle, despite not having taken Zambian citizenship said that she was simply a Zambian – 'I've felt that for a very long time.'[27] Margaret said: 'No, not a settler, no, no, no!' while not really being able to offer an alternative term.[28] Ken and Nikki said that they definitely were not expatriates, and that they felt they had been in Zambia too long to qualify as settlers – both having been born in the country. Ken said: 'We don't think of ourselves as settlers, just part of the furniture in a sense . . .' He continued: 'I believe I have the right to criticise this government, and to criticise anything here, because I'm part of the furniture. But I don't like people coming in and being here for ten minutes and then starting criticising – whether he's got a point or not, it's a different sort of . . . of an issue. Bit of a strange sort of protectiveness to the country.'[29] Alfred articulated his identity in a similar way to Ken and Nikki, as follows:

> No, no I'm not a settler – I was born here, I'm just part of it – I'm just a white variety of it! I know I've not got a Zambian passport, but . . . I suppose it's just a hang back and if you do give up your British passport it's difficult to get it back again. It's not a problem in this country, so far, having a British passport but at the same time being a permanent resident here. So, you are accepted, the only thing we can't do is we're not allowed to vote at an election.[30]

This links to another factor that emerged from the interviews, which is the importance of maintaining a non-political stance. Many of these informants are not entitled to vote in Zambian elections since they are permanent residents, and not citizens, but politics is broader than mere voter participation. It is also important to note that this is a very small sample, and there have been stayers-on who became very involved in Zambian politics. Indeed, it is interesting to note that a distinction is made by Ken between his right to criticise by virtue of his status as 'part of the furniture' and being overtly political. He elaborated this as follows: 'I've got a good lot of Zambian friends of mine, and we all talk politics, exactly what's going on and how do we see who's going to win this election [the 2006 Zambian Presidential Election].' He went on: 'Yes, so I can talk and hold my own with . . . all of us can . . . about what's happening, but you know, as a Mzungu [white person] to get in politics . . . mmm . . . it's a different world, you know.'[31] Although both Ken and Nikki have clear political views, Nikki explained that 'we've never really been actively involved in politics, no, no . . . because I think for us that would be a wrong thing. I . . . um . . . no, I don't think it's wise.'[32]

Alfred has also never actively involved himself in politics, and was, in fact, very accepting of the one-party state. He said: 'It didn't really affect us too much. I think in Africa really the best way to run a country is just having one party. I know multiparty democracy and everything goes down well elsewhere, but in some countries we just haven't quite got to that stage.'[33] Margaret was extremely well informed about local Zambian politics, although she said: 'I don't meddle in politics at all – never have done.' It was interesting that during her interview she also revealed herself to be extremely well informed about British politics, discussing all kinds of issues in great detail – among them foreign policy, the war in Iraq, education, immigration and the NHS. She concluded by saying: 'Golly – I'd better go and get my vote organised – I have the right to vote . . . not here, but in the UK!'[34]

Asked what role, if any, white people living in Zambia had today, Gabriel responded: 'Well, it depends on the person, but I don't think they contribute politically. I honestly don't think that a European's place now is to be political. It may be, I don't know. To me it's something that has gone to the African and as such, it's better to stay out of it.' She concluded her interview by returning to this point again. 'I think that provided you are reasonable in your expectations, and provided you don't go interfering, and provided you live your own life, Zambia's a wonderful place.'[35] Donald, too, tended to keep out of politics. When asked for his views on the one-party state established by Kenneth Kaunda and his United National Independence Party (UNIP), he answered: 'Well, it didn't really worry me overmuch. The one-party state. I've always said Britain's a one-party state for five years every five years! I mean, if I may say this, they talk about democracy in Britain. Britain has democracy once every five years. They'll have democracy on May 5th [referring to the 2005 General Election], but thereafter it won't have any again for a while.'[36]

When asked about the place of white people in Zambia today, John explained:

> I decided at a fairly early stage that to survive as a white in Zambia I should stay completely out of politics. Others took a different view but have not really lasted – the main reason, I think, being that they don't represent anyone but themselves. They've no large tribal blocks behind

them as the black politicians have had, they therefore carry very little weight in the cabinet and tend to become frustrated and are displaced by what are seen as more deserving black party workers. So I kept completely clear of politics.[37]

He continued, on the role of whites in Zambia:

Although we've generally steered clear of politics, we ... I think we've helped in the background by giving advice, and at times ... service, this kind of thing, to keep the show going. It was perfectly acceptable to have whites in ... largely in advisory positions, provided that the final decisions were taken by blacks, and that was as it should be. And it was in those ... in those sort of positions that I managed to survive. In fact I never had any difficulties in finding a job, despite the policy of Zambianisation, because possibly of government experience. The qualifications I had were very scarce.[38]

One theme emerged only from the second set of interviews. This was the impact of the arrival of incomers from South Africa, Zimbabwe and elsewhere on the lives of the more deeply-rooted white Zambian population. Ken and Nikki were the first to draw attention to it. Ken explained: 'What's happened here, now, is they're bringing in this word of *indigenous* Zambian, so if you're not a black Zambian you don't qualify ... you're a second class citizen in a sense.' He continued:

I think a lot of it has started because after South Africa became acceptable to the international community we've been getting a lot of South Africans coming here ... and a lot of them don't know how to behave. There are a lot of bad news people coming up from there. And, to a certain extent a lot of the Zimbabweans don't know how to behave either. They're ... a lot of them live in a time warp. And they come up here, and treat the Zambian people very poorly, and that [there] is now a sort of backlash from that.[39]

Nikki then chipped in, saying:

It also makes things very difficult for us, because not every person in the street knows you've been here all of your life, and they say 'well, you're white, so therefore you hate me', so there's that coming into, as Ken says, the picture now. We have many black friends, black Zambian friends [. . .] but I think this sort of backlash is something very new – certainly wasn't here in the Kaunda day. I think with all these people coming back ... or looking for greener pastures in Zambia, I think this is what's happening – they still have remnants of whatever way they treated black people in South Africa, and so they think it can continue here. Well, our guys ... you know with Zambia there was never really any aggro at Independence. It happened. You either accepted it or you didn't. Those that accepted it stayed. Those that didn't got out. They moved.[40]

Margaret drew attention to the same phenomenon in her interview, although she focused more specifically on Zimbabweans who had moved to Zambia, and especially what she described as the 'Afrikaner element, not the British ones'.[41] It is hard to know exactly what to make of this disquiet about 'incomers' but there was a definite sense from Ken and Nikki that it had the potential to colour any future decision they might make about staying on in Zambia for the long term.

Lastly, all of those interviewed talked about the quality of life when asked about the advantages of staying on, and most exhibited a great determination to stay in Zambia. Donald's very quick response to my question about the advantages of living in Zambia was to draw attention to the fabulous weather, which had in fact been one of the reasons that he emigrated in the first place. He went on to say:

> ... other advantages – the cost of living, I suppose. It's certainly – I mean, one grumbles about it now, but when you look around it's certainly much better than elsewhere. The friendliness of the people. I mean, wherever you are, even in the urban areas, even in the city. There's no [inaudible] – I mean, as far ... one or two places, perhaps where you wouldn't go at night, but at least you can walk where you want ... that is, well, I'll be honest, I'd be scared to go out for a walk in London, in England. And ... I don't know what else really it is ... it's just the art of living![42]

In the world of dog breeding and showing, which is his hobby, he told me that, 'I was a big fish perhaps in a small pond.' Finally, Donald told me that he'd never leave because Zambia is where his wife is buried, and went on to say, 'I shall be buried here as well.'[43]

Gabriel also began her list of advantages with the weather, before continuing: 'No – I mean, it's a lovely country – we're fortunate in that, well we ... I mean we have a reasonable house, I can contribute a certain amount – I do the stamps and things like that – I've always done them for nothing. This is just home, and I mean ... the people are pleasant.' As regards leaving, she said: 'an African country, well, it's a volatile thing. And possibly, if life became impossible here one would have to leave, but ... er, I hope not!'[44] John responded: 'I had this strong affection for the country, attachment to it, and during those years when I was with those various commercial concerns we had some very good times with the children, fishing and hunting expeditions, boating on Kariba, and this kind of thing which they would never have had if we'd gone to England or somewhere like it.' John's wife is probably less attached to Zambia than her husband, and would be willing to contemplate leaving and relocating to the UK where her sons are, but it would take a lot to uproot her husband. 'Well, if there was a Congo or Angola type of situation we'd have to consider that, but, er, I'd be very reluctant to leave.'[45]

Ken and Nikki look to the future with optimism, but do not rule out leaving if health or security considerations forced them to. Nikki said: 'Thinking of leaving . . . I think as age . . . as you get older, we worry about our health, medical facilities . . . and also becoming targets in a country where security is not good. So no, we have no plans of leaving, but I think there, you know, the thought of all that is there, you know, and we would have to . . . address it in a couple of years' time.'[46] When asked where they might gravitate if they did leave Ken found himself at something of a loss. 'I don't know, I don't know,' he said. 'We don't want to live in South Africa. The weather in the UK . . .' then he laughed.[47] Alfred contemplated leaving Zambia for Australia at one point in order to join two of his brothers, but now feels that the only thing that would make him leave would be 'if it became like a situation like it is in Zimbabwe'. For him, Zambia's advantages far outweighed the disadvantages – not just the weather, the people and the standard of living, but also the landscape. 'I just love it when I can go to the bush, just to relax, see the animals, do a bit of fishing, and rest.'[48]

This series of factors influencing people's decisions at Independence and in the postcolonial period about whether to stay on in Africa or to leave is by no means exhaustive, and it is based on interviews with a very small sample, but it is certainly indicative of people's motivations and the ways that they conceive of their identity. Much of what these interview subjects have said seems fairly obvious – particularly to anyone who has spent any time in Africa among settlers or former settler communities – but, nonetheless, there has been very little academic writing about people's reasons for staying on, and testimonies do need to be collected from this ageing cohort before it is too late.

Conclusion

This research brings into question the neat distinction often drawn between the 'settler' and the official or colonial civil servant. The distinction between 'settler' and official is a much more difficult one than the historiography sometimes suggests. It could be argued, for instance, that John started off as a colonial administrator and ended up as a settler, if indeed that is what he is. When does someone become a settler? Does it involve the purchase of land or property, or is it about a decision to stay somewhere permanently following migration? How can we best define a settler? All too often in writing on Africa (and on other colonial and imperial settings) academics do not define what they mean by the word. It is a term which many people use in quite uncritical ways, as if the definition is obvious and straightforward. Moreover, if the question of when someone becomes a settler is a difficult one, it is equally difficult to establish when someone stops being a settler and becomes something else. Gabriel would identify herself as a Zambian, having taken Zambian citizenship at Independence, but her African neighbours might judge her as a settler, based purely on the colour of her skin. Remember Nikki's concerns in this regard. And what about the term expatriate? Is this more useful in some of these cases? How people describe themselves seems important in helping us to find ways of describing them, and each of these terms were deemed problematic by my informants, who preferred instead to describe themselves as 'part of the furniture'.

These are messy categories, and it may be more useful to think of settler and official as being at two ends of a continuum, or as overlapping circles, or at least to recognise that people move between them with time and contingency. What happens when someone from the colonial administration marries someone from a 'settler' family? Might we see this as yet another category – a sort of hybrid family? There are also other white people in colonial and postcolonial Africa that fit neither the category of 'settler' or 'official' – for instance missionaries and NGO workers, described colourfully by Gabriel as 'birds of passage'.[49] Therefore, notions surrounding the complexity of the categories of 'settler' and 'official' need to be fed much more explicitly into the literature on colonialism and postcolonialism in Africa. Nonetheless, there can be real differences between 'settlers' and officialdom, notwithstanding the difficulties with the categories. For this author, the idea of home, and the intent to stay on (not necessarily fulfilled, but there, nonetheless) are key elements within defining a 'settler' as against a more temporary sojourner. However, it is crucial to remember that none of these categories is monolithic. Maybe it is time that historians moved away from talking about the 'settler view' or the 'official view' of decolonisation and Independence, and started looking towards the full range of views represented within both of these messy groups.

Notes

1 Figures from L. H. Gann and P. Duignan, *White Settlers in Tropical Africa* (London, 1962).
2 An exception to this is an excellent article on the fate of Europeans in Independent Kenya, by G. Nardocchio-Jones, which seeks to dispel the myth of a 'mass exodus' of Europeans from Kenya at Independence and reveals that there was only a 25 per cent decline in the European population between its peak in 1960 and 1967. Departures of Europeans in the years around Independence were offset by 'a continuous stream' of new European immigration in the years after it. Nardocchio-Jones draws significantly on British government documentation to paint a picture of the fate of Europeans in Kenya at the level of the group, but does not touch in detail on the drivers behind the decisions made by individuals and families. G. Nardocchio-Jones, 'From Mau Mau to Middlesex? The Fate of Europeans in Independent Kenya',

Comparative Studies of South Asia, Africa and the Middle East, 6:3 (2006), pp. 491–505. Another very short work that does deal specifically with settlers in the postcolonial period is J. R. Scarritt, 'European Adjustment to Economic Reforms and Political Consolidation in Zambia', *Issue: A Journal of Opinion*, 3:2 (1973), pp. 18–22. Other works touch on the fate of particular groups of settlers or expatriates, for instance Georgina Sinclair's work on colonial policing and the end of Empire. She observes that 'with the onset of decolonisation following the Second World War, many expatriate police officers sought employment elsewhere; a significant number stayed on within the police forces of the newly independent states or moved to other Commonwealth police forces'. G. Sinclair, *At the End of the Line: Colonial Policing and the Imperial Endgame, 1945–1980* (Manchester, 2006), p. 1.

3   G. Boynton, *Last Days in Cloud Cuckooland: Dispatches from White Africa* (New York, 1997); S. Taylor, *Livingstone's Tribe: A Journey from Zanzibar to the Cape* (London, 1999).

4   Taylor, *Livingstone's Tribe*, ix.

5   See, for instance, C. Baker, 'The Administrative Service of Malawi: A Case Study in Africanisation', *Journal of Modern African Studies*, 10:4 (1972), pp. 543–60; and W. Tordoff (ed.), *Administration in Zambia* (Manchester, 1980).

6   Figures such as Sir James Wicks, Philip Leakey and Richard Leakey in Kenya; Ivor Evans, James John Skinner, Brian Doyle and Andrew Sardanis in Zambia; Roland Brown, Derek Bryceson and Mary F. Hancock in Tanzania; or Sir Garfield Todd and a number of white MPs in Zimbabwe.

7   Baker, 'Administrative Service of Malawi', pp. 546–7.

8   P. Scott, *Staying On* (London, 1977 [reprint]), p. 231.

9   A. Ross, 'The Capricorn Africa Society and European Reactions to African Nationalism in Tanganyika, 1949–1960', *African Affairs*, 76:305 (1977), p. 519.

10   *Ibid.*

11   B. J. Phiri, 'The Capricorn Africa Society Revisited: The Impact of Liberalism in Zambia's Colonial History, 1949–1963', *International Journal of African Historical Studies*, 24:1 (1991), pp. 65–83; D. Kennedy, 'Constructing the Colonial Myth of Mau Mau', *International Journal of African Historical Studies*, 25:2 (1992), pp. 241–60.

12   The now defunct BECM in Bristol holds an extensive collection of oral history interviews relating to the Empire (in excess of 1,200). Around 70 per cent of the collection consists of interviews with former colonial civil servants and settlers, with the remainder being interviews with the formerly colonised. The collection has only a very tiny number of interviews with people who stayed on after Independence.

13   See, British Empire and Commonwealth Museum, *Voices and Echoes – Research Paper 5: A Catalogue of Oral History Holdings of the British Empire and Commonwealth Museum* (Bristol, 1999).

14   BECM, Oral History Collection: Roly Armour (Tape T/003), Tom Askwith (Tape 172), Juanita Carberry (Tape 429), Desmond Chalmers (Tapes 139 and 140), Lewis Collings-Wells (Tapes 062 and 063), Helen Haylett (Tapes 341and 342), W. Hutton (Tape 234), Sir John Johnston (Tapes 297 and 298), Mr Mackintosh (Tape 635), Christine Marsh (Tape 736), Charles Meek (Tape 707), Henry and Anna Osmaston (Tape 196), Richard Posnett (Tape 430), Ian Rand (Tape 245), Randal Sadleir (Tape 443), Robin Saville (Tape 767), David Taylor (Tapes 468 and 469), Rev. Laurence Totty (Tape 249), Nigel Walsh (Tape 671), Margaret Wood (Tape 514), Vivien Young (Tape 118).

15   My interview respondents are identified by first names rather than their full names in the text, since their identities are not important to the overall argument in this chapter. Nevertheless, each of the respondents has given full informed consent including an agreement that both their names and testimony may be published.

16   The quotations from the interviews are transcribed verbatim, and include gaps, false starts, 'ums' and 'ers', since these are indicative of the respondents' thought processes.

17   R. Holland, S. Williams and T. Barringer (eds), *The Iconography of Independence:*

'Freedoms at Midnight' (London, 2010), offers illuminating insights into many of these Independence Day ceremonies, but unfortunately Northern Rhodesia/Zambia is not among the case studies.

18 John's wife Gretta was present at my interview with her husband and sometimes prompted him or commented herself on my questions.
19 Interview with John Hudson, Lusaka (April 2005).
20 Interview with Gabriel Ellison, Lusaka (April 2005).
21 Interview with Donald Fluck, Lusaka (April 2005).
22 Interview with Ken Barron, Lusaka (August 2006).
23 Interview with Nikki Barron, Lusaka (August 2006).
24 Interview with Linelle Myers, Lusaka (August 2006).
25 Interview with Alfred Francis, Lusaka (August 2006).
26 Interview with Margaret Dodgson, Lusaka (August 2006).
27 Interview with Linelle Myers.
28 Interview with Margaret Dodgson.
29 Interview with Ken Barron.
30 Interview with Alfred Francis.
31 Interview with Ken Barron.
32 Interview with Nikki Barron.
33 Interview with Alfred Francis.
34 Interview with Margaret Dodgson.
35 Interview with Gabriel Ellison.
36 Interview with Donald Fluck.
37 Interview with John Hudson.
38 *Ibid.*
39 Interview with Ken Barron.
40 Interview with Nikki Barron.
41 Interview with Margaret Dodgson.
42 Interview with Donald Fluck.
43 *Ibid.*
44 Interview with Gabriel Ellison.
45 Interview with John Hudson.
46 Interview with Nikki Barron.
47 Interview with Ken Barron.
48 Interview with Alfred Francis.
49 Gabriel Ellison, 'A Letter to Martha', unpublished manuscript for a short story (*c.*1994).

CHAPTER 10

'I'm a citizen of the world': late twentieth-century British emigration and global identities – the end of the 'British World'?

A. James Hammerton

Serial migrants, global citizens

In 1993 Adam Salt, a single 27–year-old from a Staffordshire village, arrived at an expatriate compound in Brunei on a two-year contract to teach English as a foreign language. Adam came from a lower middle-class background, and was one of the many beneficiaries of free post-war tertiary education; in the mid-1980s he had enjoyed his years at Manchester University studying physiology and then gaining a teaching diploma. Teaching employment followed promptly, as did European travel, and he witnessed the immediate exciting afterglow of the East European revolutions. After that, he recalled, 'I was just ready to see more.' Any destination that afforded teaching work would have satisfied him, the more exotic the better, and he flirted with prospects in Jordan and Syria. But the destination was settled fortuitously with a timely advertisement for the teaching position in Brunei.[1]

This was a familiar set of motivations for young single 'sojourner migrants', or expatriates, in the post-war decades: adventure, the exotic and even a lucrative working holiday, in effect travel as consumerism. But for Adam his coming of age in the 1980s brought a further factor which was unique for many other migrants, single and married, in the 1980s and early 1990s. This was an ideological motivation which drove some to characterise themselves as 'Thatcher refugees', driven away by perceived hostile politics and the destruction of a civil society. Adam traced his convictions to the Falklands War: 'I was 16 in 1982 when the Falklands happened and I, I was disgusted and appalled by it and I still remain to this day . . . It turned me against cheap nasty jingoism . . . My reaction was to get out, I just thought oh, I just didn't see that there was any particular way back for Britain by that point.'[2] Such ideological spurs to migration might be thought to be a luxury of late twentieth-century affluent societies, but it should be noted that many of these 'Thatcher refugees' were also economic migrants, especially in the early 1980s when unemployment surpassed three million. But ideological hostility could also pave the way for lasting antagonism to Britain and thus stimulate a more mobile future and shifts in identity which might loosen commitment to a British attachment. It was not, of course, the first time that political values drove migration decisions. Similar sentiments were evident, for example, in the deep ideological disillusion expressed by many post-war British emigrants with the austerity of the decade of rationing and shortage after 1945, which could impel them to leave, often with strong antipathy to Britain.[3]

In Adam's case his Brunei sojourn extended from two to five years. Besides giving him a lifelong distaste for the bad habits of British expatriates, it enabled him to meet the Australian woman who became his wife. And while they married during a return visit to England, and his wife would have been happy to settle there, Adam preferred to re-emigrate; their next stop, in 1997, was Melbourne, for which Adam easily obtained a spouse visa and in short order they found good jobs and bought a suburban house near the beach. Eight years later, to all appearances, Adam was a largely settled migrant but, turned 40, he insisted that he remained open to further migration, particularly to the United States, and even, only at his wife's insistence, a temporary return to Britain, a country for which he now feels no special attachment and expressly no patriotic sentiments. His identity, he insists, is expressly that of world citizen, uniquely suited to his occupation. 'Somebody said we live in the age of the genuine teacher', he reflected, '[the] idea that you're able to go from place to place to place, [like] I suppose even medieval stone masons used to do.'[4]

Adam, then, has joined that increasing number of British migrants who adopt the 'world citizen', or cosmopolitan, identity, often with strong feelings of rejection of any close attachment to a single nation, whether it be their birthplace or current adopted country. A number of them, like Adam, act out the identity by becoming 'serial migrants' in youth and middle age; others become transnational 'grey nomads' in later years. Arguably, these tendencies point to ways in which personal practices reflect the broader late-twentieth century trends of globalisation. But all of them illustrate ways in which British emigration has undergone significant changes since the heyday of the immediate post-war emigration schemes to Commonwealth countries of settlement. The old loyalties, which comforted post-war British migrants that they were 'moving to another part of Britain' (albeit often shaken loyalties after arrival when they confronted the 'shock of the new'),[5] have progressively been eclipsed by a more globalised, and in some respects a

European, outlook, among migrants with a more middle-class profile than in former years.

These findings are drawn from a project based largely on personal testimonies and life histories from migrants, in oral and written form. In the absence of official data on migrant subjectivity around issues such as identity, outlook and globalising practices, personal testimony, often referred to as 'qualitative research' has become an essential resort for scholars of modern migration – sociologists, anthropologists and geographers as well as historians. Issues of representation and typicality are routinely at the heart of such research, and among oral historians there has been lively debate about ways in which 'life history research', often thick description of a 'telling case', offers a useful alternative to studies based on 'representative samples' of informants and illuminates the complex interplay between social forces and life experience.[6] This is particularly important for migration history, and the research described here goes beyond the conventional description of experience to explore the perceptions, outlooks and identities which flow from transnational migration practices. The project drew on the recorded life histories of 129 British emigrants to various destinations, mostly to the old Commonwealth, since the mid-1960s. Sixty-seven of these, or 52 per cent, had undertaken return or 'serial' migration, some returning again to the original destination, more emigrating to a second or third country. We know that such complex migration behaviour reflects wider experiences of mobility which accelerated during the second half of the twentieth century with the rise of mass travel, practices such as expatriate employment, extended backpacking and working holidays. One sociologist investigating recent British middle-class migration to Paris noted that skilled international migration had 'become a "normal" middle-class activity rather than something exclusively confined to an economic elite', part of a wave of 'middling transnationalism' comprising more complex patterns of mobility.[7] Identities like that of the 'world citizen' are, perhaps, unsurprising consequences of such behaviour.

Late twentieth century migrants and demographic change

A summary of the main demographic features of these trends should provide some context for the personal narratives. For convenience this chapter uses the term 'British Diaspora' to describe the outflow of British citizens, notwithstanding some of the persuasive reservations about its applicability which have been advanced cogently by Stephen Constantine.[8] Eric Richards has summarised the conventional wisdom that the post-war surge in emigrant numbers to old Commonwealth countries was followed by decline from the 1970s to what amounted to 'the end of the diaspora' as Britain's emigrants 'take leave of their imperial past'.[9] In relative terms there is much truth to this. The 'permanent' outflow of British nationals peaked in 1967 at over 238,000, and from the early 1970s, following tightening of admission criteria in traditional receiving countries, declined to a low point of over 102,000 in 1984. But since then the 'decline' progressively reversed itself to a high point of over 207,000 in 2004, and throughout the 1980s and 1990s the steadily increasing numbers mostly exceeded those of the 1950s.[10] So in numerical terms it is difficult to see any dramatic 'end' to the diaspora in the late twentieth century.

But there have been ongoing changes in the nature of that emigration, particularly the destinations. In the 1950s of course the old white settlement countries dominated, with Australia and Canada intermittently being the first choice of migrants. In fact, for much of the 1950s Canada was the clearly preferred destination, until 1958 when Australia became the major preference, where it has mostly remained ever since (occasionally equal with the United States), while the numbers to Canada have fallen below the second country of choice. Moreover, since the 1990s the British have remained the most numerous single country of origin migrants in Australia while in Canada they have slipped to occupying ninth and tenth. In 2002, for example the British emigrant numbers were to Australia 18,000, the USA 16,000, New Zealand 9,000 and Canada 6,000.[11]

What this focus on shifts within the 'British World' masks, however, is the steady increase, since the mid-1970s, in permanent British settlement in non-British countries, and most significantly in those of the European Union. In some recent years these have exceeded numbers emigrating to 'old Commonwealth' countries (for example in 2002 69,000 to the European Union against 44,000 to old Commonwealth and 18,000 to the USA).[12] Most strikingly, by 2006 in the lists of British citizens living 'permanently' abroad (that is for a year or longer), the top country, Australia, is followed by Spain in clear second place, and then the USA, Canada, Ireland, New Zealand, South Africa, France, Germany and Cyprus in that order. Spain and France are the new factors in this changing profile, and however much we may explain it away by newly important motives, like retirement villas for the ageing, it constitutes a major shift away from the 'British World' among emigrants from varied backgrounds, and signifies a readiness to look beyond the familiar destinations – the old 'comfort zones' of presumed cultural and linguistic familiarity for permanent settlement. This, perhaps, constitutes the strongest argument for characterising the British exodus as a genuinely globally dispersed 'diaspora' – in 2006, 9.2 per cent of the UK population were living abroad permanently, larger than the number of foreigners resident in Britain and proportionally the world's third largest diaspora.[13]

British migrants and cosmopolitanism

At the individual level, the testimony from British emigrants since the early 1970s echoes these shifting demographic profiles, at least through the lens of their recollections in taped interviews and written memoirs.[14] These sources of memory, it must be stressed, give a different impression of migrants' past lives than other personal sources might convey, for example in the series of letters that Stephen Constantine uses in this volume to explore Maidie's migration experience. They do bring to the foreground migrants' various reflections on their identity, which can be spontaneous, but to a degree at least they are solicited through questioning, and thus require care not to over-read but to approach in the context of the full life history. Statements of identity and belonging, which are grounded in the memory of life history experience, are likely to carry more conviction and authenticity than simple statements of opinion detached from their empirical foundations.

The purpose here is not to examine the migration of those who are turning in increasing numbers to European or other non-British World destinations, but rather to glimpse ways in which a creeping global outlook has influenced those British migrants who have continued to settle in old Commonwealth countries. Adam Salt, whose story is summarised at the beginning of this chapter, embarked on his journey with a complete open mind as to where he might go and where he might end, with the mindset we now associate with modern mobility, whether in travel or migration. It is usually identified with backpacking youth of the last two or three decades, but is by no means exclusive to them, as aspects of the transnational 'grey nomad' phenomenon, at the other end of the age spectrum, indicate. It is also a process that set in, in various ways, far earlier. Eric Richards reminds us that there were high rates of return migration, and to a degree serial migration, in the nineteenth century.[15] But in the mid-twentieth century we can see the habit and mentality of continuous mobility taking off in more enduring and substantial form during the heyday of the assisted Commonwealth migration schemes of the 1950s and 1960s, even among some of those who give the appearance of traditional and well settled migrants.

A British-Australian migrant, David Spurgeon, provides a good example of the shifting possibilities. David emigrated alone in 1968 to Sydney at the age of 22, and seems at first glance to be a classic 'success story' case of traditional one-way settlement, although from memory his introspective reasons for leaving appear to be modern rather than traditional. He had emerged from the lower middle class in Solihull, was disillusioned with his low-paid teaching job, and insisted that he left as a result of an 'existential crisis': 'One does naïve things as a youth . . . I was obsessed with freedom, and I loved reading Jean-Paul Sartre I remember . . . I'm sure I didn't understand it properly . . . but any story where the hero was free, to do what he wanted to do, was presumably making love to as many women as possible and spending a lot of money, I'm sure it was that conventional image, but I felt trapped in England, because I didn't have any money, and, and I couldn't get away from this terrible climate.' A holiday camping trip with his girlfriend to Spain connected his crisis with thoughts of migration. They were 'in a *tent*, north of Spain and *wow*, there was two weeks of unbroken sunshine and I thought . . . You know this is, it's possible, you know, that there is somewhere in the world where the sun does shine.'[16]

David's main narrative of his life in Australia – what might dominate if we had a collection of his letters home – is one of career success; from school teaching he ultimately became a tertiary teacher of dance at university, married an Australian, and they remained deliberately childless, in part to facilitate that 'freedom' which continued to be central to his identity. His actions and reflections on them, though, suggest other priorities, which prompt a preoccupation with his identity. Unlike the immediate post-war generation of British-Australian migrants his return trips were frequent, almost annual, and gradually moved from simple family visits to more ambitious tourism and adventure. His brother, though, emigrated to France, and although their relationship was not close the connection gradually inspired David's further mobility, so that eventually France eclipsed England in his affections. The facility of academic study leaves in Paris reinforced his attachment to France. 'If I was banished from Australia', he reflected, 'I would live in France, not England. So I've always valued my English passport because it is now a European passport. So I think of myself very much as Australian and European, and I'm very, very proud of the EU, I mean I think that that's the way forward.' David retains a residual attachment to the delights of the English countryside 'on a beautiful day. And a good pub . . . everything's got to be a beautiful day . . . the sun has to be shining'.[17] But to the extent to which national identity matters to him at all it now revolves around a transnational Australian and European attachment, and since the prospects of actually living in France have remained remote, the European attachment is one bound up with the imagination as much as a lived reality.

David's forthright Francophilia is not uncommon among his

generation of migrants, and for those who became financially prosperous enough, the genuine second home in France or Spain came within reach. Another 1968 migrant, Gerry Bullon, proud of his Jewish and Scottish heritage and his adopted Australian identity, added a further enthusiasm for France, and bought an apartment on the Riviera in 1996, where he spends several months each year; alongside the hordes of British expatriate Francophiles he finds networks of Australian, and British-Australian, settlers as well, and regularly reflects on the connections and alliances. 'I don't know *what* there is about the Australian-French thing and why that's begun, I think it's got much to do probably with the First World War. And the, the ties that *bind* the French and the Australians together; the French seem to be very respectful of Australians fighting on their soil to help them.'[18]

British migrants adopt the varieties of global and European identities described above with varying degrees of enthusiasm. In some cases, particularly when driven by ideological conviction, like Adam Salt's revulsion against Margaret Thatcher's politics, the new identity might be adopted with particular passion as a deliberate alternative to spurned British loyalties. But it is just as likely that a cosmopolitan identity will be held lightly, as a product of empirical migration experience in which new opportunities for mobility create lifestyle opportunities carrying little explicit political meaning. Indeed, a cosmopolitan outlook can work as a virtual invitation to eschew political identity or patriotism of any kind, or at least to enjoy a multiplicity of national loyalties simultaneously.[19]

Nick Collins, who was a childhood friend of David Spurgeon in Solihull, and pursued a similar migration trajectory, but to Canada rather than Australia, exemplifies this 'light cosmopolitanism'. Born in 1945, he came of age in the late 1960s when global travel was becoming accessible to increasing numbers of young people. But the source of his initial wandering was an early-developed talent for languages. 'I went to Paris when I was 11 and was amazed that I could communicate in French. By 14 I had visited 14 different countries. Heavily into languages I read Spanish and French at King's College, London. I lived in Spain for a while in both 1964 and 1965 and Paris in 1966.' Even before attending university his European travel, first with family and later alone, including three summers with a French family, acculturated him to European ways and broadened his outlook. 'I realised very quickly the world is bigger than Solihull or even the very good school that I went to.' At 18 he spent six months in the Canary Islands where he discovered an entrepreneurial flair and earned large amounts of money running his own 'language school'. His Spanish studies at university led to an external year at Madrid University in 1965, where, again, he prospered from teaching English as a second language part-time, a passport to buying a house near Alicante. The house has remained his Spanish foot in the ground, and years later, while living in Vancouver, it became a preferred attraction, rather than England, during the long summer breaks.[20]

Graduating from university in 1967, Nick was ready for further travels, and followed backpacking friends to British Columbia and the American north-west, taking any work which was offered. But opportunities in language teaching soon attracted him to Vancouver, where he eventually traded his Spanish expertise for teaching English as a second language.[21] The 'ESL' option ultimately led to a highly successful career, punctuated by marriage to an English migrant, a one-year return to England in 1973, divorce in 1996 and subsequent marriage to a Japanese wife, also a Spanish specialist. But while settlement in Vancouver proved to be highly congenial, he insists that he never, like his friend David Spurgeon in Sydney, entertained any deliberate intention of migration. Rather, his preoccupation with travel drove his decision-making until he was, virtually by serendipity, settled in Vancouver. 'So my immigration [was] really, really a slow and comfortable process. There was no moment of Eureka and, honestly, there was not ever really a plan. Things evolved and I let them develop happily.' In his memory now even his career highlights are eclipsed by his frequent travels, some of them work related, but especially the summer sojourns in Spain. 'It was hard to leave Spain sometimes, because I'd get into the whole rhythm of, of the language and the idiom and, and the people and ... I've known people there 20 years, some people in Madrid 40 years, that was nice. Also my job at Capilano sent me to Japan about five times ... I got very interested in Asia, and I also got to go to Central and South America with Spanish, and maybe go to Uruguay next year, so my job kept giving me interesting things, over and above the holidays. So I was always like, I had the next trip in my mind ... at least one ahead.'[22]

Over the years, apart from diminishing family connections, the attractions and networks in Spain, the global travel, and his enjoyment of the delights of Vancouver, have overshadowed Nick's earlier attachment to England, which now survives for him as an occasional tourist destination for theatre visits and meeting old friends in the pub. By contrast, Spain offers both climatic and cultural attractions. 'When I get on that motorway, we come out of the airport, Alicante Airport, within about 40 seconds you're on a motorway, and I know in about an hour I'll be walking into a house that I've owned for 25 years in Spain, which has got a garden and a pool and, and the next morning I'm in the village and people say: "Where have you been, I haven't seen you for a while."' We might expect this experience to translate into a throughgoing global identity. Yet Nick promptly denied any explicit 'citizen of the world' sentiment. He took out Canadian citizenship in the 1970s to 'regularise' his status and to enable him to vote, but while Vancouver gradually came to feel like 'home' it never supplanted residual feelings of belonging to England and Spain, and indeed his entrepreneurial ventures in Spain suggest that if he had wished he could have settled there just as successfully as in Canada.[23]

These are generally regarded as the preconditions for a mixed or 'hybrid identity', but it is perhaps more pertinent to note that they underline a relative lack of interest in any identity at all attached to politics and nation. Like Maidie, in Chapter 8, Nick had little interest in such matters, and his matter-of-fact attitude to his migration decisions seems to have carried over to issues of identity. His frequent mobility and his cosmopolitanism certainly underline the loosening bonds of the 'British World' among British migrants, which in his case was facilitated by his competence in foreign languages, but his role as teacher, academic and traveller do much more to define his identity than any political or cultural loyalties. Moreover, his casual approach to migration and belonging underlines the tendency in the late twentieth century for migration to become a form of consumerism.

Women 'citizens of the world' and the cosmopolitan identity

The above examples, all drawn from men's experiences, should not mislead us into thinking that global mobility in the late twentieth century was largely a masculine affair. As early as the 1950s the eager young British sojourners who seized the new, usually assisted, migration opportunities to embark on long-term working holidays around the world were as often women as men. Indeed, many female occupations, such as nursing, physiotherapy, clerical work and hairdressing, were uniquely mobile and in high demand. Young women's routinely declared motivation for these travels, which were frequently transformed from intended working holidays into permanent migration, was simply 'adventure', soon to become the virtual trademark of the backpacking generation.[24] A cosmopolitan identity, light or otherwise, was to follow.

Jenny Armati, whose eleven 'serial migrations' extended from 1971 to 2004, exemplifies some of the possibilities. She was born in 1945 in London into an unconventional middle-class family; her parents, later divorced, were dedicated communists and her mother urged her never to marry and have children. Jenny left school at 16 and went to work in a department store. Unexpectedly, this gave rise to a promising career, driven by the fashion revolution in late 1960s London, as she developed a flair for merchandising and changed jobs regularly, each time for better money. At 18 she was working for a large chain, 'Chelsea Girl', training staff in fashion promotion and presentation, all at extreme odds with her parents' ideals. At this stage there was little to drive her away from the excitements of London and a challenging and mobile career. 'Every week we'd go and do a different shop, all round the country, so in my 20s I had a fantastic time, we used to go and stay at a hotel, we'd go and work for 12 hours a day, but it was just fabulous, absolutely fun and I did that for eight years.' But while this served as a solid foundation for future career moves, after the eight years the excitement began to pall, she suffered bouts of depression, became 'fed up' with living in Earl's Court and responded eagerly to the alluring images of Australia described to her by Australian neighbours. 'I met these, oh fabulous Australians who lived in Earl's Court, and I thought I would go: "I'm off, I'm going to go, I want a bit of that."' Beginning with a short-lived sojourn with an Australian boyfriend in Hong Kong, she soon moved on to Sydney alone in search of 'adventure', thrived in her career, began another relationship with an Englishman, and stayed for seven years, with a move from Sydney to Perth.[25]

While her ultimate return to England in 1977 was motivated by family illness, it began a turbulent series of changes in Jenny's private life and places of residence. She revived her career in England but two years later was back in Australia, where she flourished again, bought her own house, and by 1982 she had met and married Douglas, an Australian, and inherited his two stepchildren. At the time Douglas was a struggling information technology consultant, and together they developed a variety of business ventures, which in 1991 took them to France, living with Jenny's expatriate brother, and later back to England in Suffolk. While Jenny revelled in the novelty of living in France, these were times of hardship, and in Suffolk she turned to cooking in pubs to make ends meet while Douglas worked on an information technology text, which they hoped would turn their fortunes. When this actually happened, in the mid-1990s, and an American company in San Francisco hired him on a lucrative contract, their lives were indeed transformed. For Jenny 'it really was like winning the lottery, because he was offered a job, you know with a huge salary and with share options ... And our life was turned around overnight, yes.' A large house in Suffolk followed, and Jenny commuted regularly to spend time with Douglas in San Francisco. The freedom of their new prosperity spurred Jenny to turn to painting, which itself became a further lucrative and fulfilling career pursuit. At the end of the contract period Douglas returned to Suffolk, where they were happy to settle permanently, but ultimately anxiety about being apart from Douglas's children in Perth drove them back to Australia in 2004. On reflection, Jenny considered that the final move back was the only one not driven by her zest for 'adventure', motivated instead for her by a sense of guilt about keeping Douglas apart from his children.[26]

Adventure for Jenny became code for openness to movement and resettlement, evident in her insistence that, 'I've always thought of myself as a global person', and that while she considers herself to be Australian after years of residence, nationality and patriotism is simply of no real importance. She struggles now to detect any overt elements of Englishness in her character. Like most British migrants she has never had time for British loyalty organisations, nor for robust expressions of patriotism, and her admitted loyalty to Australia is lightly worn. Her 'citizen of the world' identity, she acknowledges, has more to do with a willingness to live anywhere that is congenial than a political statement. 'I could go and live anywhere I think, really, as long as it had some *aesthetic* about it.' Her cosmopolitanism has grown out of her experience of serial and return migration, but it is an apolitical cosmopolitanism in which her place in the British World is of minor consequence.[27]

These trends might be dismissed as little more than the globetrotting indulgences of the wealthy First World, but from the perspective of British emigration history they illustrate the creeping globalisation of British-Commonwealth migrant habits, even among the immediate post-war generation. For migrants since the early 1990s global engagement is virtually taken for granted. Settlement might follow corporate employment contracts for expatriates of the kind we saw with Adam Salt's sojourn in Brunei. The best known of these have been in the Middle East, notably Saudi Arabia, but they can serve as the first leg of a process of 'serial migration' that leads to settlement in Commonwealth or other countries. And the children of former migrants, especially those who later returned to Britain, often carry their parents' habits of mobility into a later chapter of migration. In these ways, again, the post-war leap in migration practice has had enduring and compounding effects. But, as most of the above cases illustrate, the European Union relationship has now brought about a much greater readiness to consider the Continent as a preferred site of settlement, and for it to remain in the imagination as an alternative for those who continue to settle in old Commonwealth countries.

Two brief portrait sketches of young women migrants since the 1980s illustrate some of the ways in which Europe has become intertwined with the migrant mentality, even when the experience of it is minimal. Claire Sowerby was actually born in New Zealand, the daughter of recent migrant parents who promptly returned to England when she was only six months old, mainly because Claire's mother, with a new baby, missed the support of her own mother. Her English childhood was disrupted by her father's job mobility, and later her parents' conflict and divorce impelled her to leave home early – a common story among our migrant informants. After university she cultivated a career in fashion, a passport to routine travel around Europe, and for extended periods in India. Marriage in 1996 to Jon, a man ten years her senior, also with travel enthusiasms, crystallised a project for 'temporary' migration, with the goal of earning more money, then returning to England to renovate their house. Claire's preference, driven by her 'romantic idea' of living in Paris, was for France, but she ruefully admitted that her limited language skills ruled it out, although with lingering regret: 'But then I think if I'd gone then I would actually have got to speak French, which would be good because I'd like Eva [her child] to have a second language.' While contemplating the possibility of a contract in Saudi Arabia a job offer from Melbourne for Jon settled the issue and within seven weeks, in 1997, they were in Melbourne, with the customary visa hurdles eased by Claire's dual citizenship with New Zealand. Despite her early homesickness the one-year project became permanent, although they still discuss further moves, including to her native New Zealand, and her virtually annual return visits to England assuaged the homesickness, but now Britain feels less like home with each visit. With each of them enjoying a 'fantastic job', the attractions of Melbourne have outweighed further mobility, and any thoughts of future mobility, with India as an attractive possibility, now take for granted the assumption of ultimate return to their permanent Melbourne base.[28]

Viviane King, who emigrated to Australia in 1982, fifteen years earlier than Claire, had similar experiences and attitudes, not least in her attachment to Europe. This stemmed mostly from the heritage of her French mother, frequent sojourns in France, a year studying in Grenoble and a degree in French Studies and Politics at the London School of Economics. Her 1982 move to Melbourne extended from six to eighteen months, where she worked for companies with French connections, but after return to complete a Masters degree she promptly re-emigrated, describing herself, like Adam Salt, as an economic 'refugee from Thatcherism'. She worked for a series of politicians on the left and right in Melbourne and Sydney, and now lives in Sydney with her Australian husband and 9–year-old daughter who attends a French immersion school. While feeling that she belongs to no particular country, her attachment to Australia as home has deepened, and she now shares the common resignation that her own mobility will inevitably extend to her daughter, and not necessarily be defined by British World boundaries.

> I wonder how I'll feel if my daughter goes off to live at the other end of the world, as I did. It's inevitable that she will do this as it is part of growing up to move to other countries and experience different lifestyles. It's a lot easier to do now and of course she has British citizenship so she will have no problems doing so. Communications are a lot better now (email, Skype) so living at the other end of the world is not as drastic as it was when I arrived here in 1982.[29]

There was a further thread in common in the stories told by these two women, one which has emerged as a familiar 'lifestyle' theme among our late twentieth-century informants. Both these women were interviewed in their homes in city centre apartments in Melbourne and Sydney. In Australian cities especially this remains a relatively rare choice compared to inner or outer suburban living, especially among those with children. For both of them this was a deliberate choice, partly in opposition to suburban housing, but more emphatically in reaction to their upbringing in provincial English towns: Claire mainly in Ely, Viviane in Maidenhead. Viviane referred to 'growing up, in "white bread" England in the '60s', and like Claire fled as early as possible to life in London, which was a prelude act of migration to international mobility. And it is an irony that each sought and discovered their urban orientation again in Australia, since the previous generation of urban migrants commonly expressed their horror at the narrow conservative provincialism of Commonwealth cities like Toronto, Vancouver, Auckland, Wellington, Melbourne and Perth.[30] Most of these cities are now intensely multicultural, which adds a further attraction to migrants with a cosmopolitan orientation. It should be noted, though, that this urban theme in migration coexists with a counter trend among late twentieth-century migrants, in what is commonly referred to as 'treechange' and 'seachange' phenomena. This refers to the use of migration to effect a major lifestyle change by avoiding the city life migrants had known in Britain in favour of movement to rural bush areas, often with an ecological land care agenda, or to coastal areas with an accent on escape to a beachside lifestyle. This is the subject for a separate discussion, but it is significant that many of these migrants developed their environmental outlook in urban environments, often linked to left-wing politics, and that their approach to mobility and cosmopolitanism is not usually far removed from those with urban preferences.

The urban theme, though, underlines the cosmopolitan and transnational outlook in late twentieth-century British migration, in which

British World destinations still dominate numerically – just – but have lost their former monopoly. And even among those still arriving in British World countries, the openness to global movement, and European settlement especially, has come to complicate the old comfort zone attachment of 'moving from one part of Britain to another'. Even for those with a traditional single country migration profile, the place that Europe and the wider world occupies in the imagination, in their holiday excursion activity and in their declared identity has progressively eclipsed the Commonwealth mindset and juggling of British and Commonwealth loyalties and identities in later life. Here the sense of identity is never far removed from life experience, and often connects the migration trajectory with habits of consumerism. In the cases examined here the 'citizen of the world' identity might be held with particular passion as a matter of political conviction, but it is equally likely that it will be carried as a 'light cosmopolitanism', a reminder perhaps that migrant identities might often matter less to migrants than to historians and political analysts. These trends do not constitute the 'end of the British World' in British migration, but they underline its recent transformation into a component of a global diaspora, which is played out in the imagination of migrants as much as in their actual mobility.

Notes

1 Interview and written account, Adam Salt, Melbourne (Dromana), Victoria, 21 September 2005, LU DS10. Unless otherwise noted all references to informants derive from the 'British Diaspora' archive at the History Program at La Trobe University, Melbourne, Australia.
2 *Ibid.*
3 In a further episode of exodus driven by anger British migrants who left during the financial and currency crises and high taxation regime of the mid-1960s often speak with bitterness of their inability to get ahead in Britain.
4 *Ibid.*
5 For these aspects of the post-war migrant generation to Australia see A. J. Hammerton and A. Thomson, *Ten Pound Poms: Australia's Invisible Migrants* (Manchester, 2005), pp. 124–66 and 329.
6 *Ibid.*, pp. 19–20.
7 S. Scott, 'The Social Morphology of Skilled Migration: the Case of the British Middle Class in Paris', *Journal of Ethnic and Migration Studies*, 32:7 (2006), pp. 1105–29. See also J. V. Beaverstock, 'Transnational Elites in the City: British Highly-skilled Inter-company Transferees in New York City's Financial District', *Journal of Ethnic and Migration Studies*, 31:2 (2005), pp. 245–68; D. Sriskandarajah and C. Drew, *Brits Abroad: Mapping the Scale and Nature of British Emigration* (London, 2006), pp. 37–65.
8 S. Constantine, 'British Emigration to the Empire-Commonwealth since 1880: From Overseas Settlement to Diaspora?' *Journal of Imperial and Commonwealth History*, 31:2 (2003), pp. 19–25.
9 E. Richards, *Britannia's Children: Emigration from England, Scotland, Wales and Ireland since 1600* (London, 2004), pp. 255–77, and 303.

[245]

10 Sriskandarajah and Drew, *Brits Abroad*, appendix A, p. 104.
11 Compiled from Office for National Statistics, UK, *Annual Abstract of Statistics* (London), vols for 1959 (table 39); 1963, p. 40; 1965, p. 19; 1974, p. 22; 1982 (table 2.11); 1990, p. 19; 1996, p. 25; 2004, pp. 35–6.
12 *Ibid.*, 2004, pp. 35–6.
13 Sriskandarajah and Drew, *Brits Abroad*, viii.
14 The full 'British Diaspora' project from which this chapter is based draws on testimony from over 180 late twentieth-century British emigrants, from which 129 have been interviewed. Records are held currently at the History Program, La Trobe University, Melbourne.
15 Richards, *Britannia's Children*, p. 214.
16 Interview and written account, David Spurgeon, Sydney (Gladesville), New South Wales, 23 March 2007, LU DS85.
17 *Ibid.*
18 Interview, Gerry Bullon, Melbourne (Prahran), Victoria, 6 November 2006, LU DB85.
19 This is beyond the scope of this chapter, but it invites exploration of the relationship of migrant outlook and identity to trends of political 'anger and apathy' in British political opinion. Viewed from a political perspective the migrant identities discussed here were motivated variously by both political anger and political apathy, and may have derived to some extent from popular British political discourse. See M. Garnett, *From Anger to Apathy: The British Experience since 1975* (London, 2007).
20 Interview, Nick Collins, Vancouver, British Columbia, 23 July 2007; and written account, 11 July 2007, LU DC80.
21 Since the 1960s the popular career of teaching English as a second language has become much more common among British migrants as a passport to continuous global mobility.
22 Interview, Nick Collins, LU DC80.
23 *Ibid.*
24 For example, Hammerton and Thomson, *Ten Pound Poms*, pp. 248–63.
25 Interview and written account, Jenny Armati, Perth (Darlington), Western Australia, 20 April 2007, LU DA10.
26 *Ibid.*
27 *Ibid.*
28 Interview, Claire Sowerby, Melbourne, Victoria, 23 January 2007, LU DS75.
29 Interview, Viviane King, Sydney, New South Wales, 23 March 2007; and written account, 31 July 2006, LU DK20.
30 For example, Hammerton and Thomson, *Ten Pound Poms*, pp. 132, 139–41.

CHAPTER 11

Multiculturalism, decolonisation and immigration: integration policy in Britain and France after the Second World War

Eleanor Passmore and Andrew S. Thompson

Multiculturalism is widely considered to be a defining feature of Britain's response to post-war immigration and remains the most important – if contested – idea underpinning the British approach to integration. This chapter explores the origins of the concept of multiculturalism by comparing official rhetoric about 'new' Commonwealth immigration during the 1950s and 1960s with the social policies introduced by the government to provide for the welfare of West Indian, Indian, Pakistani and later Bangladeshi immigrants.

Today, 'integration' tends to carry two broadly overlapping meanings. First, it implies a sense of civic identity, manifested in a shared understanding of what constitute social values, beliefs and norms. Second, it refers to access to the opportunities, rights and services available to the majority of citizens, such as employment, education, health care and housing. In 2005, the head of the Commission for Racial Equality (CRE)[1] put integration firmly on the political agenda by calling into question the efficacy of multiculturalism as an ideology and a policy. More recently, scrutiny of the government's response to the emergence of fundamentalist Islamic groups in the UK has reignited the debate over the effectiveness of past approaches to integration. There are interesting parallels between contemporary debates about integration and those taking place in the 1950s, when the status and welfare of immigrants from newly independent and Commonwealth nations took on a wider political significance as the government sought to reorientate Britain's international relations during the process of decolonisation:

> The social problems of West Indian immigrants in the UK . . . have a unique significance because basically they are problems of Commonwealth relations. They pose the whole concept of a Commonwealth of Nations composed of different races in a challenging and practical form. The mixture of races in overcrowded and generally bad housing conditions

inevitably leads to racial friction with a constant threat of serious and possibly violent outbreaks of the kind already experienced.[2]

Officials were concerned not only with how to tackle the substantial problem posed by the post-war housing shortage, which they identified as a contributory factor in causing the Notting Hill riots of 1958, but with the potential repercussions of civic unrest for the UK's relationship with the Commonwealth.

This chapter seeks to demonstrate that contemporary British immigration policy – comprising border controls, the promotion of integration and anti-discrimination legislation – is, to a significant extent, the legacy of the post-war period and the political process of decolonisation. By contrasting aspects of UK policies with those adopted by France, which experienced comparable trends in migration from existing and former colonies, it also explores how far the differences between the French Republican and British multicultural models of integration influenced the development of social policies targeted at migrants.

We begin by providing an overview of immigration trends in Britain 1945–62, before comparing and contrasting British and French approaches to integration. The following section provides a more detailed examination of government immigration policy in Britain, drawing out the tensions that existed between domestic political pressures and the management of Commonwealth relations. In doing so, we provide a more nuanced account of the variety and complexity of welfare services that sought to cater for immigrants' needs. The penultimate section focuses on the introduction of restrictive immigration legislation and the measures introduced to integrate 'new' Commonwealth immigrants and tackle racial discrimination, and the interplay between them. The final section sums up the legacies of the way Britain treated migrants from the 'new' Commonwealth during the era of decolonisation for immigrant welfare – and related debates about 'Britishness' – today.

'New' Commonwealth immigration to Britain post-1945

The 1948 British Nationality Act, which granted 'new' Commonwealth immigrants the right to settle, vote and access public services in Britain represented an attempt to use British nationality as a means of maintaining close ties with the Commonwealth.[3] By virtue of the 'open door' policy that the Act created, the West Indies and South Asia emerged as two important sources of immigration to Britain during the 1950s and 1960s. An estimated two thousand people migrated to Britain from the Caribbean in 1953, followed by a further 270,000 over the following decade (see table 11.1). Many set out from Jamaica, but

Table 11.1 Estimated net immigration from the 'new' Commonwealth, 1953–62

	W. Indies	India	Pakistan	Others	Total
1953	2,000				2,000
1954	11,000				11,000
1955	27,500	5,800	1,850	7,500	42,650
1956	29,800	5,600	2,050	9,350	46,800
1957	23,000	6,600	5,200	7,600	42,400
1958	15,000	6,200	4,700	3,950	29,850
1959	16,400	2,950	850	1,400	21,600
1960	49,650	5,900	2,500	-350	57,700
1961	66,300	23,750	25,100	21,250	136,000
1962	31,800	19,050	25,080	18,970	94,900
Total	272,450	75,850	67,330	69,670	484,900

Source: Z. Layton-Henry, The Politics of Immigration: Immigration, Race and Race Relations in Post-War Britain (Oxford, 1992), p. 3. Note: 1962 figures only include first six months up to introduction of immigration controls.

all of the main islands were represented, including Barbados, Trinidad and Tobago, St Lucia and Antigua.[4] The growth of Britain's South Asian population occurred just as immigration from the Caribbean reached its peak in the late 1950s. In 1961, around 100,000 people from the Indian subcontinent were living in Britain; by 1971 this had increased to almost half a million.[5] They included Punjabi Sikhs from Jullundur and Hoshiarpur, Hindus from central and southern Gujarat, and Pakistani Muslims from the regions of Mirpur and Sylhet (after independence in 1971, the latter became part of Bangladesh).[6] There was also a smaller movement of people from Hong Kong, Singapore and Malaysia, who together formed Britain's 'Chinese community', which numbered around 96,000 by the early 1970s.

By the mid-1970s there were approximately one and a half million 'new' Commonwealth migrants living in Britain, or 3 per cent of the British population (tables 11.1 and 11.2), most of whom settled in the major conurbations of Greater London, the West Midlands, Manchester, Merseyside and Yorkshire. Other migrant groups included the 100,000 or so former members of the Polish armed forces who did not want to return to Poland under the new Communist regime;[7] 'displaced persons' from the Ukraine, Yugoslavia, Estonia, Latvia and Lithuania; people from the English-speaking world (the dominions and the USA); and the Irish, many of who had chosen to leave Ireland following the slump in the economy in 1951.[8] As a proportion of the UK's immigrant population in the 1960s, 'new' Commonwealth immigrants made up about one-third.

Table 11.2   Population by birthplace and ethnic origin: Britain, 1971

	Birthplace		'New' Commonwealth ethnic origin
Total	53,826,375		–
UK	50,514,820	(94%)	–
Irish Republic	720,985	(1%)	–
Old Commonwealth	145,250	(0.3%)	–
New Commonwealth	1,157,170	(2%)	1,486,000
India	322,670		384,000
Pakistan	139,445		169,000
West Indies	302,970		548,000
Cyprus	72,665		155,000
Africa	176,060		157,000
Other	143,355		73,000
Foreign (not stated)	1,076,935		–

Source: adapted from C. Peach, 'Patterns of Afro-Caribbean Migration and Settlement in Great Britain, 1945–1981', in C. Brock (ed.), *The Caribbean in Europe. Aspects of the West Indian Experience in Britain, France and The Netherlands* (London, 1986), p. 64.

British multiculturalism and French republicansim

France also received – and to a limited degree encouraged – immigration from its colonial territories after the Second World War, although there were significant differences in the timing, origins and history of these migratory flows, and in the policies introduced to manage them. Whereas post-war immigration in Britain came to be associated with three national groups, in France, the 'new' immigration of the 1960s was synonymous with a single region – North Africa – and with Algerians in particular.

Nor was the British government alone in viewing the welfare of migrants from existing or former colonial territories as part of a wider political debate about the future of the empire or Commonwealth. The undeclared war over Algerian independence that took place between 1954 and 1962 precipitated a significant movement of people (including both Algerians and *pieds noirs*)[9] between metropolitan France and Algeria. French sources estimated that 1,369,000 Muslims made the journey across the Mediterranean during this period.[10] According to official estimates there were between 350,000 and 510,000 Algerians resident in France by 1962, although large-scale economic migration from Algeria only began in earnest in the mid-1960s.[11] During the war and after, the sizeable Algerian population in France was subjected to surveillance and state control on an unprecedented scale, accompanied by a wide range of welfare services that sought to 'assimilate' Algerians into French society.[12] Securing the loyalty of these immigrants was seen as critical to retaining French control over Algeria itself.

Yet although there were considerable differences in the way that the French and British empires were run, and in the process by which the countries under their control gained independence, decolonisation would shape both governments response to postcolonial immigration after the Second World War. In particular, it would influence their conceptions of the modern multicultural state. In the British case, the link between the government's capacity to provide for immigrants from the former empire and the perceptions of its commitment to leading a multi-racial Commonwealth of Nations was significant. Debates about immigration policy during the 1950s and 1960s were continually being weighed against the effects they were likely to have on relations within this newly formed entity.

British 'multiculturalism' is often contrasted with, and defined against, the French model of republicanism. The essence of this argument is that the two countries represent opposing paradigms on the integration of minorities into national society. Under the republican model, French citizens were represented as individuals and absolute equals before the state, while the British approach is generally characterised by a more communitarian ideal based on recognising and accommodating the different religious beliefs, cultures, languages and traditions of minority groups. There is, however, a fundamental problem with this representation, which, in the hands of many prominent commentators and politicians, tends towards caricature rather than an interrogation of the actions of either state.[13] In what follows, we argue that the approach to integration taken by Britain owes as much to the particular policies introduced in response to postcolonial immigration after the Second World War as to differing theoretical interpretations of the relationship between citizens and the state.

During the 1950s British officials observed with growing alarm as first West Indian, then Indian and Pakistani immigrants began to arrive in Britain in search of work.[14] In spite of the hostility to 'new' Commonwealth immigration expressed privately by several frontbench MPs, successive governments resisted calls for the introduction of immigration controls, first mooted as early as 1955.[15] Britain, unlike France, did not introduce a planned immigration policy to address the post-war labour shortage. Whereas the French centralised system of economic planning placed emphasis on attracting a large number of immigrants from Europe, and a smaller but still significant number from the empire, the immigration schemes organised by the British government were limited in scale. The largest of these was the European Voluntary Worker programme, which involved relatively small numbers of migrants working under close supervision from Whitehall. The government's expressed preference for European immigrants was based on the grounds that they were more 'suitable' for the purposes of repopulating the nation. The working party on 'the Employment in the UK of Surplus Colonial Labour' published in 1948 rejected the idea of recruiting West Indian migrants on the basis that 'assimilating' them would pose too many problems and because it was believed that they lacked the requisite skills.[16] A year later the Royal Commission on Population concluded that immigration should only be accepted where immigrants were 'of good human stock and were not prevented by their race or religion from intermarrying with the host population and becoming merged with it'.[17]

In spite of a distinct lack of enthusiasm for immigration from the dependent empire, what was referred to as 'Commonwealth sentiment' initially tempered vocal demands for the introduction of controls and led the government to assert that Commonwealth citizens should not be treated differently to British nationals. Part of the reason why there was a degree of political support for the existing 'open door' regime may have been that the Commonwealth continued to be regarded as an important economic asset. Here it is worth recalling that the idea of an 'imperial political economy' had considerable purchase among some politicians and parts of a wider public well after 1945.[18] As late as 1969, two-thirds of those polled by Gallup thought it would be 'very serious' or 'serious' for Britain if the Commonwealth were to break up. While only a half of these people saw the Commonwealth as 'very important' or 'important' to Britain's military role and standing in world politics, 80 per cent were convinced that the Commonwealth was vital to British overseas trade.

Why did so many people think of the Commonwealth this way? The explanation probably lies partly in the commitment of the Labour party to the Commonwealth in the 1950s and early 1960s as a progressive force in the world, an arena not only for mutually beneficial trade, but for advancing the decidedly 'modern' cause of international aid and development. Thus the 1964 Labour election manifesto asserted that the party was 'convinced that the first responsibility of a British Government is still to the Commonwealth'.[19] The answer also lies in the shifting contours of Britain's post-war economy. Commonwealth exports supplied scarce dollars to the Sterling Area from 1945 to 1952,[20] by which time a combination of higher exports and lower imports had brought the UK's sterling problem under control.[21] Of equal importance, the years from the mid-1940s to the early 1950s also saw a significant redirection of exports toward empire markets;[22]

only from the late-1960s did this post-war preference for the products of British industry in the Commonwealth give way to expanding intra-European trade. Hence, when Britain applied for a second time to join the European Economic Community in 1967 the Commonwealth may diplomatically and militarily have begun to look like a 'broken reed',[23] but from an economic viewpoint it probably looked a much better bet.

Officials in Britain also feared that to exclude 'new' Commonwealth citizens, but not those from the old dominions (New Zealand, Australia and Canada), would be seen as an overtly racist measure by West Indian governments, India and Pakistan, a risk that the Commonwealth Relations Office was not willing to take as yet.[24] Thus the debate over controls was infused with this idea of the importance of defending 'Commonwealth sentiment'.[25] Those resisting the introduction of controls in Parliament formed an anachronistic alliance that crossed the party divide. However, their ideas about the Commonwealth they were defending did not necessarily accord. Within the Conservative Party, there were those whose views on border controls were informed by their unwillingness to see the empire disband, while some politicians on the Left not only opposed controls on an anti-racist stance but conceived of the Commonwealth as a vehicle for international solidarity. For these reasons, the two main political parties maintained an unspoken agreement to uphold the liberal entry regime for 'new' Commonwealth immigrants that had been established by the 1948 British Nationality Act, albeit their conceptions of the Commonwealth were fundamentally at odds.

In contrast to the broad interpretation of British nationality introduced by the 1948 Act, Muslims living in Algeria were only able to become French citizens on the condition that they accepted civil law over what was termed their 'personal status' as Muslims (Algerian Jews had been granted French citizenship under the Crémieux Decree of 1870).[26] In 1947 the law was revised to allow Algerians to become French citizens 'without distinction of origin, race, language, or religion' as part of a long campaign to convince Algerians, the French public and the international community that Algeria was an integral part of France, although it was not fully revoked for another nine years. Nevertheless, in metropolitan France, Algerians were governed by French civil law regardless of their status in Algeria from 1947 onwards.[27] They were therefore entitled to exercise the same rights and access the same public services as any French citizen, and they were also guaranteed the right to freedom of movement between Algeria and France, with the exception of administrative checks imposed by the French authorities until 1962.[28]

The origins of British policy on 'race relations' similarly pre-dated migration from the Asian sub-continent and the West Indies. Prior to 1945, moves for greater autonomy for the colonies and the dominions put Britain under increasing pressure to justify colonial rule by demonstrating that the nations of the empire and Commonwealth were equals in a harmonious multi-racial partnership. The new 'welfare colonialism' of the 1930s and 1940s sought to portray Britain's overseas empire as a cradle for the development of independent nations. African countries also became the target for a rejuvenated British colonialism, with the Colonial Development Acts of 1929 and 1940. The importance of sensitively handling the 'colour question' had been demonstrated to the government when West Indian soldiers were stationed in Britain during the Second World War. While British officials wanted to ensure that soldiers took home a good impression of the 'mother country', there was some irony in the fact that the British government had to accommodate racial segregation for the American troops based in the UK in spite of their concern that this would damage Britain's own reputation in the Commonwealth.[29] During the 1940s British officials were therefore made aware of the connections between the welfare of 'new' Commonwealth immigrants in the UK, and Britain's image in Commonwealth countries and the wider world. With decolonisation, demonstrating that 'new' Commonwealth immigrants received equal treatment in the UK became a part of the effort to maintain good diplomatic relations with increasingly assertive Commonwealth nations. West Indian governments in particular kept a close eye on how their citizens were treated in the UK during the 1950s and 1960s.

Welfare of immigrants during the 1950s

For as long as Britain's borders officially remained open to the Commonwealth[30] the ostensible goal of the government's policy on integration and welfare was to ensure that Britain was not seen to differentiate between British-born citizens and those holding citizenship of the UK and Commonwealth.[31] Yet the essentially domestic political questions of employing, housing or administering health care to a very small proportion of the population came under greater scrutiny as a result of their influence upon British diplomacy in the Commonwealth. Only in this context could it be claimed 'the basic concept on which the Commonwealth rests will be in jeopardy if racial friction should develop within the UK on any significant scale', when the proposed remedy was a very modest plan for a West Indian Housing Association that was eventually abandoned.

While it was important to show that 'new' Commonwealth immigrants were treated equally and without discrimination, in practice, this meant that they could expect to gain access to statutory services and little more. Whereas the French government developed a range of welfare services that officials boasted would carry Algerian immigrants from the dock to the grave, efforts to assist immigrants in Britain were the work of local authorities and voluntary bodies operating on a small scale. Until the 1960s, no government department was charged with taking responsibility for the welfare and integration of immigrants.[32]

However, the Colonial Office nominally led a network of agencies whose purpose it was to 'integrate coloured colonial people' into the UK through the Inter-Departmental Committee on Colonial People in the UK, formed in 1950. Services available to immigrants prior to 1962 included: the Migrant Services Division of the Office in the UK for the West Indies, British Guyana and British Honduras (established after the disturbances in Notting Hill in 1958 as a successor to the British Caribbean Welfare Service); welfare officers on the staff of the Indian and Pakistani High Commissions; the National Council of Social Services Group on the Welfare of Coloured Workers; Migrants Services division of the West Indian High Commission; the Institute of Commonwealth Studies; the Institute of Race Relations; the Citizens' Advice Bureau; voluntary organisations; and the churches. Immigrants, who 'found themselves at the receiving end of a formidable line up of patronage and welfare', were not benefiting from centrally organised policy but from ad hoc services, often provided by the voluntary sector.[33] Local authorities were another important source of support, although there was considerable variation in the services offered, with only a few areas, such as Birmingham, taking 'positive action' towards integrating migrants by employing a full-time welfare and assimilation officer.

Prior to the introduction of immigration controls British government policy on the welfare of immigrants was deliberately non-interventionist on the basis that Commonwealth citizens were not entitled to preferential treatment. As a result, immigrants were largely left to fend for themselves in the market for goods and services, (such as housing), that were such an important determinant of quality of life and social status in the UK. Yet new Commonwealth immigrants not only faced the prospect of securing accommodation at a time of severe shortage and learning how to navigate the expanding welfare state largely unassisted; it became increasingly evident that racism served to exclude them from services, both public and private, that were more readily available to the British population and European immigrants.

In contrast to the reactive and uncoordinated approach characteristic of immigrant welfare policy in the UK during the 1950s, the French government had established organisations to protect, assist, and keep an eye on 'indigenous North Africans' as early as the 1920s. During the 1950s and 1960s government-sponsored efforts to provide public housing, employment, health and social services exclusively to North Africans intensified, in tandem with the development of a regime of surveillance and policing operated in Metropolitan France during the Algerian war.

Border controls and integration policy from 1962 onwards

In 1960 the French government was spending 400 million francs to support 130 private or semi-public organisations to provide services to French Muslims, a programme supplemented by the work of 100 officials who specialised in 'Muslim affairs', employment and social services and were employed directly by the state. To oversee the work of these organisations and the various departments responsible for welfare policy for Algerians in the metropolis, an inter-ministerial committee was established in 1958 under Michel Massenet.

Recent work has shed further light on the close relationship between the welfare services designed to support Algerian migrants and the mechanisms of state repression, which together represented an 'attempt to insert colonial methods of policing and 'native manage-ment' into metropolitan France on a scale that was unprecedented in Europe'.[34] In a 1958 Ministry of the Interior circular officials set out the three distinct but complementary aims of departmental policy for 'French Muslim Algerians': repressive and preventative measures (to eliminate terrorism), psychological measures (to ensure that metro-politan opinion remained favourable to the majority of 'sane' Algerians whom officials insisted had not succumbed to the *Front de Libération Nationale* or FLN) and social measures to promote their integration into French society.[35]

In France, domestic departments played an important role in the campaign to win over the hearts and minds of Algerian migrants, where welfare policy played an important part. There were parallels between these efforts on the home front and General de Gaulle's Constantine Plan of 1959, which set out France's plans to promote economic development in Algeria, and was also intended to strengthen the case for French rule. A good illustration of how immigrant welfare policy was designed to serve French colonial interests was the programme for re-housing Algerians living in the shanty towns or *bidonvilles* that flourished within many large French cities during this period, and were home to Algerian nationalists, as well as migrants of many different nationalities.

The construction of 9,000 hostel beds and 4,000 other types of lodging specifically for Algerians between 1958 and 1964, and the process of clearing the *bidonvilles* explicitly served each of the aims of the Ministry of the Interior circular: eliminating terrorism by removing nationalist bases; selling the benefits of the French way of life to migrants, and advertising the munificence of the state to the French public by tackling this greatest of social needs; and integrating migrants into public housing estates and French society. Although the achievements of Massenet's committee fell rather short of his expectations, the network of welfare services for North Africans that he championed were extensive compared to those developed in Britain. Both the organisations themselves and the colonial ideals on which they were based would continue to exert an important influence over the development of France's immigration policy in the following decade.

The British government only took a more active role in providing for the welfare needs of immigrants once controls on Commonwealth immigration were introduced in 1962. This was partly the result of calls for financial assistance from local authorities in areas of high immigration.[36] Many complained that 'new' Commonwealth immigrants were placing an intolerable burden on local resources and public services, and that the demand for specialist teachers, translators, training courses and welfare officers provided evidence that councils did not feel equipped to meet their needs.

The demand for additional funding from central government raised questions about whether the social problems faced by 'new' Commonwealth immigrants were in fact any different to those facing other immigrant groups or the rest of the British population. In the case of housing, for instance, the government acknowledged that immigrants were moving to areas where overcrowding was already a problem.[37] The chronic housing shortage in post-war Britain was not the result of immigration, but it was evident that in some areas 'coloured immigrants', regardless of their country of origin, were collectively being blamed for the problem.

In Deptford, councillors claimed that 'to re-house coloured tenants over the heads of the long white waiting list would be political dynamite ... The Deptfordian rank and file regard the immigrants as a plague, the local Labour establishment as a political problem, the administrators as a social problem. All unite in seeing them as a problem to be contained ... and words like "integration" and "assimilation" are used only by outsiders.'[38] That immigration, and by implication race, was becoming a contentious and decisive political issue was demonstrated to MPs in the constituency of Smethwick during the 1964 election when a Labour seat was won by a Conservative candidate campaigning on an overtly anti-immigration platform against a nationwide swing to Labour. By 1965 the Labour Party, which had initially opposed controls on 'new' Commonwealth immigrants as racist, had joined the Conservatives in favour of controls.

Yet by the 1960s a growing body of evidence was demonstrating that West Indian, Indian and Pakistani immigrants were suffering from racial discrimination that made access to employment, housing and public services difficult, and there were increasingly vocal calls upon government to introduce anti-discrimination legislation from organisations like CARD (the Campaign Against Racial Discrimination, formed after the Notting Hill riots). Moreover, it remained important that Britain was seen to be a fair and just society to its Commonwealth partners and the outside world. British integration policy therefore took shape in a political climate of widespread support for immigration controls, pressure from local authorities to provide additional funding to deal with social problems, and a growing awareness of the problem of racism in Britain.

Prior to the 1960s, 'integration' or 'assimilation' (the two words were used interchangeably because the assumptions upon which they were based were both widespread and unchallenged) rested on the belief that immigrants would, as time passed, naturally adapt to a British way of life by relying upon existing local services and the goodwill of the British people. This represented the traditional view that immigrants would be able to 'pull themselves up by their own bootstraps and to integrate themselves', thought to be best exemplified by the upward social movement of immigrants from London's East End during the nineteenth century.[39] It was initially anticipated that this would happen for 'new' Commonwealth immigrants, but by the mid-1960s it was becoming increasingly evident that reliance on local efforts, the virtues of British citizens and the good behaviour of Commonwealth citizens was not sufficient to prevent the much feared 'social problems' from posing a threat to good 'race relations'. The inadequacy of the government's policy to date was described by Britain's first Minister for Integration, Maurice Foley, in 1965: 'Previously it had been assumed that immigrants would adjust without any help, that the social services could cope without difficulty with the burdens, and that British people as a whole were tolerant. It was becoming increasing obvious that none of these assumptions were well founded.'[40]

The government's response was to implement increasingly stringent controls on the movement of immigrants from 'new' Commonwealth countries to Britain with the 1962 Commonwealth Immigrants Act, the White Paper of 1965 that reduced the number of employment vouchers available, and the Immigration Acts of 1968 and 1971.

Restrictive border controls were a central plank of British integration policy, on the assumption that 'race relations' would improve only when the arrival of 'new' Commonwealth immigrants had been halted, both to assuage the concerns of resident white voters and to relieve the pressure on services. Integration policy was also designed to pacify those opposed to a controversial immigration bill and provide evidence to Commonwealth governments that Britain was making an effort to look after their citizens. By including a section on integration in the legislation, ministers could claim that an effort was being made to look after the interests of 'new' Commonwealth immigrants.[41] The 1962 Act was accompanied by the creation of the Commonwealth Immigrants Advisory Council (CIAC) to advise the government on matters relating to the welfare of 'new' Commonwealth immigrants, to report on whether local authorities required additional assistance from government and, if so, how this could be administered.

However, on the recommendation of the CIAC the government rejected the idea of offering additional or specialised services to immigrants of any origin because it contradicted the nominally universal reach of the welfare state and was technically very difficult to administer without changing the entire system of local authority funding. More importantly, in a context of growing political controversy over the impact of 'coloured' immigration on public services, an interventionist policy would have spelled political disaster.

This stance contrasted markedly with that of the French government, which had made a concerted effort to establish a segregated system of social support for North African immigrants. While the undeclared war over Algerian independence was being fought, French republicanism accommodated a very inegalitarian system of state-administered welfare in the name of promoting and assimilating Algerian migrants as part of a wider stratagem to hold on to power over Algeria. Although from 1961 onwards it was widely acknowledged that France would have to relinquish its claims to Algeria, French representatives hoped that by continuing to invest in the well-being of Algerian immigrants they could guarantee the safety of the *pieds noirs* in post-independence Algeria. Massenet himself contested that 'the constant preoccupation of my service has been . . . to preserve for French negotiators the modest card represented by Algerian migration, whose presence on metropolitan soil could serve as security for the Europeans of Algeria'.[42]

Even after the peace accords had established freedom of movement between mainland France and a newly independent Algeria in 1962, the repressive regime which had sought to control the lives of Algerians in France was not immediately dismantled. The justification for the continued (albeit under new names and for the nominal benefit of all

[259]

foreign workers) operation of those agencies that had been established during the unofficial war with Algeria were that the social problems facing North African immigrants had not diminished – it was certainly true that the shanty towns the government had vowed to eliminate remained a visible eyesore – partly because the government still saw Algerians as a threat to public order, and also because it was argued that demand for these services was in fact increasing as new migrants arrived. The wave of 'new immigration' from Algeria and other former or existing French colonies that began in the early 1960s in response to economic demand provided a new clientele for colonial era services long after the formal process of decolonisation had been completed.

As the French government began the process of re-badging targeted welfare services for Algerians to make them accessible to all foreign migrants, the British government turned its attention to further refining the system of support for 'new' Commonwealth migrants. In a 1965 White Paper on immigration, the CIAC evolved into the National Council for Commonwealth Immigrants (NCCI), which supervised the efforts of Voluntary Liaison Councils, the official name given to the local organisations that were to assist immigrants directly by channelling them into statutory services. The NCCI also advised the government on matters of integration but, crucially, not immigration policy. The deliberate division of responsibility for immigration (controls were stringently enforced and overseen by the Home Office), integration (handed to non-statutory bodies and mediated by representative members of immigrant communities) and anti-discrimination (dealt with by the Race Relations Board and the police) was the basis for the British 'multicultural' state. Since its inception, Britain's approach to 'integration' has been a poor cousin of immigration control, introduced to placate Commonwealth countries and British liberal opinion. Britain has never had an interventionist integration policy; multiculturalism has developed on the basis of a combination of stringent immigration policy, regulated access to statutory services and a legal framework for anti-discrimination. During the 1950s and 1960s, integration as a policy was politically expedient but amounted to very little in practice. To a large extent this was domestic policy as a diplomatic response to the pressures of decolonisation.

Conclusion

Drawing attention to the fact that, at the time of writing, 8 per cent of Britain's population is made up of families who have come to its shores, mainly from South Asia, the Caribbean and Africa, Jack Straw, the Leader of the House of Commons and former Foreign Secretary, warned, in 2007, of the dangers of a trend toward greater religious and ethnic segregation in many towns and cities. He went on to plead for the need 'to establish a (shared) sense of identity' – a set of common values, encapsulating what it means to be British.[43] As we suggested at the outset of this chapter, Straw's plea is not novel. Trevor Phillips, as chair of the CRE, had been arguing along similar lines for the previous three years. Phillips has been particularly concerned about the concept of 'multiculturalism'. He has argued that the tolerance of cultural and religious difference is all very well, yet unlikely to provide the 'glue' that will help British society to cohere. Both Straw and Phillips urge that, instead of encouraging 'separateness', the state should be actively promoting a common citizenship based on the notion that there are 'core British values' which bind us all together.[44]

Setting to one side the question of what these core or common values are – and how far they might actually be embedded in the concept of multiculturalism itself (e.g. tolerance, plurality, fairness etc.) – it is important not to lose sight of the fact that the discourse and policy of integration in Britain have always been two-sided. To be sure, the word 'integration' has long carried the connotation of a sense of civic identity, or shared values and beliefs. But 'integration' has also been consistently spoken of in terms of measures to promote 'social inclusion'. Indeed, it might well be argued that the latter is a sine qua non of the former: if immigrants do not feel that they have a 'stake' in society, and are fully a part of it, then they are unlikely to develop a strong and secure sense of British identity.

What this chapter has sought to show is that successive British governments' approach to 'integration', in terms of social welfare, has at best been haphazard – driven as much by the requirement to counterbalance restrictive entry legislation as by other considerations, and delivered through voluntary bodies as much (or more than) through state bureaucracy. Moreover, responsibility for the different facets of the immigrant experience (entry, welfare, discrimination) has been divided across government departments, to the detriment of a coherent and coordinated approach to immigrants' needs. The weight of these legacies is still keenly felt today: in terms of access to housing, education and employment, so-called 'ethnic penalties' persist for many migrant communities. Hence, however welcome, it is unlikely that new initiatives on citizenship – constitutional or educational – will of themselves address the fundamental problem that we now face. 'Integration', 'cohesion', and 'citizenship' have to be tackled more pragmatically (and fundamentally) by policy on housing, employment, education, transport, and language training and acquisition in order to prevent particular ethnic groups from becoming marginalised. Only

[261]

then, will migrants (old or new) be sufficiently involved in British society to feel that they truly belong to it.

Notes

1 The CRE is now part of the Equalities and Human Rights Commission.
2 The National Archives, London (hereafter TNA), Colonial Office papers, CO 1031/2539, 'Proposal for a West Indian Housing Association in the UK' (1958–1960). In the early 1960s the Colonial Office was relieved of its duty to care for 'colonial migrants' in the UK, and responsibility for 'integration' was gradually passed to the Home Office. The archives of the Departments of Health, Education, and Housing and Local Government also contain information on how immigrant welfare was managed by central government.
3 The Act divided British citizenship into two categories: 'UK and Colonies', and 'independent Commonwealth countries', allowing Indian nationals to retain their status as British subjects even after India became a republic.
4 C. Peach, *West Indian Migration to Britain: A Social Geography* (London, 1968), pp. 106–7.
5 R. Ballard, 'The Emergence of *Desh Pardesh*', in R. Ballard (ed.), *Desh Pardesh: the South Asian Presence in Britain* (London, 1994), p. 7.
6 That said, Gujarati settlers in Britain include a significant Muslim minority; as many as a quarter of Punjabis were Hindus; and there was a small Christian minority among those from Pakistan. See R. Desai, *Indian Immigrants in Britain* (London, 1963), p. 13.
7 J. Walvin, *A Passage to Britain. Immigration in British History and Politics* (London, 1984), pp. 105–6.
8 By the 1960s there were at least three-quarters of a million Irish-born people living in Britain, making them the largest single national group, although estimates vary depending on whether one is measuring migration or ethnic origin: see H. Kearney, *The British Isles: a History of Four Nations* (Cambridge, 1989), p. 211; Walvin, *Passage to Britain*, p. 106; and tables 12–13.
9 The name given to white settlers in Algeria.
10 Archives Nationale, Paris (AN), AN, CARAN, F1a 5056, Action Social du Ministère de l'Intérieur, Note on the civil and political rights of Algerians in the Metropolis.
11 AN, CAC, 0019770391, art. 7.
12 J. House and N. Macmaster, *Paris 1961: Algerians, State Terror and Post-colonial Memories* (Oxford, 2006).
13 M. Silverman, *Deconstructing the Nation: Immigration, Racism, and Citizenship in Modern France* (London, 1992).
14 Ceri Peach's work demonstrates that it was the economic 'pull' factor to Britain rather than the depressed economy of the West Indies or the closure of migratory channels to the USA that led to the increase in emigration to the UK (principally from Jamaica) that lasted for the duration of the 1950s.
15 Clement Attlee reportedly queried 'who organised this incursion?', cited in K. Paul, 'The Politics of Citizenship in Post-war Britain', *Contemporary Record*, 6:3 (1992), p. 453.
16 Ian Spencer, *British Immigration Policy since 1939: the making of a Multiracial Britain* (London, 1997), pp. 39–40.
17 J. Hampshire, *Citizenship and Belonging. Immigration and the Politics of Demographic Governance in Post-War Britain* (Basingstoke, 2005), p. 54; and Spencer, *British Immigration Policy*, p. 56.
18 A. Gamble, 'The European Issue in British Politics', in D. Baker and D. Seawright (eds), *Britain For and Against Europe. British Politics and the Question of European Integration* (Oxford, 1988), pp. 11–30.
19 J. Tomlinson, *The Wilson Governments, 1964–70, 3 Economic Policy* (Manchester, 2004), pp. 22–4.

20   C. Schenk, *Britain and the Sterling Area: from Devaluation to Convertibility in the 1950s* (London, 1994).
21   C. Feinstein, 'The End of Empire and the Golden Age', in P. Clarke and C. Trebilcock (eds), *Understanding Decline: Perceptions and Realities of British Economic Performance* (Cambridge, 1997), pp. 229–30.
22   G. Magee, 'The Importance of Being British? Imperial Factors and the Growth of British Imports, 1870–1960', *Journal of Interdisciplinary History*, 37:3 (2007), pp. 341–69.
23   D. Watt, 'Introduction: The Anglo-American Relationship', in Wm. Roger Louis and H. Bull (eds), *The 'Special Relationship': Anglo-American Relations Since 1945* (Oxford, 1986), p. 12.
24   The influence of the Colonial Office and Commonwealth Relations Office was undoubtedly diminishing, yet the government did not want to alienate newly independent Commonwealth governments during the 1950s.
25   TNA, Dominions Office papers, DO 175/54, MIG 58/55/2A, 'Working Party to Report on Social and Economic Problems arising from the Growing Influx into the UK of Coloured Workers from other Commonwealth Countries', minutes and memoranda (1960–61).
26   This device meant that certain personal or religious matters, including marriage, were to be governed by Islamic law, while French civil law was applied to property rights. This also suggested that this was a personal choice of colonial subjects and the product of the incompatibility of Islam with French secular society, rather than a means of subjugating Algerian Muslims.
27   AN, CARAN, F1a 5056, Action Social du Ministère de l'Intérieur, Note on the civil and political rights of Algerians in the Metropolis, Law of 20 September 1947, art. 3, para. 2.
28   AN, CAC, 0019770391, art. 2. The authorities spoke of operating a 'filtering' system to exclude terrorists and ensure that immigrants were capable of finding suitable accommodation and employment before entering France. See A. Spire, *Etrangers à la carte: l'administration de l'immigration en France (1945–1975)* (Paris, 2005), pp. 190–8, for details of the measures used to restrict the entry of migrants from DOM-TOM (départements d'outre-mer and territoires d'outre-mer) countries.
29   S. Rose, *Which People's War: National Identity and Citizenship in Britain, 1939–45* (Oxford, 2004).
30   High Commissions in India and Pakistan operated a policy of restricting the number of travel documents they issued.
31   TNA, DO 175/54, 'Working party'.
32   See also on this point D. Feldman, 'Migrants, Immigrants and Welfare from the Old Poor Law to the Welfare State', *Transactions of the Royal Historical Society*, sixth series, 14 (2003), pp. 79–104.
33   M. Phillips and T. Phillips, *Windrush: the Irresistible Rise of Multi-Racial Britain* (London, 1999), p. 88.
34   N. MacMaster, *Colonial Migrants and Racism: Algerians in France, 1900–62* (Basingstoke, 1996), p. 151; and House and MacMaster, *Paris 1961*.
35   AN, CAC, 0019770391, art. 8, circular of 10 February 1958.
36   Kensington and Birmingham sent deputations to the Ministry of Housing and Local Government on the problem of immigrant housing. Representations were also made to the Home Office from Southall, Leicester, Slough and Birmingham Town Councils about the 'influx of immigrants' between 1964 and 1972. A meeting was convened by the Parliamentary Secretary in 1965 to discuss the matter with local authorities 'with large concentrations of coloured immigrants ... who have shown themselves active in trying to grapple with the problem'. Representatives attended from Birmingham, Bradford, Brent, Hackney, Kensington and Chelsea, Manchester, Nottingham, Smethwick and Wolverhampton.
37   TNA, Cabinet Office papers, CAB 134/1468, Commonwealth Immigration Committee (1963), Section 6: Housing implications of Commonwealth Immigration. Figures from the 1961 Census showed that the presence of immigrants was unlikely

to have much effect on areas that already had high rates of overcrowding and obsolescence.

38 TNA, DO 175/203, 2–MIG 58/144/1A, 'Area Reports on Cities and Boroughs with Substantial Immigrant Settlements: Deptford (South London) and the 1964 Elections', by Alfred Sherman, Borough Officer, sent by Kenneth J. Meader, Deptford Town Clerk, to Lord Beswick, Parliamentary Under-Secretary of State for the CRO, 4 January 1965.

39 TNA, Housing and Local Government papers, HLG 118/766, 'Minutes of Proceeding at the Ministers Conference with Local Authorities on Commonwealth Immigrants', Royal Commonwealth Society, London, 21 June 1967, p. 4, comments made by the chair, J. E. MacColl MP. This was the reference point for many officials thinking on integration during the 1950s.

40 TNA, DO 175/204, 2–MIG 58/144/1B, note of a meeting between Foley and Dr Jivraj N. Mehta, Indian High Commissioner in London, 3 December 1965.

41 TNA, DO 175/194, 2–MIG 58/85/11, 'Report of the Mountbatten Mission's Visit to Commonwealth Countries', 13 June 1965. Harold Wilson used similar reasons to justify the introduction of immigration controls to the Indian Prime Minister.

42 AN, CAC, 0019770391, art. 8, report on events of October 1961.

43 'Straw plea for "British values"' and J. Straw, 'We need a British Story', *The Times*, 29 April 2007.

44 A. Thompson with R. Begum, '"Asian Britishness". A Study of First Generation Asian Migrants in Greater Manchester', *Asylum and Migration Working Paper 4*, Institute of Public Policy Research (2005), p. 9.

INDEX

Notes: t after a page reference refers to a table on that page. (n) after a page number refers to the number of a note on that page.

Boyle, M. L. 169, 170, 187(n1)
Boynton, G.
  Last Days in Cloud Cuckooland
    (1997) 214, 230(n3)
Brantlinger, P. 74
Bridge, C. xi, xvii, 128, 171
Bright, R. x, 10, 14, 19–20, 128–49
Brisbane diocese 94
British Association for Advancement
  of Science xv
British Columbia 10, 32(n58),
  33(n67), 129–43 *passim*, 161,
  169, 180, 239
British Diaspora 37(n90), 234–6,
  245(n1), 246(n14)
British Empire
  versus 'British World' 138, 143
  interconnectedness 2, 26(n8)
  raison d'être 1–2
British Empire Settlement Act (1922)
  159, 180, 197
British migrants
  and cosmopolitanism 236–40
British Nationality Act (1948) 23,
  119–20(n40), 248, 253, 262(n3)
British Overseas Settlement
  Delegation 160, 166(n14)
'British values' 261, 264(n44)
British World xiv, xv, 176, 187,
  191(n63), 192, 200
  Asian migration 128–49
  'broad themes' 2
  'end' 232–46
  'essence' 3
  outline of concept 27(n10)
  racial plurality 4
British World (Bridge and
  Fedorowich, 2003) 171
British World System xiv
'Britishness' 2, 4, 128, 134, 144–5,
  146, 171–2, 185, 187, 191(n63),
  248, 264(n44)
'Britons of Greater Britain' 5–10
Broughton, W. G. (Bishop of
  Australia) 86, 90, 100
Brown, J. M. 127(n84)
'Brunei' [Negara Brunei Darussalam]
  232, 242
Bryce, J.
  American Commonwealth (1888)
  132

Buckner, P. 189(n17)
Bullon, G. 238, 246(n18)
Burton, A. 77(n2)
Butters, Reverend W. 101

Cadbury, P. 161
California 129, 131–2, 135
Calvinistic Methodism 109
Calvinistic Methodist Archive
  (CMA, NLW) 124(n4), 125(n27)
Campaign Against Racial
  Discrimination (CARD) 258
Canada xiv, 9–10, 28(n17), 81(n80),
  134–44 *passim*, 193, 235,
  238–40
  'Anglo-British nation' 172–7,
  188–9
  'Anglo-Canadian privilege' 21–2,
  169–91
  colonists' rights 177–84, 189–90
  Middlemore Programme 152–68
Canada: Department of Immigration
  159–60
Canadian National Railway (CNR)
  169, 182, 184
Canadian Pacific Railway 194
Cannadine, D. 81(n81)
  Ornamentalism (2001) 61, 77(n3)
Cape of Good Hope 88
Capricorn Africa Society 216,
  230(n11)
Care of Children Committee (1948
  Report) 162
career migrants 18, 39(n103)
Carey, H. M. x, 8–9, 18, 72–106
Carluer, J-Y. 126(n57)
Carlyle, T. 66
Carruthers, J. 101, 102
caste 116, 118–19, 121
Catholic clergy 94–6, 99
Catholics 18, 82–93 *passim*, 102(n2),
  103(n9), 168(n71)
censuses 17–18, 20, 48, 60–81, 91–2,
  97, 174–5, 263–4(n37)
'chains of memory' (Hervieu-Léger)
  100, 106(n64)
Chamberlain, J. 137, 138
Champagnat, M. 96
Child Emigration Society
  renamed Fairbridge Society (1935)
  161

Lightning Source UK Ltd.
Milton Keynes UK
UKHW011134280619
345217UK00002B/44/P